Feminist Theory and the Study of Folklore

Feminist Theory and the Study of Folklore

EDITED BY

Susan Tower Hollis,
Linda Pershing,
and M. Jane Young

University of Illinois Press   *Urbana and Chicago*

© 1993 by the Board of Trustees of the University of Illinois
Manufactured in the United States of America
1 2 3 4 5 C P 5 4 3 2 1

This book is printed on acid-free paper.

Library of Congress Cataloging-in-Publication Data

Feminist theory and the study of folklore / edited by Susan Tower
    Hollis, Linda Pershing, and M. Jane Young.
        p.   cm.
    Includes bibliographical references.
    ISBN 0-252-02009-X (cloth : alk. paper). — ISBN 0-252-06313-9
(paper : alk. paper)
    1. Women—Folklore.   2. Women in literature—History and
criticism.   3. Feminist theory.   4. Feminist criticism.   I. Hollis,
Susan T.   II. Pershing, Linda.   III. Young, M. Jane, 1950-   .
GR470.F48 1993
398'.042'082—dc20   93-18645
                                                                CIP

Contents

Susan Tower Hollis,
Linda Pershing,
and M. Jane Young

Preface

This book had its genesis in 1985 in the efforts of a group of six women scholars, both teachers and graduate students, who were associated with the Folklore Program at the University of Texas at Austin. Believing that folklore, like all academic disciplines, operates within certain paradigms that reflect the ideologies of the academic period in which they arise, these women met to discuss their concerns about the conscious and unconscious gender biases that pervade the discipline. They had found, through their teaching experience and research, that such biases may be reflected in an absence of the female and/or dominance of the male or they may appear as the denigration of female experience, all of which serve the interest of male privilege. Concerned that feminist theory was not being adequately addressed or developed within contemporary folkloristics, together Linda Pershing, Patricia Sawin, Suzanne Seriff, Beverly Stoeltje, Kay Turner, and M. Jane Young formulated and organized, with the help of many others, an all-day symposium on folklore and feminist theory. The conference, which was officially entitled "A Feminist Retrospective on Folklore and Folkloristics," was part of the 1986 annual meeting of the American Folklore Society in Baltimore, Maryland. The purpose of the symposium was to discuss and debate not only women's folklore, as had a 1979 women and folklore conference held at the University of Pennsylvania and two earlier volumes on women's folklore (Farrer, 1975; Jordan and Kalčik, 1985), but also, and more important, to introduce feminist theory into the study of folklore and bring folklore scholarship to bear on feminist theory. This included the consideration of why and how the analysis of women's lore changes the study of all folklore, why studying any folklore with a feminist eye makes a difference, and how folklorists can contribute to the growing body of feminist scholarship that is developing in many disciplines.

In response to the initial call for papers, over forty submissions were accepted and delivered at the conference, and it is from this group, with one addition (Phillips), that this book was formulated. In reviewing the papers delivered at the conference, however, we found virtually no mention of feminist approaches to the folklore of women who are often doubly marginalized in our society by virtue of other factors in addition to their gender; these include women of color, lesbians, women with disabilities, and older women, who seldom have been the focus of folklore research. Hoping to address this lacuna, we attempted early in the development of the book to solicit essays that addressed these areas, but we did not have much success, probably both because we were not looking in the right places for the work that exists and because not enough has been done in these areas. We do not believe, as do some, that little theoretical research is being conducted by these doubly marginalized groups of women because they are not interested in or capable of theorizing about their expressive cultural practices. Rather, we concur with bell hooks that these women think and express themselves analytically and can provide crucial insights into and a reorientation of the development of feminist theory:

> Given the class nature of feminist movement so far, as well as racial hierarchies, developing theory (the guiding set of beliefs and principles that become the basis for action) has been a task particularly subject to the hegemonic dominance of white academic women. This has led many women outside the privileged race/class group to see the focus on developing theory, even the very use of the term, as a concern that functions only to reinforce the power of the elite group. Such reactions [only serve to] reinforce the sexist/racist/classist notion that developing theory is the domain of the white intellectual. (hooks, 1984:30)

Limited by time constraints and our inability to locate materials that were ready for publication, we have included those essays that we could find and suggest that these research areas must become more central to feminist folklore scholarship in the future.

Significant to the conception of the 1986 symposium and this subsequent volume was the intellectual challenge raised by recent debates over the very definition and subject matter of folkloristics. For example, scholarly discussions during the early and mid–1970s gave rise to a new conceptual approach to the study of folklore—one that emphasized performance and context to the extent that folklore itself was frequently described "as social behavioral process and as situated communicative interaction"

(Paredes and Bauman, 1972; Ben-Amos and Goldstein, 1975; Limón and Young, 1986:437). Whereas early definitions of folklore had implied that "the folk" were rural, lower class, and circumscribed by face-to-face interaction in small groups, this new emphasis on performance has focused less on who "the folk" are or what "products" they may produce than on a sense of folklore as the process of artful communication (Limón and Young, 1986:439). This emphasis on artistic process and communication has led folklorists to maintain that one must take an "emic" approach to one's subject (a contextually grounded approach that is located as nearly as possible within the social-cultural group being studied) rather than an "etic" approach (one that is based almost entirely on an analytical framework that is imposed from outside the group being studied, with little regard for the context and values that inform the lifeways of that group).

For convenience, folklorists frequently had divided their subject matter into oral tradition (or verbal art) and material culture (or visual art), each with its own specific genres. For example, oral tradition encompassed myth, folktale, legend, memorate (a subcategory of legend that is usually defined as based on personal experience), joke, riddle, proverb, and similar categories. Material culture, on the other hand, generally focused on nonlinguistic, product-oriented genres, such as folk housing, foodways, costume, and varieties of arts and crafts.

The performance-centered "new perspective" on folklore has greatly influenced these traditional categories in the same way that it has led to a different orientation to the discipline of folklore itself. The recent emphasis on process has dissolved the rigid boundaries between verbal and visual art (or oral tradition and material culture) because such categories are not fixed, nor impermeable, especially in an event-centered context. For example, although a quilting bee may seem to focus on the production of a material object, the process through which this is accomplished is of the utmost importance. Additionally, verbal genres such as joke-telling and story-telling are often integral and, indeed, inseparable from the activity of making the quilt. Thus, we see in this new approach "a reorientation of the concept of genre away from genres as fixed normative, mutually exclusive categories to a consideration of genres as malleable social phenomena open to emergence, transformation, communicative use, and interrelatedness" (Ben-Amos, 1976; Limón and Young, 1986:438). Unfortunately, although this new perspective has greatly benefited the practical and theoretical study of folklore in general, it has done little to give the folklore of and about women its proper place in folklore scholarship (Limón and Young, 1986:439, 451)—an omission we feel that this book addresses in its emphasis on women's artistic communication.

Nine chapters in the present volume appeared in some form in 1987 in a special issue of the *Journal of American Folklore*. Since that 1986 symposium the essays have been revised and updated extensively. The result is a book that we believe achieves a new degree of sophistication in feminist approaches to the study of folklore, calling into question not only case studies but also any theoretical formulations that fail to take into account women's experiences and perceptions. This book is an attempt to provide a resource for those seeking a more comprehensive view of the research recently being conducted on the intersection of feminist theory and folklore. The book is divided into three parts, each addressing a specific theme: feminist reexamination of folklore theory and the development of the discipline, new ways of looking at the types of materials conventionally studied by folklorists, and the exploration of hitherto unapproached or little-recognized materials in folklore and feminism.

The editing and production of this work has been very difficult and slow. We know of no other edited volume that has undergone such extensive revision and scrutiny as has this one. With a commitment to the sometimes cumbersome task of sharing equally in the work, we found the involvement of three editors who live in different parts of the country made editing a collection such as this one an ominous task. The large number of contributors and many outside evaluators for each essay presented immense coordination problems, complicated for all three of us by moving to new locations and new jobs during the several-year process of pulling the book together. And the process of actually getting the book published took much longer than we hoped. Nevertheless, the birth has taken place, and we, the editors, are most grateful to those who have assisted in it. Our many thanks to the organizers of the day from which this collection arose, the contributors for their skill and insight, the outside readers for their thoughtful and helpful comments, and all those who not only waited patiently but also supported this effort.

References Cited

Ben-Amos, Dan, ed. 1976. *Folklore Genres*. Austin: University of Texas Press. Originally published in *Genre* 2, nos. 2–3 (1969): 91–301, and *Genre* 4, no. 3 (1971): 281–304.

Ben-Amos, Dan, and Kenneth S. Goldstein, eds. 1975. *Folklore: Performance and Communication*. The Hague: Mouton.

Farrer, Claire R., ed. 1975. *Women and Folklore*. Austin: University of Texas Press.

hooks, bell. 1984. *Feminist Theory: From Margin to Center*. Boston: South End Press.

Jordan, Rosan A., and Susan J. Kalčik, eds. 1985. *Women's Folklore, Women's Culture*. Philadelphia: University of Pennsylvania Press.

Limón, José E., and M. Jane Young. 1986. "Frontiers, Settlements, and Development in Folklore Studies, 1972–1985." *Annual Review of Anthropology* 15:437–60.

Paredes, Américo, and Richard Bauman, eds. 1972. *Toward New Perspectives in Folklore*. Austin: University of Texas Press.

Prologue | *Rayna Green*

"It's Okay Once You Get It Past the Teeth" and Other Feminist Paradigms for Folklore Studies

Years ago, I wrote an essay about my grandmother's bad mouth, or about southern women's "expressive culture" as we were then newly inclined to call it (Green, 1977). Included in my homage was a signal story, one that came to be a primary reference for many folklorists (male and female) for years after the essay emerged. Quite simply, the story concerned my maternal grandmother, an East Texas, German-Jewish storyteller and generally frisky lady, as she was exiting from the bathtub one summer afternoon. One of my sisters observed that Granny was "getting bald on her private parts," to which my grandmother retorted, "Grass don't grow on a racetrack." Granny's entertaining, vivid, and smart-mouthed boast about her active sexual history (seven husbands for starters) was hardly alien to the female family members who were most often the delighted recipients of her instructive verbal creativity. Still, this comment and others that typified her comic genius came to be the hallmark, the sign of a different strain of female expressive culture, if not entirely of a different female world, than had theretofore been described.

Just what did Granny mean when she said, "Grass don't grow on a racetrack"? Was she bragging about sexual encounters, and if so, why would she boast about that? As if seven husbands weren't enough of a disgrace to a lady born to a decent German-Jewish farming family, one turned very Texas and Protestant, nay, Baptist, by the time I came along in 1942. Nice women didn't say such things and mean it, though plenty of nice ladies hung around Granny just waiting for her to say the next outrageous thing. Did her repertoire make Granny a bad lady, a strange one, or should it cause us to reconsider our categories for understanding?

She took as much delight in upsetting our notions of proper behavior, it's true, as she took in the utterance of something outrageous, so perhaps the outrageous act was as much of a genre for her as word play, recitation of doggerel, the embellished story, or a gospel hymn. Was she a feminist or a performer who favored shocking material? Whatever the case, she upset folks and folklorists alike, because her life, her repertoire, her style refused to allow us a comfortable analysis. In the process, she created a folklorist —me—and gave us more fodder for the ruminations we call scholarship.

When I, as scholar, confronted my grandmother's stories, songs, and comments as something more than instruction and entertainment, I was compelled then to ask serious questions about the social and political relationships in the world bounded by her vision and behavior. In the rush of the postsixties feminism, most of us subscribed to the assertion that women had been silenced by male oppression. Granny, however, gave the lie to that assertion. The thought that she might have been a closet feminist, with her politics framed in artistic shrouding, did cross my mind once or twice. Could it be, I asked, that some women had not been silenced or might their sense of oppression be expressed in surprising and creative ways? Was there something missing from folklorists' and feminists' descriptions of women's narrative, indeed of their very lives? Had we missed some point somewhere, and if so, what point had we missed? Possibly, I told myself, Granny was just deviant . . . but then, my entire female family, maternal, paternal, and steppaternal, had to be deviant because they had minds, mouths, and repertoires just like Granny's. That thought threw me, as a nascent scholar of things folkloristic, into a theoretical spasm because my paternal and maternal families stem from radically different cultural groups while sharing some socioeconomic and geographic traditions. Did gender move across class and region? All theory aside, some descriptive problems emerged as I considered Granny's tale. With theory included, some challenges arose. Did it take one to know one, as the phrase goes? Had ladies from an upperer class than I missed out on hearing what lower-class women have to say and the way they have to say it because they were always acontextually situated, more or less theoretically out? Had no one ever just sat around and listened to ordinary women talk? Had we all expected to find what we wanted in the glorious genres of big ballad and grand story and, failing that, assumed there was little else? Had we looked too hard at the obvious, at ritualized texts of formal ceremonials, and thus found women wanting in whatever it was that made us think there were only men of words and deeds to study?

To put it in reverse, had we accepted the characterizations offered by male folklorists, male singers, male tale-tellers, male artists, male translators

—both of the material and of what the material actually meant—and thus missed entirely what the women had to say? Certainly most notable female performers' repertoires and venues for performance closely resembled those of male "stars," or had we simply treated them as though they did? The possibility that all our notions about artistry were flawed was deeply unsettling, but nevertheless intriguing. There's no little bit of Granny in me, so the provocative questions came to be as compelling as her provocative performances. While I was asking myself these questions, many other female folklorists had begun to ask them as well. Inspired by the rise of feminist theory and practice in literary and historical domains and honed by French studies of everyday life and American performance theory, feminist folklorists had begun to challenge everyone's notions about expressive culture. The first studies of women's expressive behavior were, of course, primarily corrective simply in their focus on women's expression, but that focus, in turn, shifted studies to an increasingly revisionist examination of the kinds of materials and contexts operative in female repertoires (Farrer, 1986). Newly understood genres, reframed analyses, recontextualizations—all became possible in a gendered perspective.

That new perspective made Granny seem less peculiar, though even more delightful. This book is about Granny and other women, like and unlike her. Still, the book does not contain solutions to the problems raised. I am accustomed to telling my students and colleagues that scholars appear to have forgotten that theory is intended to pose interesting questions, not to give final, for-all-time answers. This volume is certainly more about those interesting questions than about answers. It does begin to address the many questions we all have about women, they way they talk, what they think, and how they think and talk about the world they inhabit. Certainly, what they think and talk about is less about men than men would have imagined and possibly hoped. As with the expressive repertoire of other "oppressed" peoples, the oppressors are not the only or primary topic. A surprise perhaps, but an even more important surprise or disappointment to many. Home and family, kinship, relationships, food and kitchen, sex—all the "traditional" female topics are what women talk about and share, though in the most surprising forms—a ribbon around the Pentagon, a sermon, a joke, an altar built of bread. Should we have thought they would speak of machines, of guns, of brave deeds, or hoped, just a little bit, that they would express a desire to run things? So perhaps they do, and so the analyses here of their expressions of desire and hope and even of revolution honor the surprises folklorists may experience when confronted with material and people that simply do not fit the forms.

Thus we have here not an affirmative action *cri de coeur* simply chronicling and complaining about what we cannot comprehend, yet hoping to set the balance right by including women or retitling old ideas. It would not be enough to redeem "gossip" by calling it a conversational genre or by replacing the liar's bench. Also, as Rachelle H. Saltzman says, she does not intend her inquiry to create yet other models for paradox and contradiction, but rather to "hear what our informants say." That would have suited Granny fine, because she thought that all my questions were silly, while she thought my interest in all those "old things" and my devoted attention to her entirely appropriate. Still, she would have liked it if we got it right, especially if we explained it in comprehensible language. I cannot say that this book goes that far, but it does go a long way to setting us right. This book is as much about the way that we, as folklorists, have learned to think and talk about women—and men—as about the women and men themselves. In this series of essays, the ladies have a go at folklore theory and, of course, by inference and direct attack, at all the linguistic, literary, and anthropological theory that create the house that Jack built. Whether tackling Romantic nationalism, cultural relativism, notions about genre and the maintenance of boundaries, Western scientific explanatory models, or even current feminist deconstructions of "male and Yale" theory, standard notions about expressive life do not find a comfortable home here.

It's How You Jiggle the Bucket

Once, many years ago, in a gathering of my younger sisters and several of their friends at my home, the assembled ladies consulted Granny for some advice in matters of the heart and body. Was it true, one asked, that the genital size (mainly of tallywhackers, as she phrased it, but woollyboogers as well) made a difference in people's sexual enjoyment? "Well, honey," replied Granny advising her, "it don't matter how deep the well or how long the rope, it's how you jiggle the bucket." I took the statement then, as now, as a theoretical one, certainly as a comment on the significance of process. This collection of essays acts, like Granny's irreverent refusal to ascribe to popular and male-centered theory, as a countervalent and corrective to theory gone astray. Process finds a happy niche here, while there is much less emphasis on product or outcome. Like the feminist scholar (whose name, forgive me, is long lost to memory) who once suggested that data henceforward be referred to as wet or dry, rather than hard or soft, feminist folklorists are making an attempt to reshape older and dysfunctional notions about performance so that those notions reflect the world as it is, not as a few would imagine it.

It's Okay Once You Get It Past the Teeth

While teaching introductory folklore courses years ago, I insisted students keep a journal of their folkloristic encounters. A male student reported a story-telling session by his fellow premed students in which a story was repeated concerning the *vagina dentata* motif. In the story, a dentist who was afraid of women because his mother told him women had teeth "down there" eventually dates and marries a receptionist in his office. On their wedding night, after repeated urgings on her part to get into bed with her and not be afraid, he becomes brave enough to look "down there" and reassure himself that no "teeth" are present. "Why, of course, you don't have any teeth," he exclaims after reluctant close examination, "look at the condition your gums are in."

Coincidentally, the very week of reportage of this male version of the motif, I experienced firsthand a female version. In my "rap" group, a feminist artifact of the seventies consciousness-raising phenomenon, a member of the group recounted her first use of a tampon—a classic women's horror story (Kalčik, 1975). She told of her innocence of such things and repeated the saga of her first use of tampons—urged on by her roommates and friends as she sat in the bathroom in their college suite—while simultaneously, her friends in the rap group were encouraging her to tell what was for her a difficult story (Kirshenblatt-Gimblett, 1975). At one point, she, like the tampon of the narrative, could go no farther, both inhibited in their passage by fear. And, as she haltingly repeated the tale of her college friends urging her on, one of her present-day friends said, "You know, it's okay once you get it past the teeth." The members of the group collapsed in laughter, two of the group members hugging the tearful but happy narrator. The absurdity of the male-centered myth, which in the male version of the story creates fear for men and humiliation for women, became real, was rejected and reshaped in a female-centered, healing, and real-world version. Certainly, such a process characterizes what feminist scholarship has tried to accomplish. While scholarship certainly cannot claim to empower or dignify anyone, it can reveal the ways in which empowerment and authorization take place. Such scholarship can, like textual exegesis of any kind, give a name and status to process. Renaming as a form of reclamation the process through which moral authority is reshaped and reestablished insists on the presence, worth, and, indeed, the very centrality of female genres, female forms, and female-centered meaning. The folklorists who reexamine performance are reexamining the very shape of artistic text, statement, object, iteration, and act and reclaiming them in the name of those who found themselves outside the boundaries of definition, of meaning itself.

My grandmother's specialties in performance were the comic song and recitation, formulaic sage and comic advice, the comic crack and comeback, and the comic real-world narrative about ordinary people and strange happenings. In three instances, these genres have generally been thought to be reserved for men; in two others, they have scarcely been recognized as genres at all. Curious that, because I was raised in a sex-separated world where women were the narrators for all the amazing things I had ever heard. I believed men to be the silent and silenced ones. In my youthful world, women alone had the power of speech, of performance; only school and the world beyond my family appeared to operate by different rules. It was both the intrusion of those different rules and the feminist critique of women silenced by the patriarchy that caused me to ask hard questions about both the rules and the critique. To find the lyrical female voice solely as a reaction to or rebellion against the patriarchy would be to grant to it more power than real-world examination would sustain; still, to find or construct a deviant expressive world where no venues, domains, and boundaries matched those of men would beggar the imagination. No such discoveries will be found in these pages. Rose Red has not replaced Snow White *or* Prince Charming in the essays herein; she just gets equal time and several new tools for getting her way.

Be Sure and Wash Ol' Possible

"When you go off to college," Granny advised me, "don't drink out any strange toilets; when you wash, wash up as far as possible, down as far as possible, and then wash ol' possible. Before you get involved with any ol' hairy-legged boy, look carefully into his jeans. And remember that snakes might not hurt you, but they will make you hurt yourself." I've tried to remember and act on all her good advice, whether I took it literally or otherwise. All the things she told me have been instructive, both in negotiating the small rigors of daily life as well as in the more substantial rigors of work, politics, relationships, and ethical behavior. All the ways in which she told me what she had to say gave me a voice, the Word, the power of song and story, the sense of myself as both speaking and spoken for. At the heart of understanding, which is what scholarship is supposed to be about, rests the work and lives of women who, like my grandmother —through their singing, game-playing, altar-making, sewing, talking, bed-making, story-telling—establish their own versions of their past and present. The realities of their lives are often forged in white-hot troubles—poverty, physical pain, loss—or abandoned as well to an existence of little conse-quence to anyone. Scholarly interpretation of their lives and work, in this context, if it be what it might, would offer a new means of getting down their versions, their own meanings for their own lives. If we do our job, as I believe the writers of these essays have done, their authority and creativity will speak through time, even while the barriers of scholarly inhibitions get between them and the truth.

While theory enhances Rose Red's magic power by giving it a shape, her work here, however, is informed deeply by two commodities that often elude the most earnest of scholars—practicality and common sense. Like Granny's advice, the work herein is not only entertaining but useful. Still, as they explore the "missing link between philosophy and practice" in women's lives, as Kay Turner and Suzanne Seriff put it, the questions the authors draw from and pose to the data here are, in most respects, the questions all humans ask of their peers, their parents, their world. What does it tell us? What can we learn? More important, these exegeses ask, not coincidentally like women's performance, *how* can we learn? Will what we know make our lives, the lives of our relatives better? What will enable our peoples to survive? The interest in these questions, on the whole, can here be taken as a ritualized form of respect, a kind of homage from women who make essays, not chants or pots. It is a form of artistry, the artistry of inquiry, that these women practice. In social-scientific ritual, it is a learner-teacher relationship commemorated and explicated. In most of the rituals, the object is to raise the status of the learner, to develop or explicate theories that will give status to the theorist. Here, the intent, like that of female-centered expression, is to express, sustain, and reconstruct relationships that are durable, powerful, and replicable. Like the "different voice" that Gilligan (1982) sees in the development of female moral judgment, these essays offer a way to hear that voice—cooperative, competitive, competent. As women "author" themselves in their texts and their performances, so these essays on the aesthetics and genres of everyday life establish and track the worth, centrality, autonomy, and potency of their vision while they explore the "connectedness and continuities with" other humans and the natural world.

It is this latter exploration that folklorists and their domains of study can and must seek. To search for them within this framework and for these good reasons is to find them within the boundaries of a feminist or genuinely humane ontology. Granny used to say that what I did, after asking lots of seemingly senseless questions, was "just to lay up and write," the equivalent in her terms of "laying up drunk." Still, she read every word, and not, I believe, simply because "her baby" wrote them. Other people's lives and art fascinated her, whether she encountered them in a television soap opera, on someone's kitchen stove, or on someone else's porch. What she would find compelling in these pages is what she found right with my own work once I'd got it according to her notions of rightness. That came about only when I was finally able to talk about and take joy in talking about home, family, relationships, myself—real things and in the language of real people. To find those connections and continuities and to find the right words to give them life, an often and perpetually painful exploration, I had to locate myself in what I was writing. The authors here find themselves in their work; more significantly, they acknowledge their own presence in the intellectual constructs they present. There is little pretense of objective distance from what they've legitimately been part of. That acknowledgment of legitimacy and place, not to say power, resonated even for those who examined old documents as well as for those who trafficked in living traditions. "This really counts," they are saying; "this really matters" for all of our abilities to negotiate creative survival. If the art matters, our form of caring about it must also matter. After having "laid up and written," what we hope for is a renewed sense of connection with the subjects and objects of our writing, the women who transform the landscapes of our past and future.

References Cited

Farrer, Claire R. 1986. "Introduction." In *Women and Folklore: Images and Genres,* ed. Claire R. Farrer, xi-xxi. Prospect Heights, Ill.: Waveland Press.

Gilligan, Carol. 1982. *In a Different Voice: Psychological Theory and Women's Development.* Cambridge: Harvard University Press.

Green, Rayna. 1977. "Magnolias Grow in Dirt: The Bawdy Lore of Southern Women." *Southern Exposure* 4:29–33. Reprinted in *The Radical Teacher* 6 (1977): 26–30.

Kalčik, Susan. 1986. " . . . like Ann's Gynecologist or the Time I Was Almost Raped": Personal Narratives in Women's Rap Groups. In *Women and Folklore: Images and Genres,* ed. Claire R. Farrer, 3–11. Prospect Heights, Ill.: Waveland Press.

Kirshenblatt-Gimblett, Barbara. 1975. "A Parable in Context: A Social Interactional Analysis of Storytelling Performance." In *Folklore: Performance and Communication,* ed. Dan Ben-Amos and Kenneth S. Goldstein, 105–30. The Hague: Mouton.

PART ONE

M. Jane Young and Kay Turner

Challenging the Canon: Folklore Theory Reconsidered from Feminist Perspectives

For at least the past fifteen years, members of the women's section of the American Folklore Society have heard certain questions raised about the relationship between feminism and folklore (even if not couched in those specific terms) that continue to reverberate—in our writing, our teaching, our professional membership in this particular scholarly society, our academic careers, and our personal lives. These questions include the following and their ramifications: Why, when there are so many female graduate students in folklore departments, are there so few female faculty in such departments? Why aren't courses concerning gender and folklore standard offerings for all folklore curricula? Why does the expressive behavior of male members of a given "folk" group receive more attention than that enacted by females in the same group—i.e., why are male performance genres so privileged in our discipline? Why aren't a significant number of academic writings by female folklorists on the Ph.D. reading lists of the major departments? Are such writings simply being ignored by patriarchal institutions? Or are women not writing theoretical works—either because their scholarly interests/focuses are elsewhere; their activist participation concerning issues of race, class, ethnicity, and gender takes too much time; or they are too devoted to family matters that male faculty members can relegate to their wives? Or is the reason (Goddess forbid) that women lack the skills to produce scholarly works in folklore that have a strong theoretical basis? Of course, all of these questions lead to a more general question: Have other disciplines been more productive of, or hospitable to, the development of feminist theory than has folklore? The answers to these questions have been slow in coming; indeed, even polite attention to such concerns is often lacking. What, then, does a feminist folklore scholar do in the face of such damaging silence? Some of us have thrown up our hands in despair at what seems to be the "tunnel vision" of folklore scholarship as it is mediated through the major folklore programs in the country; through the academic journals and presses given over to publishing the finest examples of current folklore scholarship; through the workshops, paper sessions, and special symposia of the annual meetings; and, of course, through the decisions made by the Executive Board of the American Folklore Society. Some have left the discipline entirely, finding a more receptive home in academic departments and professional organizations that provide the sort of environment in which feminists can find a voice, can express themselves and their concerns; others have remained, but have grown tired and bitter with the struggle to survive and to do productive research within a startlingly patriarchal framework—one that gives only lip service to issues of race, class, ethnicity, and gender; others have said, "There is no struggle at all, this is a discipline that concerns itself with these very issues and has much to offer"; others have taken up the gauntlet and attempted to change the orientation of the discipline by demonstrating the importance of feminist ideology within the framework of folklore scholarship in every way available to them (Farrer, 1975; Jordan and Kalčik, 1985; Jackson, 1987; Stoeltje, 1988a; Radner, 1993).[1] It is these others who have made it possible to answer the question "Can women do theory?" with the response "Read on." All of the authors whose words appear in this volume have contributed to the strength of this response, but, in this introduction to Part 1, we are most concerned with those who have directed their words and thoughts to the theoretical issues surrounding the conjunction of feminism and folklore.

Jennifer Fox addresses the problem of the lack of feminist concerns in folklore scholarship directly, pointing out that a "negative conception of women" has been engendered in the discipline of folklore since its inception, adding that this sort of bias has "contributed to the relative lack of concern with women's perspectives and activities among the people we study and to the relative suppression of women's voices in the practice of folklore." Fox suggests that before we can begin to change the current biases in our discipline we need to look backwards—to the scholars and motivating ideas that had a lasting impact on the discipline, spawning certain generative ideas that remain with us today. Recognizing that there are a number of such "founding fathers," Fox chooses to focus on Johann Gottfried von Herder—"the father of Romantic Nationalism"—whose ideas concerning "tradition, patriarchalism, and unity" have "infiltrated and informed the scripts of folklore research," operating "explicitly and implicitly to the detriment of women." Herder regarded tradition (received and propagated by men) and the patriarchal order as essential components of human nature and, thus, inviolable. In addition, Herder's principle of unity suggests that women are "other" than men in the sense of lacking something essential, and should, therefore, be subsumed under the "mantle of a higher unity." The principle of unity thus eliminates all considerations of gender, race, class, and ethnicity, holding that such diversity within a nation "is a sign of cultural degeneration." The solution that Fox suggests to folklorists and the discipline as a whole is that we first recognize the bias inherent in our scholarship from its very inception and then work to change the situation through our academic writings and through dialogue, but she sees this as adopting a radical stance that entails more than merely pointing out the existence of this bias: "it is through discourse that challenges and disrupts established symbolic structures . . . that women may actively redirect their experience."

In her discussion of Herder's notion that patriarchy is essential to human nature, Fox introduces a debate that is addressed, both directly and indirectly, by most of the contributors to this volume—a debate that has been argued vehemently by supporters and detractors of feminist theory for many years. Sherry Ortner succinctly sums up the issue in her article entitled "Is Female to Male as Nature Is to Culture?" (1974:67–87). Put simply, one can rephrase this question as follows: Is the secondary status of women in society natural (or biologically determined), as Herder would argue, or is it culturally created? A further ramification of this question is expressed by the following query: Is the creativity of women centered in their natural ability to reproduce life, whereas male creativity is manifested externally, "through the medium of technology and symbols" (Ortner, 1974:75)?

A related point of dispute concerns the spheres of activity in which women and men enact their roles (determined either biologically or culturally or influenced by both). If we respond positively to the above-mentioned query, claiming that the domain of women is "naturally" one of privacy and domesticity, whereas men control the public arena of technology and culture, a logical extension of this claim is that the sphere and role of women is one of relative powerlessness that can only be overturned if women enter the public, male-dominated realm or "create a public world of their own" (Rosaldo and Lamphere, 1974:36). Certainly, in Rachelle Saltzman's essay we see Rose Kerrigan and her female colleagues entering the public arena of politics and work; indeed, they may be said to take Fox's advice, for they challenge and disrupt the symbolic structures they find there. But the other chapters in Part 1 point to a more subtle shifting of traditional modes of control. Amy Shuman discusses a woman who strengthens her position by transforming the "accepted" interpretation of a parable, and Debora Kodish delineates the way in which female folksingers skillfully manipulate the male folklorists who have intruded on their domain. In the latter case, the women never question their own power, but it is obvious that the men do not even perceive the way in which they are managed and marginalized by those they seek to study. Nevertheless, the power of these women does not depend on male recognition to be valid; nor does the potency of the women's altar-giving discussed by Kay Turner and Suzanne Seriff rely for its efficacy on the acknowledgment of the men who take a secondary role in the creation of the St. Joseph's Day feast.

Of course, folklore is not alone in exhibiting the bias and enacting the sort of suppression that these authors and other feminists challenge. It is a common assertion of contemporary feminism that women's experiences, values, and meanings have been excluded from what have been designated and reported as *any* society's experiences, meanings, and values (Spender, 1982:7). Within patriarchy, the history and values of men are considered to be the only valid frame of reference for society as a whole, and "it is therefore in patriarchal interest to prevent women from sharing, establishing and asserting their equally real, valid and *different* frame of reference, which is the outcome of different experience" (Spender, 1982:5). Historically, women's difference from men has been used to deny them access to the opportunities and privileges granted by and for the majority culture. The exclusion of women is written into the very foundations of Western thought and has been institutionalized over the course of a three-thousand-year history.[2]

In her classic study, Simone de Beauvoir outlined the terms in which man first constructed woman as the primary "other," the negative "other," and hence "the second sex": "This humanity is male and man defines woman not in herself but as relative to him" (1974:xviii). She is different and therefore suspect; she is different and therefore objectified. In woman, man discovered the prototype for the negative inscription of difference, and in Western history patriarchal privilege became the first construction of dominance[3] that eventually gave rise to all others, including racism and colonialism (Lerner, 1986:212–29).[4]

Unfortunately, de Beauvoir accounted for woman's secondary status as the result of *her* failure to bring about change: "women lack concrete means for organizing themselves into a unit which can stand face to face with the correlative unit [man]. They have no past, no history, no religion of their own" (1974:xxii). What de Beauvoir failed to account for was the way in which women themselves perceive their difference and how they use their understanding of it to counter their secondary status.

Many of the authors in this volume and in earlier publications have focused on women's expressive genres to further an understanding of symbolic modes that serve women's own interests. Such symbolic modes, the general currency of thought and the basis for social and cultural life, have too frequently been regarded as produced by men or controlled by them (Smith, 1978:281–82). As stated by Turner and Seriff:

> Folklore and feminism conjoin in the critical attention both disciplines pay to forms of women's symbolic expression that are hidden from, or considered unimportant to, the majority culture. The combined efforts of folklore and feminism enlarge our understanding of the way in which women create or use symbolic modes within the dominant culture of the patriarchy. Folklore provides a unique data base of the traditional artistic means women have employed to express their own view of the world, and feminism offers a theoretical handle on that expression.

Feminist scholarship "undertakes the dual task of deconstructing predominantly male paradigms and reconstructing a female perspective and experience in an effort to change the tradition that has silenced and marginalized us" (Greene and Kahn, 1985:1).[5] But much of women's folklore gives evidence that this project is not necessarily a new one, nor is it exceptionally the project of academic or otherwise "politically aware" women.[6] From generation to generation, women's traditions have had their own part to play in countering the patriarchal tradition that has marginalized and silenced women.

A number of folklore scholars have documented situations in which women either use expressive behavior as a means of appropriating genres normally reserved for men or exert power that is seen by them as an inherent part of their domain, whether that power is officially recognized or not.[7] In their chapter in this volume, Turner and Seriff point out that when they cut the all-important traditional fig cookies for the St. Joseph's Day feast, Sicilian-American women frequently employ tools from the masculine domain, such as a man's pocketknife or the metal casing of a shotgun shell. They "joke about the special nature of these tools that have been borrowed from the male-centered realm of hunting and outdoor sports and reappropriated for this most domestic of tasks." Saltzman explores a more dramatic example: Rose Kerrigan, her Marxist/feminist respondent, tells Saltzman that she and her female colleagues in the factory often told "blue jokes" that denigrated women, and she recited some particularly vivid examples of such jokes. Although initially dismayed by this, Saltzman learns from Rose that the women used these jokes, which would normally be described as portraying sexist stereotypes of women, in a consciously oppositional manner. In this particular performance context, they appropriate and subvert male genres to gain power in a new way, by inverting the situation so that it is the males who are stereotyped as these jokes become vehicles for portraying women's views on male language usage. Similarly, Shuman's parable teller challenges traditional interpretations, quite consciously giving voice to her own unique experience. This issue of knowledge of one's power also pervades the essay by Turner and Seriff and links it with other chapters in this volume that delineate situations of explicit and implicit power. The Sicilian-American women are central figures in the religious process of "giving an altar"; they create a feast for St. Joseph and other saints—a feast that exhibits the efficacy of their ability to sacrifice, acted out in this elaborate offering of thanks. These women do not explicitly articulate the power embodied in their role, at least not within the parameters of Turner and Seriff's chapter, but awareness of the significance of their role as feeders and nurturers seems to underlie their actions in giving this feast.

Rather than delineating an instance of female appropriation of elements from the male realm, Kodish discusses the all-too-frequent example of women exerting power within their own realm that is not recognized by men who are blinded by their own perceptions of their importance. Kodish's examples thus serve to illustrate Fox's point that the patriarchal biases of Romantic Nationalism still wield considerable influence on contemporary folklore scholarship. Kodish focuses on two field situations in which male folklorists see themselves as veritable heroes "discovering" female folksingers, who, from the folklorists' perspective, have been until that point passive and silent.[8] By turning the tables so that we see these encounters through the eyes of the folksingers, Kodish shows us two women who are "fully aware of the worth and power" of their performances. From this perspective, the folklorists take on a more marginal position—for in the narratives of the female folksingers, the "folklorists are not powerful heroes but visitors well managed." Thus, from the emic perspective, these encounters constitute simply one more situation to be skillfully handled in the everyday lives of these women—a situation that they see within the framework of their responsibility to manage the varying tasks of the homemaker. Similarly, Saltzman offers an interesting example that underscores the importance of recognizing and allowing the informant her own voice, her own particular way of looking at the world. She cites her own fieldwork and the contradiction that she, as a feminist, saw in Rose Kerrigan's commitment to Marxism and feminism and her decision to raise a family. Significantly, as Saltzman points out, Rose saw no such contradiction. As she listens to Rose's explanation of her choices, Saltzman realizes that "people can and do make conscious choices within their historical constraints, choices that are not always consistent with *our* theories about *their* ideologies." Turner and Seriff also argue that an analysis of an expressive event such as the St. Joseph's altar tradition celebrated by second- and third-generation Sicilian-American women in a central Texas town must not be based on externally derived preconceptions of the meaning of the event. They suggest instead that folklorists recognize "the strategic way in which the participants themselves organize and reorganize the meaning of this festival according to what they consider valuable."

Summing up such encounters and perspectives, Kodish suggests that they exemplify the following problems with folklore fieldwork in general. First, folklorists fail to see informants as individuals within their communities; thus they are "too much or too little voiced" in folkloric accounts. Furthermore, folklorists do not recognize the alternative texts that the "folk" construct to explain interactions with folklorists from their own perspectives. Saltzman, Turner, and Seriff concur with Kodish, suggesting that folklorists begin to pay more attention to what the informants themselves say about the interrelationship of form, function, and audience in their expressive behavior. Secondly, Kodish points out that gender issues are frequently ignored in fieldwork and in the plethora of texts and practical handbooks that focus on how to do fieldwork in the discipline of folklore.[9] She demonstrates, therefore, how one can read this *absence* as an ideological *presence;* the omission of gender issues from the canon is not a slight oversight but a direct statement about the central concerns of the discipline. This point is, of course, useful in the analysis of all situations that involve the unequal distribution of status and power, not just those that are gender-focused. Saltzman extends this point, stating that the "contradictions inherent in combining folkloric and feminist perspectives," both in conducting fieldwork and analyzing data, exist "largely because folklore theory and research have tended to privilege male informants and masculine forms of expressive culture—even when women and their lore are examined." The solution to this dilemma offered by Kodish from the perspective of feminist scholarship echoes Fox's earlier-mentioned model for change. Kodish suggests that one must "deconstruct male paradigms" and then "reconstruct models attentive to women's experiences." Thus, Fox, Kodish, and Saltzman point to alternative and oppositional means by which to challenge the persistent male-oriented paradigms that make up the folklore canon.

Whereas Kodish has voiced a concern with the politics of cross-gender fieldwork interaction and the subsequent manner in which the folklorist writes about such interactions, Shuman focuses on the way in which respondents determine their own positions in relation to given circumstances, texts, and contexts. She portrays a situation in which a woman challenges authority and accrues power by using a well-known folklore genre—the parable—in a new context that undermines its traditional interpretation, transforming the traditional to fit it to her own interpretation of her unusual experience. This woman, an outcast in a country not her own, gives voice to her particular position by using two genres, one embedded in the other, competing for somewhat different interpretations. By creating this discrepancy between voices, this performer disrupts any carefully constructed system we might design to explain the performance. This example has led Shuman to a consideration of the politics involved in genre theory in general and to a realization that, from the perspective of feminism, neither neutral texts nor neutral contexts exist. Shuman's theories about genre explicitly critique concerns voiced by the anthropologist Clifford Geertz. Although Shuman might agree with Geertz's point that scholars in the humanities and social sciences can no longer lay "claim to moral neutrality" in the analysis of their data (1980:178), she challenges his discussion (exemplified in the following quotation) of the necessity to go beyond rigid boundaries and accept situations that give rise to multivocal interpretations:

> The properties connecting texts with one another, that put them, ontologically anyway, on the same level, are coming to seem as important in characterizing them as those dividing them; and rather than face an array of natural kinds, fixed types divided by sharp qualitative differences, we more and more see ourselves surrounded by a vast, almost continuous field of variously intended and diversely constructed works we can order only practically, relationally, and as our purposes prompt us. It is not that we no longer have conventions of interpretation; we have more than ever, built—often enough jerry-built—to accommodate a situation at once fluid, plural, uncentered, and ineradicably untidy. (Geertz, 1980:166)

Shuman counters Geertz's focus on pluralism of voice and interpretation, suggesting that constructedness, not flexibility, is the connection between gender and genre; she adds that such supposed flexibility is only an illusion. Shuman's concern is not one of transcending boundaries or making them fluid; rather, she takes issue with the boundaries themselves, raising questions concerning entitlement ("who determines the boundaries"), appropriation ("how is authority appropriated by the dominated"), and the significance of such categories.

Like Shuman, Saltzman is dissatisfied with the imposition of a false neutrality both in the conduct of folklore fieldwork and the analysis of data. She suggests that "we stop trying to force our data into neat models" and "instead focus on the alternative, sometimes paradoxical issues" that arise in fieldwork situations. Thus, she is in accord with the perspectives of those who advocate new or reflexive approaches to ethnography, emphasizing in particular that objective fieldwork or writing about such fieldwork is impossible (Ruby, 1982; Clifford and Marcus, 1986; Marcus and Fischer, 1986; Clifford, 1988; Van Maanen, 1988). Saltzman points out a serious problem that occurs when feminist fieldworkers interview women, particularly other feminists, who become their friends—in this case, she says, "the person keeps messing up the model." Saltzman encourages us to let our informants speak "more honestly," both in the fieldwork dialogue(s) and in the way we write about such interactions, emphasizing that our informants may offer us "alternative theories for the way women use and interpret their folklore."

The essays by Fox, Kodish, Saltzman, Shuman, and Turner and Seriff demonstrate that when they are interwoven, folklore and feminism can fabricate a new understanding of women's marginal status in defined cultural contexts. On the one hand, women's marginality is imposed; patriarchy enforces the rule of men from the very center of a society's organization (i.e., through the formation of laws, customs, and institutions that promote and preserve male domination) and leaves women at its periphery. In even more damning terms, Barbara Babcock states that under patriarchy "marginality is constitutionally feminine" and that the feminine is therefore "always suppressed and appropriated." On the other hand, marginality lends women the capacity to remain detached from the status quo. Their peripheral position may also reference an incompatibility with established norms, leading to innovation, especially in expressive domains. In reviewing women's expressive culture from a feminist stance it is particularly important to look for ways in which women use their marginal status to creatively undermine "the reality system" by the invention or maintenance of traditions that signal the viability and appropriateness of a different system. As Babcock further suggests, women's "marginality [also] gives access to a new definition of center."[10]

Saltzman's concerns about the dangers of forcing data into neat models or absolute categories are quite valid. Still, we suggest that it is possible to construct flexible models that permit one to situate the details of women's folklore within a larger perspective, widening the scope of folklore theory by drawing on scholarship in other disciplines. One way that folklorists can clarify and enlarge on the details of the "illusive center" discussed by Babcock is through an attempt to create new models for thinking about women's folklore. This does not entail negating the issues raised by Saltzman, for we posit that one can create models that aid in the analysis of one's data, while at the same time these models are based on expanded perspectives—they illustrate how women creatively negotiate certain situations to transcend a domain traditionally regarded as powerless. For example, grounding their ideas in a central, yet malleable, paradigm, Turner and Seriff develop a theory about women's participation in the St. Joseph's Day feast that centers on an *ideology of reproduction:* "these women are engaged in constant communication about, and evaluation of, the practice of caring for and nurturing others." Although they are living within a community that has strong patriarchal roots, it is clear that certain ethnically keyed traditions become the context within which these Sicilian-American women display their extensive and autonomous kin-based power (for similar examples among Italian-American women, see di Leonardo, 1984, 1987). Turner and Seriff make it quite clear, for instance, that the men in this community are on the periphery of the activities involved in preparing for and presenting the St. Joseph's Day feast, while the women, and their networks of kin-based labor, are central. Although the men help prepare certain food items, the most significant items are prepared and displayed by the women. Food is obviously vitally important to the feast—"a symbol of life and the labor of women" that highlights "binding relationships that are symbolically created and promoted on this day between the heavenly family and the earthly family." The activity of these women may revolve around the domestic realm, but they strategically employ their kin-related networks to transform this realm from an arena for the enactment of unpaid labor to one in which they achieve power and satisfaction.

Citing the research of Nancy Hartsock (1983), Turner and Seriff emphasize that "women's labor in every society differs from men's," but they point out that this distinction arises both from socially constructed roles and a sexual division of labor derived from women's reproductive labor, which, in turn, gives rise to a focus on relational values. According to Hartsock, this generates a distinctive women's worldview that leads in an opposite direction from male experience and social relations—"toward opposition to dualisms of any sort, valuation of concrete, everyday life, [a] sense of a variety of connectednesses and continuities both with other persons and with the natural world" (1983:298).

The notion of ideology (particularly the ideology of reproduction as it applies to women's expressive behavior) developed by Turner and Seriff is crucial because it asserts an autonomous source of women's knowledge and power even though important life activities of women such as motherwork and housework have "consistently been held by the [patriarchal] powers that be to be unworthy of those who are fully human most centrally because of their connections with necessity and life" (Hartsock, 1983:301). The pertinence of forwarding a claim for a female-centered ideology of reproduction is made against the inadequacy of most Western philosophies for assessing women's lived experience within the domestic realm. In fact it might be said that all philosophies developed under patriarchy—especially liberationist philosophies such as Marxism and Freudianism—fail to account for female dimensions of experience. Such philosophies ignore or devalue the concrete and material aspects of female life activity, including but not limited to reproductive control, childbirth, and the relations between women and children (O'Brien, 1981). The task of feminist epistemology is to uncover how patriarchy has permeated both our concept of knowledge and the actual content of bodies of knowledge, even those claiming to be emancipatory (Flax, 1983:269). In addition, feminist epistemology invites a broader conception of the knowledge, practice, and beliefs that constitute women's own understanding of their experience and labor.

This mode of philosophical inquiry in part finds its political locus in recognizing ethical and moral concepts based on women's traditional labor or work, the most traditional being reproductive labor and its extension into maternal practice (Ruddick, 1980) and kin work (di Leonardo, 1984, 1987). Since 1980, several feminist philosophers have undertaken the task of reevaluating the social relations of women's reproductive labor on its own terms. Productive and reproductive labor each produce values and create new needs, but as Mary O'Brien states, the "values and needs are not...commensurable....[The] productive process creates values and needs for the producer: in any form, reproductive labour creates another and needy human" (1981:16). Reproduction in this sense serves the necessary regeneration of sociability, the human responsibility for, and coming together with, others.

As Turner and Seriff point out, the philosophical stance that has emerged from recent feminist reinterpretations of reproduction insists upon a recognition of a gender-related "distinction between modes of thought, patterns of relationship, and ways of being in the world." They further note that this stance privileges women's reproductive experience and the use of this experience as a ground for philosophical inquiry and critique, as expressed by feminist scholars in the following terms:[11] "Mary O'Brien (1981) has called this a 'philosophy of birth'; Sara Ruddick (1980) has called it 'maternal thinking'; Alison Jaggar (1983) describes it as a noncoercive form of power that asserts 'the social development of human capacities'; and Carolyn Whitbeck (1983) and Nancy Hartsock (1983), anticipating the most recent rethinking of the essentialist argument, have proposed what Whitbeck calls a 'feminist ontology' and Hartsock refers to as a 'feminist standpoint.' "

The ideology of reproduction exemplifies the potential for discovering epistemological, ontological, and ideological structures in women's lore that characterize the power of women's difference. What feminist theory can bring to the interpretation of women's lore is a commitment to understanding that lore as it arises from and promotes this woman-centered ideology. Both folklore and feminism conjoin in their mutual validation of the regenerative and regenerating aspects of social and cultural life.

No doubt other paradigms and theories will also emerge and prove equally valuable as folklorists continue to refine the relationship between folklore and feminism. Still, the ideology of reproduction is a starting point for formulating a theory of women's folklore that can account for historical, culturally specific modes and expressions of women's power and its ramifications.

We have discussed various ways in which feminist theory, particularly scholarship that centers on the ideology of reproduction, can contribute to expanding and enhancing folklore theory. We are not, however, describing a one-way process. Women's folklore can also provide new data for, and affirmation of, theories that underlie feminist scholarship. By providing a cross-cultural spectrum of traditional texts in various aesthetic media that either affirm or critique gender-related difference, women's folklore in a very important way validates a critical feminist prospect articulated in no uncertain terms by Catherine Stimpson:

> The unravelling of male hegemony, the knitting up of a female heterodoxy at once independent and interdependent, is inseparable from feminist criticism's ... study of sexual difference itself; of what is "male" and what is "female"; of the causes and inscriptions of difference.... Because feminist criticism is feminist, the study of sexual difference is a study of hierarchy, of power differentials, as well.... For theories of sexual difference have more than intellectual interest. They influence the political imagination. (1988:118–19)

A claim for the value of traditions that formulate female-centered considerations presupposes a need to allow folklore to speak for and about the traditions of women's difference as this is manifested in their material life activities and then given voice through a range of expressive means. As Hartsock suggests, it seems certain that the specific features of women's material life activity carry important epistemological and ontological consequences for understanding and constructing all social relations (1983:299).

Folklore, as much as any other discipline or perhaps more than any other, can elucidate the full politics of women's domestic and maternal powers, both as these powers intersect with other forms of power and as they make their own critical claims. The distinctive world of women poses a paradigmatic challenge. The problem of women's inclusion—our equality—generally means that only woman's sameness to man—our humanity, not our feminine specificity—can be discussed or ultimately approved (Gross, 1987:191). Still, the fact of women's difference need not be construed as necessarily oppositional. The significance of women's traditions mentioned in Part 1 (specifically women's folksongs, women's oppositional use of humor, women's political use of certain parables, women's role in the production of the St. Joseph's Day feast) is in their furtherance of inclusivity, care, relationship, and connection. The authors in this part propose that women's understanding of the primacy of these social constituents should be taken seriously and that they should be granted their place in the construction of human relations so that all people will enjoy the benefits both of their independence and of their interdependence (Tronto, 1987).

Notes

Much of the material on the conjunction of folklore and feminist theory in this introduction is derived from certain sections of Kay Turner's Ph.D. dissertation (1990). In the spirit of "femmage" (see, for example, Pershing, this volume), Young undertook the task of melding this theoretical material with her introduction to Part 1.

1. We note here not every work written recently that addresses the relationship between feminism and folklore but the major ones that have focused on this topic.

2. Several feminist authors provide studies that document and interpret the misogynist underpinnings of Western thought and philosophy. We especially recommend Ruether (1974, 1975); Vetterling-Braggin, Elliston, and English (1977); Clark and Lange (1979); Elshtain (1981); Harding and Hintikka (1983); Gould (1983); Lloyd (1984); Suleiman (1986); and Grimshaw (1986).

3. The literature on the historical evolution, practice, and meaning of patriarchy is extensive. We have been influenced in our own thinking on the subject by readings that include de Beauvoir (1974); Daly (1968, 1973, 1978); Rosaldo and Lamphere (1974); Ortner (1974); Reiter (1975); Rubin (1975); Rich (1976); Etienne and Leacock (1980); Eisenstein (1981); Moraga and Anzaldúa (1981); Ortner and Whitehead (1981); Sanday (1981); Gray (1982); Frye (1983); Kelly (1984); Lloyd (1984); Keuls (1985); Keller (1986); Lerner (1986); and Stimpson (1988).

4. It is of critical importance to recognize that an understanding of women's domination by men has significant ramifications in further understanding other modes of domination. On this continent alone the story of women's subjection to male domination reverberates in the historical dynamics of Native American genocide, black slavery, anti-Semitism, and other forms of oppression characterized by hatred and xenophobia. Moreover, women's strategies for countering their

domination are linked to and share similarities with the counterhegemonic strategies of all oppressed people.

5. Throughout this essay we use the term *paradigm* in the sense suggested by Thomas Kuhn. According to Kuhn, paradigms are "concrete . . . models from which spring particular coherent traditions of scientific research" (1970:10–11). Thus, for our purposes, *male paradigms* are models that have been established on the basis of male perspectives and experiences, forming male-oriented traditions of folklore research. Feminist scholarship asserts that such models are inappropriately privileged, thus marginalizing female perspectives and experiences.

6. While early studies of folklore collected from women or about women offer a wealth of data, they accomplish little with regard to how gender affects folklore creation or performance. See, for example, Thiselton-Dyer (1906), Abrahams (1970), Bunzel (1972), and Azadovskii (1974); also see Farrer (1975), who edited the first feminist-oriented collection on women and folklore; de Caro (1983), who compiled an extensive bibliography on women and folklore; and Farrer and Kalčik (1988), who provided a selected bibliography of entries on women's folklore in the *Journal of American Folklore* from 1888 to 1988. Certain works from the 1970s (see Green [1977] and Weigle [1978]) did point to the potential for a more directed feminist analysis of women's folklore. But as Kodish complained almost ten years ago, "Seldom have folklorists even asked how a woman's power and place relate to her performance of folklore. Rare is the interest in women's symbolic forms *qua* women's symbolic forms rather than as barometers of some *other* issue" (1981:11). Happily, in recent studies folklorists have turned their focus to women's symbolic forms and the gendered aspect of these forms has begun to receive attention. See Mitchell (1978); Ice and Shulimson (1979); Caraveli-Chaves (1980); Kodish (1981, 1987); Turner (1982, 1983, 1990); Lawless (1983, 1987, 1988); Ice (1984); Kligman (1984); Jahner (1985); Jordan (1985); Roach (1985); Webber (1985); Yocom (1985); Babcock (1986, 1987); Limón (1986); Brady (1987); Radner and Lanser (1987); Turner and Seriff (1987); Young (1987); Sawin (1988); Stoeltje (1988b, 1988c); and Weigle (1982, 1989).

7. See, for example, the references listed in note 6.

8. Seriff (1989) brilliantly discusses the way in which a number of contemporary folklorists, especially those who study individual folk artists, write about their fieldwork as if it were a romantic adventure in which they "discovered" the folk artist—who, presumably, was passively waiting for this all-important discovery.

9. Although not by academic orientation or training a folklorist, Wax (1971) does a superb job of discussing gender issues that arise during fieldwork. See also Golde (1970) and Spradley and Mann (1975). A recent issue of *Southern Folklore* focuses specifically on gender and sex in folklore fieldwork. See Collins (1990).

10. As quoted here, Barbara Babcock's remarks were made in her role as discussant on a panel entitled "Women and Folklore: Empowering Marginality," in 1987 at the annual meeting of the American Folklore Society, Albuquerque, N.M.

11. We would like to expand this quotation from Turner and Seriff by adding to their list the writings of two other feminist scholars who also create a special

terminology to discuss the ideology of reproduction: Hilde Hein (1983) names it a liberated philosophy that puts an end to the "dichotomy of matter and spirit," and Catherine Keller (1985, 1986) names it "the ethic of inseparability."

References Cited

Abrahams, Roger D. 1970. *A Singer and Her Songs: Almeda Riddle's Book of Ballads.* Baton Rouge: Louisiana State University Press.

Azadovskii, Mark. 1974. *A Siberian Tale Teller.* Translated by James R. Dow. Center for Intercultural Studies of Folklore and Ethnomusicology Monograph Series, no. 2. Austin: University of Texas Center for Intercultural Studies of Folklore and Ethnomusicology. Originally published as *Eine sibirische Märchenerzahlerin.* Helsinki, 1926.

Babcock, Barbara A. 1986. "Modeled Selves: Helen Cordero's 'Little People.'" In *The Anthropology of Experience,* eds. Victor W. Turner and Edward M. Bruner, 316–43. Urbana: University of Illinois Press.

———. 1987. "Taking Liberties, Writing from the Margins, and Doing It with a Difference." *Journal of American Folklore* 100 (398): 390–411.

Brady, Margaret K. 1987. "Transformations of Power: Mormon Women's Visionary Narratives." *Journal of American Folklore* 100 (398): 461–68.

Bunzel, Ruth. [1929] 1972. *The Pueblo Potter: A Study of Creative Imagination in Primitive Art.* New York: Dover.

Caraveli-Chaves, Anna. 1980. "Bridge between Worlds: The Women's Ritual Lament as Communicative Event." *Journal of American Folklore* 93 (368): 129–57.

Clark, L., and L. Lange, eds. 1979. *The Sexism of Social and Political Theory: Women and Reproduction from Plato to Nietzsche.* Toronto: University of Toronto Press.

Clifford, James. 1988. *The Predicament of Culture: Twentieth-Century Ethnography, Literature, and Art.* Cambridge, Mass.: Harvard University Press.

Clifford, James, and George E. Marcus, eds. 1986. *Writing Culture: The Poetics and Politics of Ethnography.* Berkeley: University of California Press.

Collins, Camilla A., ed. 1990. *Folklore Fieldwork: Sex, Sexuality, and Gender.* Special issue of *Southern Folklore* 47:1.

Daly, Mary. 1968. *The Church and the Second Sex.* New York: Harper and Row.

———. 1973. *Beyond God the Father.* Boston: Beacon Press.

———. 1978. *Gyn/Ecology: The Metaethics of Radical Feminism.* Boston: Beacon Press.

de Beauvoir, Simone. [1953] 1974. *The Second Sex.* New York: Alfred A. Knopf.

de Caro, Frank. 1983. *Women and Folklore: A Bibliographic Survey.* Westport, Conn.: Greenwood Press.

di Leonardo, Micaela. 1984. *The Varieties of Ethnic Experience: Kinship, Class, and Gender among California Italian-Americans.* Ithaca: Cornell University Press.

———. 1987. "The Female World of Cards and Holidays: Women, Families, and the Work of Kinship." *Signs* 12 (3): 440–53.

Eisenstein, Zillah R. 1981. *The Radical Future of Liberal Feminism.* Boston: Northeastern University Press.

Elshtain, Jean B. 1981. *Public Man, Private Woman: Women in Social and Political Thought.* Princeton: Princeton University Press.

Etienne, Mona, and Eleanor Leacock, eds. 1980. *Women and Colonization: Anthropological Perspectives.* New York: Praeger.

Farrer, Claire R., ed. 1975. *Women and Folklore.* Austin: University of Texas Press.

Farrer, Claire R., and Susan J. Kalčik. 1988. "Women: A Selected Bibliography from the *Journal of American Folklore,* 1888–1988." *Folklore Women's Communication* 44–45:3–48.

Flax, Jane. 1983. "Political Philosophy and the Patriarchal Unconscious: A Psychoanalytic Perspective on Epistemology and Methodology." In *Discovering Reality: Feminist Perspectives on Epistemology, Metaphysics, Methodology, and Philosophy of Science,* ed. Sandra Harding and Merrill B. Hintikka, 245–81. Boston: D. Reidel.

Frye, Marilyn. 1983. *The Politics of Reality: Essays in Feminist Theory.* Trumansbury, N.Y.: Crossing Press.

Geertz, Clifford. 1980. "Blurred Genres: The Refiguration of Social Thought." *American Scholar* 49:165–79.

Golde, Peggy, ed. 1970. *Women in the Field: Anthropological Experiences.* Chicago: Aldine.

Gould, Carol, ed. 1983. *Beyond Domination: New Perspectives on Women and Philosophy.* Totowa, N.J.: Rowman and Allanheld.

Gray, Elizabeth Dodson. 1982. *Patriarchy as a Conceptual Trap.* Wellesley, Mass.: Roundtable Press.

Green, Rayna. 1977. "Magnolias Grow in Dirt: The Bawdy Lore of Southern Women." *Southern Exposure* 4:29–33.

Greene, Gayle, and Coppélia Kahn, eds. 1985. *Making a Difference: Feminist Literary Criticism.* London: Methuen.

Grimshaw, Jean. 1986. *Philosophy and Feminist Thinking.* Minneapolis: University of Minnesota Press.

Gross, Elizabeth. 1987. "What Is Feminist Theory?" In *Feminist Challenges: Social and Political Theory,* ed. Carole Pateman and Elizabeth Gross, 190–204. Boston: Northeastern University Press.

Harding, Sandra, and Merrill B. Hintikka, eds. 1983. *Discovering Reality: Feminist Perspectives on Epistemology, Metaphysics, Methodology, and Philosophy of Science.* Boston: D. Reidel.

Hartsock, Nancy C. M. 1983. "The Feminist Standpoint: Developing the Ground for a Specifically Feminist Historical Materialism." In *Discovering Reality: Feminist Perspectives on Epistemology, Metaphysics, Methodology, and Philosophy of Science,* ed. Sandra Harding and Merrill B. Hintikka, 283–310. Boston: D. Reidel.

Hein, Hilde. 1983. "Liberating Philosophy: An End to the Dichotomy of Matter and Spirit." In *Beyond Domination: New Perspectives on Women and Philosophy,* ed. Carol C. Gould, 123–41. Totowa, N.J.: Rowman and Allanheld.

Ice, Joyce Ann. 1984. "Quilting and the Pattern of Relationships in Community Life." Ph.D. diss., University of Texas at Austin.

Ice, Joyce, and Judith Shulimson. 1979. "Beyond the Domestic: Women's Traditional Arts and the Creation of Community." *Southwest Folklore* 3:37–44.

Jackson, Bruce, ed. 1987. *Folklore and Feminism.* Special issue of *Journal of American Folklore* 100 (398).

Jaggar, Alison M. 1983. *Feminist Politics and Human Nature.* Totowa, N.J.: Rowman and Allanheld.

Jahner, Elaine. 1985. "Woman Remembering: Life History as Exemplary Pattern." In *Women's Folklore, Women's Culture,* ed. Rosan A. Jordan and Susan J. Kalčik, 214–33. Philadelphia: University of Pennsylvania Press.

Jordan, Rosan A. 1985. "The Vaginal Serpent and Other Themes from Mexican-American Women's Lore." In *Women's Folklore, Women's Culture,* ed. Rosan A. Jordan and Susan J. Kalčik, 26–44. Philadelphia: University of Pennsylvania Press.

Jordan, Rosan A., and Susan J. Kalčik, eds. 1985. *Women's Folklore, Women's Culture.* Philadelphia: University of Pennsylvania Press.

Keller, Catherine. 1985. "Feminism and the Ethic of Inseparability." In *Women's Consciousness, Women's Conscience: A Reader in Feminist Ethics,* cd. Barbara Hilkert Andolsen, Christine E. Gudorg, and Mary D. Pellauer, 251–63. Minneapolis: Winston Press.

———. 1986. *From a Broken Web: Separation, Sexism, and Self.* Boston: Beacon Press.

Kelly, Joan. 1984. *Women, History, and Theory.* Chicago: University of Chicago Press.

Keuls, Eva C. 1985. *The Reign of the Phallus.* New York: Harper and Row.

Kligman, Gail. 1984. "The Rites of Women: Oral Poetry, Ideology, and the Socialization of Peasant Women in Contemporary Romania." *Journal of American Folklore* 97 (384): 167–88.

Kodish, Debora G. 1981. "Never Had a Word between Us: Pattern in the Verbal Art of a Newfoundland Woman." Ph.D. diss., University of Texas at Austin.

———. 1983. "Fair Young Ladies and Bonny Irish Boys: Pattern in Vernacular Poetics." *Journal of American Folklore* 96 (380): 131–50.

———. 1987. "Absent Gender, Silent Encounter." *Journal of American Folklore* 100 (398): 573–78.

Kuhn, Thomas S. [1962] 1970. *The Structure of Scientific Revolutions.* Chicago: University of Chicago Press.

Lawless, Elaine. 1983. "Shouting for the Lord: The Power of Women's Speech in the Pentecostal Religious Service." *Journal of American Folklore* 96 (382): 434–59.

———. 1987. "Piety and Motherhood: Reproductive Images and Maternal Strategies of the Woman Preacher." *Journal of American Folklore* 100 (398): 469–78.

———. 1988. *God's Peculiar People: Women's Voices and Folk Tradition in a Pentecostal Church*. Lexington: University Press of Kentucky.

Lerner, Gerda. 1986. *The Creation of Patriarchy*. New York: Oxford University Press.

Limón, José E. 1986. "*La Llorona*, the Third Legend of Greater Mexico: Cultural Symbols, Women, and the Political Unconscious." In *Renato Rosaldo Lecture Series Monograph Vol. 2. Series 1984–1985*, ed. Ignacio M. Garcia, 59–93. Tucson: Mexican American Studies and Research Center, University of Arizona.

Lloyd, Genevieve. 1984. *The Man of Reason: "Male" and "Female" in Western Philosophy*. Minneapolis: University of Minnesota Press.

Marcus, George E., and Michael M. J. Fischer. 1986. *Anthropology as Cultural Critique: An Experimental Moment in the Human Sciences*. Chicago: University of Chicago Press.

Mitchell, Carol. 1978. "Hostility and Aggression toward Males in Female Joke Telling." *Frontiers* 3:19–23.

Moraga, Cherríe, and Gloria Anzaldúa, eds. 1981. *This Bridge Called My Back: Writings by Radical Women of Color*. Watertown, Mass.: Persephone Press.

O'Brien, Mary. 1981. *The Politics of Reproduction*. London: Routledge and Kegan Paul.

Ortner, Sherry B. 1974. "Is Female to Male as Nature Is to Culture?" In *Woman, Culture, and Society*, ed. Michelle Zimbalist Rosaldo and Louise Lamphere, 67–87. Stanford, Calif.: Stanford University Press.

Ortner, Sherry B., and Harriet Whitehead, eds. 1981. *Sexual Meanings: The Cultural Construction of Gender and Sexuality*. Cambridge: Cambridge University Press.

Radner, Joan Newlon, ed. 1993. *Feminist Messages: Coding in Women's Folk Culture*. Urbana: University of Illinois Press.

Radner, Joan N., and Susan S. Lanser. 1987. "The Feminist Voice: Strategies of Coding in Folklore and Literature." *Journal of American Folklore* 100 (398): 412–25.

Reiter, Rayna R., ed. 1975. *Toward an Anthropology of Women*. New York: Monthly Review Press.

Rich, Adrienne. 1976. *Of Woman Born: Motherhood as Experience and Institution*. New York: W. W. Norton.

Roach, Susan. 1985. "The Kinship Quilt: An Ethnographic Semiotic Analysis of a Quilting Bee." In *Women's Folklore, Women's Culture*, ed. Rosan A. Jordan and Susan J. Kalčik, 54–64. Philadelphia: University of Pennsylvania Press.

Rosaldo, Michelle Zimbalist, and Louise Lamphere, eds. 1974. *Woman, Culture, and Society*. Stanford, Calif.: Stanford University Press.

Rubin, Gayle. 1975. "The Traffic in Women: Notes on the 'Political Economy' of Sex." In *Toward an Anthropology of Women*, ed. Rayna R. Reiter, 157–210. New York: Monthly Review Press.

Ruby, Jay, ed. 1982. *A Crack in the Mirror: Reflexive Perspectives in Anthropology*. Philadelphia: University of Pennsylvania Press.

Ruddick, Sara. 1980. "Maternal Thinking." *Feminist Studies* 6 (2): 342–66.

Ruether, Rosemary. 1974. *Religion and Sexism.* New York: Simon and Shuster.
———. 1975. *New Woman, New Earth: Sexist Ideologies and Human Liberation.* New York: Seabury Press.
Sanday, Peggy Reeves. 1981. *Female Power and Male Dominance: On the Origins of Sexual Inequality.* Cambridge: Cambridge University Press.
Sawin, Patricia E. 1988. "Lönnrot's Brainchildren: The Representation of Women in Finland's *Kalevala." Journal of Folklore Research* 25 (3): 187–217.
Seriff, Suzanne K. 1989. " 'Este Soy Yo': The Politics of Representation of a Texas-Mexican Folk Artist." Ph.D. diss., University of Texas at Austin.
Smith, Dorothy. 1978. "A Peculiar Eclipsing: Women's Exclusion from Man's Culture." *Women's Studies International Quarterly* 1 (4): 281–96.
Spender, Dale. 1982. *Women of Ideas.* Boston: Routledge and Kegan Paul.
Spradley, James P., and Brenda J. Mann. 1975. *The Cocktail Waitress: Woman's Work in a Man's World.* New York: John Wiley and Sons.
Stimpson, Catherine R. 1988. *Where the Meanings Are: Feminism and Cultural Spaces.* London: Methuen.
Stoeltje, Beverly J., ed. 1988a. *Feminist Revisions in Folklore Studies.* Special issue of *Journal of Folklore Research* 25:3.
———. 1988b. "Gender Representations in Performance: The Cowgirl and the Hostess." *Journal of Folklore Research* 25 (3): 219–41.
———. 1988c. "Introduction: Feminist Revisions." *Journal of Folklore Research* 25 (3): 141–53.
Suleiman, Susan Rubin, ed. 1986. *The Female Body in Western Culture: Contemporary Perspectives.* Cambridge, Mass.: Harvard University Press.
Thiselton-Dyer, T. F. 1906. *The Folklore of Women.* Chicago: A. C. McClurg.
Tronto, Joan C. 1987. "Beyond Gender Difference to a Theory of Care." *Signs* 12 (4): 644–63.
Turner, Kay F. 1982. "Mexican American Home Altars: Towards Their Interpretation." *Aztlán: International Journal of Chicano Studies Research* 13 (1–2): 309–26.
———. 1983. "The Cultural Semiotics of Religious Icons: La Virgen de San Juan de Los Lagos." *Semiotica* 47:317–61.
———. 1990. "Mexican American Women's Home Altars: The Art of Relationship." Ph.D. diss., University of Texas at Austin.
Turner, Kay F., and Suzanne Seriff. 1987. " 'Giving an Altar': The Ideology of Reproduction in a St. Joseph's Day Feast." *Journal of American Folklore* 100 (398): 446–60.
Van Maanen, John. 1988. *Tales of the Field: On Writing Ethnography.* Chicago: University of Chicago Press.
Vetterling-Braggin, Mary, Frederick A. Elliston, and Jane English, eds. 1977. *Feminism and Philosophy.* Totowa, N.J.: Rowman and Allanheld.
Wax, Rosalie H. 1971. *Doing Fieldwork: Warnings and Advice.* Chicago: University of Chicago Press.
Webber, Sabra. 1985. "Women's Folk Narratives and Social Change." In *Women and the Family in the Middle East: New Voices of Change,* ed. Elizabeth W. Femea, 310–16. Austin: University of Texas Press.

Weigle, Marta. 1978. "Women as Verbal Artists: Reclaiming the Sisters of Enheduanna." *Frontiers* 3:1–9.

———. 1982. *Spiders and Spinsters: Women and Mythology.* Albuquerque: University of New Mexico Press.

———. 1989. *Creation and Procreation: Feminist Reflections on Mythologies of Cosmogony and Parturition.* Philadelphia: University of Pennsylvania Press.

Whitbeck, Carolyn. 1983. "A Different Reality: Feminist Ontology." In *Beyond Domination: New Perspectives on Women and Philosophy,* ed. Carol C. Gould, 64–88. Totowa, N.J.: Rowman and Allanheld.

Yocom, Margaret R. 1985. "Woman to Woman: Fieldwork and the Private Sphere." In *Women's Folklore, Women's Culture,* ed. Rosan A. Jordan and Susan J. Kalčik, 45–53. Philadelphia: University of Pennsylvania Press.

Young, M. Jane. 1987. "Women, Reproduction, and Religion in Western Puebloan Society." *Journal of American Folklore* 100 (398): 436–45.

The Creator Gods: Romantic Nationalism and the En-genderment of Women in Folklore

> There is nothing abstract about the power that sciences and theories have, to act materially and actually upon our bodies and our minds, even if the discourse that produces it is abstract.
>
> —Monique Wittig

I begin with Peggy Sanday's observation that there tends to be a "congruence between the gender of a people's creator god(s), their orientation to the creative forces of nature, and the secular expression of male and female power" (1981:6). Focusing on the symbolic representations of a culture, Sanday has investigated why different societies select different styles of interaction between the sexes. She argues that such representations operate as "cultural scripts," encoding patterns that can be correlated with actual gender roles in the "acts" of everyday life.

While Sanday's work is based on the interplay between symbolic forms and gender relations among non-Western peoples, a reflexive twist brings her method into the service of understanding gender's place in our own production of scholarly discourses, or "régimes of truth," to borrow a concept from the French social theorist Michel Foucault (1980:132). By envisioning the founding fathers of Romantic Nationalism as the metaphoric "creator gods" of folklore (the discipline) and treating certain assumptions embedded in the ideological foundations of their doctrine as "scripts," I examine here the negative conception of women en-gendered in the discipline "in the beginning."

Underpinnings

Although I use the term *creator god* metaphorically and somewhat play-fully in this context, the approach I am advocating hinges on recognizing that the conceptual underpinnings—the scripts—of a scholarly discipline are themselves symbolic forms internalized as plans for action. By viewing our own symbolic constructions through a lens that we normally reserve for others, we may gain insight into our own biases—in this case, biases that operate to the detriment of women. In folklore such biases have contributed to the relative lack of concern with women's perspectives and activities among the peoples we study and to the relative suppression of women's voices in the practice of folklore (for which this volume at once provides evidence and corrective action).[1] While there have been numer-ous women folklorists, these women have generally adopted models for the collection and interpretation of data generated by men operating within a male-biased Western framework. When such models are inherently misogynistic, women may unwittingly participate in their own oppression. Romantic Nationalism is, of course, only one of many bodies of thought influencing folklore studies, yet its founding status and ongoing influence in various incarnations makes it an appropriate starting point for the agenda I outline here.

The approach I advocate also gives central place to discourse as the ground of material social relations and political struggle (see Foucault, 1972, 1980; Rabinow, 1984; Williams, 1977). Symbolic representations—from creation myths to the paradigms of a scholarly discipline—are realized in discourse, which itself constitutes and creates the conditions for social action. That is, discourse helps shape our vision of the world and structures our roles and relationships in ways that need not, and frequently do not, register on a conscious level. In part because of discourse's capacity to create experience, contemporary French feminist theorists have targeted it as a primary agent for the oppression of women (Marks and de Courtivron, 1980:3). And it is through discourse that challenges and disrupts established symbolic structures, they argue, that women may actively redirect their experience.

Here, with regard to challenging established symbolic structures, Foucault's insights on scholarly discourses are especially germane. Foucault suggested that the development of a discipline necessarily entails the establishment of acceptable discourses, or "régimes of truth." His work emphasizes the need to recognize the historically and socially contingent—versus the ontological or universal—status of "truth" as such (see, e.g., Foucault, 1972, 1979). No subject or category of thought reflects some prior reality or fundamental truth; rather "truth," as the science fiction writer Ursula Le Guin aptly suggested, "is a matter of the imagination" (1976).

And indeed, it takes little imagination to realize that the category of gender itself is a social construct whose associations permeate our own scholarly discourses. If we are to alter existing gender-based power relations, the concept of gender must be viewed as both socially and historically contingent and politically charged. In the words of the American literary critic Alice Jardine: "To recognize the ways in which we surround ourselves with our fictions is a step toward finding new ways for thinking the organization of sexual difference as grounded in cultural and political reality without positing that reality—man or woman, for example—as somehow preexisting our thought and fictions" (1985:47). The question of how the category of woman has been en-gendered in discourse has in fact preoccupied many American feminist literary critics (see, for example, Greene and Kahn, 1985; Showalter, 1985). Their inquiries into the discourses of literature and literary theory have helped reveal the extent to which women have lacked a voice in defining our own experience in these areas. As Josephine Donovan stated, "the 'social construction of reality' has been done by males, and that construction has cast women in the role of other and seen their experience as deviant, or has not seen it at all" (1984:102). Following the example of feminist literary critics, it is to the question of how women have been en-gendered in the founding paradigm of folklore that I now turn.

En-genderments

As every folklorist learns in her introductory folklore course, the eighteenth-century German theologian Johann Gottfried von Herder is the "father of Romantic Nationalism." Although Herder would apparently have considered himself neither a Romantic nor a Nationalist per se (Aris, 1965:234), his writings stimulated the marriage of these two distinct lines of thought.

Enlightenment philosophy with its emphasis on rational thought, empiricism, antitraditionalism, and universal truths provided the intellectual backdrop for eighteenth-century Europe—for learned males, in any case (a small but influential percentage of the population), of which Herder was one. The source and center of Enlightenment thought was an economically and intellectually vigorous and politically strong France. Herder's Germany, in contrast, was a loose confederation of petty states, each linguistically and culturally distinct from the next and divided into several sharply defined classes. Contemporary writers such as Goethe complained that it was difficult to write for a German audience, citing the lack of a "creditable average standard of cultivation" produced by this political, social, and cultural fragmentation (Bruford, 1939:45). Members of the German nobility viewed their own cultural heritage with contempt and looked instead to France for cultural inspiration. Herder formulated his ideas in response to this state of affairs in his native Germany and to what he perceived as the spiritual impoverishment of Enlightenment thought.

At the heart of Herder's schema is the concept of *das Volk,* meaning "folk" or "nation." In Herder's thought this nation is the most fundamental social collective, and the existence of multiple, diverse national groups represents the natural order. The quintessential nation constitutes a culturally homogeneous, organic whole with a stratified, patriarchal form of social organization much like the nuclear family upon which it is modeled; Herder conceived of the nation literally and figuratively as a family writ large. The hallmark of each nation is a shared language, history, and environment, all of which contribute to the collective consciousness (*Volksgeist*) of a people. Language occupies a privileged position in the Herderian framework, and its expressive forms—folksong, poetry, proverb, and the like—are perceived as voicing the collective consciousness and embodying the shared tradition of a *Volk.* According to Herder, members of a healthy nation feel a genuine reverence for their shared tradition, one that encompasses the wisdom of the forefathers.

Viewed against the foil of Enlightenment thought, which elevated human reason as the agent of progress, Herder's ideas take on a nostalgic cast. His doctrine glorified what he considered to be a more basic form of social organization and salutary way of life that he saw passing with Europe's urbanization and industrialization. Specifically, he envisioned a strong and unified German nation built on the model of this idealized *Volk* society.

Herder's ideas fell on particularly fertile soil in Germany, coming as they did around the time of the French Revolution of 1789. The cachet of revolutionary thought was the doctrine of popular sovereignty and individual rights, inspired by the philosophy of Jean Jacques Rousseau. The need to define a people—the body politic that was to govern itself—stimulated a wave of nationalism on both philosophical and political levels in numerous European countries, Germany among them.

In Germany's struggle for self-definition, however, the initial acceptance of revolutionary ideals on a philosophical level was met with a conservative backlash when the political implications of revolution became clear.[2] Germany, whose social order still bore the stamp of feudalism, was not ready to accept a revolutionary leveling of society. Yet when the Revolution occurred in France, Germany's elite had to balance the desire to maintain class distinctions with the need to become more unified against the threat of Napoleonic conquest. As the historian Reinhold Aris observed, the German reaction was "to find a refuge in the historic past and a belief that Germany could only be saved if it trusted to tradition and the law of historic continuity rather than to rational experiments" (1965:219). Herder's model at once provided a formula for German unification and legitimated preservation of the old order. His ideas thus helped stimulate the rise of German nationalism in its Romantic incarnation.

Since Romanticism was a movement of the educated upper classes who had an economic stake in maintaining the existing social order, the conservatism of Herder's framework held a special appeal. The Romantics readily assimilated Herder's nationalistic vision, based as it was on the elevation of tradition. Aris noted that "the Romantics started as literary revolutionaries, shocking the people . . . and cultivating the past as a protest against the present. A few decades later, fairy tales, folksongs and stories of knights and witches had become the common property of the people and had greatly strengthened the national consciousness, so that Germans became interested for the first time in their literary and poetic treasures" (1965:219). Individuals like the Grimm brothers, in turn, were stimulated by this line of thought, answering the Herderian call to attend to language and folk expression. Herder's ideas were also instrumental in the use of folk expression to establish the national identity of various countries such as Finland and the Slavic nations when they fought for their political independence. And, of course, his ideas helped form the basis for the study of folklore as a scholarly discipline.

While Herder is to be credited with a number of important contributions to Western thought—the promotion of cultural relativism and the recognition that expressive language use conveys much about the worldview of a people, for example—there are three interwoven themes in the Herderian framework that operate explicitly and implicitly to the detriment of women: tradition, patriarchalism, and unity.[3] These themes, I suggest, are not innocuous indices of an antiquated doctrine, but ideas that have infiltrated and informed the scripts of folklore research.[4]

Tradition

Although the concept of tradition is not in itself a tool for the oppression of women, Herder's understanding of the term is. Tradition for Herder is synonymous with education, which he believed to be humanity's most precious tool for propagating and upholding the values of a nation. Herder wrote that "all education must spring from imitation and exercise, by means of which the model passes into the copy; and how can this be more aptly expressed than by the term tradition?" (1800:227). Herder's vision of education contrasts sharply with mainstream Enlightenment thought, in which education has a fundamentally progressive social role. Education in the latter view means to acquire the skill of subjecting all principles to the test of reason before allowing them the status of truth. Tradition is accordingly devalued and subordinated to reason, and reason is the key to progressive social change. Conversely, Herder felt that change—if it is to be beneficial—must be gradual, immanent, and effected with reference to tradition. Herder's conservative view of education as tradition was designed to uphold the social order. In practical terms, upholding the social order in eighteenth-century Germany included keeping women uneducated. But there is a more subtle manner in which Herder's concept of tradition operates to exclude women as well.

In Herder's thought the very essence of tradition is masculine. Whereas the maternal province is to provide physical nourishment by the breast, the paternal role is to provide spiritual nourishment by instilling tradition. As Herder would have it: "Paternal love . . . is best displayed by a manly education. The father early inures his son to his own mode of life: teaches him his art, awakens in him the sense of fame, and in him loves himself, when he shall grow old, or be no more. This feeling is the basis of all hereditary honour and virtue: it renders education a public, an external work: it has been the instrument of transmitting to posterity all the excellencies and prejudices of the human species" (1800:216). Besides being the propagators and receivers of tradition, men are also its ultimate source. Tradition springs from the insight of the forefathers, which is encapsulated and passed on in folk expression. From authorship it is a short step to authority: the "sayings of the fathers," in Herder's words, are "always the fountainhead of all wisdom" (Herder, quoted in Barnard, 1969:229) and a nation's most precious possession (Berlin, 1976:165). Tradition thus conceived effectively excludes women on all levels. Women are, quite simply, irrelevant to its workings. Because tradition is passed from father to son and sanctified "as a holy relic" (Herder, quoted in Barnard, 1969:229), it is rendered a self-perpetuating and inviolable (hermetic) system.

Patriarchalism

Beneath Herder's conception of tradition, passing as it does through the male line from father to son, is a more general patriarchal orientation—a patriarchal idiom permeates the discourses of Romantic Nationalism. In Herder's framework, patriarchy represents nothing less than the "natural order" of the world (Berlin, 1976:154). His writings treat the family as a universally patriarchal institution that represents the perfect "government in miniature" (Herder, quoted in Barnard, 1969:229). As such it is both the template for all other, more complex forms of government and the source from which they spring. Men, it follows, have the natural right to authority on all levels of government from the family to the nation.

For Herder, the "natural" occurrence of the family as a patriarchal institution also gave rise to the first articulations of religious sentiment. In a passage that presages Durkheim, Herder suggests that

> from the father of the family came the analogy of the Father of mankind: the God of their fathers appeared, as it were, in the friendly guise in which he was first perceived; the hut became a temple, the table an altar, and the fathers, along with their first-born, became the priests. All the oldest religions are full of these family traits, and how could mankind be more gently introduced to, and improved by, the learning, wisdom, custom, religion and virtue, which was so necessary to it, than through these gentle ties of paternal rule? (Herder, quoted in Barnard, 1969:230)

The patriarchal order thus pervades all levels of society and, like tradition, is made inviolable by rooting it in human nature and vesting it with religious sanction.

Given this patriarchal orientation, it is not surprising that the discourses of Romantic Nationalism also incorporate the all-important concept of the "fatherland" (*Vaterland*) as an inalienable aspect of nationhood. Because the natural environment helps determine the culture and national character of a *Volk,* an analogy is established whereby father is to individual as fatherland is to nation. Just as the fathers shape posterity in their position as the source and conduit of tradition, the fatherland has a seminal and ongoing role in the development of a nation. And just as the individual must honor the fathers, honoring the fatherland, as the historian Carleton Hayes suggested, is the "*sine qua non* of solid, genuine development" for a nation (1927:731).

The language of patriarchy in the discourses of Romantic Nationalism thus pervades and determines the conception of a *Volk.* Tradition and authority resonate with the voice of the fathers while the voices of the mothers are suppressed.

Unity

Although Herder saw endless diversity in the world around him, he continually sought to subsume such diversity under the mantle of a higher unity. Remember that foremost on Herder's agenda was the creation of a strong and unified German nation. Unity thus emerges as a powerful motif in his writings, constituting perhaps the most subtle and ramifying means by which his framework operates to exclude women.

The ideal nation in the Herderian model is a culturally and linguistically homogeneous, organic whole. Because each nation is a unique entity deriving from its distinct environmental setting and historical development, diversity among nations represents the natural order. Internal diversity, on the other hand, is a sign of cultural degeneration. In Herder's words, "the most natural state is *one* people with *one* national character" (Herder, quoted in Hayes, 1927:735, emphasis mine). The concept of individuality, a central concern in eighteenth-century thought, is transferred to the nation in Herder's framework: the nation is likened to an individual with a distinct personality and life history (Aris, 1965:243). The history of a nation is accordingly reduced to the singular and envisioned as a linear, unified development.

Herder was a theologian by training, and the unity he envisioned in the natural order bears the distinctive signature of the Judeo-Christian tradition in which he was steeped. Like the Hegelian dialectic that seeks to resolve difference in the form of contradiction through transcendence to a higher unity (Seem, 1973:125), Herder's framework is similarly informed by the Judeo-Christian concept of the One. The principle of unity, like tradition and patriarchy, is consequently made sacrosanct. And indeed, the unifying principle in history was identified by Herder as the Christian God himself (Aris, 1965:240).

Herder's talent for distilling unity from diversity operated efficiently to elide difference in the ideology of Romantic Nationalism. In light of the patriarchal bias and masculine conception of tradition in his framework, a major category overlooked is woman. Woman is defined in relation to man as that "creature . . . dissimilarly similar to himself" (Herder, 1800:210), and in the discourses of Romantic Nationalism those dissimilarities are assimilated by the unity that is man. Woman, as the French theorist Luce Irigaray (1985) argues to be the case generally in Western systems of representation, is ultimately en-gendered as the silent, inert mirror for man. Herder's own words evoke this image:

> Happy is it, that Nature has endowed and adorned the female heart with an unspeakable affectionate and powerful sense of the personal worth of man. This enables her to bear also his severities: her mind willingly turns from them to the contemplation of whatever she considers as noble, great, valiant, and uncommon in him: with exalted feelings she participates in the manly deeds, the evening recital of which softens the fatigue of her toilsome day, and is proud, since she is destined to obedience, that she has such a husband to obey. (1800:214–15)

Cracks

Herder wrote that "every where woman has been . . . from her nature . . . the first failing stone in the human edifice" (1800:212). Since the human edifice in the Western tradition has been constructed by men, women can use this position as "the first failing stone" to topple the structures that confine us. Romantic Nationalism, which is at once a product of the Western tradition and a reaction to it (viz., the rationalism of the Enlightenment, the liberalism of the French Revolution), lends itself well to the task. When the discourses of Romantic Nationalism are viewed in the general context of Western thought, a counterdiscourse emerges from the cracks—those areas where contradictions or lapses in logic occur—between the tellings of the two.

The first crack concerns the land, which in Western thought is traditionally gendered as feminine and, like women, made the object of conquest. In the language of Romantic Nationalism, however, it is masculinized and exalted as the Fatherland. Endowing the land with male genitalia, if you will, sanctifies and empowers it with an impenetrability not accorded a femininely conceived land. One crack leads to another: in Herder's writings the natural environment in its Fatherland incarnation is treated as the progenitor and molder of culture. This reversal of the traditional Western assertion of culture's power to transform nature challenges the clear-cut pairing of male/culture and female/nature. The final crack derives from the elevation of intuition, imagination, and emotion over reason in the discourses of Romantic Nationalism. Herder's writings, as I have suggested, assign a masculine value to these qualities, which are traditionally viewed as feminine in Western thought. From insight emanates the wisdom of the fathers, which is handed down through the male line as tradition, the most precious possession of a *Volk*.

Examination of these cracks reveals a fundamental paradox: what is generally associated in the Western tradition with the feminine and given a negative value in comparison to its masculine counterpart is reversed in Romantic Nationalist ideology. A case in point is the structuralism of Claude Lévi-Strauss, which goes so far as to assert the universality of the traditional associations of woman/nature/emotion and man/culture/reason by rooting them in the structure of the human mind—a view that has been effectively challenged by the recent work of anthropologists such as Eleanor Burke Leacock (1981) and Catherine Lutz (1986). Ironically, the en-genderments of Romantic Nationalism also challenge these traditional Western gender associations, thereby containing the potential for a subversive "feminist" critique of the prevailing male-biased tradition (something that most assuredly did not cross Herder's mind). Yet like the tradition it counters, Romantic Nationalism elevates the masculine and vests its own discourses with patriarchal authority. Because patriarchal authority is invoked in the service of two contradictory frameworks, however, it is inadvertently subverted. Comparison of these two discrepant views reveals the cultural—rather than the natural or universal—status of such authority. This paves the way for alternative constructions that allow more equality between the sexes.

Rewriting the Scripts

I end with a note about "felt" oppression: discourses that devalue the feminine may be internalized by women and men alike, shaping both our self-perceptions and our perceptions of the "other." Such discourses constitute forms of oppression in themselves as well as blueprints for action that excludes or denigrates women. As long as we maintain that our scholarly models are either neutral or materially inconsequential, we can continue to justify the acts encoded in the scripts. By reviewing our models through a gender-sensitive lens, we may discover latent sexual politics at work and cracks in the discourses that give us the leverage to change the existing patriarchal order. By discovering and exploring such cracks in our own received traditions, we may indeed begin to rewrite the scripts.

Notes

An earlier version of this essay appeared in 1987 in the *Journal of American Folklore* 100 (398): 563–72. Thanks to Beverly Stoeltje, whose suggestions helped shape this work in innumerable ways; to Laura Long, Lynn Gosnell, Patricia Sawin, Bruce Jackson, and the coeditors and anonymous readers of this volume for comments on earlier drafts; and to Richard Bauman for inspiring my interest in Herder.

1. See Farrer's pioneering and insightful discussion (1975) on the problem of women and folklore.

2. The ideology of the Revolution gave rise to an upsurge of feminist activity in France. The emphasis on individual freedom gave women the opportunity to assert their rights as individuals, which is precisely what they did (see Marks and de Courtivron, 1980:15–16). In his publications, Condorcet championed the cause of women as well, demanding that they be given political rights. Although I do not pursue the issue here, I speculate that part of the German backlash against

the Revolution was motivated by this upsurge of feminism and the imagined threat of women being elevated to the same status as men.

3. Although a number of Romantic Nationalists—such as Müller, Novalis, and Schleiermacher—adopted and elaborated on these themes, I limit myself here to Herder and his writings. I discuss only those aspects of Herder's work that helped form the core of Romantic Nationalist ideology. I have used the English translations of his works, checking key words and concepts against the originals with the assistance of a German speaker.

4. Although Romantic Nationalism is no longer a working paradigm used by folklorists, the Romantic Nationalist–inspired notions of tradition as the crux of "folk" expression and the embeddedness of such expression in a unified community are implicit in many writings in the field of folklore. As a representative, see, for example, Richard Dorson's classic volume on folklore and folklife (1972). For an example of the implicit patriarchal perspective that also continues to inform contemporary folklore, see Debora Kodish's chapter in this volume. The point here is that Romantic Nationalism is the model on which folklore as a discipline was founded and that many of its underlying assumptions have continued to inform folklore studies even as the field has changed through time.

References Cited

Aris, Reinhold. 1965. *History of Political Thought in Germany from 1789–1815.* New York: Russell and Russell.

Barnard, Frederick M., ed. 1969. *J. G. Herder on Social and Political Culture.* Cambridge: Cambridge University Press.

Berlin, Isaiah. 1976. *Vico and Herder: Two Studies in the History of Ideas.* New York: Viking Press.

Bruford, W. H. 1939. *Germany in the Eighteenth Century: The Social Background of the Literary Revival.* Cambridge: Cambridge University Press.

Donovan, Josephine. 1984. "Toward a Women's Poetics." *Tulsa Studies in Women's Literature* 3 (1–2): 99–110.

Dorson, Richard M., ed. 1972. *Folklore and Folklife: An Introduction.* Chicago: University of Chicago Press.

Farrer, Claire R. 1975. "Women and Folklore: Images and Genres." In *Women and Folklore,* ed. Claire R. Farrer, vii-xvii. Austin: University of Texas Press.

Foucault, Michel. 1972. *The Archaeology of Knowledge.* Translated by A. M. Sheridan Smith. London: Tavistock. Originally published as *L'Archéologie du savoir.* Paris, 1969.

———. 1979. "What Is an Author?" In *Textual Strategies: Perspectives in Poststructuralist Criticism,* ed. Josué V. Harari, pp. 141–60. Ithaca: Cornell University Press.

———. 1980. *Power/Knowledge: Selected Interviews and Other Writings, 1972–1977,* ed. Colin Gordon. New York: Pantheon.

Greene, Gayle, and Coppélia Kahn, eds. 1985. *Making a Difference: Feminist Literary Criticism.* London: Methuen.

Hayes, Carleton J. H. 1927. "Contributions of Herder to the Doctrine of Romantic Nationalism." *The American Historical Review* 32 (4): 719–36.

Herder, Johann Gottfried von. 1800. *Outlines of a Philosophy of the History of Man.* Translated by T. Churchill. New York: Bergman Publishers. Originally published as *Ideen zur Philosophie der Geschichte der Menschheit.* Riga, 1784.

Irigaray, Luce. 1985. *Speculum of the Other Woman.* Translated by Gillian C. Gill. Ithaca: Cornell University Press. Originally published as *Speculum de l'autre femme.* Paris, 1974.

Jardine, Alice. 1985. *Gynesis: Configurations of Woman and Modernity.* Ithaca: Cornell University Press.

Leacock, Eleanor Burke, ed. 1981. *Myths of Male Dominance: Collected Articles on Women Cross-culturally.* New York: Monthly Review Press.

Le Guin, Ursula K. 1976. *The Left Hand of Darkness.* New York: Ace.

Lutz, Catherine. 1986. "Emotion, Thought, and Estrangement: Emotion as a Cultural Category." *Cultural Anthropology* 1 (3): 287–309.

Marks, Elaine, and Isabelle de Courtivron, eds. 1980. *New French Feminisms: An Anthology.* New York: Schocken.

Rabinow, Paul. 1984. *The Foucault Reader.* New York: Pantheon.

Sanday, Peggy Reeves. 1981. *Female Power and Male Dominance: On the Origins of Sexual Inequality.* Cambridge: Cambridge University Press.

Seem, Mark D. 1973. "Liberation of Difference: Toward a Theory of Antiliterature." *New Literary History* 5 (1): 121–33.

Showalter, Elaine, ed. 1985. *The New Feminist Criticism: Essays on Women, Literature, and Theory.* New York: Pantheon.

Williams, Raymond. 1977. *Marxism and Literature.* Oxford: Oxford University Press.

Wittig, Monique. 1980. The Straight Mind. *Feminist Issues* (Summer): 103–11.

Absent Gender, Silent Encounter

In her examination of ways in which female characters and images are repeatedly read (or, better, strongly misread) by Yale school critics, Barbara Johnson (1984) makes it clear that, as in many "schools" of thought, "the Yale School has always been a Male School." Despite an apparent lack of interest in matters of gender, these critics have constructed an implicit theory of gender in their theory and practice (see Bloom, et al., 1979). Johnson illustrates a "repeated dramatization of woman as simulacrum, erasure, or silence," effectively tracing how a female presence is consistently, if variously, effaced by Yale School theory and within readings elaborated by school "members" (Johnson, 1984:101, 111). Johnson's work traces fundamental ways in which gender and language determine one another.

As Johnson has shown for the Yale school, Gilbert and Gubar for Bloomian theory in particular, and Schweickart for reader-response theory, the apparent absence of gender in texts may instead be read as a present, if implicit, theory of gender (Johnson, 1984; Gilbert and Gubar, 1979; Schweickart, 1986). Where folklore scholarship is concerned, the explicit mention of gender has seldom been made but gender relations are constantly present as subtexts, as powerful and present themes within the stories that folklorists tell themselves.

Like anthropologists, travel writers, and other professional and semiprofessional strangers, folklorists have produced a large literature describing fieldwork experiences. Introducing collections of folksongs, appearing in the liner notes to records, or told as anecdotes among colleagues, folklorists' descriptions of their first encounters with traditional artists reiterate common themes and depend upon repeated conventions. Recent analyses of the poetics and politics of ethnographic writing should encourage consideration of folklorists' narratives (see Clifford, 1983; Crapanzano, 1986; Pratt, 1986; Rose, 1982).

Anthropological "tales of entry" often cast the anthropologist as an "awkward simpleton," someone who is not fully able in the foreign world into which she or he has stumbled (Crapanzano, 1986:69). "Fables of rapport," in turn, "narrate the attainment of full participant-observer status" (Clifford, 1983:132). These new readings are subtle and enlightening, but they do not usually consider the gender of observers and observed. In what follows, I point to some patterns that arise in descriptions of gendered characters in such tales. I also suggest some patterns that seem to characterize accounts told by women and men (respectively observed and observers in these examples, although this is not always the case in folklore fieldwork). I will use as my examples four texts describing two encounters. But I will begin with some generalizations about the larger genre of folklorists' first-encounter tales.

First, they are tales of marvels. Like some wonder tales, folklorists' accounts of their own first encounters with traditional artists emphasize the magical or marvelous character of the event. The openings of such personal narratives often describe the difficulties of the search, the obstacles overcome on the quest. Once encountered, the traditional singer or storyteller often testifies to the special quality of the meeting. Thus, it is often noted that storytellers as well as singers seemed to have been preparing for a folklorist's visit for decades (see Azadovskii, 1974:14; Mackenzie, 1919:ix, 13, 19, 20; Szwed, 1970:152).

Closings also help to establish the marvelous character of the event. It is commonly observed that the singer or storyteller sings or talks all the night long, without ever repeating a song (Kodish, 1983:133). If this is not a magical halting of the sun's course, then, in this real-life version of the fairy tale world, it is a token of the transformation of the ordinary natural round. Even more important is the production during this magical night-time of voicedness of a seemingly endless volume of riches: stories, songs, folklore.

Such familiar conventions deserve attention as significant features of folklorists' own narratives. A closer examination of contrasting accounts of first encounters may suggest how recurring motifs and formal features (including openings, closings, quoted speech, silence, and elaboration) work within a narrative and, more important to this essay, how gender is constructed.

Examples readily come from the well-documented encounters of folklorists with the singers Almeda Riddle and Jeannie Robertson (Abrahams, 1971, 1977; Abrahams and Kodish, n.d.; Gower, 1983; Niles, 1986; Wolf, 1967). Both women are described as having an extraordinary surplus of songs. John Quincy Wolf recalled that on his first meeting with Almeda Riddle, in 1952, she listed a hundred titles that she could sing for him. She promised that when he was finished recording those, she would sing a second hundred songs (Wolf, 1967:108; also see Azadovskii, 1974:14; Morris, 1944:133; Niles, 1986:84–85).

Writers describe both women as becoming suddenly conscious, awakened to the new worth of their heritage, transformed by the folklorist's visit. Writing about Jeannie Robertson, Herschel Gower generalizes this pattern for traditional singers as an encounter between the outside world and a singer who "wakes up one morning" with a sudden new consciousness of the value of his or her traditional legacy. Gower writes that the singer "may be jolted into this awareness . . . [through] the knock on his [*sic*] door by a professional folklorist with tape recorder" and in other ways: by hearing his or her songs on the radio or seeing them in print, for example (Gower, 1983:133). As if asleep, the unselfconscious singer is roused into self-consciousness by the knock of the scholar or by the sound of the mass-mediated version of the singer's own identity. One way or another, the traditional artist is represented as testifying to the importance of the encounter.

Hamish Henderson's version of his first encounter with Jeannie Robertson emphasizes his own quest, his attempts to get past Jeannie Robertson's resistance. He knocks at the door and like some fairy-tale hero uses wits and words to win entrance. When talk fails, he turns to song. He is admitted when Robertson hears what a bad job he is doing on her song. Invited in, he recalls the "fantastic feeling" that "rolled over him," the "Nunc Dimittis feeling."[1] Henderson mentions that Robertson gives him tea and that he records against her will, long into the night (Niles, 1986:84–85).

Such conventions do not only establish the marvelous character of meetings between folk and folklorist but, as told by male scholars, these accounts resonate with a marked, if unacknowledged, sexuality. They contain a rich, if implicit, symbolism of gender, describing the new awakening of an often- silenced woman, an awakening brought about by the near-magical appearance of a young and powerful male outsider and resulting in the new or newly appreciated voicedness of the woman. Male collectors appear as powerful, magical outsiders, folktale heroes initiating action and reestablishing value. Female informants appear as passive vehicles, unwitting receptacles of knowledge, silent, unspeaking, to be wooed and won into speech. The process of collecting folksongs (or tales) resembles the awakening of a silently sleeping beauty or, as the language may often suggest, a sexual conquest.[2]

Descriptions of the silenced folk waiting for some discovery by outsiders has registered, entering and affecting theory in many ways. Taking these accounts at face value, some scholars have debated the marginal status of some expressive and creative individuals within folk society. While opportunities for creative expression may vary within small-scale rural communities (especially for women), it is still true that the depiction of such encounters has the power of a convention, functioning as symbol rather than fact. However marginal, individuals have voices and identities within their communities. That folklorists describe the folk as too much or too little voiced, overflowing with song or sulkily silent, reminds us of the symbolic nature of the convention (Renwick, 1980:14–16).

One purpose of feminist scholarship is to deconstruct male paradigms; a second is to reconstruct models attentive to women's experiences. Another tradition of first-encounter stories—those told by the people "discovered" or observed—provides an alternate way of understanding the experience discussed above.

I have chosen the particular examples above because there exist, fortuitously, alternative "texts" for these encounters. The women visited by folklorists in these two cases have reported on their own perspectives, and differences between the two accounts of first encounters are instructive. For example, Jeannie Robertson herself denies any mystery to her first encounter with Hamish Henderson. She acknowledges her awareness of Henderson, other folklorists, and their business. Long before outsiders find their way to her door, she comments to her family that she knows exactly the types of songs they seek (Gower, 1983:133).

She considers, when Henderson does find his way to her, that his timing is poor. She "had spent that day keeping her sister-in-law's two children and they had gotten on her nerves to such an extent that she tried to put Henderson off. She wanted to 'fa' doon to [her] bed' and rest before singing" (Gower, 1983:133). Her account of this first encounter stresses her part in caring for children. In her account, the children sing for the stranger before she does—something unmentioned by Henderson. Talking about her own first encounter with this outsider, Robertson sets it within the context of her responsibilities. She uses the singing as a way to mind and divert her charges. "But after the older bairn had sung several of his Auntie Jeannie's sangs, Hamish stayed on to tea and I sung for him steady till two o'clock in the morning. I never got my rest—nae rest that day, you see. And that's the God's truth if I never rise from this chair" (Gower, 1983:133).

Providing for the needs of the collector is one more of the responsibilities and courtesies described by Jeannie Robertson. In fact, the story of her first encounter is framed as a common type of women's narrative: a conventional account of how she manages the expected and unexpected tasks of a homemaker. With this narrative, Robertson is able to testify to her own skills without setting herself apart as seeking such attention or praise. As well, her account describes a traditional pattern of coaxing, by which singers move from talk into singing; her use of the children to make that transition is a significant difference from the usual descriptions of the pattern (see Posen, 1988:89).

Almeda Riddle had long balanced her own need to sing against family values, which held that singing publicly, devoting time to singing, and considering music as an art or profession were utterly outside the realm of acceptable or appropriate behavior for a young Ozark woman. In describing her own first encounter with the folklorist John Quincy Wolf, she uses many of the same conventions employed by Robertson: children are a means to her performance and justification for it; she performs with modesty and propriety for a stranger whom she decides to please; her performance is a calculated and self-conscious one.

Like Jeannie Robertson, Riddle is having a difficult day dealing with children and tasks. Hot and tired, she is called into a neighbor's kitchen to sing for the visiting scholar; she obliges. Almeda Riddle puts a child at the center of her own story of this first encounter. She tells a family story, an account about the humorous sayings of a child, referencing this story type in her introduction: "And a funny thing happened the first tapes that I cut for Doctor Wolf. Did I tell you that? About my little granddaughter?"[3]

Riddle then describes how she had been watching her grandchildren, how she happened to be over at the Starks' fetching water, and how she was called up to the house and asked to sing, which she did. Later, at supper, the granddaughter is asked what she did that day, and Riddle quotes the girl:

> She said, "I seen a gray wolf. A man named gray wolf. He had on a gray suit." And said, "Daddy, I got so mad that I'm *still* mad." And he said, "Well, what'd he do?" "Well now," she said, "Granny was *hot* and she was *tired,*" and said, "she had to tow old blue-eyes. . . ." Said, "she had to carry him up the hill. He wouldn't walk." And said, "Granny was just so tired and hot." Said, "she pulled off her bonnet and sat down and sung." Said, "Uncle Don went in the kitchen and cried." And . . . she said, "that wolf feller." Said, "he sat there and just wiped his eye, cryin'." And now said, "Daddy, she didn't sound as good as she does sometime, but she didn't sound that bad either."
>
> She thought they was cryin' because I was makin' a mess of the song. "She didn't sound good," but said, "she didn't sound that bad either."

By quoting the humorous misunderstanding of a small child, Riddle pays modest compliment to her own artistry and to the effect of her performance upon the scholarly visitor. Like Jeannie Robertson, Almeda Riddle is fully aware of the worth and power of her own performance.

Both women express these opinions comfortably within native narrative genres.

Like Jeannie Robertson, Almeda Riddle describes both the disruption and the toll of her everyday domestic routine. The importance of family and housework in these women's accounts ought not to be overlooked (Spivak, 1985:128). Unmentioned by folklorists, family and housework are important frames of reference for Jeannie Robertson and Almeda Riddle. Housework and family normalize and define the first encounters of these women and strangers. Folklorists within these narratives are not powerful heroes but visitors well managed. In these women's lives folklorists provide opportunities, and from the very outset both Robertson and Riddle are capable of taking advantage of these new possibilities. Looking back, they minimize the significance of the first encounter and the resulting differences in their own role or status by their emphasis on the everyday.

Other differences between the two types of accounts, those of observer and of woman observed, are instructive. The accounts by Robertson and Riddle emphasize not only women's presence and agency but also their control and authority. In their narratives women describe their home lives, the contexts for their encounters. These worlds, their inhabitants (children and kin), and everyday labors and activities into which folklorists intrude—all are absent from male folklorists' accounts. Like the travelers' accounts brilliantly studied by Mary Louise Pratt, folklorists' accounts erase present context. Travelers to Africa replaced present people and activity with their own reveries of future European and colonial productions (Pratt, 1986:145–46). In the previous examples, folklorists replaced present contexts with their own reveries: accounts of the textual production of isolated subjects, sexualized accounts of the overpowering and awakening of silent women. Folklorists writing about these women "folk" are, in fact, writing about themselves.

Other differences orient the two women's accounts. The convention of the discovery, used by folklorists to suggest the heroic nature of the active outsider, becomes the convention of the unexpected visit, in which a woman acts as a capable manager and a skillful performer, satisfying and pleasing her company (and not producing songs or stories valuable only as goods). No sleeping beauties, these are active working women. Not silent, these are women who know well the worth of their words and their songs. No stories of romance, these first encounters are tales of household labors and of making a life. Not accounts of the relations between single strange men and solitary native women, these are accounts filled with family and kin, adults and children (Kodish, 1983:140–41, 144).

Accounts of first encounters, told differently by these women "folk" and men folklorists, are reminders of ways in which assumptions about gender condition our understandings of field research experiences. But perhaps more important, these brief two-sided examples of single encounters should suggest that the texts of both folklorist and "folk" are fictive forms, shaped by convention and oriented by particular perspectives.

Additional examination of first-encounter stories, with careful attention paid to features of the genre, can help us to explore the hidden theories of gender within which we all work—for there are many variations within this genre. Other types of first encounters—told by women folklorists as well as by men—emphasize the development of friendship or the blossoming of a relationship, the sudden and unexpected discovery (rather than the careful quest), the role of the folklorist as simple or unobtrusive recorder, the planned "trick" or the use of deception, or the power and control of the folk performer (often viewed as a negative matter by the folklorist who is duped) (Oxreider, 1975; Muir, 1965:37–41; Gordon, 1938:9; Mackenzie, 1919:ix, 13, 19, 20).

Some of these other accounts emphasize connectedness. Folklorists' inquiries into the traditions of familiar people with whom they have some relationship—their kin, students, servants, neighbors, or members of vacation communities—may both defamiliarize and alter these ties. The first-encounter tales that I've cited here depend upon the folklorist's investigation of unfamiliar people and places. More starkly than those accounts in which folklorists become tourists in their own lands and homes, first-encounter tales remind us of the complex power relations that condition the "collection" of folklore and the even more complex ways in which our narratives may conceal and reveal such relations. Power differentials are especially obvious when the folklorist is male, the "folk" female, and the conventions of their encounter draw solely from one (male) point of view. Motifs in all of these accounts give weight to different elements of a complex form of interaction and transaction, and one upon which this entire discipline has been founded. All of our texts, theories, and histories stand in some relation to encounters such as those described above.

We know altogether too little about such encounters and have too seldom considered (despite the rise of contextual and performance studies) how such encounters are presented or obscured and how they shape our thinking. Taking accounts of first encounters as facts rather than fictions, we have largely ignored the implications of scholarly suppression of gender consciousness. But the implications are far-reaching, affecting not only versions of field experiences and the collection and production of texts but all aspects of folklore theory and history.

How might this be so? Remember only the ways in which Almeda Riddle and Jeannie Robertson orient their accounts above so that children and housework are significant, so that women are active agents, so that the visit of a folklorist interrupts but does not displace the everyday routine—and consider how folklore theory would be reordered if it was guided by these encounter stories rather than those inscribed (or hidden) by folklorists. These women's narratives construct different kinds of agents (performers, tradition-bearers), performative intentions, and textual forms. Interruptions, "fragmentary" texts, and performances that allow women to maintain several identities at once (mother, homemaker, performer) gain new importance.

For women in some communities, it might turn out that "reporting" and "repeating" were preferable to "authoritative" models of performance (which might instead be understood as overly aggressive or assertive). "Reporting" or "repeating" might be viewed as elegant performance forms in which a woman might present narrative or song along with its lineage and its context, crediting those others from whom she learned.

As well, songbooks and ballad books (often created by women who thus remain keepers of a tradition without taking center stage in an assertive performance) might be considered performances in their own terms, not documents of texts, secondary to performance. These lasting written versions of songs and clipped periodical accounts of tales might instead be privileged over ephemeral oral versions. The "fragmentary" performances of women singers might be considered significant in their own right. And that "fragmentary" genre, the lyric, might long ago have been celebrated for its implicit and metonymic structure.

No such reorientation is likely. When theory and practice are reconsidered, it is in regard to the changing perspectives of academics. Relatively recently claimed genres (like recitation) continue to elaborate a contrast between seemingly coherent and fragmentary or monologic and dialogic genres: again extending a definition that privileges men's speech roles and social norms. We continue to understand oral performance as ephemeral and of the moment, as masterful, authoritative, aggressive, dominant, and coherent.

In each of these cases, and like written acts of procreation, a metaphor of male paternity and performance is constructed. Folklore theory (no less than literary theory, writing, or ethnography) is constrained by powerful and patriarchal subtexts. In the differing accounts discussed above, Almeda Riddle and Jeannie Robertson are our guides in deconstructing standard or canonical texts. At the very least, their examples should remind us that gender is never absent and that encounters are never one-sided. At best, their presence and actions, so utterly familiar to so many of us, may help us imagine and inhabit roles—as folks and folklorists—allowing equity, pleasure, and satisfaction in good measure.

Notes

For Sarah, whose own first encounter with the world delayed this essay's original presentation. An earlier version of this essay appeared in 1987 in the *Journal of American Folklore* 100 (398): 573–78. Thanks to Dorothy Noyes and Margaret Kruesi for their comments, to Suzi Jones for her usual clarity and precision, and to the anonymous readers and editors of the present volume for their good suggestions.

1. "Nunc Dimittis" is "now let depart," from the canticle in the Anglican liturgy: "Lord, now lettest thou thy servant depart in peace, according to thy word, for mine eyes have seen thy salvation." This is spoken when the Christ child is presented in the Temple—e.g. "now I can die"—and by extension, spoken after a moment of revelation. Thanks to Dorothy Noyes for this reference.

2. Also see Mackenzie (1919:20), who instructs the collector like an "ardent lover" to dissemble.

3. This quotation, and the story that follows, are from a tape-recorded interview by Debora Kodish with Almeda Riddle, Greer's Ferry, Arkansas, Oct. 22, 1983. The tapes are in the author's possession.

References Cited

Abrahams, Roger D. 1971. "Creativity, Individuality, and the Traditional Singer." *Studies in the Literary Imagination* 3:5–34

———. 1977. "Moving in America." *Prospects* 3:63–82.

Abrahams, Roger D., and Debora Kodish. n.d. "Preserving Even the Scraps: Songs and Stories from Almeda Riddle of Greer's Ferry, Arkansas." Ms.

Azadovskii, Mark. 1974. *A Siberian Tale Teller.* Translated by James R. Dow. Center for Intercultural Studies in Folklore and Ethnomusicology Monograph Series, no. 2. Austin: University of Texas Center for Intercultural Studies in Folklore and Ethnomusicology. Originally published as *Eine sibirische Märchenerzahlerin.* Helsinki, 1926.

Bloom, Harold, Paul de Man, Jacques Derrida, Geoffrey Hartman, and J. Hillis Miller. 1979. *Deconstruction and Criticism.* New York: Continuum Press.

Clifford, James. 1983. "On Ethnographic Authority." *Representations* 1 (2): 118–46.

———. 1986. "Introduction: Partial Truths." In *Writing Culture: The Poetics and Politics of Ethnography,* ed. James Clifford and George E. Marcus, 1–26. Berkeley: University of California Press.

Crapanzano, Vincent. 1986. "Hermes' Dilemma: The Masking of Subversion in Ethnographic Description." In *Writing Culture: The Poetics and Politics of Ethnography,* ed. James Clifford and George E. Marcus, 51–76. Berkeley: University of California Press.

Gilbert, Sandra, and Susan Gubar. 1979. *The Madwoman in the Attic: The Woman Writer and the Nineteenth-Century Literary Imagination.* New Haven: Yale University Press, 1979.

Gordon, Robert Winslow. 1938. *Folk-Songs of America.* Washington, D.C.: National Service Bureau, Federal Theater Project, Works Progress Administration.

Gower, Herschel. 1983. "Analyzing the Revival: The Influence of Jeannie Robertson." In *The Ballad Image: Essays Presented to Bertrand Harris Bronson,* ed. James Porter, 131–47. Los Angeles: Center for the Study of Comparative Mythology, University of California.

Johnson, Barbara. 1984. "Gender Theory and the Yale School." *Genre* 17:101–12.

Kodish, Debora. 1983. "Fair Young Ladies and Bonny Irish Boys: Pattern in Vernacular Poetics." *Journal of American Folklore* 96 (380): 131–50.

Mackenzie, W. Roy. 1919. *The Quest of the Ballad.* Princeton: Princeton University Press.

Morris, Alton C. 1944. "Mrs. Griffin of Newberry." *Southern Folklore Quarterly* 8:133–98.

Muir, Willa. 1965. *Living with Ballads.* New York: Oxford University Press.

Niles, John D. 1986. "Context and Loss in Scottish Ballad Tradition." *Western Folklore* 44:83–106.

Oxreider, Julia. 1975. "Elmira Hudson New, Friend and Informant: Folklore from Anson County, North Carolina." *Keystone Folklore Register* 21 (1): 3–12.

Posen, I. Sheldon. 1988. *For Singing and Dancing and All Sorts of Fun.* Toronto: Deneau.

Pratt, Mary Louise. 1986. "Scratches on the Face of the Country; or, What Mr. Barrow Saw in the Land of the Bushmen." In *"Race," Writing, and Difference,* ed. Henry Louis Gates, Jr., 138–62. Chicago: University of Chicago Press.

Renwick, Roger deV. 1980. *English Folk Poetry: Structure and Meaning.* Philadelphia: University of Pennsylvania Press.

Rose, Dan. 1982. "Occasions and Forms of Anthropological Experience." In *A Crack in the Mirror: Reflexive Perspectives in Anthropology,* ed. Jay Ruby, 219–73. Philadelphia: University of Pennsylvania Press.

Schweickart, Patrocino. 1986. "Reading Ourselves: Toward a Feminist Theory of Reading." In *Gender and Reading: Essays on Readers, Texts, and Context,* ed. Elizabeth A. Flynn and Patrocino Schweickart, 31–62. Baltimore: Johns Hopkins University Press.

Spivak, Gayatri Chakravorty. 1985. "Feminism and Critical Theory." In *For Alma Mater: Theory and Practice in Feminist Scholarship,* ed. Paula A. Treichler, Cheris Kramarae, and Beth Stafford, 119–42. Urbana: University of Illinois Press.

Szwed, John F. 1970. "Paul E. Hall: A Newfoundland Songmaker and His Community of Song." In *Folksongs and Their Makers,* ed. Henry Glassie, Edward D. Ives, and John Szwed, 149–67. Bowling Green, Ohio: Popular Press.

Wolf, John Quincy. 1967. "Folksingers and the Re-creation of Folksong." *Western Folklore* 26:101–11.

A Feminist Folklorist Encounters the Folk: Can Praxis Make Perfect?

I don't believe in charity. I believe in justice.
　　—Rose Kerrigan

My concern in this essay is with the contradictions inherent in combining folkloric and feminist perspectives—in doing the fieldwork and in analyzing the data. Although such contradictions don't have to exist, they frequently do—largely because folklore theory and research have tended to privilege male informants and masculine forms of expressive culture—even when women and their lore are examined. And while a neo-Marxist feminist ideology would indicate that we ought to treat our informants as equal partners, scholars have a tendency to assume that we as outside observers of culture can know more than our informants about their folklore (cf. Clifford and Marcus, 1986; Stocking, 1985; Turner and Bruner, 1986). One way of dealing with these dilemmas is to confront them directly by exploring specifically with our informants the relationships between women's choices of expression and their sense of belonging to a larger culture. That is what I have attempted to do in my ongoing discussions about Communism and feminism with Rose Kerrigan, the subject of this chapter.

This may seem an obvious approach, but few have chosen it. Some feminist scholars frame their analyses with the assumption that women have universally been oppressed by men, as culture has oppressed nature (Ortner, 1974; Rogers, 1978; Rosaldo and Lamphere, 1974). For example, Louise Lamphere states that

this issue was clearly set forth in several articles in *Woman, Culture and Society,* which argued that in every known culture women are considered in some way inferior to men. . . . Rosaldo suggests that women's role as mother and primary socializer of children . . . sets up the possibility of a distinction between a domestic and a public sphere, the former the province of women, the latter of men. . . . Generally, the more complex the society, the more heterosexual subgroups are differentiated from each other and, in addition, women in each group, even the dominant ones, are subordinate to their own men. (1977:613–14)

Yet, the alternative route of exploring notions of women's power within their own spheres frequently and implicitly reflects such a dichotomy (Christ, 1979; Lamphere, 1977:617; Sanday, 1981), for women's culture cannot be defined independently of men's. As Peggy Sanday notes in her introduction, "This book is intended for an interdisciplinary audience interested in a global view of female power and male dominance in tribal societies" (1981:1–2). Although Sanday (1981:2–3) disagrees with Sherry Ortner (1974) regarding universal female subordination, she does believe in the cultural subordination of Western women thanks to

two of the guiding symbols of Western male dominance—the patriarchal, decidedly masculine God and the sexual, inferior female who tempts the male from the path of righteousness. . . . Collective sentiments centering on maleness and masculine symbols acquire coercive power by defining females as the "other" and feminine symbols as evil. . . . [But] the resurrection of goddess symbols by contemporary feminists shows, once again, that people seek to align sacred and secular sex-role plans. (215, 231)

Unfortunately, such approaches exclude those areas of overlapping experience, the anomalies informants often relate, and the polysemy of such concepts of nature and culture even within Western society. We also construct such models according to spheres of power and authority, competition, ownership, and forward progress. The boundaries are drawn, the models follow in neat "scientific" packages, and we can claim that separate but equal cultures really do exist for men and women.

I would like to suggest, as an alternative, that we stop trying to force our data into nice neat models, which are admittedly great fun to construct and have the virtue of making us look very efficient and knowledgeable about our field, and instead focus on the alternative, sometimes paradoxical issues. Although this is not a new approach in and of itself, it is one that few explore (e.g., Farrer, 1986; MacCormack and Strathern, 1980; Stoeltje, 1986; Young, 1987). Because certain structural contradictions, as well as the more taken-for-granted implicit cultural categories, especially concerning women in Western societies, don't tend to be logical or easily resolved in our models, many scholars have overlooked or undervalued them (see Kodish, this volume).[1]

The fieldwork experience is supposed to teach us to apprehend the "other"—out there and within ourselves. This is particularly true of those of us with a feminist commitment: the women we interview often become our friends, and this can often pose problems when we objectively try to analyze the material we have collected. The person keeps messing up the model. But such interference can keep us and our subsequent writings more honest in the theories we do construct and more ethically aware that we are dealing with thinking, reacting people—not with cultural objects. The interpretations that our informants offer us may also provide alternative theories for the way women use and interpret their folklore.

During the course of my dissertation research in London, I met Rose Kerrigan, then an eighty-three-year-old, Irish-born woman, whose Russian-Jewish parents raised her in the socialist milieu of early twentieth-century Scotland. Responding to a letter I'd put in the *Morning Star*, a national Communist newspaper, Mrs. Kerrigan told me that she was a Communist from Glasgow and had some stories to tell me. Much to my amazement, Rose turned out to be a reservoir of folksongs, jokes, and memorates—a folklorist's dream come true. And—to top it all—not only was she a founding member of the Scottish branch of the Communist party but she had been an outspoken feminist since her early teens. Clearly I had made quite a find!

It wasn't until my third or fourth interview with Rose Kerrigan that I actually began to get to know her and regard her as more than a highly interesting cultural object. Once I finally listened to what Rose was telling me about her folklore, I began to understand a bit of how she had managed and manages to negotiate her identity within the constraints of her admittedly broad-based culture (Royce, 1982). According to Rose, and contrary to Dave Harker's exposé (1985:236–53),[2] the Communist party in Great Britain, especially the Scottish branch, was not only a political hotbed but also a rich source for the exchange of folksongs, many of which were about freedom and ways to achieve it. Yet several of the songs, which she had habitually performed in the past and then sang for me, also revealed a humorous skepticism about tales of utopian bliss elsewhere and a romantic sense of justice, which to her meant that men should marry their lovers. Such a song repertoire not only encompassed many of her personal and community ideals but also enabled Mrs. Kerrigan to make exchanges of songs and verses on an egalitarian basis with male and female party members. In the presence of a male colleague of mine a more restricted side to Mrs. Kerrigan's identity as a woman also emerged. While she was telling us about her role in organizing factory women into a union, Rose mentioned that her workmates exchanged confidences with her and among each other and also told a great many jokes—jokes that she refused to tell in mixed company.[3] These jokes and other anecdotes of her own tended to portray men as fools and women as the tricksters who duped them. Yet they did not always seem to reflect her egalitarian beliefs. Her choice of such expressive forms was particularly suited to persuading others to her point of view, whereas her songs tended to be more reflective of her stated values and exchanged with others who felt similarly. For Rose Kerrigan, different folklore genres (i.e., songs and jokes) function differently: thus she performs them for different audiences (Hall, 1980:129).[4]

Faced with this wide assortment of data, which also included Rose's thoughts on feminism, Communism, and methods of achieving both, I wondered how *I* could reconcile Mrs. Kerrigan's outspoken radical views (both feminist and Marxist) with her choice to raise a family of three and care for her home. How could she continue to consider herself neither subjugated nor suppressed? Traditional feminist (e.g. Friedan, 1963)[5] as well as Marxist feminist (e.g. Leacock, Safa, and Contributors, 1986; Ortner, 1974; Rosaldo, 1974:17–18, 21–25; Sanday, 1981)[6] theorists would have said that her identity was indeed secondary to that of her husband, a national party leader—that she was not conscious of her own situation. When I asked her about this seeming contradiction, Rose's response was that it had been *her* choice to raise her family, work, and serve the party in whatever way she and her husband *both* decided was important.

Rose Kerrigan's comments serve to emphasize that people can and do make conscious choices within their historical constraints, choices that are not always consistent with *our* theories about *their* ideologies (Barth, 1969; Jackson, 1988:276–92; Jansen, 1965:43–56; Tedlock, 1983; Turner and Bruner, 1986). Recognizing the different functions and contexts of jokes and songs for Rose led me to realize that the theoretical contradictions between her Marxism, which led her to believe in the necessity of universal liberation, and her feminism, which did indeed speak to the oppression of women by men, were in my mind, not hers. Though she rejected God early in life, her socialist and Jewish upbringing instilled in her the importance of justice as opposed to charity—the former implies that people have a right to equal treatment, the latter that it comes at the whim of those in power. Various experiences in her life convinced her that women are the more compassionate sex; as such, they should set an example for men rather than strive to be like them. For Rose, these lessons came together in a mixture of feminism and Communism, both of which dictate working toward a just society and the liberation of all men and all women. Feminism—liberating women via the enlightenment of men and women—as Rose Kerrigan practices it, is one way of achieving Communism.

Examining data in the light of their performance and situational use-value (Abrahams, 1981:320; Bauman, 1983:4–5; Limón, 1983:49–50) demonstrates that what we see as ideological paradoxes only appears as such if certain values are privileged over others.[7] In Rose Kerrigan's narratives what appeared to me as outright contradictions did not seem that way to her. For example, she was able to explain the reasons for such apparent contradictions as an avowed Marxist's manipulating people to make them buy things they were unsure they needed. To get a farmer to buy a pair of trousers, she told me that she would offer to hem them while he went about his other shopping. But she did this without her employer's knowledge and at no extra charge: "Now the difference between him and me was, I was concerned about people, wasn't I? I've always been concerned about people. So nobody went out of that shop except I knew that they were satisfied—that I had really tried to fit them or get them something. So the result was they came back to me from the country, you see? . . . They were satisfied and they sent their friends in, so the shop did well." When the same employer refused to keep her on if she got married, since he didn't believe married women could both work and care for a home, Rose again bent the truth by just not telling him when she did marry—thus proving her competence as a woman as well as a salesperson. When he finally found out, eighteen months later, he "sacked me. I'm not boasting, but within two years he was closed down."

But Rose did not believe that men's oppression of women was the entire source of their trouble; she also held women partly responsible for not doing what they could to improve their situations:

You know, there's very few people who've been a women's libber as long as me! You know I started at twelve! Or younger even than that! But their idea of it [today] is different to me. We held . . . a kind of a convention . . . about three or four years ago, and I was asked to discuss with another woman who was very strong on this women's lib business about women. And some of my remarks weren't the kind of things that they expected. . . .

The women themselves have been a lot to blame for what happens to them; it's true that it's been a man's world, but I can remember in my lifetime! Women who wouldn't have a woman doctor! . . . They fall for the prejudice and they didn't work it out for themselves.

And, in my opinion, it's been birth control that's mostly freed women, because if a woman had a family of five or six children or more, what chance had she to break away from the chains? . . . How can she say no to sex if he's the breadwinner? . . . When I was a child some of these married women had . . . ten and twelve children! . . . The little girls were all drudges bringing up the one that's coming after them, and so on and so on and so on. And it was always the women.

In my husband's family, because his mother didn't have a girl till the fifth child, he did all that. That's why he was such an understanding man. . . . And because he felt for his mother. . . . But if he was the type who said, "Oh, I'm not doing that," and went out to play football, . . . she wouldn't have done anything to him! She appealed to his better feelings, and he did it. . . . It is a man's world, and we're breaking it down. But the . . . women's libbers . . . forget that we put in the spade work, we women who fought for birth control, which is now their right as it were, who fought for attention for abortion when it was a back door thing and people died of it. These are the things you've got to remember. . . . You're not only doing it for yourself, you're doing it for the generation that comes after you.

In dealing with people, she told me, "You find your common denominator, and if it's lower than what you think it should be, then you try to bring it up. Don't try to do it all in a day, you can't! You can't bring them 100 percent to yourself, but you can bring them away from slipping the other way." Rose applied this approach to the women in the factory she organized, in her own relationships with other workers, within the Communist party, and in trying to get new members for the party.[8] In the factories she exchanged what she called "blue" (sexually obscene) jokes with the women, she was always willing to listen to others' problems, and she tried very pointedly not to alienate the other women by flaunting her often greater work skills. Thus while saying quite freely that women ought to take responsibility for changing their own condition, she was also willing to go along with the factory women's view of the male sex and to exchange blue jokes that denigrated men, because those were the constraints of the situation. The audience context clearly affected the choice of expression—the common denominator, as she calls it. What is peculiar about these jokes, however, is the way that they use "male" or sexist stereotypes of women to make quite the opposite point. That they can do so is due entirely to their performance context, without which they lose their situated and relevant meanings. For instance:

> This girl told me this. She worked in the factory. She said, this man met his friend, and as he was getting on a bit, his friend said to him,
> "Why don't you get married?" he said.
> "Oh well, I'm waiting for my ideal wife."
> And he said, "Well, what is your ideal wife?"
> He says, "Well, my idea of a good wife would be one when she walked down the street she would look like a lady, in bed she would act like a prostitute, and in the kitchen, she'd be economical."

A few years later he met his friend again and he said, "Did you get your ideal wife?"

"Ah, no, not exactly," he says. "My wife, when she walks down the street, she looks like a prostitute. In the kitchen, she acts like a lady. And in bed she's economical."

I was a bit surprised to hear Rose tell this joke, which didn't exactly reveal a heightened feminist consciousness according to my definition— quite the opposite, in fact. But then she went on to explain my misinterpretation of the joke. "That, for instance, shows us real chauvinistic—how can you put it? That man, that joke! But really, it . . . shows him up . . . [by showing] what women might do to upset him sort of thing. He's really reacting to the fact that he wants perfection, but he's not always prepared to give perfection! You see? Is he? You see they're always looking for perfection in the female." In a recent letter (1992), Mrs. Kerrigan explained, "The *chutzpa* is that his desires have to be satisfied sexually & culinarly; selfishness is portrayed here. What does he get. She pleases herself and puts him in his place! Victory for her."

In my original paper, presented at the 1986 American Folklore Society meeting, I used a different joke here, the one that Rose refused to tell me in the presence of a male colleague. Upon reading that paper, however, Mrs. Kerrigan reminded me that that joke was not appropriate for a general audience, especially not one with men present, and certainly not for publication. She told me that she could not show the paper to her daughters with that particular joke cited. Although she did not explicitly ask me to take it out, Rose did "give" me the joke quoted above in its place and added her own analysis of its meaning. In doing so, she not only preserved what she considered to be appropriate behavior for the circumstances but she also was able to add her own interpretation in place of mine (as she has continually done) and assert her role as an active participant in this endeavor rather than as passive object to be analyzed.

Another of Rose's blue jokes, which she said could be told in mixed company, is about a prostitute:

> We would always joke about the Catholic girl who went from Ireland to England to work. And she couldn't make a living, and she became a prostitute. And then she come to see her mother, she come back to Dublin, and her mother said,
>
> "Oh, Molly! Haven't you done well!" she says. "You've come all dressed up, in a fur coat and looking very smart."
>
> And she says, "Yes mother." She says, "I've had to turn prostitute." And her mother immediately fainted, and when she came to, she said to her, when she explained to her what happened, she said,
>
> "Oh, glory be to God! I thought you'd said you'd turned Protestant!"

Rose's fondness for this joke was a bit easier to comprehend—or so I thought. I assumed that to her it wasn't an ethnic joke about how loose the Irish were, but rather an anti-English joke. Like the Mexican "stupid American" jokes (Paredes, 1966), it seems to comment on a dominant Protestant English culture that purports to be highly moralistic in its judgments about Irish Catholics while simultaneously exploiting them and other British peoples. What amused Rose, I thought, was that the mother would rather see her daughter be a prostitute than a Protestant. She herself has more respect for prostitutes who honestly offer a service in exchange for money than for the hypocrisy of the English culture's dating system. This subtext, which could be garnered only from extended conversation with Rose about other issues, seemed to make clear why she did not mind having this joke told in mixed company. While discussing her girlhood she told me:

> I was terribly contemptuous of my girlfriends who went out with boys and were boasting about how they'd dodged them, they went out to the pictures with them, [how the boys] bought them chocolates. They were only out for what they would get. . . . I said to one of my friends, and she was horrified, I says, "You're worse than prostitutes! You want to take and not give, at least they give something for what they're getting." . . . I always felt myself that if you let boys see you home and all that sort of thing, you become beholden to them. . . . I wouldn't go out with anybody unless I paid my own way. And the boys, . . . that got under their skin, the idea. . . . I had an instinctive dislike from having been brought up with three brothers who'd got it so easy, and I was always the drudge! I was determined that I wasn't going to be caught out with it. . . . I wanted to be accepted on the basis of being equal always, you see?

Upon reading an earlier draft of this essay, Rose wrote to me with the following refinements, which disagreed somewhat with my interpretation of this joke given above. "The satire of the Irish joke is a swipe at bigotry. Prostitution is a 'sin' which the mother tolerates but the hypocrisy [is that] both Catholic and Protestant are Christian. The Catholic changing to Protestant is unacceptable—Bigotry."[9] Although Rose's explanation differs with my more specific interpretation, I believe that her "Irish" joke can still be understood to function more or less as I have suggested. According to Mrs. Kerrigan's refinements, however, it is bigots in general who are "stupid"—as opposed to people of a particular nationality or religion.

Before Rose gave me her latest interpretation of these jokes, I had presented the following as further illustration of the British/"other" cultural conflict about the relationship between men and women:

The best one I ever heard was a joke against the English language, which is, how foreigners have to put up with the language when they're trying to learn English, you know?

There were three foreigners . . . waiting for somebody, talking to pass the time.

One said to the other, "Are you married?"

He says, "Yes, I'm married."

"Have you got any children?"

He says, "Oh no! I'm sorry, but my wife, she's unbearable."

So the chap, the other one butts in, and he says, "I think you've got that wrong," he says. "This English language, very difficult. But I think you've got that wrong. I think what you really mean is that your wife is inconceivable."

So the other one, the third one says, "Well, I'm sorry to contradict each of you" he says, "because I've been longer here than you, and I know that English is difficult, but what you really mean is that your wife's impregnable."

Is that not a good joke?

From one point of view this joke is about men's views about women, but more particularly it is implicitly about a woman's views on male language usage. As Rose stated, the joke concerns the words available in the English language to describe women who don't have children. Women who are unbearable are unpleasant to be around, inconceivable or unimaginable is the woman who doesn't have children, and fortress-like, a challenge to men, are impregnable women.

According to my understanding of this joke's contextual meaning, Rose was emphasizing the way the joke exemplifies the irrationality of the English—for having such a confusing language. Rather than being a joke that criticizes childless married women, which would be odd for her, it is one that seems to laugh at the language and culture that creates the context for such beliefs. According to Mrs. Kerrigan, however, only the implicit meanings that I noted were in accord with her own intentions.[10] As she wrote, "this [joke] is a satire on our language & the difficulty foreigners find in understanding it." Rose does not, however, include a critique of the English as part of the joke's subtext.

For me, as audience, the common thread running through all three of these "blue" jokes is that sex for its own sake is worthless. To Rose, however, her jokes denoted something else. As she wrote to me in April 1992, "if you will forgive me . . . your conclusions especially with regard to the 'jokes' are completely out of line. Altho' we (Brits) & Americans speak the same language sometimes interpretations are different. . . . First of all the thing that makes all of these jokes, good jokes, is that they contain *satire*. . . . I feel I must point out my point of view because, I feel you have come to the wrong conclusions & I hope you will understand."

According to my interpretation, the woman in Rose's jokes—figures objectified by men, English culture, and religion—regained their autonomy and became subjects only because of Mrs. Kerrigan's reports of the jokes' performance contexts. Women told these jokes to other women, enabling the narratives to function like Paredes's "stupid American" jokes. The texts by themselves disparage women for not fulfilling the desires of men, for not bearing children, for using sex as a commodity—in other words, for not acting like "good" women. But the performance contexts (both the ones in which I participated and the ones that Rose reported to demonstrate to me the female control in those situations) invert this meaning and make the women into trickster figures. Such female tricksters— by retaining control of their bodies, of their sexuality, by withholding from men and from the dominant culture—maintain their autonomy and can exert a certain power over men.[11]

For Rose Kerrigan, sex without love has no meaning. For women to emulate men, to turn sex into a market commodity, would be to lose its proper use-value for her. As she told me upon reading the original version of this essay:

> I suppose some of the conclusions . . . were more feminist than I personally am. . . . The objection I have to all feminists is this: In my young day, they always talked about [how] . . . you couldn't trust [the men]. They were always running about "for one thing," as the saying is. . . . They just took, went elsewhere if it suited them, didn't believe in the loyalty and all that. . . . And now when women are freed from the fear of becoming pregnant and . . . make their own way . . . , they're acting the same, some of them, acting the same way as these men acted towards women in the past. And *that* is not what I call women's liberation, you see! That's my strong point about that!
>
> . . . In my opinion, because we are so much better in outlook . . . we should set an example. We, the women, should be the example. Not that we should emulate the men, but the men should come round to emulating women, who have got a more peaceful, less aggressive outlook on life, more caring—because it's always the women who've looked after the sick. Always the women who look after the people that are in trouble—it's always the women! Don't find very many men rushing around to help somebody in distress. . . . So if we want a better world, we've got to push forward our own advantages we have over men, the better feelings that we have, the more consideration that we really are capable of. We should be bringing them to be like us and not—we don't want to emulate them if they don't care about each other. . . . It's flattering to their ego, [but] it's not getting them anywhere.
>
> . . . [There should be] more respect on both sides. . . . I believe that you should give and take. . . . Really and truly, one has to recognize that the best way to live is to have someone you care for and who cares for you. . . . That

doesn't necessarily mean you've got to take their name, that doesn't necessarily mean you've got to have children if you don't want them.

In reconciling her ideas with actual practice, Rose emphasizes the importance of justice, whether between individuals or at a societal level. It takes concrete actions to change the world:

> My life's been spent in trying to . . . activize everybody. You see, as a Communist, I never was a very rigid dialectic—discusser or any of that. I mean, I would try to do things. For twelve years in Glasgow I was the chairperson of a tenants' association. . . . No matter what job I did, and I worked in different kinds of things—I was an active member of my union.
>
> . . . Communism in general is my real aim in life, but along the road you've got to get down to the common denominator with the ordinary person and find out how far you can bring them along the road. . . . So now I work with the pensioners. I don't go into great arguments with them about whether we should have socialism or not. . . . I tell them what I think, and at the end they can agree with you because you're putting forward a simple argument of life. And you're agreeing with them when they're grumbling about something, you're helping them along, pointing out why it should be like that, and why it shouldn't be like that. So that's always been my attitude to things. Mostly, I went along.
>
> When I was at school, they used to call me the professor. . . . They'd say, "Go and ask Rose, she knows all about it."
>
> When I worked in the factory, girls would say, "Ask Rose, she'll tell you."
>
> And I'd say to them, "Now there's somebody in charge of your bench. You should ask her about that."
>
> "Oh no, she's old, Rose." And she'd be a good ten or fifteen years younger than me! . . . You could get to their level as it were without downing them, always trying to bring them up a little bit higher towards you, never looking down on anybody, even how stupid their arguments are.

Rose used the same technique to reveal the hypocrisy of men in the party:

> The socialists that I met who made an effort to teach somebody else about socialism never had anything to do with it in the home; [they'd say] . . . "Oh she's not interested"—without finding out.
>
> . . . I used to say to them . . . if we had a social or anything, "Bring the wife along, get to know us!" Because otherwise there was this antagonism in the home. The man went out and did all these things at night; she was left at home with the children. So, this attitude of antagonism to the husband and his views could build up, and I could always see that that was wrong, always. Even as a young person I could see it. . . .
>
> I said, "Well I'm a woman! I'm interested, how did I become interested?"

I would say to them, "You've never tried, have you, to interest them," you see? And then we would have women's groups sometimes. Now some of the women in the movement always resented that.

"Why should we have to have divisions like that, women's group? If they're interested, they'll come along." But they always needed that little bit extra, so I was always in favor of having a women's group where women could express themselves and not feel they're being looked down upon by the men, you see?

Interestingly, Rose's songs reflect this mixture of scolding, exhorting, and encouraging the workers, as well as her own hope for a just society. After hearing her sing her "favorite revolutionary song" (a version of Percy Bysshe Shelley's "Song to the Men of England" [Shelley, 1946:270–71]), I commented that many of her songs, which include Negro spirituals[12] and several of her father's Yiddish songs,[13] seemed to reflect themes of liberation. Rose replied that of course her songs had to do with freedom—it was a part of being a Communist for her. But she also said that she sings a great many love songs (popular and folk), such as "The Spinning Wheel," "Juanita," "Oft in the Stilly Night," "The Gentle Maiden," and "Mary of Argyle," which end with marriage, or at least a proposal.[14] As she puts it: "Oh yes ... what appeals to me besides the music of a song are the words, ... the old songs that you sing. Today the love songs, for instance, they're just love songs and they talk about love, but the songs of the past always ask the women to be a bride. There's a difference there, and it's a historical reality."

But her attraction to songs about loyal lovers is not mere romantic escapism:

My understanding is that women should have an equal right with men and an equal opportunity for everything—culture wise ... and in every way and in every facet of life. ... But if women think that feminism is emulating the things that they condemn the men for! It's not my understanding of feminism. That's doing as bad as them!

... Too much is made of this promiscuity. ... From what you see on the TV, a man's bound to get the impression that any woman'll jump into bed with him at the crack of a whip or just to be asked, or sometime not even to be asked. The women half the time on the TV make the running, all because everything's been cleared away for them! That isn't my idea of living together. It's not love! There's no such thing as love, if it's only sexual intercourse for the sake of a moment's passion or something like that. I might be old-fashioned and wrong; I don't think I am. ... It's equality at work, equality in the home, equality sexwise. ... You have the right to say no either way, and a right to try and make it possible always ... if you've got a proper love between people, if you've got the proper idea that courtship takes place, which makes it possible—that's what I always had all my life.... Women shouldn't need to demand it, or men demand it. No man has any right to demand of a woman that she sleep with him and live with him.... If a woman goes just because she thinks, "Oh well, I can stay with him, but I can leave him any day"—it's wrong! You must know what you're living with.

More recently, Rose wrote to tell me: "My remarks re the songs was to show the historical difference there was & is on the marriage situation. I don't promote marriage as such, in present day attitudes, a genuine relationship where children are not stigmatised as they were before is all right by me. I move with the times."

These pages only begin to give a sense of the sort of woman Rose Kerrigan is, to explain how she chooses among a wide variety of strategies to persuade others of her views on feminism and Marxism. I have tried to show how her choices of folkloric expressions function according to her reports of their performance context and how they fit into her personal ideology. Clearly, Rose Kerrigan's choices of songs, jokes, and anecdotes are derived from her life's experiences and her firm commitment to Communism. But they are also influenced by her age and the historical constraints that inform her sense of what is and is not correct behavior for women. Her explanations of her beliefs, not coincidentally, come from her sense of the unique contribution a woman's point of view and behavior can make to the world and to Communism. The sort of Marxist feminism that Rose expresses emphasizes that women are to serve as models for men. In her opinion, women are the more humane and caring sex and thus obligated not to indulge in uncompassionate behavior that dehumanizes those involved. As noted above, her preference for justice rather than charity comes directly from her Jewish background, particularly from her socialist and religiously observant father who always sought to persuade others rather than to dispute their beliefs.

Mrs. Kerrigan's style and choice of folkloric expressions make clear that, for her, hierarchical relationships and competition between men and women, as well as between different classes and countries, can and should be overcome by interacting with others as human beings—not as objects or impersonal forces. Individual folksongs she sings or jokes she tells may not always be ideologically consistent with each other—because she believes that different situations require different tactics. Her own explanations for acting in a specific way, for performing a certain song or joke, help to reconcile these apparent contradictions by switching the focus from the more obvious subject matter of individual texts to their particular use and context.

Rose quite consciously regards herself as a performer. She works at learning her songs and jokes so that she can relate them properly. Regarding the transmission process, Rose explained, "If you tell a joke, my thing is, if I hear something good . . . , I tell it to myself more than once in order to try and memorize it." The process is similar with songs, although she also writes down the words in order to learn them. Thus, while her political use of folkloric materials may be unconscious (i.e., in the workplace or at Party meetings she did not perform jokes, songs, or stories to persuade others to her point of view but to fit in or entertain), her decision to learn and tell a particular song, joke, or anecdote is quite explicit.

Rose Kerrigan is hardly an exploited woman in need of having either her class or her feminist consciousness raised. Her methods and ideas may not be in accord with others in her party or of her sex. And the content of the folklore that she chooses to express her views or those of others may seem incompatible with a standard feminist ideology (not Rose's) that insists that women are oppressed by men; such a notion implies that turning the tables on the oppressor is the only way to topple the hierarchy (not Rose's view at all). It also implies that women are objects and victims, not autonomous subjects with their own methods of achieving their own goals.

In fact, Rose's songs and jokes are consistent with her own methodology of persuasion and compromise, despite the often "sexist" topics of her jokes or the politically "simplistic" recommendations of her songs. But such apparent contradictions between subject matter and intent become reconciled only when both their performance context and their use-value are considered and understood. We should not, therefore, dismiss what some may call rationalizations—for if we truly listen to our informants and hear what they say, we may well come to appreciate and learn from their theories about the ways in which women (and men) use and interpret their folklore.

Notes

I'd like first to thank Rose Kerrigan, without whose friendship, patience, help, and time this could not have been written. Her comments are quoted from interviews conducted during 1985–87 and our correspondence that dates from 1986 to 1992. Also crucial to my research was the *Morning Star,* which published my original letter requesting information about volunteers in the 1926 General Strike. I'd also like to express my appreciation to Patricia Sawin for our ongoing dialogue about folklore and feminism, to Debbie Fant for her editorial comments, and to the editors of this volume, Jane, Linda, and Susan, for their indescribable patience and tolerance. Finally, I'd like to acknowledge Steve Roud, Doc Rowe, Marion Bowman, and Craig Fees, some of the folklorists in England without whose cultural translation and continuing friendship my work could not have been accomplished. This essay and a version published in 1987 in the *Journal of American Folklore* 100 (398): 548–62 are based upon research conducted during 1985–86 and 1987 in London, England, the latter portion made possible by a Grant-in-Aid from the Wenner-Gren Foundation for Anthropological Research.

1. Roger deV. Renwick (1980) has addressed the importance of paying heed to these cultural "commonplaces" in his analysis of English folk poetry, and I owe much interpretive inspiration to his methodology and tutelage over the years.

2. According to Dave Harker (1985), folksongs and ballads do not reflect the "soul" of the "people" of Great Britain. Instead they were collected, co-opted, and manipulated by middle-class scholars as well as socialist organizations and governments to create a false consciousness about "the people." Concepts like "folksong" and "ballad" are bourgeois constructs imposed from above and as such are useless for comprehending working-class culture.

Harker's efforts to deconstruct the history of British folksong scholarship do successfully reveal the classist and self-conscious creation of "folksong" as a historical construct. But while Albert Lloyd and Ewan MacColl may have appropriated aspects of folk culture for their own purposes, this does not mean that folksongs do not exist or that individuals, whatever their class, are incapable of recognizing them as authentic parts of their own culture—whether borrowed from "above" or extracted from "below."

3. "Some of the jokes I heard at the factory from the women I couldn't repeat to anybody! Oh no! I couldn't! . . . Not in front of any man! I could tell you! But I couldn't tell him."

4. While the notion that form, function, and audience are interrelated structures is not a revolutionary concept, it is one that researchers often forget in the midst of fieldwork—or back in the ivory tower.

5. According to Carol Rogers, "One of the most important strategies of American feminism . . . was 'consciousness-raising,' an institutionalized process by which neophyte feminists learned first, that they are subordinated, and second how and in what forms this subordination occurs. The development of this kind of awareness was seen as an essential first step to political awareness. . . . A number of feminist anthropologists have continued this process by demonstrating that women are universally subordinated. To them, the notion that women in other societies may not be, or do not believe themselves to be, subordinated is evidence of 'false-consciousness' " (1978:138).

6. For instance, Eleanor Leacock, Helen Safa, and Contributors start with the basic assumption that women are oppressed—at home, in the workplace, and in society. Leacock and Safa's preface to *Women's Work* notes that the various chapters "deal with the issue of gender inequality both at the family or household level and at the level of the community or society—or in what have been called

the private and public domains. Much of the debate among feminists over whether patriarchy or capitalism is the primary contemporary basis for women's subordination has focused on which domain is more important. . . . [Despite] somewhat differing views . . . , all agreed on the inseparable link between the gender division of labor at the household level and such a division at the societal level, demonstrating that no strategy of change confined to one level alone can succeed in eradicating female subordination, *even under socialism*" (Leacock and Safa, 1986:x, emphasis mine).

7. Following José Limón (1983) and Roger Abrahams (1981), I am using this Marxist terminology to describe folklore "as 'gift giving' . . . nonalienated labor, and the denial of commodity fetishism. . . . All [folkloric performances] . . . may be displays of 'the possibility of hanging on to the *use* and value of things . . . in the face of those who would turn all of life into acts of consumption' " (Limón, 1983:49–50).

8. It has occurred to me over the course of conversations with Rose, and in writing the various versions of this essay, that she may have also been using my interest in feminism and folklore to persuade me of the rightness of her cause: Communism. Clearly Rose was attempting (and continues in letters) to pass on to me her values and to convince me of their rightness. Thus there may be other interpretations of the discourse between the two of us (Hall, 1980:137–38).

9. In a letter (1992), Rose further cautioned that "if you include that joke you may alienate Catholics, who may resent the implication, & I think it would be diplomatic not to include it." Since the implications were derived from *my* interpretation of the joke, not Rose's, and since she gave me her permission to use it, I decided to include it along with her reservations.

10. In the April 1992 letter, Mrs. Kerrigan interpreted the joke as follows: "A woman bears a child (giving birth). To be unbearable is to be impossible. A woman conceives a child. To be inconceivable is lacking in understanding. A woman is pregnant (with child). To be impregnable is to be impenetrable. The root word is confusing to foreigners, but the joke is cleverly funny. And it's the *satire* that is good."

11. I stress at this point that the interpretations expressed in this chapter present my attempts to reconcile Rose Kerrigan's folklore with my own feminist understanding of them and what she conveyed to me of her worldview; other readings (hers included) are clearly possible, and those articulated here are not meant to exclude them.

12. As Rose told me: "I learned a lot of my songs from the gramophone in the early days, I learned Paul Robeson's song when he sang:

> "Oh by and by, by and by,
> I'm gonna lay down this heavy load.
> Oh one of these mornings, bright and gay,
> I'm gonna lay down my heavy load.
> I'll tickle my wings and cleave the air
> I'm gonna lay down this heavy load."

I learned that from the grammophone. You see, that's because I've got a good ear."

13. For example, she sang one about "the history ... in Europe, after the Inquisition, the Jews lay dormant, nothing—friends from everywhere started to knock on the door, 'Rise up!' ... It means, the words mean, 'Rise up, don't sleep so long, there are things for you to do. Israel says, "Stand up!" ' And it's a real nationalist song, my father used to sing that, and I learned it. And you know how I learned it off him? Writing it down phonetically, I like wrote the words down. . . . Aye, he explained it all to me! You see, it starts ... 'From Asia to Europe ... I slept for 1700 years,' like a Rip Van Winkle thing. You see, they lay dormant after the Spanish Inquisition, the Jews. I ... never heard anybody else sing it."

14. To illustrate her point, I include the transcription of two of her songs: "Juanita," an English popular song, and "The Spinning Wheel," a Scottish ballad.

> Soft o'er the fountain,
> Lingering falls the southern moon.
> Far o'er the mountain
> Breaks the day too soon.
> In thy dark eyes tender
> Where the warm light longs to dwell
> Weary looks yet tender
> Sing thy fond farewell.
>
> Nita, Juanita,
> Ask thy soul if we should part
> Nita, Ju-an-ita,
> Lean thou on my heart.
>
> When in thy dreaming dreams
> Like these shall shine again.
> And daylight beaming
> Prove thy dreams are vain.
> Wilt thou not relenting
> To thine harps and lover's sighs
> In thy heart consenting,
> To a prayer gone by.
>
> Nita, Juanita,
> Wilt thou lie there by my side,
> Nita, Ju-an-ita,
> Be my own fair bride.

"See what I mean? There's a difference. Now I'll sing you a Scottish song that's got the same kind of theme" (stanza breaks correspond with Rose Kerrigan's phrasing):

> As Jean sat by her spinning wheel.
> A bonny laddy he passed by.

As Jean sat by her spinning wheel,
A bonny laddy he passed by.
She turned around and viewed him weel,
For oh-oh he had a glancin' eye.

She looked aroound and viewed him weel,
But aye she turned her spinning wheel.
She looked aroound and viewed him weel,
But aye she turned her spinning wheel.

Her snow white hands he did extol.
He praised her fingers neat and small.
Her snow white hands he did extol.
He praised her fingers neat and small.

He said there was na lady fairer
Whose hands with her he could compare
His words into her heart did steal,
But aye she turned her spinning wheel.
And aye she liked his words so weel,
She laid aside her spinning wheel.

He said lay by your rock, your reel,
Your winnings and your spinning wheel.
He said lay by your rock, your reel,
Your winnings and your spinning wheel.
And come and be-ee his bonny bride.
And aye she liked his words sae weel,
She laid aside her spinning wheel.

"See the difference? I mean, they all want to get married!"

References Cited

Abrahams, Roger D. 1981. "Shouting Match at the Border: The Folklore of Display Events." In *"And Other Neighborly Names": Social Process and Cultural Image in Texas,* ed. Richard Bauman and Roger D. Abrahams, 303–22. Austin: University of Texas Press.

Barth, Fredrik, ed. 1969. *Ethnic Groups and Boundaries.* Boston: Little, Brown.

Bauman, Richard. 1983. *Let Your Words Be Few.* Cambridge: Cambridge University Press.

Christ, Carol P. 1979. "Why Women Need the Goddess: Phenomenological, Psychological, and Political Reflections." In *Women Spirit Rising,* ed. Carol P. Christ and Judith Plaskow, 273–87. San Francisco: Harper and Row.

Clifford, James, and George E. Marcus, eds. 1986. *Writing Culture: The Poetics and Politics of Ethnography.* Berkeley: University of California Press.

Farrer, Clare R. 1986. "Introduction." In *Women and Folklore,* ed. Clare R. Farrer, xi-xxi. Prospect Heights, Ill.: Waveland Press.

Friedan, Betty. 1963. *The Feminine Mystique.* New York: W. W. Norton.

Hall, Stuart. 1980. "Encoding/Decoding." In *Culture, Media, Language: Working Papers in Cultural Studies, 1972–1979,* ed. Stuart Hall, Dorothy Hobson, Andrew Lowe, and Paul Willis, 128–38. London: Hutchinson.

Harker, Dave. 1985. *Fakesong: The Manufacture of British "Folksong"—1700 to the Present Day.* Philadelphia: Open University Press.

Jackson, Bruce. 1988. "What People like Us Are Saying When We Say We're Saying the Truth." *Journal of American Folklore* 101 (401): 276–92.

Jansen, W. Hugh. 1965. "The Exoteric-Esoteric Factor in Folklore." In *The Study of Folklore,* ed. Alan Dundes, 43–56. Englewood Cliffs, N.J.: Prentice-Hall.

Lamphere, Louise. 1977. "Review Essay—Anthropology." *Signs* 2:612–27.

Leacock, Eleanor, and Helen I. Safa. 1986. "Preface." In *Women's Work,* Eleanor Leacock, Helen I. Safa, and Contributors, ix–xi. South Hadley, Mass.: Bergin and Garvey.

Leacock, Eleanor, Helen I. Safa, and Contributors. 1986. *Women's Work.* South Hadley, Mass.: Bergin and Garvey.

Limón, José E. 1983. "Western Marxism and Folklore: A Critical Introduction." *Journal of American Folklore* 96 (379): 34–52.

MacCormack, Carol, and Marilyn Strathern, eds. 1980. *Nature, Culture, and Gender.* Cambridge: Cambridge University Press.

Ortner, Sherry. 1974. "Is Male to Female as Nature Is to Culture?" In *Woman, Culture, and Society,* ed. Michelle Zimbalist Rosaldo and Louise Lamphere, 67–87. Stanford: Stanford University Press.

Paredes, Américo. 1966. "The Anglo-American in Mexican Folklore." In *New Voices in American Studies,* ed. Ray Browne, 113–28. West Lafayette, Ind.: Purdue University Press.

Renwick, Roger deV. 1980. *English Folk Poetry: Structure and Meaning.* Philadelphia: University of Pennsylvania Press.

Rogers, Susan Carol. 1978. "Woman's Place: A Critical Review of Anthropological Theory." *Comparative Studies in Society and History* 20:123–62.

Rosaldo, Michelle Zimbalist. 1974. "Woman, Culture, and Society: A Theoretical Overview." In *Woman, Culture, and Society,* ed. Michelle Rosaldo and Louise Lamphere, 17–42. Stanford: Stanford University Press.

Rosaldo, Michelle Zimbalist, and Louise Lamphere, eds. 1974. *Woman, Culture, and Society.* Stanford: Stanford University Press.

Royce, Anya Seton. 1982. *Ethnic Identity: Strategies of Diversity.* Bloomington: Indiana University Press.

Sanday, Peggy Reeves. 1981. *Female Power and Male Dominance: On the Origins of Sexual Inequality.* Cambridge: Cambridge University Press.

Shelley, Percy Bysshe. 1946. "Song to the Men of England." In *The College Survey of English Literature,* vol. 2, ed. B. J. Whiting, Fred B. Millett, 270–71. New York: Harcourt, Brace.

Stocking, George W., ed. 1985. *Observers Observed: Essays on Ethnographic Fieldwork.* Madison: University of Wisconsin Press.

Stoeltje, Beverly. 1986. " 'A Helpmate for Man Indeed': The Image of the Frontier

Woman." In *Women and Folklore: Images and Genres,* ed. Claire R. Farrer, 25–41. Prospect Heights, Ill.: Waveland Press.

Tedlock, Dennis. 1983. *The Spoken Word and the Work of Interpretation.* Philadelphia: University of Pennsylvania Press.

Turner, Victor W., and Edward M. Bruner, eds. 1986. *The Anthropology of Experience.* Urbana: University of Illinois Press.

Thompson, E. P. 1971. "The Moral Economy of the English Crowd in the Eighteenth Century." *Past and Present* 50:76–136.

Young, M. Jane. 1987. "Women, Reproduction, and Religion in Western Puebloan Society." *Journal of American Folklore* 100 (398): 435–45.

Gender and Genre

Feminist studies of folklore are always faced with the conflicting possibilities of traditional forms as oppressive or liberating. In this study of how a woman appropriates a traditional parable to describe her liberation, I suggest that genres are not neutral classification systems but are part of a politics of interpretation in which meaning and the authority to propose and ascribe categories is contested. My text is a parable embedded in a life-history narrative collected from a Mexican woman with three children living without legal documents in California. Her story, and how she has constructed her past, forms the basis for the questions I am asking about how people negotiate the categories that are imposed upon them and, more particularly, how a person defined by others as an outcast can envision a future of possibilities rather than a destiny of failure. My path to understanding the woman's story and her parable led to a reexamination of how folklorists have conceptualized the problem of genre.

Theories of gender and genre converge in their exploration of the problems of classification and the disruption of boundaries.[1] Genre is often gendered, and a great deal of feminist scholarship concerned with cultural texts (literary, political, traditional) has focused on the ways gender boundaries have been reinforced by generic ones. Generic boundaries, the systems for classifying different sorts of texts, are never fixed, and our investigations usually tell us more about the edges and crossovers than they do about the centers. Gender scholarship questions how cultural categories are reproduced and under what conditions women are complicit with or resistant to the reproduction of conventions. Among other possibilities, women can be seen as the bearers of tradition, or the women's domains can be seen as separate, as standing outside of or in competition with what is identified as "the culture."

I will examine five areas of folklore genre theory from a feminist perspective. The first area concerns the problem of genre classification and the question of whether or not the concept of "ethnic genres" can address some of the issues of hierarchy, status, and privilege that concern feminists. While the idea of ethnic genres (roughly that each ethnic group has its own criteria for sorting types of texts) serves as an important corrective to the alternative concept of universal fixed categories, the question for feminists is whether this particular instability, between universal and particular systems of classification, can address another sort of instability, between centers and margins of categories. My second area of concern is the relationship between texts and the worlds they putatively represent. Here we find that interpretations are always motivated, never neutral, and that no matter how extensive our research, we cannot remedy the gap between representations and experiences; our attempts to give voices to silenced women do not remedy their marginalized position. I suggest a shift away from concerns with the accuracy of interpretation, which are in essence attempts to fix meaning, and toward understanding how particular systems of meaning become privileged or abused. I briefly consider, as a third area of concern, the incompatibility between the folkloristic premise of cultural relativism and the feminist insistence on evaluating cultural constructions. While feminists and cultural relativists might share claims for multiple interpretations as opposed to monolithic truths, feminists accept neither neutral nor "cultural" descriptions as the alternative. My fourth issue is how genres have been examined as holistic, totalizing worldview systems rather than cultural constructions motivated by particular interests that are constantly maintained or renegotiated. My final concern is to develop a politics of genre in which we can ask questions about how understanding genre classification can contribute to an understanding of how people comply with or undermine authoritative discourses.

The Appeal of Genre

By calling attention to the ways in which genre classification systems could represent the values of a culture, the performance focus of folklore scholarship laid a foundation for investigating the ways in which boundaries are maintained, reproduced, transgressed, or shifted.[2] The study of genres as conventions and as part of conventional attitudes opened the door to the study of genres that had previously received little scholarly attention and to questions of the unconventional or of competing conventions.

Building upon earlier discussions of the concepts of emic and etic categories, Dan Ben-Amos (1976) proposed the concept of ethnic genres as an alternative to universal analytic categories. An ethnic genre system is a group's own terms for communicative categories.[3] One appeal of ethnic genre systems is the possibility of correlating ways of categorizing forms of communication with ways of comprehending other aspects of social life and with worldviews generally (Gossen, 1972). However, the correspondence between genre systems and worldviews depends upon an impossibly homogenous group in which communication consistently reflects worldviews. Genre systems are as much about disputes, the maintenance and shifting of boundaries, as they are about correspondences, and the idea of homogeneous groups is as invented as are the generic categories themselves.

The concept of ethnic genres depends upon a concept of an isolatable group. In the case of gender, genre classification systems often compete with those of the larger group. Of course, classifications by any group, including class, race, nationality, or culture, as often as not involve competing systems. As Marie-Laure Ryan points out, "There is no such thing as *the* native taxonomy" (1982:114).

Competing genre systems involve more than a lack of fit in particular generic categories. The classification systems themselves are ideological, and, as will be discussed, ideology includes both the dominant and the suppressed views, the complicit as well as the resistant,[4] and is not the same as a holistic concept of worldview.[5] Disputes over what counts in a classification system lead to larger issues, such as the grounds for privileging, canonizing, or authenticating particular kinds of texts. Susan Stewart's studies of graffiti and other "crimes of writing," including plagiarism, forgery, pornography, and distressed genres, call attention to the ways in which genre classifications are ideological. Speaking of graffiti, she writes, "In practices of production and apprehension, aesthetic valuation is a process of repression and emergence, erasure and reinscription" (1987:163).

The competition for privilege, for aesthetic valuation, or, more crudely, for what counts and for who will do the counting, is among genre *systems,* not genres, even though the discourse about genres often frames the disputes in terms of some proposed attributes of particular genres. This point is particularly salient for a feminist study of genres in which particular characteristics might be proposed as "essentially" belonging to women's communicative forms. Genres do have identifiable characteristics in particular social, historical moments. However, those characteristics and their significance are not fixed or inherent to the genre, and questions of the status of particular genres are best addressed in terms of the relations among genres. These relationships provide an opportunity to ask questions about the status of women's genres as privileged, trivial, or marginal, questions about the relations among genres in terms of hierarchies, authorities, or privileged representations, and questions about differences among contexts of use based on gender.

The Appeal of Accurate Description

A companion to the appeal of ethnic genre systems as less ethnocentric than universal analytic categories for genres is the appeal of the possibility of neutral descriptions. Both cultural relativism and feminism propose the possibility of comparison between essential units, whether between cultures or between male and female portrayals of women. Feminist readings begin from the thesis that a neutral text is impossible (Newton and Rosenfelt, 1985:xv-xxxix). As Denise Riley has put it, "Feminism never has the option of putting forward its own uncontaminated, self-generated understandings of 'women': its 'women' too, is always thoroughly implicated in the discursive world" (1988:68).

While feminists share with folklorists the recognition that categories such as genre or gender are cultural constructions, there is a profound difference between the feminist's explicit evaluation of texts in terms of the way women are or are not portrayed and the folklorist's attempt to value only the integrity of cultures. Both feminist readings invested in feminist portrayals of women and folkloric descriptions of performance as culturally relative are based upon a basically formalist, certainly modernist, and somewhat positivist set of assumptions about the relationship between experience and representation.[6] Both can too easily ignore the ways in which representations are constructions of reality. What neither entertains is the investigation of the ways cultural knowledge and power are distributed: who shares culture with whom, who imposes culture upon whom, and who appropriates culture from whom.

As Toril Moi points out, some feminists argue that the "highest goals of literature" should be the "more or less faithful *reproduction* of an external reality to which we all have equal and unbiased access" (1985:45). On the face of it, such a demand does not seem far from the cultural relativist's interest in describing cultures as they are. However, the difference is that the feminist rejects the essentially male portrayal of the oppressed female, and a cultural relativist rejects no portrayals. The similarity is that both depend upon a face-value reality and on the possibility of representing it in textual form.

The Appeal of Cultural Relativism

Just as the hidden appeal of neutral representations is essentialism, the accurate portrayal of something as we know it or want it to be, the hidden appeal of cultural relativism is an escape from the crisis of representing general laws about particular situations. (The explicit appeal is the equally problematic project of attempting to see cultures on their own terms.) When we ask, for example, whether Middle Eastern women who wear veils are oppressed or are representing a different tradition that cannot be judged according to Western standards,[7] we are caught in what Clifford Geertz has described as "an hermeneutics of legal pluralism," an attempt to represent the "other" without transforming it into our terms (1983:225).

Geertz suggests that we focus on the vernacular, on what he calls "local knowledge" rather than "placeless principles" (1983:218). However, the concept of local knowledge does not resolve the dispute about whether the use of local terminology or local accounts from the culture's own viewpoint is either less oppressive or more accurate. Ultimately, the problem is not a matter of deciphering local knowledge, describing more accurately, or discerning realities through appearances. More contextual detail will not lead us closer to "the truth." Rather, contextual information is essential for understanding the grounds on which ownership of "the truth" is contested, including the ways in which we as investigators are implicated in truth claims.

The Appeal of Homogeneous Worldview

The move, in folklore research, to study ethnic genre classification systems, rather than individual genres, was a move toward the study of the ideological agendas behind the classification systems. The discussion of genre classification in terms of worldviews could be seen as a mistaken route in that investigation. Genre classifications and the different uses of particular genres by men and women are significant parts of and indicators for how people construct their social worlds and are constructed by them.[8] The problem is that just as people have divergent ways of classifying genres, they have divergent worldviews, and at best (or worst), the worldview paired with the genre classification system represents a dominant view. Rather than assume consistency between worldview systems and genre systems, we can ask questions about what the privileged status of particular genres can tell us about discrepancies in social status and about who benefits from maintaining such systems. Claims for a "harmonious world view matrix" (Dundes, 1971:99) suppress questions about the position that is being suppressed. Once we observe that views on genre hierarchy correspond with worldviews, the question is, to what extent is this correspondence traceable, and what can it tell us about privileged and stigmatized communication?

Holistic, totalizing models set up a hierarchical contrast between the allegorical, which supports the holistic model, and the epiphenomenal, a category for any text that does not fit.[9] The discrepancy here is not between the sign (the text) and its referent (a particular worldview). The allegorical and the epiphenomenal do not exist side by side but engage each other in confrontation. While one interpretation claims the status of worldview, the other works to undermine it (de Man, 1979:10; Morson, 1981:110–11).

The difficulty is to abandon the privileging of worldview without giving in to artificially neutral, or culturally relative, descriptions. Cultural relativism is often criticized for its lack of determined meaning (Jarvie, 1975:262), but that is not the criticism here. Meaning is situated, but, and this is the point of divergence from cultural relativism, it is also contested; the contest is part of the context, and the boundaries of the context are also contestable. As Richard Terdiman puts it, "Conflict is thus as characteristic of the semiotic realm as of the social" (1985:36). The problem with a totalizing worldview model is that it only presents the dominant part of the contest: "The *meaning* of the sign is thrown open—the sign becomes 'polysemic' rather than 'univocal'—and though it is true to say that the dominant power group at any given time will dominate the intertextual production of meaning, this is not to suggest that the opposition has been reduced to total silence. The power struggle *intersects* in the sign" (Moi, 1985:158).

Appeals to worldview or other holistic systems of meaning are nothing more than attempts to fix meaning, to privilege a particular system. The alternative is to study the processes for privileging meaning, the cultural constructions of genre or canon that grant status to particular kinds of texts and performances. Holistic meanings do not then disappear, since, as Julia Kristeva points out, they are part of language, as a signifying system (1986).

Correspondence between genre systems and worldviews are allegorical; they grant authority to a particular narrative explanation for the relations between genres. Discussions of genre are especially useful for exposing the problems of reductive allegories built into claims for an alliance between a genre and a worldview.[10]

Resisting Appeals: A Politics of Genre

Studies of genre begin with questions of classification: a text is designated as a this and not a that.[11] The discovery of permeable boundaries has led both to investigations of dual membership (a this and a that at the same time) and to discussions of authority and authenticity (Retallack, 1987). A politics of genre classification is concerned with questions of resistance as well: the refusal to be named as a part of a particular category or the act of undermining authority or authenticity claims. Feminist readings remind us that all interpretations are about hierarchies. The exploration of genres invites the investigation of the relationships between forms, of which hierarchies are but one type.

Genre classifications are themselves cultural artifacts or constructions, positioned in historical and political situations. The distribution of resources, power, and knowledge become important in understanding the relation between text and text and between text and either worldview of experience. In a sense, genre studies epitomize problems of textual referentiality. The three major schools of thought—the universal genres proposed by Aristotle and others, based upon qualities inherent in the forms and reactions they produce in the addressee; the analytic or formal classification of genres based not upon universal principles but upon relations between texts; and the ethnic genres based upon a combination of the above two, founded on culturally specific principles of worldview and relations between genres—all propose that genres contain extratextual information about reading.[12] Even the debates about genre correspond to a problem of referentiality. Basically, they ask, are genres universal or culturally specific; are they informed by worldview or by literary convention? These are questions concerned with finding a set of referents for genre. Instead, we might ask, how does genre classification utilize the distribution of power, knowledge, and authority? What kinds of authority does the system appeal to: to the authority of male tradition or to gendered genres? Genre classifications, in the case discussed here, are a supreme example of gendered cultural constructions.

"A Marketplace of Opinions"

Folklore genre scholarship has been more concerned with how genres are defined in relation to each other (what makes a riddle different from a proverb) rather than the relation between genres used in a particular speech event.[13] I will offer an example of how the meaning of one genre depends upon its challenges to authority through the relationship to another genre used in the same speech event. The problem here is not a text that does not fit a genre but the use of a particular genre, a parable in a new context that undermines the parable's traditional interpretation. Building upon Barbara Kirshenblatt-Gimblett's study "A Parable in Context" (1975), I will discuss a parable told in a conversational context. Kirshenblatt-Gimblett's parable was told in the context of a conversation and reported in the context of an account of the situation generally. The following parable was told in the context of a life-history narrative. The life-history narrative and parable were collected from a Mexican woman living in San Jose, California. The collection was part of a larger research project conducted by Diane Schaffer concerning the feminization of poverty. When the researchers learned that this particular women was in the United States illegally, she was determined to be ineligible for their study, and instead, with her permission, the tape was made available to me.[14] The interviewer is a Chicana graduate student.

In her four-hour-long life-history account, the woman tells how she was abandoned (her term) by her husband in Compostela, Mexico, shortly after the birth of their first child. She describes how, as an abandoned wife, she was categorized and treated as an outcast. She believed her husband would return, but other people did not. He did return but abandoned her again after the birth of their second child. After several years, he returned and she persuaded him to let her join him in San Jose, California. He abandoned her again after the birth of a third child, and the years that followed were even more difficult since she had almost no network of support. Her life story is one of constant struggles against both the obstacles of the traditional social attitudes that branded her as an undesirable outcast and the contemporary problems of living in a country where she does not speak the language, cannot work legally, and must provide for three small children. Her account consists of two genres, a parable embedded in a life history narrative, both competing for somewhat different interpretations. In her life history narrative, she describes how she resisted accepting the idea that she had been abandoned. She did not work at first because married women did not work in her community and she did not want to "dishonor" her husband. An abandoned woman was neither married nor single, and her story is about the financial and emotional difficulties of being a noncategory and thus not having access to the resources and possibilities of either category. She said (translated from Spanish): "Well, some people said I had been abandoned because I was dumb, that I should have done this, that, and who knows what else, that it was my fault that he had left me, because I was proud, and I should have begged him, followed him. Um, others, 'No good it's better that they split up. She can find work herself and do more than with that old man. He's no good company.' And still others said, 'Poor thing, it's really hard without a husband.' Well, it was a, a (laughing) marketplace of opinions."

This account was followed by a discussion of how she had managed as an undocumented worker and a single mother. At the time of the interview, the narrator had a job cleaning houses and was exchanging child care with a neighbor. She was hopeful that her life would improve. The interviewer asked: "Ah, how are you trying to achieve these things that you want?" And she responded:

I have done many, many things, but how shall I say, when I was small and I went to school, there was a lesson in a book about a pair of little frogs that were jumping, jumping around near a window. They were in the garden in a basin. So, they were looking around to see what there was outside the garden. They jumped, jumped up to the house and fell through the window onto the dining room table. And they fell into a bowl of *natas* [skin that forms on milk when it boils]. Then they were scared because it wasn't mud, it wasn't water, it wasn't grass, it wasn't, they didn't know what it was, no? They were, they were, they were drowning. So they started to kick their legs, kicking, kicking. And uh one of them got very frightened, very scared, and she began to drown. She drowned, she drowned in *natas*. The other one kept on kicking, kicking, kicking, kicking. And if you beat them a lot, if you beat them again and again, it turns to butter. So the little frog was kicking, kicking, kicking, kicking. And that stuff began to get hard underneath. She kept on kicking kicking until she could, could, could support herself on what was becoming hard. And she jumped out of [the bowl], you see? She wasn't familiar with where she was. And no one told her what to do or how to do it.

My situation is similar. There is someone who tells me what to do, what I should do. But I can't because I don't have, I don't have, in the first place, to begin with, eh, I'm in this country illegally, I don't have papers. There's no one who can tell me, I can give them to you. I ask in one office, I asked in another. They say ask that notary. I go there to that notary; they say in that place there's someone who worked for the community who can give you guidance about immigration. And there I go to ask. They say in the welfare office there's someone who, who can tell you what to do. So I go to welfare. And it's like that, see? And nowhere has anyone given me the answer to that. Everywhere I go they tell me I can't.

But I've been like the frog. I can't, it's not my environment, it's not my country, but I keep on kicking (laughing). I don't want to drown, you see? I want to get out, even if it's just out of the country. And that way, if I can't do anything, at least, at least get out and say, but I tried, no. I tried to do it, I couldn't do it, but I did try. And that's what I'm doing here, trying to, trying to get papers.

The parable is a conversational genre. Parables are told as part of a particular situation, and they work metaphorically to convey a point.[15] This parable draws a clear parallel with the life-history narrative in which it was told: the woman, like the frog, is on her own in an unfamiliar situation, and she intends to continue to struggle to survive. However, differences between the two genres suggest questions. What does she perceive her adversity to be? What is her relationship to her companions in the struggle? Does the parable provide the voice of tradition, the voice of consensus or shared understandings? Does she give greater authority to the parable than to her own words? Does the parable make her story more exotic or more typical?

Parables are a form of reported speech. As Bakhtin warns us, reported speech can be parodic as easily as it can be referential (1981:342–43). That is, when we borrow another's words, and traditional phrases and stories are not only another's words but are the words of the anonymous and sometimes authoritative, traditional "other," we negotiate between the world the authority describes and the world we describe.

Parables do not contain referents for either social situations or worldviews, though as a form of authoritative discourse (Bakhtin's term to describe privileged, powerful, fixed, persuasive [traditional] discourse), parables suggest a connection between situations and a worldview. The connection between the parable and the woman's life is part of a construction that works in two directions: she shapes her understanding of her situation in terms of the parable and she relies upon her interpretation of the parable in making her choice to tell it. She may even change the parable to better suit her situation.

Throughout the interview, the woman used many traditional phrases to describe her situation. For example, to describe the problem of returning home to live with her mother she says she was "flour from another sack"; she did not really belong there. The use of traditional material is part of her discourse, but traditional knowledge is not necessarily a constraint; it can be a resource for rethinking oppressive categories. For example, according to the conventions of the community in which she grew up, a single woman, a term used to refer to women who have been away from home, is a dangerous person, and unmarried women living at home are not permitted to associate with her. The use of the parable is a way of redefining her situation.

Parables and other allegorical forms propose fixed meanings: they appeal to *the* universe for meaning.[16] However, the appropriate use of a parable and what it represents depend upon a teller's and listener's relation to that universe.[17] Each telling invites new meaning or confirms or undermines existing interpretations. However, the question for feminist studies, and especially for feminist studies concerned with the concepts of tradition and change, is, what constitutes a rupture in the status of proposed fixed meanings? Further, do new interpretations stand alongside the old ones or do they disturb the status of the fixed meanings? In this case, a new interpretation involves shifting the privileged status of genres in relation to each other.[18]

Although the frog parable adequately represents the woman's situation, it also presents a startling contradiction in her adoption of it to counter her community's perception of her situation. She self-consciously presents the contradiction as part of her claim that she has remade her life. She insists upon her rejection of her community's characterization of her failures and instead proposes that her problem is that of a person in new surroundings who has only to persevere in finding a way to survive. In the parable, the struggling frogs are on their own; they stumble into adversity unknowingly and without blame. The parable is not about a person who was the victim of abandonment. In the life-history narrative, the woman presents not her own but her community's perception of her as an outcast. Although her situation is a common one, she claims to be providing a new interpretation or at least some new choices.[19] The parable could be a story told to anyone in unfamiliar surroundings: to someone taking on a new job, for example, and certainly we can see the parallels between crossing the border and jumping into the *natas*. But women in Compostela are not supposed to have to take on something as drastically unfamiliar as a new country, language, and way of life by themselves.

The use of the parable within the life-history narrative creates several new relationships. The woman uses a traditional parable to describe a contemporary situation, a situation that is quite different from the community where the authority of the parable resides. Further, that juxtaposition changes our interpretation of the parable. The woman uses the parable to represent her voyage to unfamiliar territory, but in Compostela it is inappropriate for a woman to make this voyage on her own. Here the voyage to the unknown has been appropriated by a female member of the culture, though many abandoned women face similar struggles and might similarly reinterpret their outcast status. One possible scenario, one construction of reality, has been substituted for another. Flour in another sack and frogs in *natas* are similarly in unfamiliar surroundings, but the flour is more like the first frog; the situation is hopeless. The second frog does not get more accustomed to the *natas;* this is not a parable about the unfamiliar turning into something good. There is only the chance to get out or, if not, to keep on kicking and to transform the situation, to turn the *natas* into butter, to acquire the necessary legal documents. The solution itself is ambiguous, and we do not know whether the goal is to get out, to escape, or to transform the current situation, to triumph over it. The virtue of the parable embedded in the life-history story is that it can support this ambiguity. It is not that any given text can have unlimited interpretations, depending upon the perspective of the viewer, but that the perspective of the viewer can encompass ambivalence and polysemy. The unstable relations of the genres (what I have called a lack of fit) become resources for sustaining the contradictions and discrepancies that are part of the complex cultural situations. It is astonishing that we (folklorists at least) ever associated parables with fixed meaning.

The traditional discourse from Mexican culture is transformed by its transplantation, and what is important here is not two equivalently valid systems but two invalid systems, two places in which the system does not work, two worlds that differently create the category of an abandoned woman as unfamiliar, dangerous, impure, or illegal. All cultures categorize appropriate and inappropriate behavior, and it is these categorizations that are sometimes treated as relative. However, relativism is more than a classification problem, more than a question of assigning a genre. A feminist reading insists upon an interruption in the hierarchy of interpretations rather than a peaceful coexistence between possible interpretations.

In these particular texts, the parable and life-history narrative undermine each other. They compete for status in a number of ways. Most evidently, in the parable the heroine overcomes obstacles, and in the life-history narrative the struggle is ongoing.[20] In addition, the parable is a traditional genre with the authority of tradition, even if it is newly applied to the woman's situation. However, the parable's insertion in the text places it in the role of an example, a possible allegory with a variety of interpretations, in contrast to the status of the everyday struggles of a real person. Parables often undermine other narratives by reclassifying events, but their use always calls into question or reaffirms the status of those who claim the power to classify. As Kirshenblatt-Gimblett points out throughout her discussion of the use of a parable to reinterpret a situation, the use of a parable can be a less disruptive way of making such entitlement claims (1975). Whereas Devora, in Kirshenblatt-Gimblett's account, uses the parable to subtly persuade her listeners of another way to interpret an awkward situation, the woman telling the frog parable uses it to provide an alternative ending for her ongoing story. Devora puts herself at risk for intervening in someone else's narrative; the Mexican woman is at risk for applying a traditional lesson to her nontraditional situation. In both cases, the teller of the parable intervenes, the first relying upon the authority of the parable, as if she herself had not spoken, the second borrowing the parable and asserting her own authority to apply it.

It is here that I find an interruption in the hierarchy of traditional genres. The content of the stories might be explored for their feminist qualities, but such an exploration can too easily create an alternative, relative, equally oppressive worldview. For example, for feminists, the texts are conveniently liberating; in both the life-history narrative and in the parable, the woman rejects the world of her oppressors. Additionally, and to the delight of structural feminists and particularly to those who look for the destruction of the oppressed view as part of the creation of the liberated view, the parable provides two frogs, one that dies confined to a limited perspective and the other that lives.

Not only the San Jose woman's use of the parable but also any use is a construction. A different Compostela telling, hypothetical or collected, and the San Jose telling are not relative. Once we have the San Jose example, any purportedly more authoritative example is permanently undermined; every telling that would be seemingly homogeneous with "the Compostela patriarchal worldview" must admit the possibility of ironic usage. Bakhtin argued this position in terms of authoritative voice, and such terms are particularly helpful for demonstrating the nonneutrality of any text; authority itself can as easily be called into question as invoked (1981:342–43). Genres exist only in relation to other genres; they are what Bakhtin has termed "texts bearing upon texts" (Todorov, 1984:22–23).

The story of the two frogs acts as a parable by appealing to and under-mining the voice of tradition and authority at the same time. The life history narrative might be seen to refer to the same general set of possible events and worldviews as the parable. However, the point is not the similarity of the referents but the startling discrepancy between voices. A feminist reading demands that we take account of that discrepancy, not as a matter of the relationship between two genres, nor as a contest for discovering the right interpretation, nor as evidence for multiple (and relative) possible interpretations. By taking a stand, the performer disrupts any carefully constructed system we might design to explain the performance.

On one level, this claim is quite simple. We have to examine the ways in which performances take a stand and the ways in which we interpret the taking of stands. Pressed further, on another level, this claim calls into question the relation between text and experience, both in terms of the relations between genres negotiated within the context of the interview and in terms of the relations between the interview as a text and the larger experience of the woman's ongoing life.

A politics of genre is not simply the recognition of new kinds of genres or embedded genres. It rests neither on kinds of reading nor on kinds of texts, though, in the case of studies of women's folklore, women's texts and feminist readings have led to political questions. Through the discovery of what might have looked like boundary transgressions, boundaries themselves have become an issue. We begin with questions of entitlement: Who determines the boundaries? Observations of appropriation follow: How is authority appropriated by the dominated; how are standard genres put to nonstandard purposes? Finally, any classification itself is questioned in order to ask what the categories signify: What is the significance of the ordinary/artistic, the ephemeral/classic, or the high/low culture distinctions? The marketplace of opinions invites both appropriations of ready-made genres (and appeals to their authority) and entitlement claims: "this does not speak for me." A feminist approach to genre (as one aspect of a feminist folkloristics) is concerned with identifying the gendered instabilities in classification systems through which women can negotiate and thereby appropriate traditional forms for their own purposes.

Notes

I am grateful for a grant from the Ohio State University Center for Women's Studies for transcription funds and to Katharine Young, Sally Meckling, Susan Ritchie, Suzanne Seriff, Nan Johnson, and the editors for their comments on the manuscript.

1. See Denise Riley (1988) and Jacques Derrida, who writes, "Thus, as soon as genre announces itself, one must respect a norm, one must not cross a line of demarcation, one must not risk impurity, anomaly, or monstrosity" (1980:57).

2. As Roger Abrahams has suggested, the concept of genre is implicated in our understanding of tradition: "Genres give names to traditional attitudes as traditional strategies which may be utilized by the performer in [his/her] attempt to communicate with and affect the audience" (1976:193).

3. Ben-Amos surveys several approaches to the study of genre and proposes an "ethnic system of genres," a metafolklore, "understood to mean the conception a culture has of its own folkloric communication as it is represented in the distinction of forms, the attribution of names to them, and the sense of the social appropriateness of their application in various cultural situations" (1976:226).

4. As defined by Newton and Rosenfelt, "ideology, then, is not a set of deliberate distortions imposed on us from above, but a complex and contradictory system of representations (discourses, images, myths) through which we experience ourselves in relation to each other and to the social structures in which we live" (1985:xix).

5. For a folkloric discussion of worldview, see Dundes (1971).

6. For a more extensive discussion of the relationship between experience and representation, see Shuman (1986).

7. Cheryl Bernard points out, "Like the research that came out of the academic wing of the black movement, the anthropology (and the sociology) of women took a skeptical view of 'value-free' science, arguing that it had too often been a trick on the part of the power-holders to rationalize existing inequities." She suggests that those who claim cultural relativism as a reason for not criticizing oppressive acts "are affected by a kind of Third World trauma that has overtaken all Westerners of liberal persuasion.... The sight of the Third World masses marching through the streets in millions to demand the return to the chador [veil], the reinstatement of religion, and a chance at martyrdom on the warfront has left many Western observers with the paralyzing feeling that their standards of understanding are really and totally inadequate" (1986:278–79).

8. See Giddens's concept of agency and social construction (1981:54).

9. There is always the danger, in cultural studies, of seeing events or institutions as epiphenomena, reflective of rather than constitutive of culture. See Edward Bruner (1984:3).

10. Aijaz Ahmad discusses the dangers of reductive allegories and proposes his own Marxist allegory in his critique of Jameson (1986).

11. See James Clifford, "Allegory prompts us to say of any cultural description not 'this represents, or symbolizes, that' but rather, 'this is a (morally charged) story about that' " (1986:100).

12. See Ryan (1979, 1981) and Ben-Amos (1976) for general discussions of the classification of genres.

13. Richard Bauman offers an example of the study of the relation between genres in context in a discussion of Bakhtin's concept of dialogic genres (1992:132–43).

14. While it is imperative that parables be collected in the context of their conversational use, one is fortunate to be able to tape-record the conversational telling of a parable. Like Kirshenblatt-Gimblett, I was not present during the telling. In this case, a lengthy interview turned sufficiently conversational to allow for the telling of the parable.

15. For a discussion of proverb and metaphor, see Peter Seitel (1977). E. Ojo Arewa and Alan Dundes discuss the importance of understanding proverb in its contextual use (1964).

16. Literary scholars from Samuel Taylor Coleridge to Northrop Frye (1957) have discussed allegory as restricting meaning. "Allegory says one thing and means another," writes Angus Fletcher (1964:2). According to such a scheme both the thing said and the thing meant are considered as fixed meanings, and the problem is the fit between them. Alternatively, Kenneth Burke suggests that proverbs "name typical recurrent situations" (1973:293) and thus puts the burden on strategies of classification rather than the fit between the name and the experience.

17. See Katharine Young's discussion of the distinction between realms in the story, the story-telling situation, and the world inhabited by the participants (1986:chaps. 5, 6).

18. According to Mary Louise Pratt, "Structuralism has taught us that genres are never completely autonomous but are always defined within the genre system with respect to each other" (1981:180). See Terdiman (1985) for a discussion of the limitations of structuralism for understanding power relations.

19. I am using the term *choice* here in the sense of an alternative scenario rather than a choice to make one's life different. I recognize the difficulties of the term *choice* insofar as it implies that one has the power to change a situation. For example, see Catharine A. MacKinnon (1987:14).

20. I have discussed the relations between ongoing and completed narratives throughout *Storytelling Rights,* 1986.

References Cited

Abrahams, Roger. 1976. "The Complex Relations of Simple Forms." In *Folklore Genres,* ed. Dan Ben-Amos. Austin: University of Texas Press.
———. 1984. "Goffman Reconsidered: Pros and Players." *Raritan* 3:76–94.
Ahmad, Aijaz. 1986. "Jameson's Rhetoric of Otherness and the 'National Allegory.'" *Social Text* 15:65–68.
Arewa, E. Ojo, and Alan Dundes. 1964. "Proverbs and the Ethnography of Speaking Folklore." *American Anthropologist* 66:70–85.
Bakhtin, M. M. 1981. *The Dialogic Imagination.* Edited by Michael Holquist. Translated by Caryl Emerson and Michael Holquist. Austin: University of Texas Press.
———. 1986. *Speech Genres and Other Late Essays.* Edited by Caryl Emerson and Michael Holquist. Translated by Vern W. McGee. Austin: University of Texas Press.
Bauman, Richard. 1992. "Contextualization, Tradition, and the Dialogue of Genres: Icelandic Legends of the *Kraftaskald.*" In *Rethinking Context: Language as an Interactive Phenomenon,* ed. Alessandro Duranti and Charles Goodwin, 125–46. Cambridge: Cambridge University Press.
Ben-Amos, Dan. 1976. "Analytical Categories and Ethnic Genres." In *Folklore Genres,* ed. Dan Ben-Amos. Austin: University of Texas Press.
Benard, Cheryl. 1986. "Women's Anthropology Takes the Chador." *Partisan Review* 53 (2): 275–84.
Bruner, Edward. 1984. *Text, Play, and Story: The Construction and Reconstruction of Self and Society.* 1983 Proceedings of the American Ethnological Society. Washington, D.C.: American Anthropological Society.
Bunch, Charlotte. 1987. *Passionate Politics.* New York: St. Martin's Press.
Burke, Kenneth. [1941] 1973. *The Philosophy of Literary Form: Studies in Symbolic Action.* Berkeley: University of California Press.
Clifford, James. 1986. "On Ethnographic Allegory." In *Writing Culture: The Poetics and Politics of Ethnography,* ed. James Clifford and George E. Marcus, 98–121. Berkeley: University of California Press.
———. 1988. *The Predicament of Culture: Twentieth-Century Ethnography, Literature, and Art.* Cambridge, Mass.: Harvard University Press.
de Man, Paul. 1979. *Allegories of Reading: Figural Language in Rousseau, Nietzsche, Rilke, and Proust.* New Haven: Yale University Press.
Derrida, Jacques. 1980. "The Law of Genre." *Critical Inquiry* 7 (1): 55–81.
Dundes, Alan. 1971. "Folk Ideas as Units of World View." *Journal of American Folklore* 84 (331): 93–103.
Farrer, Claire R. 1975. "Women and Folklore: Images and Genres." In *Women and Folklore,* ed. Claire R. Farrer, vii–xvii. Austin: University of Texas Press.
Fernandez, James W. 1983. "Convivial Attitudes: The Ironic Play of Tropes in an International Kayak Festival in Northern Spain." In *Text, Play, and Story: The Construction and Reconstruction of Self and Society,* ed. Edward Bruner, 199–229. 1983 Proceedings of the American Ethnological Society. Washington, D.C.: American Anthropological Society.

————. 1986. *Persuasions and Performances*. Bloomington: Indiana University Press.

Fletcher, Angus. 1964. *Allegory: The Theory of a Symbolic Mode*. Ithaca: Cornell University Press.

Frye, Northrop. 1957. *Anatomy of Criticism*. Princeton: Princeton University Press.

Geertz, Clifford. 1983. "Local Knowledge: Fact and Law in Comparative Perspective." In *Local Knowledge: Further Essays in Interpretive Anthropology*, 167–234. New York: Basic Books.

Giddens, Anthony. 1981. *A Contemporary Critique of Historical Materialism*. Berkeley: University of California Press.

Gossen, Gary. 1972. "Chamula Genres of Verbal Behavior." In *Toward New Perspectives in Folklore*, ed. Américo Paredes and Richard Bauman. Austin: University of Texas Press.

Hamburger, Kate. 1973. *The Logic of Literature*. Translated by Marilynn J. Rose. Bloomington: Indiana University Press.

Herskovits, Melville. 1973. *Cultural Relativism*. Edited by Francis Herskovits. New York: Random House.

Jarvie, I. C. 1975. "Epistle to the Anthropologists." *American Anthropologist* 77:253–66.

Kirshenblatt-Gimblett, Barbara. 1975. "A Parable in Context: A Social Interactional Analysis of Storytelling Performance." In *Folklore Performance and Communication*, ed. Dan Ben-Amos and Kenneth S. Goldstein, 105–30. The Hague: Mouton.

————. 1988. "Mistaken Dichotomies." *Journal of American Folklore* 101 (400): 140–55.

Kristeva, Julia. 1986. *The Kristeva Reader*. Edited by Toril Moi. New York: Columbia University Press.

Lambropolous, Vassilis, and David Neal Miller, eds. 1987. *Twentieth-Century Literary Theory*. Albany: State University of New York Press.

MacKinnon, Catharine A. 1987. *Feminism Unmodified: Discourses on Life and Law*. Cambridge, Mass.: Harvard University Press.

Moi, Toril. 1985. *Sexual/Textual Politics: Feminist Literary Theory*. London: Methuen.

Morson, Gary Saul. 1981. *The Boundaries of Genre*. Austin: University of Texas Press.

Newton, Judith, and Deborah Rosenfelt. 1985. "Toward a Materialist-Feminist Criticism." In *Feminist Criticism and Social Change: Sex, Class, and Race in Literature and Culture*, ed. Judith Newton and Deborah Rosenfelt, xv-xxxix. London: Methuen.

Pratt, Mary Louise. 1981. "The Short Story: The Long and the Short of It." *Poetics* 10:175–94.

Radner, Joan N., and Susan S. Lanser. 1987. "The Feminist Voice: Strategies of Coding in Folklore and Literature." *Journal of American Folklore* 100 (398): 412–25.

Retallack, Joan. 1987. "Post-Scriptum-High-Modern." *Genre* 20:483–512.

Riley, Denise, 1988. *"Am I That Name?" Feminism and the Category of 'Women' in History.* Minneapolis: University of Minnesota Press.

Rorty, Richard. 1979. *Philosophy and the Mirror of Nature.* Princeton: Princeton University Press.

Rosaldo, Michelle. 1983. "Moral/Analytic Dilemmas Posed by the Intersection of Feminism and Social Science." In *Social Science as Moral Inquiry,* ed. Norma Haan, Robert N. Bellah, Paul Rabinow, and William M. Sullivan, 76–95. New York: Columbia University Press.

Ryan, Marie-Laure. 1979. "Toward a Competence Theory of Genre." *Poetics* 8:307–37.

———. 1981. "On the Why, What, and How of Generic Taxonomy." *Poetics* 10:109–26.

Schaffer, Diane M., Amy Shuman, and Sabra Webber, with Artemis Leontis. 1992. "Rethinking 'Think Globally, Act Locally.'" In *Changing Traditions: Crosscultural Perspectives on Women,* ed. Marilyn Waldman, Muge Galin, and Artemis Leontis. Papers in Comparative Studies 7. Columbus: Ohio State University Press.

Seitel, Peter. 1977. "Saying Haya Sayings: Two Categories of Proverb Use." In *The Social Use of Metaphor: Essays on the Anthropology of Rhetoric,* ed. J. David Sapir and J. Christopher Crocker, 75–99. Philadelphia: University of Pennsylvania Press.

Shuman, Amy. 1986. *Storytelling Rights: The Uses of Oral and Written Texts among Urban Adolescents.* Cambridge: Cambridge University Press.

Stewart, Susan. 1987. "Ceci Tuera Cela: Graffiti as Crime and Art." In *Life after Postmodernism: Essays on Value and Culture,* ed. John Fekete. New York: St. Martin's Press.

———. 1988. "The Marquise de Meese." *Critical Inquiry* 15:162–92.

———. 1991. *Crimes of Writing: Problems on the Containment of Representation.* New York: Oxford University Press.

Terdiman, Richard. 1985. *Discourse, Counter Discourse.* Ithaca: Cornell University Press.

Todorov, Tzvetan. 1984. *Mikhail Bakhtin: The Dialogic Principle.* Minneapolis: University of Minnesota Press.

Tomashevsky, Boris. 1978. "Literary Genres." Translated by L. M. O'Toole. *Russian Poetics in Translation* 5:52–93.

Young, Katharine. 1986. *Taleworlds and Storyrealms: The Phenomenology of Narrative.* Dordrecht, the Netherlands: Martinus Nijhoff.

"Giving an Altar to St. Joseph": A Feminist Perspective on a Patronal Feast

The St. Joseph's altar tradition—dating back to the sixteenth century in Sicily—continues to be celebrated in Sicilian-American enclaves in Texas, Louisiana, California, and elsewhere. The tradition is said to have originated in Sicily when families offered food and prayers of thanks to St. Joseph at the end of a major famine that ruined the yearly crops and claimed many lives. Today many Sicilian-American communities still honor San Giuseppe, the patron saint of Sicily, the family, and the poor, through the creation of elaborate floor-to-ceiling altars composed primarily of food and traditionally dedicated and displayed in the home (see fig. 5.1). Individual families host the St. Joseph's Day celebration, but it is the women who actually "give" the altar, orchestrating and overseeing the entire range of feast-day activities, including the preparation and building of the altar in honor of St. Joseph, the ritual enactment of Mary and Joseph's search for lodging in Bethlehem, and, finally, the celebratory feasting of the entire community. This folk religious-altar tradition provides a splendid case in point for understanding family-centered folklore practice and performance from a feminist orientation.

Folklore and feminism conjoin in the critical attention both disciplines pay to forms of women's symbolic expression that are hidden from, or considered unimportant to, the majority culture. The combined efforts of folklore and feminism enlarge our understanding of the way in which women create or use symbolic modes within the dominant culture of the patriarchy. Folklore provides a unique data base of the traditional artistic means women have employed to express their own views of the world, and feminism offers a theoretical handle on that expression. At the very

Figure 5.1. A completed St. Joseph's Day altar comes close to filling an entire room in the host's home. (Photo by Suzanne Seriff)

core of the feminist critique that has helped shape our understanding of the St. Joseph's tradition is the insistence that women's reproductive capabilities—both physical and social—must no longer be considered, a priori, as the primary source of women's dependence and subordination within patriarchy.

In this essay we examine the St. Joseph's altar tradition as it is enacted among second- and third-generation Sicilian-American women in a central Texas town that we call Chase, Texas. This tightly knit community of Sicilian Texans is culturally bound by its common region of origin in Sicily—most of the families hailed from three small farming communities in the impoverished capital region of Palermo—and by its early immigrant history in Texas between 1880 and 1914 as a settlement of river valley cotton farmers. Based largely on the self-contained and semi-isolated nature of these early settlements, the Sicilians in this area developed a particularly strong sense of ethnic loyalty and identity, promoted through the early establishment of a number of local societies whose membership was based on common nationality and religion (Belfiglio, 1983:105–6).[1]

The ethnic presence and religious focus of this community is still very much in evidence today. For one thing, many Sicilian families still live and work in the fertile, if flood-prone, farmlands that their parents and grandparents bought and cultivated around the turn of the century. Others who have become merchants, business people, and civic leaders—and have moved with their families closer into town—still retain strong ties to their ethnic community through involvement in church-related activities and extended family gatherings. Two-thirds of the current membership of Chase's St. Anthony Catholic Church—which was founded by Sicilians in 1896—is still represented by families of Sicilian descent (Belfiglio, 1983:106). Thus, although today the effects of class distinctions between farmers and merchants are more in evidence,[2] the community's common ethnic identity and heritage are repeatedly emphasized among its members—especially during ethnically keyed festive events such as the St. Joseph's Day celebration.[3]

Over the past several years we have observed and participated in the preparation of six separate St. Joseph's Day altars given by families of differing classes and occupational statuses in this community. While we have observed significant differences in the size, aesthetic composition, and social distribution of individual altars—differences that reflect a complex variety of sociomaterial factors[4]—we have been struck by certain commonalities in the ways in which the altars are planned, constructed, anticipated, and evaluated by the altar givers and their kin-based assistants. Much of this aesthetic and operational accord is undoubtedly attributable to the collective ethnic identity of the altar givers and their families; however, we feel that it is important to consider, as well, the ways in which gender is inscribed in the constructions of this ethnicity and its traditions.

As we listened to our informants—both male and female—talk about the St. Joseph's Day altar tradition, we realized that for them, this elaborate folk Catholic celebration was considered one of a complex of related activities that are enacted and maintained through women's networks in this Sicilian community. These activities include intrafamilial sharing of responsibilities for child care and care of the elderly; preparations and promotions of life-cycle celebrations, such as weddings, showers, funerals, and births; and a variety of folk religious and church-related activities that move the community through an annual cycle, including Easter, Christmas, the annual summertime church-sponsored spaghetti suppers, and church bazaars. Even though many of the women in this community work outside the home,[5] daily and primary attention is given to these acts of community and familial support that assure the growth and well-being of blood relations as well as an extended, extrahousehold network of relations. And what is equally important is the reflexive nature of these acts. We noted that these women are engaged in constant communication about, and evaluation of, the practice of caring for and nurturing others.

Based on our growing awareness of the value that these activities hold for the women themselves, we came to understand the importance of gender in theoretically defining the St. Joseph's Day celebration. The introduction of gender into the discussion of this celebration is particularly important in attempting to understand the traditional expressive behaviors of a community whose familial, economic, and social relations have retained the historically and culturally defined patriarchal inheritance of the *pater familias*. Simply put, it is an inheritance in which the father is defined as the head of the household; in him is vested the putative right to dominate the family. Ethnicity, in turn, is largely identified with an idealized patriarchal past in which women stayed at home and served men and children (di Leonardo, 1984:228).

It is this "feminine ideal" of submission and selflessness that might seem, on the surface, to be validated in the Sicilian religious tradition of women sacrificing an altar to St. Joseph, the male patron of the Catholic Holy Family. This interpretation, raised by Diane Christian in a critique of an earlier version of this essay, mirrors the official liturgical reading of Catholic doctrine and narrative as supportive of a "willing embrace of the patriarchy" (Christian, 1988:54). Christian broadly asserts, for example, that Mary's maternity is a *male* miracle, that her life-giving power is subordinated to her son, and most important, for our purposes, that her nurturing power is subordinated to her husband, Joseph, who is, after all, the true protagonist of this festival (1988:54).

From the standpoint of the hierarchy of the church, Christian is right in noting the way in which female power generally tends to be reorganized into male power. In most major historical religions the birthright of the mother is narratively refigured to give the legitimizing edge to paternity. While we recognize the patriarchal bias posed by such Catholic narrative— and echoed in the surface structure of the social system—we draw from our ethnographic and historicoliturgical data to suggest a significantly more complex reading of the St. Joseph's Day feast. This reading is predicated on the fact that the figure of Joseph, alone among all the many saints in the Catholic pantheon, is in fact depicted in this ritual not as a model of patriarchal domination but rather as a marginal and contingent figure—indeed the only Catholic saint whose presence automatically implies the presence of mother and child and the primary interrelationship between them. As Pamela Quaggiotto astutely points out in her in-depth ethnographic study of the St. Joseph's tradition in contemporary Sicily, "the altar ritual presents a paradox in that while it is ostensibly performed to honor Saint Joseph, and by extension the husband/father of the family ... the ritual simultaneously undermines many of the premises of the male role" (1988:288).

We therefore maintain that an analysis of the St. Joseph's tradition must derive not from externally imposed preconceptions of religious meaning but from the strategic way in which the participants themselves organize and reorganize the meaning of this festival according to what they consider to be valuable. What emerges from this reexamination of the St. Joseph's Day feast is an image of the feast—not as a symbolic or material expression of women's subordination to men—but rather as a kind of communitywide expression of the power of women's work both within the context of the St. Joseph's story and the social practice of everyday life.

It is for this reason that we feel that the elaborated tradition of "giving an altar" must be seen, first, in the wider sociopolitical context of women's work, in general, and the kind of work Micaela di Leonardo has termed "the work of kinship," more specifically. As defined by di Leonardo, kin work refers to "the conception, maintenance, and ritual celebration of cross-household kin ties including visits, letters, telephone calls, presents, and cards to kin; the organization of holiday gatherings; the creation and maintenance of quasi-kin relations; decisions to neglect or to intensify particular ties; the mental work of reflection about all these activities; and the creation and communication of altering images of family and kin vis-à-vis the images of others, both folk and mass media" (1987:442–43). Di Leonardo's conception of kin work is important for understanding the full extent of women's material-symbolic involvement in this ethnically keyed tradition and the political nature of this involvement—that is, as a source of women's extensive kin-based power.

Secondly, we make a claim for understanding the religious narrative (the official reading that poses St. Joseph as the Holy Patriarch of the church and of the family), the exaggerated symbolic imagery, and the activity surrounding the feast day as an expression of the relational and maternally derived values and intentions that underlie this work of kinship. In terms, first, of the religious narrative of St. Joseph, we note the impact of a discursive shift enacted by the participants whereby the patronal prerogatives of St. Joseph are transposed and finally transformed by a more inclusive dramatization of the power of affiliation. St. Joseph is never separated out as the sole recipient of devotion. Indeed, on this day that is dedicated to St. Joseph alone in the Catholic calendar, the ritual necessarily entails the presence of Mary and Jesus also, and the emphasis shifts to tell a story about the attributes of the family, not the individual saint. In fact, the women in our study have made use of the malleability of a range of religious symbols to forward a scenario in which an entire coterie of sacred personages is honored; in addition to the Holy Family, the altars we observed generally hosted a wide range of personally chosen saints, both female and male.

Both this religious tableau and the particular symbolic imagery that is promoted on the St. Joseph's table give dramatic and aesthetic recognition to the sustaining values of nurturance, care, comfort, and support—values embodied in what we have called an ideology of reproduction. If the ideology of reproduction can be said to be embedded in the very core of women's everyday life, the St. Joseph's Day celebration becomes instrumental in annually highlighting the importance of this ideology. In the following section, we provide a detailed description of women's strategic involvement in both the material and symbolic domains of this feast day in order to better understand the full meaning and significance for those who choose to sacrifice an altar on St. Joseph's behalf.

St. Joseph's Day in Texas

Let us begin, then, with a description of the most salient visual image of the St. Joseph's feast day: the symbolically loaded altar. Sometimes referred to as a "table," the altar is constructed only for presentation on or around the feast day, March 19. This highly elaborate altar tradition finds its counterpart in the maintenance of home altars, or specially reserved sites for housing images of the saints at home, a folk practice widespread among Catholic women of Mediterranean descent. On an everyday basis women take primary responsibility for invoking the protection and help of holy personages; women bring them into family membership through the display of their images and through active daily communication with them in prayer. The altar marks a site for communication between the heavenly family and the earthly family. It bridges sacred and secular realms by providing a locus of communication, a place for the performance of belief. While the home altar is usually an unobtrusive, fixed assemblage in the private quarters of the home, the St. Joseph's table is most often grandiose in its multitiered display of sacred statues and pictures of the saints, the Virgin, and Jesus, surrounded by mounds of specially prepared and carefully displayed food.

Altars of this type can occupy the greater part of the largest room in an altar giver's home. Built up against a wall, the understructure of the altar consists of five or six wooden platforms, each about eight feet long, arranged in a step pattern. A carpenter from the local Sicilian community builds this structure to conform with the altar giver's specifications. A large table is set in front of the raised platforms, all of which are completely covered with white cloth.

Statues of St. Joseph and the Holy Family are generally placed in the center of the uppermost altar shelf. The Holy Family is flanked on either side by a variety of other saints and holy personages chosen at the discretion of the woman giving the altar. It is not unusual for a woman to honor fifteen to twenty different saints. Directly below the saints, set out prominently on the next two shelves, are large wreath-shaped breads, one for each of the saints (see fig. 5.2). Attached to these breads are decorative fig cookies shaped in the form of the saint's defining emblems, such as the lily-crowned staff for St. Joseph. The centers of the breads are filled with whole pieces of fruit (oranges, grapefruits, and bananas), and each bread is accompanied by a carafe of red wine. Interspersed among the breads are flowers, candles, and cookies shaped like hearts or other symbols associated with the festival of St. Joseph. Images of the saints and their symbolic breads serve as the focus of the altar. Below these on the remaining shelves and table are found an abundant array of cakes, pies, and trays of traditional cookies and pastries. At the center of the table is an image of the infant Christ, and in front of it is a book-shaped cake emblazoned with sugar rosary beads. Written on the cake is a prayer chosen by the altar giver, such as the Prayer of St. Francis.

The altar is filled almost to overflowing, but care is taken to give the whole arrangement a symmetrical and finished look. Food is raised high and grandly displayed via the multitiered, vertical thrust of the altar's construction. In fact, the highest altar is considered best: the taller it gets, the more food it can display. At the sides of the main altar, long, cloth-covered tables stretch into the room. These side tables are overloaded with donated pies, cakes, trays of cookies, and other sweets that cannot be contained on the altar proper. Participants readily express their overwhelming sense of the altar's beauty, its abundance, and its signifying powers as a testament to women's labor and love. They stand before the altar, comment on its particular aesthetic qualities, and verbally note their admiration for specific women who they know to have been responsible for certain items or aesthetic arrangements.

The altar makers choose the particular saints and holy personages to be honored on their altar in accordance with the role these saints have played in granting help and favors throughout the women's lives. They either use their own personal statues and holy pictures or ones loaned to them for the occasion by friends and family members. Some of the more commonly chosen saint's images include St. Lucy (eye trouble), St. Teresa (general favors, especially for young women), St. Anne, the mother of Mary (women in labor), St. Jude (impossible causes), St. Anthony (good love matches and lost things), St. Gerard Majella (childbirth and pregnancy), St. Michael (prevention of crime and robbery), and St. Peregrine (cancer). Various representations of the Virgin Mary—including her portrayal as Mother of Mothers, the Immaculate Conception, and Our Mother of Mt. Carmel—may also be chosen, as can certain favored images of Christ,

Figure 5.2. Close-up of a completed St. Joseph's Day altar showing saints' images, the saints' breads, fruits, cakes, cookies, flowers, and votive candles. (Photo by Kay Turner)

such as the Holy Infant Jesus, the Holy Infant of Prague, and the Sacred Heart of Jesus. We note that several of these saints (e.g., St. Peregrine) are not officially recognized by the church, but have become unofficial patrons for various needs.

The decision to give an altar is based upon a private promise made between a person and St. Joseph, sometimes years in advance of the actual offering. Both women and men make promises to St. Joseph, but it is the women who fulfill them by actualizing the creation of the altar. The St. Joseph's altar is always made in thanksgiving for an answered prayer. Family members might petition St. Joseph for help in curing illness, rectifying financial setbacks, bringing a loved one safely back from war, or bringing a healthy child into the world. As one of the senior members of the community, Rose Restivo, explained, "If someone in your family is sick, you make it for him—you ask St. Joseph—and it works. It sure does work." In essence, St. Joseph stands as that protector of the integrity of the family who is called upon whenever the close-knit fabric of family relations is in danger of being rent.

When the altar tradition was at its peak in this Texas community (after World War II and the Korean War) as many as twenty to thirty individual altars were made in private homes. "They used to have them all the time," altar maker Rosalie Gullo offered. "A long time ago we used to have so many neighbors, they had one in each house. They get through eating at one house and they go to another. It's really a great tradition. It's really great. It's a lot of work. But some things are worth it." Today, in urban centers such as Houston, the tradition has become a public one held in the church.[6] In Chase it is still a home-based tradition, although only three or four different altars are made each year. The number of altars is dwindling, but the importance placed on the event has certainly not diminished. If anything, the altars themselves have become increasingly more elaborate, and the responsibility for maintaining the tradition within the community assumed by individual altar makers has become increasingly complex.

Today, for example, a single family can count on hosting the feast for anywhere from five hundred to one thousand guests. Obviously, the expense of giving an altar is not to be underestimated. In the 1960s it cost about five hundred dollars to give a fancy altar; the cost now is in the thousands of dollars. However, the host family rarely carries the entire financial or material burden. Gifts of time, money, and goods are pledged by other family and community members, often as promises to St. Joseph or other saints in order to insure blessings. For example, Sally Cantarella's aunt had cancer. To stay healthy, she promised to make eight cakes for Sally's altar. Sally continued, "Different ones will make different donations. I mean, it just all goes together."

Detailed knowledge of, and expertise in, constructing the altar is usually passed down among women in a family, from mother to daughter or from grandmother to granddaughter. As one woman told us, "My mother used to fix a big one almost every year. I learned everything from her." And Sally Cantarella explained, "When you live with someone, they sort of tell it to you all the time. I learned from my grandmother. She had one every time one of her boys came back from the service. She had four boys." Further knowledge of the tradition is gained in crosshousehold exchanges among women friends and kin.

Once a petition has been answered, the woman and her family begin to make preparations for the giving of the table. Many weeks in advance of the feast day the altar giver chooses the women in the community—kin and friends—to serve as her primary helpmates. It is at this point, too, that she selects the family members and friends whom she wants to participate in the ceremony that accompanies the presentation of the altar. This ceremony—a ritual reenactment of Joseph and Mary's search for lodging in Bethlehem—requires that these individuals play the roles of the Holy Family members and those additional saints who are represented on the altar. The ceremony is centered around a ritual feasting of these impersonated saints.

The altar is constructed over a nine-day period previous to the date the altar will be publicly displayed. This period constitutes a novena,[7] and each day of preparation is concluded with the saying of a novena and a rosary in honor of St. Joseph. The rosary invokes St. Joseph's counsel, comfort, and refuge. It names his attributes and expresses the desire for a relationship with him, saying, in part: "St. Joseph, you were the Father—you were a virgin like the Mother. . . . Mary the Rose; Joseph the Lily . . . Immaculate Patriarch, beloved custodian of Jesus, gentle spouse of Mary . . . St. Joseph give me comfort, the comfort I need to save my soul." While the text of the Rosary to St. Joseph is largely standardized, the altar giver augments it with her own personalized tributes to each of her honored saints, thanking them for specific intercessions on behalf of her husband, her children, her parents, or her friends.

During these nine days, the women center their activities around the cooking and baking of the huge quantities of special foods that will either adorn the altar or be served at the feast itself. Early in the preparation period the women bake certain of the fancy pastries and cookies used to decorate the altar. Of utmost importance is the baking of the traditional *cosi figli*[8]—giant fig cookies made in the shape of the saints' identifying symbols: the Sacred Heart of Jesus, the rosary of Mary, the rose-encrusted cross of St. Teresa, the plain cross of St. Gerard, and the book of St. Ann are a few examples. These will be attached to special wreath-shaped breads, the *cucchidagli,* one for each saint on the altar. Until recently both the *cucchidagli* and the *cosi figli* were made at home by women, but now the bread is purchased at a local Italian bakery.

Usually a full day is devoted to preparing the *cosi figli;* the process for making them is slow and requires patience, dexterity, and as many skilled workers as possible. The cookies are made from a stiff dough of flour and water with very little shortening. The dough is rolled out and the fig paste (composed of ground dried figs, raisins, oranges, and spices, such as cinnamon, allspice, cloves, and nutmeg) is spread evenly over the bottom layer of dough and hand-shaped into a form such as a cane (representing the staff of St. Joseph) or a heart. This is then covered over with a second layer of dough.

Now the intricate work of cutting designs and patterns into the forms begins. The women use tools (a pocketknife, a pecan picker, scissors, and the metal casing of a shotgun shell) that are reserved just for this purpose; (see fig. 5.3) in fact, they are sometimes handed down from mother to daughter as treasured implements of the tradition. Lena Tratta proudly showed us the pocketknife her mother had used and then passed on to her over forty years before.

Figure 5.3. Making *cosi figli,* the traditional fig-filled pastries created in the shapes of the saints' identifying symbols. (Photo by Kay Turner)

These days the tools could easily be substituted by store-bought pastry-decorating items, but the women retain a particular affection for the traditional implements of this festival trade. The women joke about the special nature of these tools that have been borrowed from the male-centered realm of hunting and outdoor sports and reappropriated for this most domestic of tasks. One woman laughingly told us she hoped she would never be stopped by police on her way to make *cosi figli:* "What would they say about the 'weapons' I'm carrying?" And Mary Ponzio had everyone in the room laughing when she reported, "My bullet bit the dust. I called Miss Lucy and asked her if she had an extra bullet. And she said 'No,' but she'd get her brother to go shoot a gun to get one for me."

With scissors and knives the women cut away at the top layer of dough creating decorative designs where the dark fig paste shows through against the white dough that remains. The pecan picker is used to manipulate the dough and, along with the bullet, is used to press ornamental circles, half moons, and edging marks onto the dough. Depending upon the intricacy of the form and design, this process alone can take from thirty minutes to two hours to complete. Then the cookies are baked and ready to be attached to the bread wreaths.

In the Chase community certain women are known for their expertise in making particular *cosi figli* forms. Mary Ponzio is usually called upon to make the intricately cut *spado* (monstrance) that occupies a central place on the altar and is the *cosi figli* emblem that is kept as a remembrance by the family hosting the altar. Women or girls who are just learning the tradition start out making the Sacred Heart form, which is considered the easiest to create.

In the days that follow, women continue to meet at the altar giver's home, where more perishable sweets such as pies, cakes, and the Italian pastries including *canolis* are made, as well as dozens of different kinds of cookies. Certain of these are considered traditional for inclusion on the altar: *pupa cu lova* (peacock-shaped dough containing a hard-boiled egg), *pignolati,* usually referred to as "haystacks" (fingerfuls of fried dough stacked to resemble a pinecone, symbolically referencing the legendary pinecones that Jesus is said to have played with as a child), *sfinge* (fried ricotta cheese rolled in powdered sugar), sesame seed cookies, cookie knots with anise centers, and the colorful sugar-coated ring cookies.

During the intense final days of preparation, the women spend ten- to twelve-hour days in the altar maker's home, where extra stoves, refrigerators, and utensils have been moved in to accommodate the massive culinary activity. It is not unusual to find fifteen to twenty women working in a crowded kitchen or spread out into other parts of the house. In addition to preparing the pastries and cookies, the women must wash, chop, and fry all of the vegetables (often as many as thirty different kinds), peel and decorate the sour fruits, and make the final preparations for the fish and pasta courses that will be fed to the saints.

As the nine-day preparation period wears on, women increasingly take over the altar giver's house. The exaggerated activity of the women is further underscored by the role men play—or, in a sense, the role men do not play—in the preparation of the feast. Men occupy space on the periphery of the busy altar-making scene. They willingly defer to the women's authority, doing whatever they are asked to facilitate the success of the event. They undertake heavy physical tasks, such as building the understructure of the altar, erecting the outdoor serving tents, stirring the large vats of pasta, and setting out the table and chairs for the huge communal meal. But this is essentially a time when the women must do what they do best. The men joke among themselves that they have "nothing to do"; as one man said, "The women do it all, they really put out."

Two days before the celebration the altar giver and her closest friends and kin begin to arrange the altar in one of the largest rooms of the house, usually the dining or living room (see fig. 5.4). Women in the community share general knowledge of how the altar should be arranged, although

Figure 5.4. Friends of the altar giver work out the decorative details in the creation of a St. Joseph's altar. (Photo by Kay Turner)

each altar giver has a considerable amount of leeway in deciding the final aesthetic composition of her altar. Pertinent factors considered and generally agreed upon by the women include a concern for symmetry and balance, the proper placement of the saints' statues up high or focally centered, and a visual forwarding of the saints' emblem breads, placed in conjunction with their statues or lined up in a row beneath them. Rosalie Gullo explained to us that with the exception of the breads and certain other singularly important items, "you need to have two of everything on the altar, one on each side to make it look right." And we also heard a somewhat dismayed discussion of the aesthetic difference between past and current altars with regard to the contemporary use of mass-produced Easter candies and sweets (e.g. marshmallow chickens, brightly colored sugar eggs, and so on). In the past the handmade saints' breads did not have to compete with these store-bought decorations. In fact, Rose Restivo told us that the wreathed breads used to be much larger; each one held three or four different saint's emblems and were the primary focus of the table.

The day before St. Joseph's, the host family oversees the cooking of the huge vats of linguini and sixty or more gallons of sugar-sweetened tomato-based gravy. This constitutes the basic entrée that will be served to the guests after the ceremony. Men perform this labor-intensive job outside in the garage or in a tent erected specifically for this purpose. Because St. Joseph's Day falls during Lent, meat in the gravy is not allowed; instead, hard-boiled eggs are served with the sauce. Both men and women boil and peel the eggs—sometimes as many as 1,500—the night before the feast. Men take shifts throughout the night to stir and season the huge vats of sauce. The altar giver and her female companions oversee this process, coming out to the tents every couple of hours to check on the seasoning, temperature, and thickness of the sauce. According to Sally Cantarella, "The men are just the ones who can handle [the pots]. The *ladies* supervise."

Once the altar has been completely set—sometime on the day or evening before the feast—the local parish priest comes to the house to bless the altar and the family sponsoring it. On the day of the altar's presentation hundreds of people, most from the immediate area, participate in the feast. The celebration begins at 9 A.M. with the principal participants reciting the Rosary to St. Joseph and the other saints for the last time. This is followed immediately by the ceremony that dramatizes Joseph and Mary's search for lodging. The party of chosen saints, led by Joseph and Mary, must knock on three different doors of the house before they will be allowed to enter by the host family. In days past the saints were dressed in homemade biblical costumes. Now the one remaining costume feature is the handmade lily-wreathed staff carried by St. Joseph at the head of the procession. Once inside, the saints are seated at the elegantly set table at the foot of the altar.

Then commences the ceremonious feting of the saints; gifting the saints with food serves as the central ritual act. The altar giver chooses four to six people, usually men, to serve the saints at the table. It is their job to place the food in front of the saints and to clear the table after each course. They encourage the saints to eat up to and beyond their capacity. It is not unusual to see the servers cutting up portions of food, wiping dirty mouths, and even spoon-feeding the honored guests, especially those played by young children. In a manner typical of mothers and grandmothers, the servers do everything possible to cajole the saints to "Eat! Eat! Have just a little bit more." According to custom, the saints must eat some of every kind of food. As many as fifteen courses are served, each course containing a sampling of three or four different types of food. Emphasis is placed upon ensuring that the saints are honored through extreme culinary indulgence.

While a select group of men do the actual serving of the plates of food to the saints, dozens of women take the honor of presenting the food as gifts to them. This presentation, traditionally reserved for women and open to any woman who attends the feast, is a devotional act that community members refer to as "making a wish." Women form a line from the kitchen to the altar site, each woman holding one plate of food that she will hand off to the server when she arrives at the saint's table. According to custom, each woman is allowed to present three different courses, lining up anew each time until her third round is given. At the end of the third round, she may make a wish. As Ann Scarmardo told us, "You can ask for anything, something you need, or anything you want to be." This is not a conventional devotional act in which the believer is making prayers of petition, confession, or reconciliation; rather, it is an open-ended ritual act that allows for a basically nonreligious moment of wish fulfillment. So popular is this custom that in this community as many as a hundred or more women go through the process of presentation.

The feast always begins with sour citrus fruits (symbolic of the original famine in Sicily that gave rise to the tradition hundreds of years ago), proceeds through several courses of traditionally prepared vegetables such as *finocchio* (sweet fennel), burdock, and artichoke, then moves on to the fancifully decorated whole fish, followed by a course of the meatless pasta, and ending with three or four courses of each kind of sweet that is found on the altar. The meal culminates at the moment when the saints can ask for seconds of their favorite sweets directly from the altar. After the saints have been feted, the host family escorts them from the table and positions them in a line to receive homage from those in attendance. Typically, the host family first washes the saints' hands, and then people pass from saint to saint, kneeling to kiss their right hands and touch their feet. These acts anticipate the symbolic gestures associated with Christ and his disciples at the Last Supper.

This ends the ritual procedures of the day, and at this point, friends, relatives, and community members who have gathered go outside and line up to fill their plates with the food the saints have "left behind." Everyone is served heaping portions of spaghetti and egg, which is then eaten on the lawn beneath a huge tent. Once the spaghetti has been consumed, women attending the altar begin dispensing its contents, bringing trays loaded with the various sweets that only recently had decorated the sacred site. Since all the food has been blessed, it is not allowed to go to waste; the object is to clear the altar completely by the end of the day.

In accord with the initial purpose of the feast day—that is, to feed the poor and the hungry—any food that is not consumed is given to charity. Sally Cantarella explained how, at the conclusion of her St. Joseph's dedication, she and her husband would "box it [the leftover food] up and take it to the nursing home or the orphanage." They always did this, she said, "because it's all blessed and it's not to be thrown away. It's taken to the needy." Rosalie Gullo added, "This (custom) was from the old country, that's where it all started from. . . . Then they used to give it to the poor, to the real poor people."

Before the representative saints leave at the end of the day they are each given one of the fancy breads and a fig cookie made in the shape of their saint's attribute (e.g., cane, heart, and so on). Those who have played the saints often save their symbolic breads and cookies and display them during other holiday occasions. While the beautiful breads are reserved as gifts for the saints, there is a token on the altar for everyone. Fava beans and chick peas symbolize good luck, and bowls of these dried beans are always found somewhere on the altar. While the saints' ceremony begins with the serving of sour fruit, a remembrance of the bitterness of the famine, the fava bean provides a parallel reference to the famine at the end of the feast. The bean reminds one not of bitterness but of sustenance. According to legend, fava beans and chick peas were the only foods that kept people alive during the drought. All the guests know that they can pick up a dried bean at the end of the day and carry it home with them for good fortune during the year until St. Joseph's Day is celebrated again.

The Work of Kinship and the Politics of Relationship

Even the most casual observer of the preceding spectacle could not help but be impressed with the overstated grandiosity of the altar on the one hand and the primacy of women's involvement in its creation on the other. Usually occurring during Lent, the feast momentarily overrides this season associated with fasting and personal denial. In a season that anticipates Easter's blood sacrifice of Christ's Passion, a day is given over to a different kind of sacrifice that signifies not death, but the abundance of life. Food display and consumption become the order of the day. As a religious feast, St. Joseph's Day is structured through symbolic exaggeration, and food is the key symbol. In the sacred calendar of this Sicilian-American community no other feast day or holy day emphasizes the ritual display and consumption of food quite like St. Joseph's Day.

Food—as a symbol of life and the labor of women—is the binding element in the St. Joseph's Day feast. Food performs multivalent symbolic functions in the feast, some of them obvious, others not. In an obvious way, food—a conventional gift to the gods—is ritually presented as a gift to the saints. But we also suggest that food can be seen as a key symbol for indicating women's power to forward values of relationship, interconnection, nurturance, sustenance, and growth. Because food is so symbolically central to the meaning of the feast, we want to attend to the particular ways in which the women in this community instill symbolic significance into its production and consumption.

In the first instance, the production of the festive foods is materially and symbolically framed in terms of the value of relationship and interconnection among women in this community. More than during any other holiday, celebration, or community-based activity, the intensive and specifically woman-identified labor of St. Joseph's Day provides an opportunity for women to express their commitment to their families and, especially, to each other. Women unite with other women in an extended kin network to cook, clean, bake, decorate, construct, serve, and do all things necessary to assure the successful fulfillment of their promise. According to Quaggiotto, "The preparation of an altar provides a context in which women can create an object of great aesthetic value, however ephemeral, which is based on their domestic skills" (1988:75). Even more important, she continues, it becomes a time when women receive recognition for these skills and accomplishments in a culture that otherwise provides few opportunities for such blatant acknowledgment.

Although the initial petition to St. Joseph is a highly personal and individual act, the gifting is realized as an elaborately orchestrated act of kin collaboration and cooperation. As one altar giver put it, "When you're helping someone else you're actually doing the labor. And it really is [labor]." The nature of this help is fundamentally cooperative and negotiated; no one woman has expertise in every aspect of the altar's preparation. Instead, each woman brings with her a special talent, recipe, or other resource, which is pooled, discussed, and negotiated throughout the process of altar construction. Di Leonardo argues that this negotiating process of taking on or ceding tasks "is clearly related to acquiring or divesting oneself of power within kin networks" (1984:445). And moreover, it is a process that is carried over from year to year as the different women in the community alternate among themselves the responsibilities of hosting, food preparation, errand-running, and gift-presenting. Sally Cantarella gave us a firsthand account of the way in which the St. Joseph's feast promotes this kind of alternation and negotiation of responsibilities:

> It's such a beautiful devotion, really. I feel like I did more work at Mrs. Emola's altar than I'm doing now [at my own], because now I'm just actually sort of advising: "Where do you want this?" "How do you want this?" and making sure they [her helpers] have all their supplies. Everyone has a job. That's what makes us feel relaxed. Like I have certain ladies that'll be in charge of the kitchen, of getting all the food ready to start making the plates. . . . And everyday someone furnishes lunch so you don't have to stop working.

Di Leonardo suggests further that holiday celebrations such as St. Joseph's Day serve for women as "foci of kinship power" (1984:218); the planning and presentation of holiday food and other rituals, she says, are ways in which women extend and cement the bonds between them. The primacy of women's collaborative work during St. Joseph's Day is echoed in the words of altar helper Angelina Rizzo, who asserts, "These women get together, and it's all women, and they really know how to work together. And I really enjoy helping." The days of preparation are filled with activity, talk, prayer, reminiscence, joking, eating, shared decision-making, and argument. Women engage in an exaggerated display of the interconnection with each other. Several of the women take days off from work to participate. Explaining her involvement in the tradition, Ann Lampo said, "I took off three days last week when we started. This is a time when we ladies can all be together. Everyone is so busy the rest of the year. I wouldn't miss it. It's so beautiful the way everyone helps out." The day's work is only interrupted by the noonday lunch—a veritable feast in itself—which is provided by other women who are not cooking for the altar. Before eating, the women gather in a circle to pray; the prayer is offered by the altar giver. On one such occasion, Marianne Marino first thanked St. Joseph for his help and care, then followed by thanking him for "the beautiful friendships that make all this possible."

Of course the common goal behind this festival-related work of kinship is the ritual feeding of the saints. The collective knowledge of women's domestic labor is aimed at providing symbolic sustenance and nurturance to the Holy Family and the other saints. The bonds that are created between the women engaged in this labor are, in turn, mirrored in the binding relationships that are symbolically created and promoted on this day between the heavenly family and the earthly family. At this feast the saints are solicitously treated as family members. They are considered to literally *own* the home of the altar giver for the day. That the saints are honored and feted with sweet and fancy foods is indicative of women's desire and capacity to host the saints appropriately, to labor excessively for them, and thereby to further solidify the continuing benefit of reciprocal relationship with them. Food—ephemeral, earthy, sustaining, pleasurable—and in this culture the product of women's work and kin work—becomes a primary symbol for acknowledging the desire and capacity to fulfill the commitments of relationship to the heavenly family and to the earthly family.

The sacred recipients of all of this food—that is, the saints—are holy figures who have been nurtured in relationships with the altar giver throughout her life. Each woman's choice of saints and holy personages is a highly personal and emotion-filled act—one that serves to symbolically mark her reliance on the saints during the most important events and crises in her life. The primacy of a woman's personal relationship with her saints is demonstrated in Sally Cantarella's explanation to us about the reasons why she had chosen particular saints for her altar:

> All the saints on my altar—they're the ones that I've prayed to all my life, that I made novenas to. . . . These are the saints that I have. This is St. Peregrine—that is for cancer—he is the patron saint of people with cancer. He was cured of cancer. [Sally petitioned St. Peregrine on behalf of her best friend and business partner who had cancer and subsequently died.] St. Anthony is the saint we pray to when you lose something. Then the Guardian Angel—I have her because my daughter was coming home one day and it could have been a terrible accident. . . . I said, 'The Guardian Angel must have put her arm around her, and I said, "I have to honor her," because I feel like the Guardian Angel really had put her arms around her. Then the Holy Family is who I prayed to to help Joe [her husband], to keep him healthy and strong to fulfill his obligations of everyday living. Then St. Jude [patron of impossible causes]—in my younger days I prayed to him for special favors, so I'm honoring him. St. Michael the Archangel is the saint for [protection against] crime and robbery, and I feel like we're in business and we need the protection the way things are. . . . And St. Teresa I also—in my younger days—prayed to for special favors. And the Infant Jesus of Prague was Katherine's, my partner's. We had a dress shop together, and then she died of cancer. This was her statue. I told her, I said, "Katherine, don't you worry." She said, "I won't be here for your altar. . . ." And I said, "That's something we don't know. None of us has a guarantee. But I will promise you that if you're not with us, your Infant Jesus will be on my altar." And this [pointing to an old, ornately framed picture of the Holy Family] is my grandmother's. And I felt—with her not being with us—I wanted to have as many memories as possible.

Statues on the altar honor relationships with different saints but, as Sally's explanation also demonstrates, the statues represent relationships with, honor of, and love for kin and friends as well. This means that, in effect, each altar is tailored to represent a personal narrative that is specific to the altar giver. Every woman's altar therefore encompasses and reflects her entire lifetime, not just the specific promise made to St. Joseph for the feast day.

The drawing together of earthly and heavenly relationships is further marked in the ceremony enacted during the feast. The woman giving the altar chooses the adults and children whom she wishes to represent the saints on her altar. This process of choosing the saints is a further testament to the power—and the rewards—of women's kin and quasi-kin networking skills. In explaining who she chose to represent her saints and why, Sally Cantarella unwittingly highlighted to us her process of creating, acknowledging, and maintaining her personal network of kin and quasi-kin: "My mother and father are going to represent St. Joseph and Mary. I have a little boy of a dear friend of ours who will be the Baby Jesus. The Infant Jesus of Prague is one of my godchildren. St. Teresa is another godchild. The Guardian Angel is my niece. St. Peregrine is the child of another friend." These representatives are given the honor of symbolically personifying the saints, but equally they are honored in that they index the woman's gratitude for, and recognition of, important social relationships.

This celebration of the woman's personal pantheon also can be seen as a way of elaborating the conventional narrative of this feast day. Joseph is never portrayed as the exclusive protagonist of the St. Joseph's Day story; rather, his story is embedded in the narrative of the whole family and, indeed, community. Certainly Joseph is accorded a central place in the ritual event and in the participants' sentiments on this occasion. But what the women never lose sight of is the familial relationships that surround and support his personage. In this ritual Joseph is portrayed not as an isolated patriarch but as a "handmaiden" to Mary and the impending family. Indeed, as Quaggiotto points out, in every way "Joseph is a subsidiary actor in the Nativity and the surrounding events" (1988:288).

The Sicilian women's sacrifice of labor for St. Joseph's Day honors the man who lovingly sought shelter for his wife's trial, but it also marks the ultimacy of Mary's gift to the world: the birth of the Christ Child.[9] Joseph is not only peripheral to this supernatural drama, he is, as Quaggiotto remarks, also "marginal to the major human interaction that occurs within the family, which is centered around mother and child" (1988:288).

As the Holy Mother prepares to give birth, the earthly mother prepares a nurturing setting for the sacred birth to take place. It is through her capacity as caretaker and nurturer that the earthly mother is able to facilitate this most sacred of events through her gift of hospitality to the Holy Family. Although the day is dedicated to St. Joseph, the male patron of the family, the central story around which the day's events are constructed focuses not on him alone, but on the women who lodge and feed his Holy Family. The dramatic pinnacle of the narrative enacted on this day is the moment when the altar giver finally opens her doors to the holy pilgrims, inviting them into her home and heart. With tears of joy in her eyes, altar giver Sally Cantarella opened the door of her house to embrace her Holy Family and saints with the traditional words,

> There is room for Jesus, Joseph and Mary
> This is no longer my house,
> It is that of Jesus, Joseph and Mary.

In giving over her home to the Holy Family, the altar giver offers the very heart of her own worth. Her gifts of food and lodging are gifts of cooperation and collaboration with Mary, symbolically ensuring the continuity of the human race through one more generation and the safe delivery of the Blessed Redeemer for all time.

In sum, we view these women's symbolic appropriation and adaptation of the Bethlehem story (traditionally told and dramatized during Christmas) for the St. Joseph's Day feast as a tactical discursive act designed to forward an essentialist agenda of relationship and identification with the mother. St. Joseph's conventionally discursive power as "patron" of the family ultimately is mediated by a promotion of values centered in the importance of woman's power of relationship.

Conclusion: The Ideology of Reproduction in the St. Joseph's Day Feast

In the previous sections we have attempted to demonstrate that the St. Joseph's Day feast can be fruitfully understood as a folk religious celebration predicated on the material and symbolic display of women's power. As dramatically demonstrated in the feast day and in activities accruing to it, this power is largely defined by women's capacity and desire to create and sustain positive ties of relationship among family, friends, and community. As Quaggiotto also affirms for her informants in Sicily, "Beyond and through the altars to Saint Joseph one hears the great unsayable in Sicilian culture: women's desires for identity, recognition, power, and prestige, which are expressed through but are not reducible to the interests of the family. The ritual both provides a glimpse of these desires and masks them, as it must" (1988:314).

Our analysis might end here, but we would like to conclude our essay by setting out the meaning of women's investment in the St. Joseph's feast in more specific feminist theoretical terms.

The work that women do in connection with the St. Joseph's feast is made possible through the extended and extensive networks of female kin and friends that have evolved intergenerationally and across households over time. As we have suggested earlier, the organization and implementation of this kind of major celebratory event is a direct result of "the work of kinship."

These and other kinds of women's activities and work have been the focus of recent attention among feminist scholars, who have begun to formulate new understandings about the relations among gender, kinship, and the larger economy. Di Leonardo defines two theoretical trends, in particular, that she feels are keys to the reinterpretation and revaluation of women's work and the domestic domain (1987:441). In the first, identified by di Leonardo as the "household labor approach," feminist scholars have focused on certain of women's nonmarket activities—especially housework, child care, service to men, and care of the elderly—and insisted that these activities be defined as distinct forms of women's labor to be counted as part of the overall social reproduction of the family and the community. The second approach, which di Leonardo calls "the domestic network perspective," makes a claim for the importance of understanding the role of women's domestic and kin-related networks in the sociopolitical lives of women. These scholars see kin-related networks as "products of conscious strategy . . . , as sources of women's autonomous power and possible primary sites of emotional fulfillment and, at times, as vehicles for actual survival and/or political resistance" (1987:441). Where the first approach tends to construct a view of women as sentient and goal-oriented—yet ultimately self-interested —actors, the second, concerned primarily with women's ties to others, tends to depict women primarily in terms of nurturance, other-orientation— and, in short, a somewhat lopsided female altruism (di Leonardo, 1987:441).

What is particularly helpful for our purposes is di Leonardo's attempt to fuse and thereby to reconcile these two potentially opposing perspectives with her notion of "kin work." The concept of kin work, embodying notions of work and love and crossing boundaries of households, helps us to see both the interrelations of these phenomena and women's roles in creating and maintaining these interrelations (1987:452).

Our consultants in Chase accept their primary responsibility for housework and the care of dependent children, but for these women the domestic domain is not only an arena in which much unpaid labor must be undertaken but also a realm in which they gain what di Leonardo suggests are human satisfactions—and power—not available in the labor market. The concept of kin work, as developed by di Leonardo, reveals the actual labor involved in what we "culturally see as love" and helps us to give consideration to the political uses of this labor. As di Leonardo puts it, kin work is not only women's labor from which children and men benefit, it is also labor that women undertake in order to create obligations in men and children to gain power over one another (1987:452). Di Leonardo maintains that viewing women's domestic labor through the kin work lens helps to bridge the gap in the feminist discussion of the difference between altruism and self-interest in women's actions. Altruism and self-interest need not necessarily be considered mutually exclusive. Certainly in the St. Joseph's celebration women promote both their willingness to give to others—the feast is after all a sacrifice and called such by altar makers—and an unmitigated sense of the value and worth of the domestic labor that they consider to be their expertise.

While di Leonardo provokes a needed reassessment of the political consequences of the kind of women's kin work exemplified in the context of St. Joseph's Day, she does not examine the epistemological consequences of this kind of sexual division of labor. In other words, she does not come to terms with the "moral division of labor" (Held, 1987:111) that structures and consistently informs the power of kin work as we have observed it among Sicilian-American women in Texas. We suggest that St. Joseph's Day can be understood as the paradigmatic expression of this kind of division. On this day women not only engage in kin work with each other—as they do on all other holiday occasions—but they particularly forward the values of nurturance, care, comfort, and support—the birthright of the mother. Here religious belief is specifically wedded with what we call an "ideology of reproduction," that is, the ideology that arises from women's experience of giving birth to children and rearing them into human persons. In other words, it is through the care and nurturance shown to the Holy Family on this day that the importance of women's daily caretaking of the earthly family is also sacralized. What is so clearly signified in the St. Joseph's ritual is no less than an ontological state that, as Quaggiotto similarly argues, "refers to women's role in creating life, in bringing new members into the species and recruiting new members into the family; it refers to the processes of change, growth, and progress of human life which are made possible by women" (1988:313). This "moral division of labor," made symbolically evident in the St. Joseph's feast, sets the terms for further understanding women's kin work as an aspect of their reproductive labor wherein morality, values, beliefs, attitudes, and ways of knowing are founded centrally in activities associated with birth and mothering.

Since 1980, several feminist philosophers have undertaken a reevaluation of the social relations of women's reproductive labor in the industrialized West. The philosophical stance that has emerged from their writings insists upon a recognition of a gender-based distinction between modes of thought, patterns of relationship, and ways of being in the world. Mary O'Brien (1981) has called this a "philosophy of birth"; Sara Ruddick (1980) has called it "maternal thinking"; Alison Jaggar (1983) describes it as a noncoercive form of power that asserts "the social development of human capacities"; and Carolyn Whitbeck (1983) and Nancy Hartsock (1983), anticipating the most recent rethinking of the essentialist argument, have proposed an entirely distinct ontology, what Whitbeck calls a "feminist ontology" and Hartsock refers to as a "feminist standpoint."

Hartsock's argument for a "feminist standpoint" is perhaps the most relevant for our interpretation of the St. Joseph's Day altar tradition. Like di Leonardo, Hartsock is interested in refocusing and expanding an understanding of women's labor, but she begins by reasserting the potential for the Marxian category of labor to include both the interaction with humans and with the natural world. In so doing, she avoids the false dichotomy that characterizes women's labor as either natural or social. She invites a viewpoint on the sexual division of labor that includes the full range of practices that constitute women's material life and activity and can account for women both as contributors to subsistence and as mothers (1983:284). Women's labor in every society differs from men's, but this difference is never purely a socially constructed distinction. Hartsock emphasizes the *sexual* rather than the gender-determined division of labor in an effort to forward the universally invariant fact that women's labor includes birthing children and the nearly invariant fact of rearing children. The bodily and sensuous practices of mothering—the labors of reproduction—structure social relations in a particular way.

This is not to ignore the fact that women in capitalism contribute to both production for wages and production of goods in the home, but, as Hartsock maintains, there is a profound difference between the productive labor of women and that of the male worker because only a part of women's labor is represented by her contribution to subsistence:

> Women also produce/reproduce men (and other women) on both a daily and a long-term basis. This aspect of women's "production" exposes the deep inadequacies of the concept of production as a description of women's activity. One does not (cannot) produce another human being in anything like the way one produces an object.... Much more is involved, activity which cannot easily be dichotomized into play or work. Helping another to develop, the gradual relinquishing of control, the experience of the human limits of one's actions—all these are important features of women's activity as mothers.... Women as mothers, even more than as workers, are institutionally involved in processes of change and growth.... In addition, in the process of producing human beings, relations with others may take a variety of forms with deeper significance than simple cooperation with others for common goals—forms which range from a deep unity with another through the many-leveled and changing connections mothers experience with growing children. (1983:293–94)

Women's reproductive labor has epistemological and ontological consequences that result in the construction of female existence as centered in relational values. This, according to Hartsock, leads to a distinctive women's worldview that opposes dualisms, maintains a valuation of concrete, everyday life, and senses a variety of connectednesses and continuities both with other persons and with the natural world (1983:298).

Echoing Hartsock, Carolyn Whitbeck defines "feminist ontology" as that sense of being that is based upon a conception of the self-other *relation* that is significantly different from the self-other *opposition* that underlies the history of Western patriarchal thought and practice. A feminist ontology restates the terms of being within a framework that is neither oppositional nor dyadic. She locates this ontology not in an abstract or reductionist theory but in a certain type of general practice. Whitbeck herself defines this practice as "the mutual realization of people." She assumes, but does not document, that this practice is found in a variety of particular forms, most, if not all of which, are discoverable in women's work and are therefore largely ignored by the dominant culture. Among these are child-rearing, nursing the sick, care of the dying, the organization of family gatherings, and a variety of spiritual practices centered upon the well-being of the family.[10]

Both of these philosophers point to the political significance of a maternally derived ideology of reproduction that emphasizes social practices based on affiliation, concern for others, sharing, caring, gifting, and noninstitutionalized religious belief. But Whitbeck, Hartsock, and the others are in the business of rewriting philosophy. What is absent from all of their work, as O'Brien recognizes, is a more concrete sense of the specific social forms that emerge from and embody the dialectics of this reproductive process (1981:92).

We, as folklorists, recognize that women's traditional expressive culture may offer the missing link between philosophy and practice. The reality of women's lore such as that made so obvious in the St. Joseph's feast unravels the abstractions of philosophy and weds them to the very content and practice of women's lives. We feel there is a crucial claim to be made for an ideology discoverable in much of women's lore that is based on their own expression of the power of reproductive labor.

Notes

We would like to thank all the women and their families who invited us into their homes to learn the St. Joseph's tradition from them. Their gracious acceptance of strangers afforded us the opportunity to closely observe and participate in this intimate expression of family and community life. This essay serves as an introduction to our continuing work on the St. Joseph's Day altar tradition in Texas. In order to protect the privacy of our informants, we have here employed pseudonyms for all personal and place names. An earlier version of this essay appeared in 1987 in the *Journal of American Folklore* 100 (398): 446–60. We would like to thank Pamela Quaggiotto, Amy Shuman, Paula Manini, and the editors and outside readers of this manuscript for their many insightful comments on earlier drafts.

1. For further information on the Sicilian community in Texas, see, especially, Belfiglio (1983, 1985) and the Institute of Texan Cultures (1973). For a more general introduction into the Italian immigrant communities in America, see Marinacci (1967), Nelli (1983), and Pellegrini (1956).

2. Also in evidence are the lingering effects of an age-old rivalry between descendants of the Sicilian cities of Corleone and Poggioreale, whose families spoke different dialects, venerated different patron saints, and settled on opposite sides of the river upon their arrival in this part of Texas (Belfiglio, 1983:109).

3. The tight-knit nature of this enclave was made immediately apparent to us when we initiated our fieldwork by agreeing to meet Sally Cantarella at a local Italian bakery and restaurant where community members congregate for coffee and conversation. While waiting for Sally, we met Joe Lampo, who, upon gaining a sense of our mission, questioned us saying, "How come you know Sally and I don't know you? Are you Catholic, are you kin, are you married?" Those questions shortly summarized the basic social alliances that bind this community together.

4. The altars reflect the beliefs, tastes, aesthetic predilections, family history, and class status of their makers. As one woman told us, "Everybody has their own way. Everybody does it a little bit different." At this point in time the tradition in this part of Texas is characterized by the building of large, very elaborate altars. This is due in part to the fact that not as many altars currently are being given; those that are receive the benefit of a larger base of women in the community who work on and provide donations of food for them. While this kind of spectacular altar presentation is typical, the tradition is also expressed in other, less grandiose ways. There is a distinction between, for example, altars that are promised as a long-term devotion—some for five years, ten years, or a lifetime—and those that are dedicated singularly for one year only. One woman who dedicates an altar every year told us that because she and her husband don't have much money, they tend to "keep it plain and simple." In 1984, this woman mounted the altar on their kitchen table, covered with a lace tablecloth, and it consisted simply of a large, heirloom lithograph print of the Holy Family in front of which were set four undecorated St. Joseph's Day breads, a votive candle lighted for St. Joseph, a statue of St. Anthony, and a small assortment of cakes and pies, two of each. At the end of the feast day the breads and sweets were given to a niece, a friend's daughter, and to strangers—two young couples in the neighborhood who were jobless and had recently become parents. The differences among the altars we have observed is certainly something to be accounted for in more detail as we continue our study of this tradition. But despite their differences, all the altars we have seen or heard about give primary evidence of women's kin work in their creation. As di Leonardo suggests in looking at women's traditions in another Italian-American context, it is important to recognize "that kin work is *gender* rather than class based," and this important fact "allows us to see women's kin networks among all groups" (1987:449).

5. By concentrating on these acts of community and familial support, however, we do not mean to imply that the Sicilian-American women in our study do not

also participate in the labor market outside the home. Indeed, a majority of the altar givers we interviewed either work alongside their husbands in jointly owned businesses or farms, retain clerical or secretarial jobs in town, or have started their own small businesses by themselves or in partnership with other women from the community.

6. The folklorist Nicholas Spitzer reports another variation on the tradition as it is produced in Louisiana, where altars are constructed in public places, not necessarily the church (personal correspondence, Oct. 1986). Spitzer suggests that the change from the private to the public domain has resulted in consonant changes in the ways in which men and women participate.

7. A *novena* is a nine-day period of prayer, especially a period for praying the rosary, which was instituted by Mary in her aspect as the Virgin of the Rosary. Catholic scholars trace the meaning of novenas to a commemoration of the nine months of Mary's pregnancy with Jesus (Hilgers, 1911:141–44). The number of people who come to the altar giver's home during these nine days to pray the rosary is seen as further testament to the kin-based influence and power of the altar giver. As Sally Cantarella remarked, "Like I said, it's been standing-room only. And Father John said it's because they like [me]."

8. This spelling of the traditional fig cookie was offered on several occasions by women who make them in the community. The literal translation would be "things made of figs," *cosa de fiche.*

9. The figure of St. Joseph, as he is treated both within the Texas-Sicilian community and in the larger tradition of Christianity, invites commentary concerning his ambivalent status as a patriarch. In certain suggestive ways St. Joseph may be considered the patriarch who, by standard definition, does not qualify or act as one. Indeed, he appears to be the only Catholic saint whose presence automatically implies the family. We recall that in the biblical story of Christ's life, Joseph somewhat reluctantly takes on the burden of marrying a woman who is to birth a child that is not his. And as the life history of Jesus progresses we find that it is his mother, not his earthly father, who plays a central and continuous part in Jesus' life, including the critical moments of his death and his resurrection.

On the community level, in the rosary said in his honor for the feast, St. Joseph is characterized as patriarch, but is called "Immaculate Patriarch"; he is called "Father," but is immediately referenced thereafter as "a virgin like the Mother"; and he is prayed to as the one who is "predestined" by God for the service of God's "eternal Son and His Blessed Mother and made worthy to be the spouse of this Blessed Virgin and the Foster Father" of Jesus. Interestingly, St. Joseph is rendered in Marian terms. In essence, St. Joseph is called to render service to the Virgin Mary, the Blessed Mother. St. Joseph, unlike a true patriarch who establishes power and dominance through the bloodline, has no blood claim in the birth of Christ. Only Mary, who gave bodily birth to the Christ Child, has such a claim, and Joseph serves the woman who gave birth to the world's saviour. Both Mary and Joseph serve their son, but it is not said that Mary serves her earthly husband. Women in the Chase community nominally refer to St. Joseph as the head of the household, but when they speak of him personally in terms of their day-to-day relationship with him, they call him "my friend," "my closest pal," and "my daily companion." And it should be noted that this is not unlike the way they personally refer to their own husbands, not as heads of household, but as partners in life. We speculate that St. Joseph's ambivalence as a male patriarch lends itself to the unique way in which the St. Joseph's Day feast can articulate women's power—maternal power—in a celebration that formally honors a male saint. See Quaggiotto (1988:288–303) for an excellent history of the cult of St. Joseph and the signifying power of his marginal status in the St. Joseph's Day ritual in Sicily.

10. Without directly saying so, Hartsock and Whitbeck adopt what we would call a "new essentialist" position. On the one hand they each recognize and give a positive slant on the sexual difference between women and men. But they want to hang this difference on the hook of social practice, thereby linking essential difference not wholly to cause but more to its effect. This yields a position that is open to change and potentiality. The fact that women exert an essential maternity—an ideology of reproduction—in the St. Joseph's Day feast is one way of determining, symbolizing, and affirming the value of their daily social practices as women.

The essentialist position has been argued—for and against—throughout the past twenty years of feminist critique. For the most part essentialism has been negatively critiqued in American feminism; innate difference or sexual difference has been overridden in favor of gender theory keyed to the social construction of male/female difference and its poststructural interpretations. (For detailed discussion of the essentialist critique see, for example, Alcoff, 1988; Moi, 1985; and Stanton, 1986.) But essentialism is enjoying a positive reinvigoration in more recent feminist theory that attends to the notion of essentialisms, including but not limited to sexual difference, that are played out in various realms, such as social, sexual, and symbolic practices, wherever female subjectivities are being constructed. (For discussion of the "new essentialism" see De Lauretis, 1989; Fuss, 1989; and Schor 1989.)

References Cited

Alcoff, Linda. 1988. "Cultural Feminism versus Post-structuralism: The Identity Crisis in Feminist Theory." *Signs* 13 (3): 405–36.
Belfiglio, Valentine J. 1983. *The Italian Experience in Texas.* Austin: Eakin Press.
———. 1985. *Best of Italian Cooking, Texas Style: With Love, from the Italian Texans.* Austin: Eakin Press.
Christian, Diane. 1988. "No New Truths and All the Old Falsehoods." *Journal of American Folklore* 101 (399): 53–55.
De Lauretis, Teresa. 1989. "The Essence of the Triangle; or, Taking the Risk of Essentialism Seriously: Feminist Theory in Italy, the U.S., and Britain." *Differences* 1 (2): 3–37.
di Leonardo, Micaela. 1984. *The Varieties of Ethnic Experience: Kinship, Class, and Gender among California Italian-Americans.* Ithaca: Cornell University Press.

————. 1987. "The Female World of Cards and Holidays: Women, Families, and the Work of Kinship." *Signs* 12 (3): 440–53.

Fuss, Diana. 1989. *Essentially Speaking: Feminism, Nature, and Difference.* New York: Routledge.

Hartsock, Nancy. 1983. "The Feminist Standpoint: Developing the Ground for a Specifically Feminist Historical Materialism." In *Discovering Reality: Feminist Perspectives on Epistemology, Metaphysics, Methodology, and the Philosophy of Science,* ed. Sandra Harding and Merrill B. Hintikka, 283–310. Boston: D. Reidel.

Held, Virginia. 1987. "Feminism and Moral Theory." In *Women and Moral Theory,* ed. Eva Feder Kittay and Diana T. Meyers, 111–28. Totowa, N.J.: Rowman and Allanheld.

Hilgers, Joseph. 1911. "Novena." In *The Catholic Encyclopedia,* vol. 11, ed. Charles G. Herbermann, 141–44. New York: Robert Appleton.

Institute of Texan Cultures. 1973. *The Italian Texans.* San Antonio: University of Texas at San Antonio Press.

Jaggar, Alison J. 1983. *Feminist Politics and Human Nature.* Totowa, N.J.: Rowman and Allanheld.

Kuykendall, Eleanor. 1983. "Toward an Ethic of Nurturance: Luce Irigaray on Mothering and Power." In *Mothering: Essays in Feminist Theory,* ed. Joyce Trebilcot, 263–74. Totowa, N.J.: Rowman and Allanheld.

Marinacci, Barbara. 1967. *They Came from Italy: The Stories of Famous Italian Americans.* New York: Dodd, Mead.

Moi, Toril. 1985. *Sexual/Textual Politics: Feminist Literary Theory.* London: Methuen.

Nelli, Humbert. 1983. *From Immigrants to Ethnics: The Italian Americans.* Oxford: Oxford University Press.

O'Brien, Mary. 1981. *The Politics of Reproduction.* London: Routledge and Kegan Paul.

Pellegrini, Angelo M. 1956. *Americans by Choice.* New York: Macmillan.

Quaggiotto, Pamela. 1988. "Altars of Food to Saint Joseph: Women's Ritual in Sicily." Ph.D. diss., Columbia University.

Rich, Adrienne. 1976. *Of Woman Born.* New York: W. W. Norton.

Ruddick, Sara. 1980. "Maternal Thinking." *Feminist Studies* 6 (2): 342–66.

Schor, Naomi. 1989. "This Essentialism Which Is Not One: Coming to Grips with Irigaray." *Differences* 1 (2): 38–58.

Speroni, Charles. 1940. "The Observance of St. Joseph's Day among the Sicilians of Southern California." *Southern Folklore Quarterly* 4 (3): 135–39.

Stanton, Domna C. 1986. "Difference on Trial: A Critique of the Maternal Metaphor in Cixous, Irigaray, and Kristeva." In *Poetics of Gender,* ed. Nancy K. Miller, 157–82. New York: Columbia University Press.

Turner, Kay. 1982. "Mexican American Home Altars: Towards Their Interpretation." *Aztlán* 13 (1–2): 309–26.

Whitbeck, Caroline. 1983. "A Different Reality: Feminist Ontology." In *Beyond Domination: New Perspectives on Women and Philosophy,* ed. Carol C. Gould, 64–88. Totowa, N.J.: Rowman and Allanheld.

PART TWO

Margaret R. Yocom

Waking Up the Dead: Old Texts and New Critical Directions

Not long ago, two of my fortyish women friends got glasses for the first time in their lives. "Well, I can see better," one told me. "Not that my vision was really bad before, just a little fuzzy on the edges. But the thing that's really startling is not my vision; it's the idea of having to get glasses, my mortality, you see. Facing that. But you know what's good? Now, I think I look even more like the person I am."

Trying to see better, by whatever means, often takes us through a rather complicated process, one that brings us in touch with a great deal of discomfort and, simultaneously, with the comfort of knowing that the journey has its rewards.

Adrienne Rich wrote of the rewards and perils along this path of change before many of us started to walk it. In "When We Dead Awaken: Writing as Re-vision," she explains, "Re-vision—the act of looking back, of seeing with fresh eyes, of entering an old text from a new critical direction—is for women more than a chapter in cultural history: it is an act of survival. Until we can understand the assumptions in which we are drenched we cannot know ourselves.... But there is also a difficult and dangerous walking on the ice, as we try to find language and images for a consciousness we are just coming into" (1979:35).

The essays in Part 2 all examine traditional materials that have been analyzed by folklorists before. But by looking once again and using, this time, the lens of feminist theory with its focus on the intersection of gender, race, power, and class, the games and quilts, oral histories and epics, tall tales and sermons all stand transformed.

The first three essays reexamine folklore texts by focusing on the process of creation rather than on the cultural product. The next three question the way women's roles in early texts have been perceived by other scholars and offer rereadings. And the last two essays look at women's performances in male-dominated arenas and identify strategies that women employ to survive and create. In addition, I suggest several meeting places of folklore and feminist theory, especially within the present dialogues on difference, power, and the concept of woman.

Re-viewing Process

One way to see old texts anew is to highlight the process of creation instead of the product, alone, that traditional exchanges produce. When we pay attention to how a game is played, how a quilt is put together, how an interview is conducted, new interpretations of the products and of the roles of women players and creators stand before our eyes.

Linda A. Hughes's research on girls' games provides, as she describes it, "a much-needed counterpoint to the current rhetoric of deficit and deficiency surrounding girls and their games." By focusing not on the game of foursquare itself but primarily on how the game was played by a friendship group of white girls at a private Quaker school near Philadelphia, Hughes found that girls used their rhetoric of "niceness" and being friends to manage—not avoid—competition within a complex group structure. Girls, she reminds us, "are quite capable of taking highly stereotypical themes and pastimes and doing quite unstereotypical things with them." Hughes proposes that girls may prefer activities in which they, and not the activity, determine who will vie against whom and where competing parties represent meaningful social divisions rather than more arbitrary or skill-determined groupings. But she also suggests that studies on how games are played are likely to reveal significant areas of overlap across gender lines as those lines are now drawn by scholars in the field.

In an essay that also looks at girls' games and the ways girls play, Marjorie Harness Goodwin argues that girls do compete, negotiate, and make hierarchical arrangements. Examining how African American working-class girls in West Philadelphia begin and direct their games, Goodwin demonstrates that games that involve tasks are structured cooperatively and that pretend play, such as "house," is structured hierarchically. After negotiation takes place, play is not disrupted. Taking issue with studies that suggest that girls' games are simple and noncompetitive and thus do not prepare girls for successful performance in adult institutions, Goodwin presents girls' sociodramatic play as highly complex activity that poses a range of problems absent from other play. Since girls' social organization varies across different kinds of games, she encourages study of a variety of games, urging that all such studies be grounded in context.

Arguing against an artifact-centered approach to quilting, Joyce Ice advocates examining the quilting process in terms of women's lives and work, concentrating on what women say about their work and what it means to them. This approach allows Ice to see the women's definitions of work, their own folk aesthetic, their willingness to compromise in a group setting, and their shifting aesthetic evaluations of the quilts. A focus on process enables Ice to discover how conversation holds the group together much like quilting holds the layers of a quilt together. It is through the quilting process, Ice affirms, that quilts "come to externalize a set of aesthetic and social values derived from a shared sensibility."

Re-viewing Actions

By focusing on the actions of women and their interactions with men, Patricia E. Sawin, Susan Tower Hollis, and M. Jane Young formulate different visions of women's roles in Finnish epic, Egyptian myth, and Western Puebloan society from those put forth by earlier scholars. Their essays re-view the acts of women, especially those acts that have seemed insignificant to other researchers. The work of Sawin and Young underscores the findings of Judith Newton who, quoting Berenice Carroll, maintains that "female power 'can lodge in dangerous nooks and crannies' " (1981:7). It is patriarchal presuppositions that deem one act valuable and another not; and it is these presuppositions that the authors of this volume seek to eliminate. Re-viewing actions demands questions that describe and analyze women's actions and interactions, detail the historical conditions of the action, explore the intersection of private and public actions, and present women's contributions as part of a system.[1]

Sawin and Young's studies also support the observations of Judith Fetterley who, in her work with male-authored texts of the American literary canon, remarks:

> Consciousness is power. . . . To expose and question that complex of ideas and mythologies about women and men which exist in our society and are confirmed in our literature is to make the system of power embodied in the literature open not only to discussion but even to change. Such questioning and exposure can, of course, be carried on only by a consciousness radically different from the one that informs the literature. . . . Clearly then, the first act of the feminist critic must be to become a resisting reader rather than an assenting reader. (1978:xx-xxiii)

Susan Tower Hollis also explores women and their actions, but her work urges us to move carefully as we assess women's power. She challenges earlier feminist scholarship that seeks to convince us that the presence of powerful female figures in a society's mythology indicates that power would also reside in that same society's mortal women.

In her revisionist essay, Patricia Sawin takes a fresh look at a canonical text, the *Kalevala,* and transforms this national epic of heroic victory into a tale of tragedy. The editor, Lönnrot, assembled the texts that became the *Kalevala* to provide an unambiguous, glorious past for the Finns; his compilation portrays national forefathers destroying their enemies, often women, in its pages. Sawin suggests that the *Kalevala* can be read as a tragedy about a society that, having tasted of equality and cooperation between men and women, changes back to one that upholds the patriarchal values of strength and violence.

Sawin examines the speech acts in Ilmarien's courtship of Louhi. She demonstrates that the women's questions and riddles enable them to separate the men who cannot "read" their language from those who can. Thus, they choose the best mate for Louhi, one who works cooperatively with her to solve the nation's ills. This time of cooperation lasts only for a moment as Ilmarien shifts back to his earlier patriarchal language and ways that valorize strength and violence, battle with women, and the blaming of women for society's ills. If we look through the lens of the resisting reader, Ilmarien brings on tragedy.

Turning to ancient Egyptian texts, Susan Tower Hollis, like Patricia Sawin, focuses on texts generated early in a people's history and commented on by a host of scholars. Given her interest in both ancient historical texts and mythology, Hollis sets out to explore a theory of congruence ascribed to by both Lauri Honko and Peggy Reeves Sanday that suggests if women are portrayed as powerful in their culture's mythology then the society is likely to have women in positions of power as well.

Although the Egyptian night sky goddess Nut and the more ancient goddesses Neith and Hathor performed acts of cosmic and earthly necessity, their power did not, Hollis notes, translate itself into power for mortal women. Using Egyptian primary documents—histories of rulers; iconographic representations, such as statues, pyramids, and paintings; language; legal documents; instructional texts; and love songs, Hollis argues that royal and upper- and middle-class Egyptian women had only limited independence and political influence. They did not have the substantial societal influence as posited by several earlier scholars. Hollis calls for an exploration of the power of women of all levels within a given society and cautions against assuming that powerful mythological goddesses signal power for earthly women.

M. Jane Young rethinks the role of women in Western Puebloan religion. Although earlier accounts of the culture focused almost exclusively on the ritual activities of men, implying that women have had no significant role in religious practice, Young argues that women are central to the ideological basis of the religion, since much of the ritual behavior of the men imitates the reproductive power of the women.

Young, relying on Native American commentary about men's and women's roles and looking closely at the intersection of women's acts with men's ritual acts, finds balance and equity.[2] Men tend the crops and give life to corn; all Western Puebloans believe that crops spring from the womb of Mother Earth. In kiva rituals, men sprinkle the kachinas (masked god impersonators) with sacred cornmeal, ground by women. Thus, men imitate the women's role as feeders. Though women do not enter the kivas (secret underground chambers) once they are built, they plaster the walls of the kiva and leave their handprints on the roof beams. Men, during ceremonies, look up and are reminded of their mothers, wives, and daughters. Citing other acts as well, Young maintains that in this "culture that focuses on reproduction and life, neither women nor men are regarded as dominated or dominating. Both are seen as partners operating in an interdependent manner to keep the heart of the village . . . alive and strong."

Re-viewing Power

In the last two essays in Part 2, the authors take women's performances in male-dominated arenas as their texts and interpret them by asking questions about power, both covert and overt. Theirs is no simple task, for to "insist upon women's power in the past, and in the present," as Judith Newton asserts, "is to challenge the most dominant and most entrenched of social relations" (1981:xix). These essays on fundamentalist women preachers and women tall-tale tellers explore how these women have used their positions to maneuver within their worlds and to reconstruct their images and roles within the larger social and political entities that surround them—family, religious congregation, class, region, and nation. In doing so, these essays raise questions about the nature and the effects of women's power; they lend support to the research of Joan Radner and Susan Lanser who maintain that "in the creations and performances of dominated cultures one can often find covert expressions of ideas, beliefs, experiences, feelings and attitudes that the dominant culture—and perhaps even the dominated group—could find disturbing or threatening if expressed in more overt forms. We further suggest that such coded messages may ultimately help to empower a community and hence to effect change" (1993:4).

Vera Mark examines tall tales that were told at a liar's contest in the Gascon region of France during the late 1970s and early 1980s to explore women's performances in this male-dominated genre. In their stories, the male tellers use a great deal of sexuality and picture women negatively. The two women who won the contests employed similar strategies: though they used some sexuality, they embedded the sexuality within positive images of the region, and they emphasized their status as grandmothers and as motherly women. Thus, they reproduced social conventions and, by doing so, were able to put a contest-winning image of a positive, powerful woman before the audience. A third woman's story defined the boundaries of male-oriented social conventions by transgressing them: her story featured overt sexuality and pictured a woman besting a man at hunting. She received no prize. Men's tales, Mark concludes, reveal their discomfort with women's sexual and reproductive power, while women's tales reflect their ambivalence toward performing at a male event and their desire to put forward positive images of themselves.

Elaine J. Lawless, studying white women in the Pentecostal churches of southern Indiana and central Missouri, asks how women become preachers, given the scriptural foundation for the muted subjection of women. She finds her answers in the maternal, reproductive images that the women use as strategies to "strip their presence behind the pulpit of its most threatening aspects." The women also demean their capabilities, stress their handmaiden status, and acknowledge their subservience to God and men. The source of their power, Lawless suggests, lies in the congregation's perception of women preachers as more pious and closer to the values of home and family than many men preachers, who are more likely to be identified with the secular world.

Difference and the Concept of Woman: Folklore and Feminist Theory

In the 1980s and 1990s, one of the primary discussions within feminist theory has centered on the concept of difference and its relation to the idea of "woman." The essays in this part contribute to this continuing effort to find new ways to discuss women and men, free from self-defeating strictures.

"The concept of woman," writes Linda Alcoff, "is a problem." Summarizing the difficulty, she explains that "woman" as category has been the necessary point of departure for people who want to reevaluate and change women's lived experience in contemporary culture, but that "woman" is also problematic because it invokes the idea of limits, of "other" that has been placed on it by patriarchal constructions (1988:405).[3]

Alcoff outlines the two major theoretical responses to the problem, one of cultural feminism, the "ideology of a female nature or female essence reappropriated by feminists themselves in an effort to revalidate undervalued female attributes," and another, following poststructuralism, that rejects the possibility of defining woman, since in doing so "we duplicate misogynist strategies when we try to define women, characterize women, or speak for women, even though allowing for a range of differences within the gender" (1988:408).

Several theorists, including Alcoff, offer new responses to difference by stressing context, woman as positionality, and gender as a social construction. Here, I present these responses and suggest how the folklore essays that follow contribute to feminist research.

Arguing for an understanding of woman that foregrounds specific contexts, Joan Scott explains that she wants to avoid the male/female binary opposition that "serves to obscure the differences among women. . . . It is not sameness *or* identity between women and men that we want to claim, but a more complicated historically variable diversity than is permitted by the opposition male/female, a diversity that is also differently expressed for different purposes in different contexts. . . . It does not deny the existence of gender differences, but it does suggest that its meanings are always relative to particular constructions in specified contexts" (1988:45–47).

Linda Alcoff develops the concept of woman as positionality. Such a theory, she explains, "shows how women use their positional perspective as a place from which values are interpreted and constructed rather than as a locus of an already determined set of values." It stipulates that woman is a "relational term identifiable only within a (constantly moving) context" and that the "position that women find themselves in can be actively utilized (rather than transcended) as a location for the construction of meaning, a place from where meaning is constructed, rather than simply the place where a meaning can be *discovered* (the meaning of femaleness)" (1988:434).

Presenting an understanding of gender as a construction, a process, a reflex that is located within situations that change, Nancy Chodorow insists that we "can only understand gender difference, and human distinctness and separation, relationally and situationally." Women do not find themselves in positions, they are co-responsible for them. Women

> participate in the creation of these worlds and ideologies, even if our ultimate power and access to cultural hegemony are less than those of men. . . . To see men and women as qualitatively different kinds of people, rather than seeing gender as processual, reflexive, and constructed, is to reify and deny *relations* of gender, to see gender differences as permanent rather than as created and situated. . . . Feminist theories and feminist inquiry based on the notion of essential difference, or focused on demonstrating difference, are doing feminism a disservice. They ultimately rely on the defensively constructed masculine models of gender that are presented to us as our cul-

tural heritage, rather than creating feminist understandings of gender and difference that grow from our own politics, theorizing, and experience. (1980:16)

Like Chodorow, Scott, and Alcoff, bell hooks argues that going beyond the male/female debate would open feminism to more powerful analyses. "By repudiating the popular notion that the focus of feminist movement should be social equality of the sexes," she argues,

> our own analysis would require an exploration of all aspects of women's political reality. This would mean that race and class oppression would be recognized as feminist issues with as much relevance as sexism. When feminism is defined in such a way that it calls attention to the diversity of women's social and political reality, it centralizes the experiences of all women, especially the women whose social conditions have been least written about, studied, or changed by political movements. When we cease to focus on the simplistic stance "men are the enemy," we are compelled to examine systems of domination and our role in their maintenance and perpetuation. (1984:25–26)

The authors of the essays in this volume add their voices to this polyphonal chorus of ideas and, by locating gender relations within particular national, ethnic, racial, or religious groups functioning at specific historical moments, they underscore the value of positionality. Patricia Sawin, in viewing the *Kalevala* at a particular moment in Finland's history, sees Lönnrot's construction of the text as establishing a male/female split to create a national identity. M. Jane Young explores the men's and women's roles in Western Puebloan religion and finds that the group stresses balance and equality. She also shows how, given different historical moments, the same values obtain. Vera Mark, while affirming her decision to study the image of "woman," nevertheless finds, in dealing with such a specific context, that class, region, and gender intersect. And in her work with white Pentecostal women preachers from Missouri and Indiana, Elaine Lawless shows how gender differences were constructed by both the women and men of the congregation and how women preachers manipulate those same ideologies so they can preach both at home and all around the state.

The chapters in this part based on fieldwork and contextual analysis illustrate what viewpoints are possible when researchers focus on the context in which women informants express themselves. It is in their persistent and careful focus on interrelationships within living contexts that folklorists have much to contribute to feminist theory. Folklorists' study of individual performances that are situated in specific historical moments and cultures provide forceful examples of positionality. Hughes and Goodwin, for example, in their study of games, examine the play group and, to some extent, its features of class and race. By drawing on the group context, however, both researchers were able to see the concept of woman in new ways: Hughes found how these young girls manipulated, rather than accepted, the construct of the "nice girl," and Goodwin discovered the defect in saying "when girls play games, they . . ."

Another contribution that folklorists make to feminist scholarship lies in their continual refinement of fieldwork strategies as they work with women who are alive today. Literary critic Judith Newton hints at the challenge of dealing with contemporary women as she discusses one of the benefits of working with women's cultures of the past: "To study power and powerlessness in nineteenth-century female life," she admits, "is also to employ a strategy. It is to explore power in relative tranquility; it is to examine power struggles where we can work without having to work through a bad case of nerves" (1981:xviii). Feminist folklore fieldworkers who work with women and men in contemporary society certainly can get a bad case of nerves and more, but they have developed useful strategies that help them work closely with and also report clearly on their informants.[4] And these field experiences offer other feminist scholars already-tested methods for working with both contemporary and historical texts. For example, many of the authors in this volume searched for their informants' views of the contexts. Elaine Lawless discusses how she talked to her informants about her theories concerning them and gathered their reactions; she makes clear to us which she agrees with and which she does not. M. Jane Young solicited interpretations from her Hopi and Zuni "colleagues." Many developed close, long-standing relationships with their informants. And, to both better understand and to acclimate themselves to their fieldwork contexts, many of the authors took part in what their informants were doing: Joyce Ice quilted, Linda Hughes and Marjorie Goodwin played games, and Vera Mark told tall tales on a stage in France.

The essays in this volume also reflect the tensions between changing and competing theoretical stances in feminism. Though the contextual emphasis in folklore enables feminists to speak to positionality and diversity and to discuss women who perform together, it is also the very concept of context that can be used in an essentialist way to speak of women. Our challenge is a full and faithful investigation and presentation of context. When we as female fieldworkers look at women who quilt together or who appear on the same stage as storytellers, for example, do we see them primarily as a group of "women" and assume a unified female subject? Do we take for granted that they are a community? Or, do we look for divisions among the women—as Vera Marks does—and explore the discontinuities and the relationship between traditional expressions and debate?

These essays, then, to differing degrees and in different ways, demonstrate how folklorists through their emphasis on context and positionality contribute to feminist discourse.

Waking Up the Dead

When my girl cousins and I would get together in the early 1950s and play out behind the smokehouse on the farm in the Pennsylvania German country, we would often get into screaming contests. After all, we had heard our grandmother call our grandfather from the fields at supper time, and we had heard our grandfather call the cows just a little before our grandmother called him. Our voices, we discovered, could carry.

What we got from our grandmother for our efforts was, "You girls be quiet. Why, you could wake up the dead!" But we also saw the half-smile on her face as she listened to our soaring sounds.

Whether we develop new sight or newly found voices, hopefully the ideas in these essays about re-viewing process, actions, and power will help us to keep on delighting in our discoveries and waking up the dead.

Notes

1. Similarly, Janet M. Bujra calls for an investigation of "the relationship, the character of articulation, between domestic and non-domestic spheres of action" (1982:21–22).
2. Young's findings support the research of Peggy Reeves Sanday on dual-oriented societies and the distribution of power (1981).
3. See also Rosalind Coward's summary of the problem: "Feminism 'is a commitment to [exploring the ways of being a woman] involving a double movement: on the one hand, there is a desire to understand how it is that women as a sex are subordinated: on the other hand, there is a desire to challenge the very idea of natural sex roles. The problem is that of understanding the position of women as a sex without presuming that being a sex entails forms of natural behaviour and position.... The contradictoriness of this position is, however, only apparent' " (quoted in Meese, 1986:xv).
4. For additional discussion of strategies of women fieldworkers, see Anita Best (1991), Peggy Golde (1970), Kathryn Morgan (1981), and Margaret R. Yocom (1990).

References Cited

Alcoff, Linda. 1988. "Cultural Feminism versus Post-structuralism: The Identity Crisis in Feminist Theory." *Signs* 13 (3): 405–36.

Best, Anita. 1991. "Finding Our Way through the Field: Women's Fieldwork Strategies in Newfoundland." Paper presented at the annual meeting of the American Folklore Society, St. John's, Newfoundland.

Bujra, Janet M. 1982. "Introduction: Female Solidarity and the Sexual Division of Labour." In *Women United, Women Divided,* ed. Patricia Capland and Janet M. Bujra, 13–45. Bloomington: Indiana University Press.

Chodorow, Nancy. 1980. "Gender, Relation, and Difference in Psychoanalytic Perspective." In *The Future of Difference,* ed. Hester Eisenstein and Alice Jardine, 3–19. Boston: G. K. Hall.

Fetterley, Judith. 1978. *The Resisting Reader.* Bloomington: Indiana University Press.

Golde, Peggy. 1970. *Women in the Field.* Chicago: Aldine.

hooks, bell. 1984. *Feminist Theory: From Margin to Center.* Boston: South End Press.

Meese, Elizabeth. 1986. *Crossing the Double-Cross: The Practice of Feminist Criticism.* Chapel Hill: University of North Carolina Press.

Morgan, Kathryn. 1981. *Children of Strangers: The Stories of a Black Family.* Philadelphia: Temple University Press.

Newton, Judith Lowder. 1981. *Women, Power, and Subversion: Social Strategies in British Fiction, 1778–1860.* Athens: University of Georgia Press.

Radner, Joan N., and Susan S. Lanser. 1993. "Strategies of Coding in Women's Cultures." In *Feminist Messages: Coding in Women's Folk Culture,* ed. Joan Newlon Radner, 1–29. Urbana: University of Illinois Press.

Rich, Adrienne. 1979. "When We Dead Awaken: Writing as Re-vision." In *On Lies, Secrets, and Silence: Selected Prose, 1966–1978,* 33–70. New York: Norton.

Sanday, Peggy Reeves. 1981. *Female Power and Male Dominance.* Cambridge: Cambridge University Press.

Scott, Joan W. 1988. "Deconstructing Equality-Versus-Difference: Or, the Uses of Poststructuralist Theory for Feminism." *Feminist Studies* 14 (1): 33–50.

Yocom, Margaret R. 1990. "Fieldwork, Gender, and Transformation: The Second Way of Knowing." *Southern Folklore* 47 (1): 33–44.

"You Have to Do It with Style": *Girls' Games and Girls' Gaming*

If we are what we eat, a striking array of theorists (and feminists) have decided that we are also what we play. Tag, baseball, and hopscotch are trivial if measured by the amount of systematic research attention they have drawn. But they are far from trivial if measured by their role in theories of gender differentiation in childhood (Emmott, 1985; Gilligan, 1982; Kohlberg, 1966; Pitcher and Shultz, 1983) and by their perceived role as impediments to the pursuit of a more equitable society (Harragan, 1977; Lever, 1976).

I will explore here the significance of children's games to theories of gender differentiation in childhood, with particular attention to issues of feminist concern. I propose that a shift in focus from *what* children play (their games) to *how* they play (children's gaming) may provide a much-needed counterpoint to the current rhetoric of deficit and deficiency surrounding girls and their games. Selected observations from an ethnographic study of one girls' play group illustrate the very different images that can emerge from analyses of girls' games and of those same games in the playing.

Games and Gender

Interest in children's play groups has risen dramatically among nonfolklorists in recent years (Corsaro and Eder, 1990). There has been increasing awareness that interactions with peers are as important to development as interactions with adults and that peer interaction may differ in significant ways from the more commonly studied adult-child interaction (Hartup, 1983; Youniss, 1980).

Gender is a highly salient issue in the study of peer group structure and interaction because children's play groups are highly gender-differentiated during the elementary years (Maccoby and Jacklin, 1987; Thorne, 1986). Boys and girls tend to play within different types of play-group structures and to play different types of games (Eifermann, 1968; Finnan, 1982; Lever 1976, 1978; Sutton-Smith, 1979). These differences are often cited as evidence that boys and girls encounter very different contexts of peer-group socialization with far-reaching implications for adult gender roles. Maltz and Borker (1982), for example, have suggested that separate male and female sociolinguistic subcultures develop in the context of children's gender-segregated play groups, and Tannen (1990:47) has proposed that "the ways of speaking [that adults learn] growing up in separate social worlds of peers" are so different that male-female communication in our society constitutes "cross-cultural communication."

The basic outlines of this proposed gender-differentiated peer-group socialization are presented in Table 6.1, which summarizes the most commonly cited differences between boys' and girls' games and play groups. In general, boys' games have been characterized as more competitive, active, and aggressive and as requiring larger groups and a more complex social structure. Girls' games, in contrast, have been portrayed as more cooperative, passive, and verbal and lacking in complex social structure.

The political dimensions of children's games also become apparent in Table 6.1. The language of high-status corporate America is a highly gendered play language, and it is clearly a male play language of being "competitive," a "team player," and a "good sport" (Harragan, 1977; Schwartzman, 1978). This observation has sparked considerable concern among feminists like Lever, who believe that "boys' games . . . prepare their players for successful performance in the wide range of work settings in modern society (while) girls' games . . . prepare their players for the private sphere of the home and their future roles as wives and mothers" (1976:484).

Others, like Harragan, have been less measured in their indictment of girls' traditional games and pastimes, concluding that if women want to "play the game" well at the upper strata of our society, then girls are playing the wrong things: "Girls' games teach meaningless mumbo-jumbo . . . they teach nothing. . . . The objective of girls' games is never to beat anybody or perform under competitive stress, but merely to improve an agility in a vacuum" (1977:49–50).

Responses to these concerns have taken different forms in the political and academic arenas. In the former the dominant concern has been to change what girls play. This agenda was incorporated into public policy with passage of Title IX of the Federal Education Amendments of 1972. In the academic arena, however, the current concern is less to change

Table 6.1 Gender Differences Commonly Cited
in Studies of Children's Games

Boys' Games	Girls' Games
Involve fantasied or actual conflict and competition between groups or teams	Involve indirect competition between individuals, not groups
Require active interference with other players	Have much turn-taking in ordered sequences
Have well-defined outcomes, clear winners and losers	Have multiple, well-defined stages in play with many rules dictating every move
Require more body strength, more physical contact	Require coordinated choral activity, with many rhymes, songs, etc.
Require motor activity involving the whole body	Use only parts of the body
Result in a continuous flow of activity	Involve more audiences, in-game waiting, and solitary practice
Use larger and more outdoor spaces	Use smaller spaces and more indoor spaces
Involve larger and more age-heterogeneous play groups	Involve small, intimate play groups, often dyads or triads
Result in more fights, but last longer	Tend to break up when disputes arise

Key Contrasts

Competitive	Cooperative/turn-taking
Active	Passive
Aggressive/physical	Verbal/symbolic
Winners/losers	Coordinated choral activity
Teams/large complex groups	Individual/small intimate groups

Source: This information is compiled from Eifermann (1968); Finnan (1982); Lehman and Witty (1927); Lever (1976, 1978); Pitcher and Shultz (1983); and Sutton-Smith (1979).

what girls play than to change the value system that casts what they do as deficient in relation to what boys do. Feminists are increasingly challenging theories that characterize certain qualities and abilities as more mature than others and that portray girls and women as stuck at less mature levels.

A notable recent example is Carol Gilligan's (1982) challenge to Kohlberg's (1981) theory of moral development and subsequent attempts to develop an alternative model of female development (Gilligan, Lyons, and Hanmer, 1990). In simplest terms, Gilligan has argued that girls and women characteristically construct social reality in a way that places a high premium on social relationships and especially on close, intimate relationships with friends. This, in turn, leads them to construct morality differently than men, who characteristically approach social order in terms of individual rights and autonomous action. Her key concern has been to portray these contrasting orientations as matters of difference rather than deficits in the development of women.

Interestingly, boys' and girls' games have been central to theories of moral development since it was first delineated by Piaget in 1932 (1965), and they have remained central to attempts to recast that theory in a way that portrays women's constructions of social and moral order in more positive terms. Gilligan (1982) was compelled in her early work to explain that girls avoid activities like the competitive games common among boys because their potential for conflict is threatening to highly valued social relationships. She cited Lever's (1976) report that girls break up their games whenever serious disagreements arise to support the view that girls avoid competition in order to avoid conflict and preserve their friendships.

It is important to note the emphasis here on traditionally masculine qualities of competition and conflict in peer groups, because it represents a significant shift in focus since Piaget (1965) stressed cooperation, a quality commonly associated with girls, as the central element in peer-group interaction fostering cognitive growth. Cooperation, as the general "give-and-take" quality of peer relations that fosters more complex constructions of social and moral order (Hartup, 1983; Piaget, 1965; Youniss, 1980), has been replaced in discussions of gender by cooperation as personal qualities of "nonaggression, interpersonal conformity, restraint and nurturance or helplessness" (Kohlberg, 1966:122). The cooperative, relationship-centered social orientation associated with girls has thus come to be viewed not only as incompatible with the effective management of competition, conflict, and complex group structures but also as an impediment to critical developmental processes.

The simplest dialectic underlying all of this, of course, is that both society and theory are hierarchically organized and that both equate higher levels of functioning with traditionally masculine qualities. Gender differences in children's games enter the picture as central villains in the process of creating and sustaining patterns of inequality. Whether because of something inherent in the feminine psyche (Gilligan, 1982) or because of differential socialization (Lever, 1976, 1978), girls are seen as playing games that perpetuate values, attitudes, and skills that are inappropriate to the achievement of higher-status roles in our society.

Games and Gaming

I do not believe that the issue for feminist folklorists is whether gender is and ought to be a central concern in the study of children's games. Gender has long been a major comparative framework for the collection and study of children's games for the simple reason that gender is a highly significant organizing principle in children's daily lives (Maccoby and Jacklin, 1987; Thorne, 1986). Given the theoretical and political significance of children's games, however, I do believe that we ought to be asking whether the social reality that girls construct in their games is as bleak and limiting as current models suggest.

I believe that one way to introduce a new language into discourse in this domain is to shift the focus of analysis from children's games to gaming (Denzin, 1977; Fine, 1983; Hughes, 1991), from descriptions of *what* children play to *how* they play. There is good reason to believe that such a shift would enrich the current debate concerning games and gender, but it will require a significant shift in perspective among folklorists concerning the theoretical and political significance of children's folk culture.

To date, folklorists have not concerned themselves centrally with children's folklore beyond the occasional collection or anthology, and they have only rarely applied performance or communication approaches to its study (Bauman, 1975; Ben-Amos and Goldstein, 1975). The literature on games and gender thus shows little awareness of children's folk culture or of the creative, emergent quality of folk performance. Where current thinking about games and gender is informed at all by the work of folklorists, it reflects text over context, relying almost exclusively on comparisons of boys' and girls' games independent of the contexts in which they are actually played (Evans, 1986; Factor, 1988).

Goldstein (1971), however, demonstrated some time ago that we should not take the games children play as accurate measures of their playing or their players, cautioning that "the rules which are verbalized by informants and which are then presented by collectors in their papers and books for our analysis and study are . . . the rules by which people should play rather than the ones by which they do play" (1971:90). He presented his own observations of how children transformed the game of counting out from a "game of chance" to a "game of strategy" (see Roberts and Sutton-Smith, 1971) to propose a fundamental rethinking of this game and how it functioned in children's lives. As Maynard has observed, "The *way* a rule is used in a group may be more important than the content of the rule in describing a local group's culture. And . . . culture objects (including rules) need to be approached not by way of previously established content but by way of how they emerge and function in the communication patterns of a particular group" (1985:22).

Performance and communication-oriented studies have the potential to alter current images of girls and their games. I will illustrate by describing a group of girls who played a "girls' game" but who did not play it the way it was "supposed to be played." The image of these girls that emerges from an analysis of their game contrasts sharply with the far more complex image that emerges from an analysis of how they actually played that game.

Following Goldstein (1971), I based this study on the premise that the rules we commonly record in descriptions of games neither describe how it is actually played nor rigidly prescribe what players can and cannot do. Instead, the game rules set a general framework for collective action that is then subject to interpretation and negotiation (Brenner, 1982; Collett, 1977; Denzin, 1977; Evans, 1986; Fine, 1981; Polgar, 1976). Players can, if they collectively want to and within important limits, selectively invoke, ignore, defend, reject, reinterpret, or simply change the rules as they mold their games to suit their own agendas and purposes (Hughes, 1991; Polgar, 1976). In the process they can generate a gaming structure that differs in important ways from the stated structure of the game and, as a consequence, present very different images of their own skills and competencies.

The Foursquare Study

My observations are drawn from an ethnographic study of approximately forty children who played the game of foursquare during recess at a Friends (Quaker) school in the western suburbs of Philadelphia. I will only briefly describe this study here and only selectively draw upon its findings. A more detailed discussion of theory and methods, as well as a more extensive description of this game and its playing, can be found in Hughes (1983, 1989, 1991).

The foursquare study was originally undertaken to develop a conceptual and methodological framework for understanding how groups of children adapt their games to different social settings. The primary focus was on how rules and principles governing the social lives of children more generally interact with the rules of their games to generate qualitatively different versions of games.

The study was conducted in two phases: observation followed by interview. I observed twenty-three half-hour recess periods over a period of approximately two years. Foursquare was played during fourteen of those sessions. I then interviewed ten of the regular players about the game and its playing over a period of three months.

The Players

The players represented a naturally occurring play group, most of whom had played together regularly over a period of several years. They were entirely self-selected by their spontaneous participation in the game. Thirty-nine children (twenty-seven girls and twelve boys) were most intensively observed. They were predominantly fourth- and fifth-grade girls, though both younger and older children and a few boys were also regular players. Most came from white, middle- to upper middle-class families. Approximately 20 percent came from Quaker families.

It is important to note that while I observed boys as part of this study, I cannot report how they might have independently approached the playing of this game. The few boys who played regularly blended their style of play with that of the dominant group of girls. When large groups of boys participated in the game, the context was always a "teasing," "boys-against-the-girls" one (Thorne, 1986). These episodes revealed much about the principles underlying "normal" play as the girls responded to the boys' violations of those principles. They did not, however, shed light on how the boys themselves might have constructed this game on their own.

The Game

Foursquare is a common and widespread ball-bouncing game, which would be characterized as an individual (nonteam) game, with a "central person" (Gump and Sutton-Smith, 1971), whose outcome depends upon a mixture of strategy and skill (Roberts and Sutton-Smith, 1971). It was probably introduced via physical education classes (Fait, 1964; Farina, Furth, and Smith, 1959; Lindsay and Palmer, 1981). Interviews with current and prior students and staff at this school indicated that it has been a folk game in this setting, entirely initiated and sustained by children themselves, for at least twenty-five years.

The game is played on a square court, approximately twelve feet on a side and further divided into four equal squares, painted onto a paved portion of the playground. The "real game"[1] of foursquare, as these players define it, requires a minimum of five players, one player in each of the four squares and at least one other player waiting in line to replace any active player who is out. Play begins when the player in one of the squares, the "king," calls a set of rules for the following round of play. "Calls" most commonly invoke a set of rules, like "my rules" or "regular rules" or "Debbie rules," which are understood to allow certain "moves" and to prohibit others. Other "calls" selectively allow or prohibit one or more specific "moves" ("no slams or wings" or "spins are allowed"), and still others combine the two ("regular rules; duckfeet is out").

After "calling the rules," the "king" serves a large red rubber ball to one of the other players by bouncing it in that player's square. The ball is bounced from player to player until one of the players fails to return it to another player's square or until the ball bounces more than once in a player's square. That player is out. She or he leaves the court and goes to the end of the line of players waiting to get into the game. The remaining three players rotate toward the "king's" square, filling in the vacant square, and the first player in line enters the game at the square farthest from the "king." The "king" again "calls the rules" and serves the ball to begin another round of play.

Observations

I dictated my playground observations into a tape recorder for transcription and elaboration immediately following each recess period. Each entry included the identities of all of the players, their positions in the game, the rules in effect for each round of play, and the mode and rationale for resolving each round of play. I focused on different aspects of play during different sessions, including patterns of ball movement among players, verbatim transcripts of verbal interaction among players, and photographic documentation of nonverbal communication (Hughes, 1988b). I always paid special attention to disagreements and other contexts in which players were called upon to explain or justify their actions (Harre and Secord, 1972; Marsh, 1982; Much and Shweder, 1978). I also regularly visited classrooms and the staff lounge to gather information about the broader school context. I occasionally played the game with children.

Interviews

I then interviewed ten girls representing the "regular" players in nine half-hour to one-hour sessions. I always interviewed the players in groups to allow for discussion among participants, to encourage the use of shared terminology, and to allow the kind of side exchanges that often reveal private meanings. I also took care to interview groups comprised of girls from the same social cliques both together and in combination with girls from different social circles to encourage challenges to any one interpretation of what happened in the game.

Analysis

I used the juxtaposition of information derived from field observation, participant observation, and interviews, along with informant evaluation, to generate and check my understanding of principles underlying the playing of foursquare in this group. I transcribed all observations and interviews and indexed them for mention or occurrence of particular players, rules, and roles and for instances of events like disagreements, apologies, excuses, explanations, demonstrations, and instruction in which players were called upon to somehow explain or justify their actions.

I constructed a structural model of the game to represent meaningful gaming units (i.e., "calls," "serves," "outs") as a network of nodes (von Cranach, 1982) or junctures at which alternative courses of action were possible. I further characterized each unit and juncture in terms of variations in player action and players' responses to those variations (Hughes, 1983, 1991) in order to identify what players perceived to be acceptable versus unacceptable conduct in the game. I also constructed an elaborate glossary and taxonomy of game rules (Hughes, 1989). Players' own criteria for distinguishing among various rule types and functions provided additional evidence concerning general principles underlying play. Further analyses focused on relationships between stated rules and action, the rhetoric and pragmatics of actual rule usage, and issues of strategy and style as performances were managed and modulated toward preferred interpretations (Hughes, 1983, 1988a).

Playing Foursquare

At first glance, there is nothing remarkable about this play group or their game. Foursquare is commonly observed to be played predominantly by girls, and it has many characteristics associated with girls' games, like competition between individuals rather than teams, a central person, orderly waiting for turns, and a small play space. Further, social life among these girls, including their playing of foursquare, was regulated with a stereotypically feminine rhetoric of "niceness" and "friends" (Kohlberg, 1966; Maltz and Borker, 1982). They constantly talked about "being nice," "being mean," and "being friends" whenever actions in the game were being challenged or defended, and they consistently invoked these terms in interviews to explain why players acted the way they did (Hughes, 1988a).

What is significant, however, is that these girls used this stereotypically feminine rhetoric to support, and even demand, aggressive competition and to overlay a complex teamlike structure on a game that called for individual competition. The observation that girls can compete, and very aggressively, within the kind of cooperative, relationship-centered social orientation that is supposed to make them *noncompetitive* represents a significant challenge to the current wisdom concerning girls and their games. Girls' concerns about "being nice" and "being friends" have been cited to explain why girls *avoid* competition and competitive games (Gilligan, 1982), but they have never, to my knowledge, been used to explain *how* girls compete.

How this group of girls got from a rhetoric of "niceness" and "friends" to a demand for highly competitive, disequilibrial interaction is thus of considerable interest. One way into this system is to look at a highly unusual instance in which a player was *not* able to compete. In the following excerpt from my field notes, Donna,[2] a highly skilled and popular player, was "king." Under almost any other circumstances she would have played a very central role in determining who was "out," but in this case she was unable to play at all:

> Donna is "king." Her younger sister, Pam, is in square #3, a boy she has been trying to impress, John, is in square #2, and her best friend, Sally, has just come into the game.
>
> Donna calls, "Times," and takes her sweater off. Her sister, Pam, also calls, "Times," and fixes her hair. Someone in line comments, in a sarcastic tone, "*Everyone* has times."
>
> Donna calls, "Untimes," and bounces the ball back and forth with John. Her friend, Sally, takes her sweater off and ties it around her waist like Donna has just done. Pam does the same.
>
> Donna finally calls, "Fairsquare." (This call means that no one is supposed to try to get anyone else out.) She serves the ball to John, and then immediately calls, "Times." She bends down to fix her shoe laces, as the others bounce the ball among themselves. She calls, "Untimes," hits the ball once, and then calls, "Times" again, this time to fix a barrette.
>
> Donna fiddles with her hair while Sally tries to slam the ball past John, but the ball lands outside his square. Donna calls, "Untimes," then turns to Sally and says, "Sorry, Sally. I'll get you back in." [Donna and Sally's teacher cornered me in the lunchroom the next day to ask if I had any idea why Sally was suddenly refusing to talk to her former best friend.] (Field notes, Apr. 30, 1981, 27)

With this instance in mind, I want to return to the principles "be nice" and "be friends," situate them within this particular game, and then consider the more usual circumstance when players like Donna plunge into the fray instead of spending an entire exchange tying their shoes and fixing their hair.

In foursquare the principle that people should "be nice" meant not getting other players out and helping players who were out get back in. The problem was that it was not possible to be "*really* nice" and still "play the game." In practice almost anything these players could do to "be nice" to one person was by definition "mean" to somebody else. If they were "*really* nice" and didn't get anybody "out," this was not only boring but also "mean" to players who were left standing around waiting to get into the game. If, on the other hand, they tried to "be nice" to players in line by helping them get into the game, they had to "be mean" to somebody else by getting them out.

Players resolved this apparent dilemma in an interesting way. They reasoned that if an action that was "mean" to one player could be simultaneously "nice" to another player, then that meanness was not "*really* mean." Instead, in their own words, it was "nice-mean." The issue for players, then, was not how to "be nice," at least in the sense of being "*really* nice," but how to be "mean" without being "*really* mean."

This was accomplished by invoking the second basic principle of social life in this group, "be friends." As I saw it played, foursquare almost always involved a dozen or more players, and thus more than one circle of close friends. It was this *social* structure that allowed players to be "nice-mean":

Author: You said sometimes you had "friends." Is "friends" a rule?
Janet: No, it's just like ...
Pam: It's being nice to people.
Donna: It's a thing you do.
Pam: You try not to get them out.
Donna: ... You don't do it with everybody (laughs). (Field notes, Apr. 30, 1981, 12–13)

In the playing, the principle "be friends" meant that players were really obligated to "be nice" to only *some* of the other players. All players recognized this special obligation to friends and knew that it could not be fulfilled without also "being mean" to somebody else (nonfriends). This meanness was, in their view, not "*really* mean," because it was only the unintended, unfortunate, and incidental side-effect of the desire and, indeed, the obligation, to "be nice" to their "friends."[3]

Players often went to great lengths to reinforce this view of actions that would be "*really* mean" if not performed for the benefit of their friends. It was common, for example, for a player to turn to a friend in line just before hitting a hard "slam" past another player, and call, "Sally, I'll get you in!" The message: this "mean stuff" is *really* intended to "be nice" to Sally and not to "be mean" to the player who must leave the game in order for this to occur.

Perhaps paradoxically, then, the gaming principle "be nice-mean" provided a framework for competition among these players by specifying who *must* "be nice" to whom. But this also implicitly specified who *must* "be mean" to whom, and this explains the seriousness of Donna's dilemma in the play episode described earlier. She was supposed to "be nice" to all of the other players, but she could not fulfill this obligation without also "being mean" to one of them. She could not escape her dilemma by retreating into a series of time-outs, however, because obligations to "friends" were not limited to simply *not* getting them out. There was also a positive demand to get someone else out instead. Within the logic of play in this group, it was "mean" *not* to "be mean" if, as a consequence, you were *not* "nice" to your "friends." Among these players, the principle "be nice-mean" did not simply allow disequilibrial interaction, it required it as a positive reaffirmation of significant relationships.

Discussion

There is nothing in a description of the rules of this game (or, for that matter, in a description of the rhetoric of social life in this group) that would lead to the principle "be nice-mean" as a framework for competition among these players. It emerges only out of a complex interaction between social structure and game structure as the game is actually played. "Nice-mean" works to support competition here because patterns of inclusion-exclusion (Sutton-Smith, 1979) from social groups outside of the game ("friends") modified the meaning of acts of inclusion-exclusion within the game ("outs").

More significantly, this interaction between game text and social context generated a way of playing foursquare that differed in important ways from what the game rules prescribed. Foursquare is a game of individual competition, but these girls did not play it that way:

Amanda: It's supposed to be that you treat everyone equal and no one's your friend and no one's your enemy.... Everyone is just all for yourself.... That's the way it's *supposed* to be.... It's not *supposed* to be team on team.

Janet: It's not *supposed* to be (laughs).

Author: You make it sound like lots of times it is team on team, though.

Chorus: It *is!* (laughter). (Field notes, Apr. 27, 1981, 26)

This grafting of an informal team structure ("friends") onto a nonteam game provides a particularly striking example of the different kinds of images that can emerge from studies of what children play versus how they play. The game structure pictures a group of girls operating largely as disconnected individuals. This image is totally consistent with the notion that when girls do compete, they prefer the "simpler" and less divisive social structure of individual rather than team competition (Lever, 1976, 1978; Sutton-Smith, 1979). In contrast, the gaming structure pictures these same girls constructing a complex, large-group activity with a highly elaborate rule structure (Hughes, 1989) in which subgroups of players competed quite aggressively with each other. In short, it pictures girls doing all of the things they are not supposed to do given the cooperative, relationship-centered rhetoric of their play group.

These girls did systematically embed all individual action within a broader matrix of social relationships and responsibilities. But they used their rhetoric of "niceness" and "friends" to construct and manage competition within a complex group structure, not to avoid it. They took a game that specified competition among individuals and adapted it to a way of competing that was more consistent with the social organization and structure of their group. Small groups of close friends were a highly salient aspect of the social landscape outside of the game, so regardless of what the game rules prescribed, groups always vied with groups in the game.

In the present case, therefore, to have assumed that these girls competed as individuals just because they chose a nonteam game would have significantly distorted and grossly oversimplified the social reality. In fact, if I were to speculate about girls' apparent preference for nonteam games based upon the current observations, I would not conclude that girls choose these games because they prefer to compete as individuals. Instead, I might propose that girls (perhaps unlike boys, though this remains to be investigated) prefer activities where they, and not the activity, determine who will vie against whom and where competing parties represent meaningful social divisions rather than more arbitrary or skill-determined groupings.

I believe that this interpretation is at least as plausible as the rather convoluted argument that girls prefer to act as individuals because they value friends. This is true, however, only if we accept that girls can express and display a concern for others without retreating to a world of "nonaggression, interpersonal conformity, restraint and nurturance or helplessness" (Kohlberg, 1966:122). When these girls talked about "being nice," they clearly did not mean "*really* nice." The issue was how to "be mean" without being "*really* mean."

The gaming structure of foursquare also suggests greater complexity in the organization of girls' play groups and greater elaboration of the rule structures of girls' games than is commonly recognized. I suspect that the kind of subgroup within large-group organization employed by these players may be common in girls' play groups. It will only become salient, however, when researchers recognize that at least some girls do play in groups larger than dyads and triads and begin to look at how they structure those larger, more complex group activities.

Conclusion

The picture that emerges from this study, and from the few other carefully contextualized studies of how girls play (Goodwin, 1985, 1988; Goodwin and Goodwin, 1987; von Glascoe, 1980) is a complex mixture of themes that are both consonant and discrepant with the conventional wisdom concerning girls and their games. On the one hand, these studies consistently report strong themes of cooperation and a concern for close, intimate relationships, as Gilligan (1982), Kohlberg (1966), and others would predict. On the other, they provide little evidence that, as a consequence, girls just sit around with one or two close friends comparing skills or exchanging intimacies. All girls do not lack skills in organizing and sustaining large-group activities or games with highly complex and elaborate rule structures. All girls are not incapable of engaging in aggressive competition, and they do not all fall apart in the face of the slightest disagreement.[4]

Discrepancies between theory regarding girls' games and observations of their playing may be explained in a variety of ways. They may be purely an artifact of particular groups and settings, indicative of changes in girls' play in response to changes in gender role expectations and opportunities in our society (Finnan, 1982; Sutton-Smith, 1979), or they may be a reflection of the filtering of girls' play through the lens of predominantly masculine play theorizing (Schwartzman, 1978). I suspect all of these factors are involved to some degree. But I also suspect that shifting the focus from games to their playing in particular settings is a significant factor in generating more complex images of girls' play.

Gender, as it is realized in children's everyday lives, does not simply dictate one game versus another, one simple and the other complex. It is also a factor in how children play, shaping the agendas and purposes (Sabini and Silver, 1982) to which players mold their games and the manner or style (Harre and Secord, 1972) by which those purposes are pursued. The players I worked with, in fact, characterized differences between how boys and girls play games precisely along dimensions of goals and style:

Author: You think you're better than the boys?
Donna: Yeah, I think all the girls are.
Author: So how come the girls are saying that the boys always get them out?
Kathy: [The boys] don't think about anything else but getting you out. So maybe the girls might be better at the game, but they're better at getting people out. And that's *all* they do in the game.
Janet: Yeah.
Author: Well some people think that the game is about getting people

out, that that's the point of the game. That's not really the point
of the game?

Janet: Umm, it is, sort of.

Kathy: It is, sort of. But you don't have to do it *all* the time.

Janet: You have to do it with style, kind of. You have to do it in style.
   (Field notes, Apr. 29, 1981, 4–5)

The concerns displayed here for *how* things are done (for "style") and
for modulation of the single-minded pursuit of the stated point of the
game ("outs") in light of principles basic to the social life of the group (like
"friends") were dominant themes among these players. It is not true,
however, that boys did not share the same concerns. At least in the
contexts observed in this study, boys were quite concerned about more
than simply "getting people out." They very systematically targeted girls,
and it was this *selectivity,* along with the "*really* mean" ways they pursued
it, that so irked the girls.

Clearly both boys and girls make creative use of the performance
frames constituted by their games. This dimension of children's play has
yet to be tapped, however. It cannot be explored by studies contrasting
qualities of boys' versus girls' games or the rhetoric of social life in boys'
and girls' play groups. It requires, as Goldstein (1971) suggests, carefully
grounded description and analysis of the rules by which children actually
do play their games. Girls are quite capable of taking highly stereotypical
themes and pastimes and doing quite unstereotypical things with them.
Since this is in the nature of stereotypes, I have no reason to believe that
boys are any less capable in this regard. The conventional wisdom concerning boys' games is as much in need of reevaluation as current images
of girls and their games.

Given their theoretical and political significance, I believe that children's
games are worth another look, this time, however, from the perspective of
how children actually play them and with an eye to the variety of ways in
which both boys and girls go about initiating and sustaining complex
episodes of social life. As Thorne (1990) has argued, and Goodwin (1988)
and Goodwin and Goodwin (1987) have demonstrated, such studies are
likely to reveal significant areas of overlap across gender lines as they are
currently drawn, and to provide a counterpoint to the rhetoric of contrast,
difference, and deficit that now dominates the literature in this area.

Notes

An early draft of this chapter was presented as part of the panel "Ethnographic
Studies of Cooperation and Competition in Girls' Play" in 1986 at the annual

meeting of the American Folklore Society, Baltimore, Md. I would like to thank Barrie Thorne, Candy Goodwin, Bruce Jackson, and the editors and reviewers of this volume for helpful comments and suggestions in the preparation of the manuscript.

1. In all discussions of the game of foursquare, the children's own terminology has been enclosed in quotation marks.

2. The children's names have been changed throughout.

3. This concern for the motive and intent underlying an action over its form was a highly salient aspect of play in this setting and a significant factor in the philosophical complexity of disagreements and disputes among these players (Hughes, 1988a, 1991). Interestingly, von Glascoe described similar patterns among a group of girls she observed playing redlight in Southern California: "A surprising order of philosophical inquiry emerges in the course of (resolving disputes). Arguments are grounded in terms of player-members' doctrines of intentional acts, unconscious acts, "accidental" acts, goal-directedness of acts and fate-determined acts" (1980:229–30).

4. Contrary to Lever's (1976) report, the players I observed fought quite vigorously and quite often, but they never abandoned the game. In fact, Lever appears to be the only researcher to make this claim, even though it is very widely cited in discussions of girls' play groups. Goodwin and Goodwin (1987) not only find that disagreements are common among girls but that their structure and modes of resolution may be even more complex than those found among boys.

References Cited

Avedon, Elliott M. 1971. "The Structural Elements of Games." In *The Study of Games,* ed. Elliott M. Avedon and Brian Sutton-Smith, 419–26. New York: Wiley.

Bauman, Richard. 1975. "Verbal Art as Performance." *American Anthropologist* 77:290–311.

Ben-Amos, Dan, and Kenneth S. Goldstein. 1975. *Folklore: Performance and Communication.* The Hague: Mouton.

Brenner, Michael. 1982. "Actors' Powers." In *The Analysis of Action,* ed. Mario von Cranach and Rom Harre, 213–29. Cambridge: Cambridge University Press.

Collett, Peter. 1977. "The Rules of Conduct." In *Social Rules and Social Behaviour,* ed. Peter Collett, 1–27. Oxford: Basil Blackwell.

Corsaro, William A., and Donna Eder. 1990. "Children's Peer Cultures." *Annual Review of Sociology* 16:197–220.

Denzin, Norman K. 1977. *Childhood Socialization.* San Francisco: Jossey-Bass.

Eifermann, Rivka. 1968. *School Children's Games.* Washington, D.C.: U.S. Office of Education.

Emmott, Shelagh. 1985. "Sex Differences in Children's Play: Implications for Cognition." *International Journal of Women's Studies* 8 (5): 449–56.

Evans, John. 1986. "In Search of the Meaning of Play." *New Zealand Journal of Health, Physical Education, and Recreation* 19 (2): 16–19.

Fait, Hollis F. 1964. *Physical Education for the Elementary School Child*. Philadelphia: W. B. Saunders.

Factor, June. 1988. *Captain Cook Chased a Chook: Children's Folklore in Australia*. Ringwood, Australia: Penguin.

Farina, Albert M., Sol H. Furth, and Joseph M. Smith. 1959. *Growth through Play*. Englewood Cliffs, N.J.: Prentice-Hall.

Fine, Gary Alan. 1981. "Friends, Impression Management, and Preadolescent Behavior." In *The Development of Children's Friendships,* ed. Steven R. Asher and John M. Gottman, 29–52. Cambridge: Cambridge University Press.

———. 1983. *Shared Fantasy*. Chicago: University of Chicago Press.

Finnan, Christine R. 1982. "The Ethnography of Children's Spontaneous Play." In *Doing the Ethnography of Schooling,* ed. George Spindler, 356–80. New York: Holt, Rinehart, and Winston.

Gilligan, Carol. 1982. *In a Different Voice: Psychological Theory and Women's Development*. Cambridge, Mass.: Harvard University Press.

Gilligan, Carol, Nona P. Lyons, and Trudy J. Hanmer, eds. 1990. *Making Connections: The Relational Worlds of Adolescent Girls at Emma Willard School*. Cambridge, Mass.: Harvard University Press.

Goldstein, Kenneth S. 1971. "Strategy in Counting Out: An Ethnographic Field Study." In *The Study of Games,* ed. Elliott M. Avedon and Brian Sutton-Smith, 167–78. New York: Wiley.

Goodwin, Marjorie Harness. 1985. "The Serious Side of Jump Rope: Conversational Practices and Social Organization in the Frame of Play." *Journal of American Folklore* 98 (389): 315–30.

———. 1988. "Cooperation and Competition across Girls' Play Activities." In *Gender and Discourse: The Power of Talk,* ed. S. Fisher and A. Todd, 55–94. New York: Ablex.

Goodwin, Marjorie Harness, and Charles Goodwin. 1987. "Children's Arguing." In *Language, Gender, and Sex in Comparative Perspective,* ed. Susan Philips, Susan Steele, and Christina Tanz, 200–248. Cambridge: Cambridge University Press.

Gump, Paul, and Brian Sutton-Smith. 1971. "The 'It' Role in Children's Games." In *The Study of Games,* ed. Elliott M. Avedon and Brian Sutton-Smith, 390–97. New York: Wiley.

Harre, Rom, and Paul Secord. 1972. *The Explanation of Social Behavior*. Totowa, N.J.: Littlefield, Adams.

Harragan, Betty L. 1977. *Games Mother Never Taught You*. New York: Rawson.

Hartup, Willard W. 1983. "Peer Relations." In *Handbook of Child Psychology,* 4th ed., vol. 1, ed. Paul H. Mussen, 103–96. New York: Wiley.

Hughes, Linda A. 1983. "Beyond the Rules of the Game: Girls' Gaming at a Friends' School." Ph.D. diss., University of Pennsylvania.

———. 1988a. " 'But That's Not *Really* Mean' ": Competing in a Cooperative Mode." *Sex Roles* 19 (11–12): 669–87.

———. 1988b. "Play Space and Personal Space." Paper presented at the annual meeting of the Association for the Study of Play, Berkeley, Calif.

————. 1989. "Foursquare: A Glossary and 'Native' Taxonomy of Game Rules." *Play and Culture* 2:103–36.

————. 1991. "A Conceptual Framework for the Study of Children's Gaming." *Play and Culture* 4 (3): 284–301.

Kohlberg, Lawrence. 1966. "A Cognitive-Developmental Analysis of Children's Sex-Role Concepts and Attitudes." In *The Development of Sex Differences,* ed. Eleanor E. Maccoby, 82-173. Stanford: Stanford University Press.

————. 1981. *The Philosophy of Moral Development.* San Francisco: Harper and Row.

Lehman, Harvey C., and Paul A. Witty. 1927. *The Psychology of Play Activities.* New York: A. S. Barnes.

Lever, Janet. 1976. "Sex Differences in the Games Children Play." *Social Problems* 23 (4): 478–87.

————. 1978. "Sex Differences in the Complexity of Children's Play and Games." *American Sociological Review* 43:471–83.

Lindsay, Peter, and Denise Palmer. 1981. *Playground Game Characteristics of Brisbane Primary School Children.* Canberra: Australian Government Publishing Service.

Maccoby, Eleanor E., and Carol N. Jacklin. 1987. "Gender Segregation in Childhood." *Advances in Child Development and Behavior* 20:239–87.

Maltz, Daniel N., and Ruth A. Borker. 1982. "A Cultural Approach to Male-Female Miscommunication." In *Language and Social Identity,* ed. John J. Gumperz, 196–216. Cambridge: Cambridge University Press.

Marsh, P. 1982. "Rules and the Organization of Action." In *The Analysis of Action,* ed. Mario von Cranach and Rom Harre, 231–41. Cambridge: Cambridge University Press.

Maynard, Douglas W. 1985. "How Children Start Arguments." *Language in Society* 14:1–30.

Much, Nancy C., and Richard A. Shweder. 1978. "Speaking of Rules: The Analysis of Culture in Breach." In *Moral Development,* ed. William Damon, 19–39. San Francisco: Jossey-Bass.

Piaget, Jean. [1932] 1965. *The Moral Judgment of the Child.* New York: Free Press.

Pitcher, Evelyn G., and Lynn H. Shultz. 1983. *Boys and Girls at Play: The Development of Sex Roles.* New York: Praeger.

Polgar, Sylvia K. 1976. "The Social Context of Games or When Is Play Not Play." *Sociology of Education* 49:265–71.

Roberts, John M., and Brian Sutton-Smith. 1971. "Child Training and Game Involvement." In *The Study of Games,* ed. Elliott M. Avedon and Brian Sutton-Smith, 465–87. New York: Wiley.

Sabini, John, and Maury Silver. 1982. *Moralities of Everyday Life.* New York: Oxford University Press.

Schwartzman, Helen. 1978. *Transformations: The Anthropology of Children's Play.* New York: Plenum.

Shimanoff, Susan B. 1980. *Communication Rules: Theory and Research.* Beverly Hills, Calif.: Sage.

Shwayder, D. S. 1965. *The Stratification of Behaviour.* London: Routledge and Kegan Paul.

Sutton-Smith, Brian. 1979. "The Play of Girls." In *Becoming Female,* ed. Claire B. Kopp and Martha Kirkpatrick, 229–57. New York: Plenum.

Tannen, Deborah. 1990. *You Just Don't Understand: Women and Men in Conversation.* New York: William Morrow.

Thorne, Barrie. 1986. "Girls and Boys Together . . . but Mostly Apart: Gender Arrangements in Elementary Schools." In *Relationships and Development,* ed. Willard W. Hartup and Zick Rubin, 167–84. Hillsdale, N.J.: Erlbaum.

———. 1990. "Children and Gender: Constructions of Difference." In *Theoretical Perspectives on Sexual Difference,* ed. Deborah Rhode, 100–113. New Haven, Conn.: Yale University Press.

von Cranach, Mario. 1982. "The Psychological Study of Goal-Directed Action: Basic Issues." In *The Analysis of Action,* ed. Mario von Cranach and Rom Harre, 35–73. Cambridge: Cambridge University Press.

von Glascoe, Christine. 1980. "The Work of Playing 'Redlight.'" In *Play and Culture,* ed. Helen Schwartzman, 228–30. Westpoint, N.Y.: Leisure Press.

Youniss, James. 1980. *Parents and Peers in Social Development.* Chicago: University of Chicago Press.

Accomplishing Social Organization in Girls' Play: Patterns of Competition and Cooperation in an African American Working-Class Girls' Group

Investigations of female interaction patterns have been guided by perspectives that have limited our analysis of them. In an attempt to characterize women as speaking in a different voice recent research on female interaction has tended to examine those features of female communication that are clearly *different from* those of males to the exclusion of those that females and males share. For example, researchers have examined cooperative aspects of female language usage while they have largely ignored ways in which disagreement may be expressed.[1]

Psychologists have argued that concern for the details of legalistic dispute is critical for the development of moral judgment (Piaget, 1965:83). Recognition of girls' competence in negotiation thus has enormous import for theories of female development. Typically, however, girls are seen as avoiding direct competition and having little concern for negotiational involvements (Gilligan, 1982; Lever, 1976; Sutton-Smith, 1979). Studies of naturally occurring friendship groups, including those of Norwegian nursery school children (Berentzen, 1984); white, middle-class elementary school children (Hughes, 1988); white, middle-class junior high school children (Eder, 1990); and black, white, and Puerto Rican junior high school children (Shuman, 1986) have contradicted these interpretations of girls' interaction, which are based largely on interview data. For example, in her study of foursquare among middle-class white children, Hughes (1988 and this volume) has elegantly demonstrated that girls strategically mold and modulate the raw materials of their games in line with complex friendship alliances.

My own ethnographic studies of urban African American working-class girls also reveal the competence girls display when negotiating social order. However, the forms of social organization that girls select to carry out their play vary across play activities. Here, I will focus on sequences of directives or speech actions that try to get someone to do something (Austin, 1962) and the responses to those directives. I will examine these sequences within task activities and pretend play. In this way I will investigate how girls select different forms of a similar action to accomplish distinctive types of social order.

I will begin by examining how girls interact as they undertake a task activity—making rings to wear from the rims of glass bottles. When girls organize tasks, they select an egalitarian social structure, thereby avoiding distinctions between participants. Such a form of organization is consistent with the way in which they normally conduct their daily interactions with one another. This does not, however, provide a comprehensive picture of their modes of interaction. I have found that girls use competitive as well as cooperative talk. For example, in jumping rope (Goodwin, 1985), repairing utterances (Goodwin, 1983), or disagreeing with one another (Goodwin and Goodwin, 1987), girls use argumentative speech forms. Girls do not, however, customarily use bald commands, insults, and threats—actions that are commonplace among boys. Such actions are reserved for situations in which girls negatively sanction the behavior of one another. Across different domains girls exhibit a range of speech patterns and social organization.

Fieldwork and Theoretical Approach

The present study is based on fieldwork among a group of children in an African American working-class neighborhood of Southwest Philadelphia whom I encountered during a walk around my neighborhood. Seeing a group of girls jumping rope, I asked if I could watch them and told them that I was interested in making observations of their play over a long period of time because I was doing a study of the everyday activities of children. I informed them that I wanted as accurate a record of what went on as possible and therefore would bring a tape recorder after two months. At first I thought I would study only girls' activities; this plan changed when the boys insisted that their activities were equally as interesting and asked if I could record them as well. The parents of each child were visited and told about my purposes on the street.

I traveled with the children as they went about their activities on the street while I had a cassette recorder with an internal microphone over my shoulder. Because I used only the internal microphone, I never had to actively point something at the children to record them and could get good records of their conversations simply by staying with them. I attempted to minimize my interaction with the children so as to disturb as little as possible the activities under study. My role was different from that of most anthropologists, in that I was more an observer of the people I was studying than a participant in their activities.

The values of the children's parents are mainstream, using Hannerz's (1969:38–42) classification. The language spoken by them was Black English Vernacular; in analyzing my transcripts of the talk of these children I found it similar to that of African American speakers in Harlem (Labov, 1972:184). I observed the children (whom I will call the Maple Street group) for a year and a half (1970–71) in their neighborhood, focusing on how they used language within interaction to organize their everyday activities.[2] The children ranged in age from four through fourteen and spent much of their time in four same age/sex groups. Here I will be concerned principally with older children, ages nine to fourteen.[3]

As the children played I tape-recorded their conversation. Rather than being based on a laboratory model, the methodology I used was ethnographic and designed to capture as accurately as possible the structure of events in the children's world as they unfolded in the ordinary settings where they habitually occurred. In all, over two hundred hours of transcribed talk form the corpus of this study. Sequences of actual interaction are thus available for other researchers to conduct comparative work. The approach used in this chapter, conversation analysis, constitutes an approach to the study of naturally occurring interaction developed within sociology by the late Harvey Sacks and his colleagues.[4]

Organizing a Task Activity

The ways in which speakers shape directives and recipients reply to them provide for a range of alternative types of social arrangements between participants. Some directive/response sequences differentiate between participants and result in asymmetrical relationships. Directives may be constructed in a variety of different ways. For example they can be phrased as imperatives (i.e., "Do X!"), a format that is frequently heard by its addressee as imposing (Brown and Levinson, 1978:100–101) and thus constituting an aggravated speech act (Labov and Fanshel, 1977:84–86);

alternatively, directives may be softened or mitigated (Labov and Fanshel, 1977:84–86), for example, phrased as requests ("Could you please do X?"). Among the Maple Street boys, those assuming a position of authority utilize aggravated requests, while those occupying subordinate roles use more mitigated forms.

Girls use a variety of directives in organizing a task activity. In making rings from glass bottles, girls carefully scrape bottle rims over metal sewer covers or other rough surfaces so that the rims break evenly, leaving as few jagged edges as possible. The girls must procure and allocate resources and establish techniques for the objects' manufacture. In accomplishing a task activity, girls participate jointly in decision-making with minimal negotiation of status. The following interaction, which occurred over a two-hour period, provides examples of the types of directives typically found among the girls:

(1)   *Girls are searching for bottles to make rings.*
    Kerry: Well let's go– let's go around the corner–
              Let's– let's go around the corner where whatchacallem.

(2)   *Girls are looking for bottles.*
    Kerry: Let's go.
              There may be some more on Sixty-ninth Street.
    Martha: Come on.
              Let's turn back y'all so we can safe keep em.
              Come on. Let's go get some.

(3)   *Girls are looking for bottles.*
    Martha: Let's go around Subs and Suds.
    Bea: Let's ask her "Do you have any bottles."

Girls' directives are constructed as suggestions for action in the future. Syntactically, the forms used by the boys generally differentiate speaker and hearer. A boy playing leader orders another to do something. In addition insult terms included in the directive provide derogatory depictions of the addressee's character. Such features of gender differentiation in directive use are illustrated in the following examples, taken from a two-hour session in which boys were making slingshots. The boys have divided themselves into groups led by Tony and Malcolm.

(4)   *to a boy who attempts to join Tony's group*
    Tony: Go downstairs.
              I don't care *what* you say.
              You aren't—You ain't no good
              so go down*stairs.*

(5)   *regarding a hanger Ossie is cutting with pliers*
    Malcolm: Put your foot on it stupid.
              You afraid?

(6)   *regarding coat hangers*
Malcolm: Gimme the *things* dummies.
            If you expect me to bend em.
            Y'all act dumb.

(7)
Malcolm: PLIERS. I WANT THE PLIERS! (0.6)
            Man y'all gonna have to get y'all own wire
            cutters // if this the way y'all gonna be.
Pete: Okay. Okay.

Alternatively, subordinates make requests to team leaders:

(8)   *taking a hanger*
Tokay: Can I have some hangers?
Malcolm: Put that thing *back*.

(9)
Tommy: Could Pete be on your side,
            and I be on Malcolm's side?
            Malcolm could I be on your side?
Malcolm: *Heck* no!

The verb used by the girls—*let's*—signals a proposal rather than either a command or a request and, as such, shows neither special deference toward the other party (as a request does) nor makes claims about special rights of control over the other (as a command does). Thus, through the way in which they format their directives the girls make visible an undifferentiated "egalitarian" relationship between speaker and addressee(s). The structure of directives used to organize making rings is similar to directives used in other joint tasks, such as playing jacks (i.e., "Let's play some more jacks."), jumping rope (i.e. "Let's play 'one two three footsies.' "), or hunting for turtles (i.e., "Let's look around. See what we can find.").

When directives are formulated to place demands on recipients, they may also contain an account that provides explicit reasons for why an action should be undertaken. The leaders for the boys use directives that commonly display no obvious reason why certain tasks need to be performed, except for the leader's own whims ("PLIERS. I WANT THE PLIERS!"). By way of contrast, girls' accounts consider the benefits that will accrue to all members of the group. Turns in which this occurs are marked with arrows:

(10)
Martha: Bea you know what we could do, (0.5)
            We gotta *clean* em first,
            We gotta *clean* em.
Bea: Huh,
Martha: We gotta *clean* em first. // You know,

Bea:	I know.
→	Cuz they got germs.
	[[
Martha:	Wash em and stuff cuz just in case
→	they got germs on em.
	And then you clean em,
	[[
Bea:	I got some paints.
	(3.5)
Martha:	Clean em, and then we *clean* em and
	we gotta be careful with em
	before we get the glass cutters.
→	You know we gotta be careful with em cuz it cuts easy.

In the boys' group, directing activity is generally the purview of specific boys who assume the position of leaders (Goodwin and Goodwin, 1990); however, in the girls' group proposals for courses of action can be made by many different participants, and the girls generally agree to the suggestions of others. For example, consider the following in which the girls are bringing home a supply of bottles to make rings:

(11)

Kerry:	Hey y'all. Let's use these first
	and then come back and get the rest
	cuz it's too *many* of em.
Martha:	That *right.*
Kerry:	We can *l*imp back so nobody knows where
	we *g*ettin them from.
	(0.8)
Martha:	That's right.
Kerry:	And w— and wash our hands.
	And wash your hands when you get *f*inish now.
Martha:	If the boys try to follow us we don't know. Okay?
Kerry:	Yep.

In terms of both how directives are constructed and the way in which others respond to them, the girls' system of directive use displays similarity and equality rather than differentiation among group members. Girls characteristically phrase their directives as proposals for future activity. They tend to leave the time at which the action being proposed should be performed somewhat open. Boys acting as leaders (who in this case are in control of both the resources and the activity space), however, specify that they want tasks done on their terms:

(12)   *asking for pliers.*

Malcolm:	Gimme the thing.

Ossie:	Wait a minute. I gotta chop it.
Malcolm:	Come on.
Ossie:	I gotta chop it.
Malcolm:	Come on Ossie.
	You gonna be with them?
	Give it to me.
	I'll show you.
Ossie:	I already had it before you.
Malcolm:	So? I brought them out here.
	They mine.
	So I use em when I feel like it.

Rather than differentiating speaker from hearer, a girl issuing a directive is usually included as one of the agents in the action to be performed. Within task activities a symmetrical form of social organization is established by the girls in their same-sex group. However in other circumstances girls can select more aggravated forms and construct quite different forms of social organization.

Pretend Play in a Girls' Mixed-Age Group

Within dramatic play participants must sustain a pretend reality, differentiate social identities, and develop a story line. Throughout pretend play children may choose alternative social and interactive identities: character in the drama, member of the play group, or commenter on the interaction in progress. Much of Goffman's (1974) frame analysis is relevant here in that participants animate characters throughout their play and take up different stances vis-à-vis these characters.

To illustrate social organizational possibilities within fantasy play I will investigate a specific instance of playing house. Figure 7.1 illustrates the dramatized kinship relationships between the two separate households that Patrice and Martha, who enact sisters playing mothers, establish at the onset of this session.[5] During the dramatic play Landa (age ten) enacts the part of a childless sister of Patrice (ten) and Martha (twelve), who pretend to be household heads. At the onset of play, Bea (twelve), Brenda (eight), and Kerry (twelve) take on the roles of Patrice's children. Drucilla (seven) and Prestina (five) are Martha's children.

In the development of task activities, the girls use the directive *let's,* which includes one's self within the scope of the action, and they share in decision-making, developing an egalitarian social organization. When playing house, girls enacting the role of a mother address their children with directives that are very similar in structure to those that mothers or caretakers use. Such patterning is consistent with other research on role-playing among

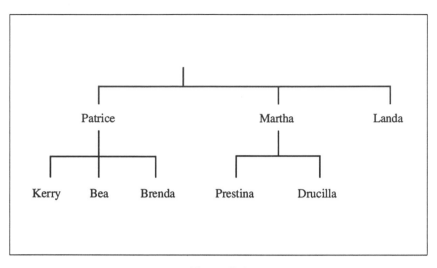

Figure 7.1

children's groups (Andersen, 1978:89; Corsaro, 1985:82; Ervin-Tripp, 1982:36; Garvey, 1974, 1977a; Mitchell-Kernan and Kernan, 1977:201–7; Sachs, 1987), which has demonstrated that directives constitute the principal means through which children realize positions of dominance and submission between characters, such as those in the mother/child relationship. In house a hierarchical form of social organization is visible in both the enactment of roles and the management of activity. Girls enacting the role of mother address their children with directives that are imperatives delivered loudly and with exaggerated emphatic stress:[6]

(13)

> Martha: BRING THOSE CARDS BACK,
> BRING THAT BOOK IN THE HOUSE AND C:OME HOME!
> Don't *climb* over that way.
> You climb over the *right* way.

(14)

> Martha: Drucilla, BRENDA, Prestina,
> GET IN THE CAR! Get in the car.
> Sheila and Brenda, and all y'all get in the car. =
> Where Drucilla at. GET IN THE CAR.
> YOU GOIN OVER *MY* HOUSE. GO ON OVER AND GET—
> UH—WHERE'S DRUCILLA AT.

Younger children, however, use mitigated directives that display their subordinate status in requests for permission, such as "Mommy may *we* go out and play?" or "Can I hold your book?"

In pretend play not only is there asymmetry in the enactment of directives but also in the management of the activity. As overseers of the unfolding drama, both Patrice and Martha monitor the actions of participants and control how roles are played:

(15)

Patrice:	HEY BRENDA YOU OUGHTA // be sleep!
Kerry:	I can't even get her in the bed.
Patrice:	I know.
Patrice:	SHE'S NOT // EVEN PLAYIN RIGHT.
	SHE NOT EVEN *PLAYIN* RIGHT.
Martha:	BRENDA PLAY RIGHT.
	THAT'S WHY NOBODY WANT YOU FOR A CHILD.
Patrice:	GET IN THERE AND GO TO SLEEP!

Girls in the position of mother can thus dictate for others the dimensions of play *outside* the frame of fantasy as well as within it. They not only can control who can play what roles but also how they play them.

Asymmetry is extended to other aspects of the activity as well. For example, while one might expect a certain equality among two girls who play mother, only one of them characteristically makes decisions for the group. In this case Martha assumes the right to change frame through pretend directives, and, in general, it is she who plays the role of stage manager:

(16)

Martha:	Hey y'all.=Pretend it's a—like—
	it's about twelve o'clock.=okay?
Patrice:	It's twelve o'clock in the afternoon
	so y'all should settle down.

Responses to pretend directives are not randomly distributed among participants. While many girls are present, generally the person responding to a request to pretend is another girl situated in an equivalent role. In these examples Patrice, a household head, is the principal party who replies to Martha's overt proposals for shifts in activity. Martha's position of authority over Patrice can also be seen in the way she gives imperatives to her:

(17)

Martha:	Where Patrice go.
	You better get your children in the *house*.

Repeatedly Martha's definition of the situation is asserted above Patrice's. In the following situation after Martha states that she has to fix dinner (line 2), Patrice (line 3) offers an alternative plan of action using a modal

verb: "*They* could eat dinner with *us.*" This suggestion is flatly opposed
in a next turn by Martha (lines 4–5), and subsequently the group follows
up on Martha's plan.

(18)

1	Martha:	Don't sit over here or stand over here
2		cuz I gotta fix dinner.
3	Patrice:	*They* could eat dinner with *us,*
4	Martha:	No *uh* uh I'm fixin—I brought all this food out here
5		and they gonna eat over here.

Not only do girls establish hierarchical arrangements among members
of their groups but in addition they form coalitions against particular girls.
Among the Maple Street girls, negotiating who is to enact the most valued
roles is an important feature of social organization. The sibling of the
principal decision maker is the most coveted position, because people in
these two positions are perceived to be best friends. Here, Martha's best
friend, Landa, had no difficulty acquiring the identity of sibling sister.
However, considerable negotiation took place regarding Kerry's identity
thirty minutes into the dramatic play, as the girls conspired to prevent
Kerry from enacting the role of Martha's sister:

(19)

1	Kerry:	I'm not your daughter.=all right? Um,
2		I'm—I'm her *sister.*
3	Patrice:	N:OO! // You—
4	Martha:	YOU CAN'T BE STAYIN WITH ME!
5	Kerry:	I know.=I'm stayin with *her*! But I
6		can-
		[
7	Patrice:	YOU—Uh *uh*! You—you *my* daughter.
8	Kerry:	Mm *mm.*
9	Patrice:	Uh *huh.* // Until *Bea* get back.
10	Kerry:	*Bea* your daughter.
11	Patrice:	I know.=I—
		[
12	Martha:	WELL HOW CAN YOU BE HER *SISTER,*
13	Patrice:	UH *HUH* BECAUSE *WE* S://ISTERS,
14		HOW CAN YOU BE *HER* SISTER.
15	Martha:	NOW HOW CAN YOU BE *MY* SISTER,
16	Patrice:	How can you be my // sister.
17	Landa:	That's r— that's right.
18		(0.8)
19	Landa:	We all three *sisters.*
20	Martha:	I *know.*
21	Landa:	Well how come you don't wanna be

22		her daughter.
		[
23	Brenda:	THERE Martha, Landa // and
24	Kerry:	I'm another sister.
25	Brenda:	There Martha and Landa is her—
		[
26	Martha:	N:O.
27	Brenda:	Is your—and // she—
28	Martha:	WELL YOU STAY HERE WITH *HER*.

The dispute about Kerry's position in playing house begins in lines 1–2, when Kerry proposes that she enact the role of Patrice's sister rather than that of her daughter. This proposal is protested by the other girls. The argument nears closure when Kerry (line 24) states, "I'm another sister." Subsequently, Martha (line 28) concedes that she can be a sister under the condition that she live with Patrice. In this way Martha terminates the dispute while distancing herself from Kerry. Thus in the midst of dramatic play, as in other interactions (Goodwin, 1982), girls take care to delineate their friendship alliances. Although there is considerable debate, the girls continue playing together for nearly an hour after the dispute is resolved.

Conclusion

Various researchers (Gilligan, 1982:242; Lever, 1976; Sutton-Smith, 1979) have proposed that the structure of games itself influences the form of social organization that children evolve. As the argument goes, because girls do not participate in complex games (team sports having a large number of players, high degrees of interdependence of players, role differentiation, rule specificity, and competitiveness) with respect to males, females are less able to develop the negotiational skills that prepare one for successful performance in a wide range of work settings in large, formal organizations (Lever, 1974:240–41).

As can be seen from the data on playing house, within a fairly unstructured form of play (that is, a form of play with relatively few explicit rules), an incipient hierarchy emerges. As within any activity requiring the close coordination of participants in differentiated roles, decisions regarding how the play is to proceed must be made from moment to moment; within house this allows for the emergence of the role of manager of the activity. Although both girls playing mother may give directives to children in the play frame, one girl in particular controls the staging of the activity. She makes frequent use of imperatives in her talk and, in general, uses aggravated directives to oversee aspects of the activity. Concurrently, those in positions subordinate to the principal character (as both characters in the drama and actors in the dramatic play) display their positions of subordination vis-à-vis those in a position of authority, thereby constructing complementary roles.

Within dramatic play, some girls further create a differentiation of participants through the ways in which they criticize certain other girls or exclude them from valued positions. Alliances of girls against particular individuals are played out in a fashion that resembles alliance formation in a gossip event called he-said-she-said (Goodwin, 1980b, 1990). Supportive evidence for girls' competence in developing elaborate forms of social organization while playing games comes from Hughes's (1988 and this volume) studies of white middle-class girls; within a nonteam game such as foursquare girls evolve quite sophisticated forms of social organization that entail contests between incipient teams.

In addition to countering several popular notions concerning the nature of girls' interaction patterns, the data presented here support the notion that the play girls prefer is highly complex. Fantasy enactments pose a range of problems absent from other play activities. At each point participants have to determine what it is that they are doing now, displaying for others what constitutes the common scene in front of them. Pretend play differs from other domains of play in that children enact vocal and nonvocal scripts appropriate to their relative positions in a pretend reality, endeavoring to sustain the definition of the situation as play. This is accomplished through skillful managing of staged identities, artful uses of a repertoire of voices, and careful attention to the framing of interaction. The competencies of girls in elaborating dramatic play argue for a view of such activities as equally as complex as those in team sports. Indeed, I would argue, as has Garvey, that pretend play is perhaps one of the most complex kinds of play conducted in childhood since it is likely to encompass most, if not all, of the resources at a child's command and to integrate them into a whole (Garvey, 1977b:79).

The form of social organization that evolves in the midst of pretend play differs from that which characterizes girls' task activities. Girls interpret task activities as needing relatively little control. In coordinating the actions of participants, events are treated as involving parallel rather than tightly interdigitated events, which are typical of a game such as jump rope or house. Girls make use of directives that include the speaker as well as others within the scope of the action and suggest, rather than demand, the next course of action. In addition, making decisions regarding what happens next is rotated among group members. When aggravated directives are used in this frame they are in some way modified, either through accounts that specify safety of the individual involved or benefits for the entire group.

Girls thus exhibit a range of different types of social organization in their activities. Many studies of gender differences tend, as Thorne argues, to promote the notion of separate worlds of males and females—to abstract gender from social context, to assume males and females are qualitatively and permanently different (1986:168). Here I have attempted to show that some features of girls' activities are hierarchically structured, resembling the ways in which boys structure their play (Goodwin, 1980a, 1990).

The findings reported here would thus seem to counter many of the prevalent notions about girls' social organization. Typically, girls are seen as avoiding direct competition and spending little time on negotiational involvements (Gilligan, 1982; Lever, 1976; Sutton-Smith, 1979). Such a view supports the perception of females as powerless speakers. As I have demonstrated within the "house" frame, girls devote considerable attention to negotiating features of their play, making use of language that expresses disagreement in an aggravated fashion. Moreover, such negotiation takes place without the disruption of the ongoing activity or a breech in social relationships, as is frequently argued to occur among girls (Gilligan, 1982:9–10; Lever, 1976:482). The form of differentiated social organization within a comparatively large cluster that girls evolve within playing house also defies the often-cited typifications of girls as interacting within small groups or friendship pairs (Eder and Hallinan, 1978; Maltz and Borker, 1983; Waldrop and Halverson, 1975). The fact that girls' social organization varies substantially across different domains makes it imperative that studies of girls' play be grounded in detailed analyses of specific contexts of use.

Notes

1. For reviews of the literature on politeness in women's talk see Brown (1976); Kramarae (1981); McConnell-Ginet, Borker, and Furman (1980); McConnel-Ginet (1983); Philips (1980); Thorne and Henley (1975), Thorne, Kramarae, and Henley (1983); West and Zimmerman (1985).

2. For a more complete description of this fieldwork, see Goodwin (1990).

3. All names of people and places are fictitious. Data are transcribed according to a modified version of the system developed by Jefferson and described in Sacks, Schegloff, and Jefferson (1974:731–33). Double obliques (//) indicate the point at which a current speaker's talk overlaps the talk of another. An alternative system is to place a left bracket ([) at the point of overlapping talk. Punctuation marks are not used as grammatical symbols, but mark intonation. A period indicates falling intonation. A comma is used for falling/rising intonation. Question marks are

used for rising intonation. Numbers in parentheses (0.5) indicate elapsed time in tenths of seconds. A colon indicates that the sound preceding the colon has been lengthened. When one strip of talk follows another with noticeable quickness an equal sign is placed between the two utterances. Arrows are used to call attention to particular lines within a longer transcript. Italic type indicates stressing and may involve pitch or volume. Uppercase indicates increased volume. Materials in double parentheses indicate features of the audio materials other than actual verbalizations.

4. Important collections of research in conversation analysis can be found in Atkinson and Heritage (1984), Button and Lee (1987), Schenkein (1978), the special double issue of *Sociological Inquiry* edited by Zimmerman and West (1980), and a special issue of *Human Studies* (1986) edited by Button, Drew, and Heritage. Turn-taking is most extensively analyzed in Sacks, Schegloff, and Jefferson (1974). For an analysis of both basic ideas in ethnomethodology and work in conversation analysis that grows from it see Heritage (1984).

5. The importance of female sibling ties among African American families has been discussed by Aschenbrenner (1975), Ladner (1971), McAdoo (1983), and Stack (1974). McLoyd, Ray, and Etter-Lewis (1985:41) and Pitcher and Schultz (1983) report that among preschool children there is generally little development of the father/husband role during pretend play.

6. The ring-making sequence occurred on September 28, 1970, while the playing house sequence took place on October 24, 1970.

References Cited

Andersen, Elaine Slosberg. 1978. "Learning to Speak with Style: A Study of the Sociolinguistic Skills of Children." Ph.D. diss., Stanford University.

Aschenbrenner, J. 1975. *Lifelines: Black Families in Chicago*. New York: Holt, Rinehart, and Winston.

Atkinson, J. Maxwell, and John Heritage. 1984. *Structures of Social Action*. Cambridge: Cambridge University Press.

Austin, J. L. 1962. *How to Do Things with Words*. Oxford: Oxford University Press.

Berentzen, Sigurd. 1984. *Children Constructing Their Social World: An Analysis of Gender Contrast in Children's Interaction in a Nursery School*. Bergen Occasional Papers in Social Anthropology, no. 36. Bergen, Norway: Department of Social Anthropology, University of Bergen.

Brown, Penelope. 1976. "Women and Politeness: A New Perspective on Language and Society." *Annual Reviews in Anthropology* 3:240–49.

Brown, Penelope, and Stephen C. Levinson. 1978. "Universals of Language Usage: Politeness Phenomena." In *Questions and Politeness Strategies in Social Interaction,* ed. E. N. Goody, 56–311. Cambridge: Cambridge University Press.

Button, Graham, and John R. Lee. 1987. *Talk and Social Organisation*. Clevedon, England: Multilingual Matters.

Button, Graham, Paul Drew, and John Heritage. 1986. *Human Studies: Special Issue.* Dordrecht, the Netherlands: Martinus Nijhoff.

Corsaro, William A. 1985. *Friendship and Peer Culture in the Early Years.* Norwood, N.J.: Ablex.

Eder, Donna. 1990. "Serious and Playful Disputes: Variation in Conflict Talk among Female Adolescents." In *Conflict Talk: Sociolinguistic Investigations of Arguments in Conversations,* ed. A. D. Grimshaw, 67–84. Cambridge: Cambridge University Press.

Eder, Donna, and Maureen T. Hallinan. 1978. "Sex Differences in Children's Friendships." *American Sociological Review* 43:237–50.

Ervin-Tripp, Susan. 1982. "Structures of Control." In *Communicating in the Classroom,* ed. L. C. Wilkinson, 27–47. New York: Academic Press.

Garvey, Catherine. 1974. "Some Properties of Social Play." *Merrill-Palmer Quarterly* 20:163–80.

———. 1977a. "The Contingent Query: A Dependent Act in Conversation." In *Interaction Conversation and the Development of Language,* ed. M. Lewis and L. Rosenblum, 63–93. New York: John Wiley and Sons.

———. 1977b. *Play.* Cambridge, Mass.: Harvard University Press.

Gilligan, Carol. 1982. *In a Different Voice: Psychological Theory and Women's Development.* Cambridge, Mass.: Harvard University Press.

Goffman, Erving. 1974. *Frame Analysis: An Essay on the Organization of Experience.* New York: Harper and Row.

Goodwin, Charles, and Marjorie Harness Goodwin. 1990. "Interstitial Argument." In *Conflict Talk,* ed. A. Grimshaw, 85–117. Cambridge: Cambridge University Press.

Goodwin, Marjorie Harness. 1980a. "Directive/Response Speech Sequences in Girls' and Boys' Task Activities." In *Women and Language in Literature and Society,* ed. S. McConnell-Ginet, R. Borker, and N. Furman, 157–73. New York: Praeger.

———. 1980b. "He-Said-She-Said: Formal Cultural Procedures for the Construction of a Gossip Dispute Activity." *American Ethnologist* 7:674–95.

———. 1982. " 'Instigating': Storytelling as Social Process." *American Ethnologist* 9:799–819.

———. 1983. "Aggravated Correction and Disagreement in Children's Conversations." *Journal of Pragmatics* 7:657–77.

———. 1985. "The Serious Side of Jump Rope: Conversational Practices and Social Organization in the Frame of Play." *Journal of American Folklore* 98 (389): 315–30.

———. 1990. *He-Said-She-Said: Talk as Social Organization among Black Children.* Bloomington: Indiana University Press.

Goodwin, Marjorie Harness, and Charles Goodwin. 1987. "Children's Arguing." In *Language, Gender, and Sex in Comparative Perspective,* ed. Susan Philips, Susan Steele, and Christina Tanz, 200–248. Cambridge: Cambridge University Press.

Hannerz, Ulf. 1969. *Soulside: Inquiries into Ghetto Culture and Community.* New York: Columbia University Press.

Heritage, John. 1984. *Garfinkel and Ethnomethodology.* Cambridge, Mass.: Polity Press.

Hughes, Linda A. 1988. " 'But That's Not Really Mean': Competing in a Cooperative Mode." *Sex Roles* 19:669–87.

Kramarae, Cheris. 1981. *Women and Men Speaking.* Rowley, Mass.: Newbury House.

Labov, William. 1972. *Language in the Inner City: Studies in the Black English Vernacular.* Philadelphia: University of Pennsylvania Press.

Labov, William, and David Fanshel. 1977. *Therapeutic Discourse: Psychotherapy as Conversation.* New York: Academic Press.

Ladner, J. A. 1971. *Tomorrow's Tomorrow: The Black Woman.* New York: Anchor Books.

Lever, Janet Rae. 1974. "Games Children Play: Sex Differences and the Development of Role Skills." Ph.D. diss., Yale University

———. 1976. "Sex Differences in the Games Children Play." *Social Problems* 23:478–83.

McAdoo, H. P. 1983. *Extended Family Support of Single Black Mothers.* Columbia, Md.: Columbia Research Systems.

McConnell-Ginet, Sally. 1983. "Review of *Language, Sex, and Gender: Does 'la Difference' Make a Difference?* edited by Judith Orasanu, Mariam K. Slater, and Leonore Loeb Adler, and *Sexist Language: A Modern Philosophical Analysis,* edited by Mary Vetterling-Braggin." *Language* 59:373–91.

McConnel-Ginet, Sally, Ruth Borker, and Nelly Furman, eds. 1980. *Women and Language in Literature and Society.* New York: Praeger.

McLoyd, Vonnie C., Shirley Aisha Ray, and Gwendolyn Etter-Lewis. 1985. "Being and Becoming: The Interface of Language and Family Role Knowledge in the Pretend Play of Young African American Girls." In *Play, Language, and Stories: The Development of Children's Literate Behavior,* ed. L. Galda and A. D. Pellegrini, 29–43. Norwood, N.J.: Ablex.

Maltz, Daniel N., and Ruth A. Borker. 1983. "A Cultural Approach to Male-Female Miscommunication." In *Language and Social Identity,* ed. John J. Gumperz, 196–216. Cambridge: Cambridge University Press.

Mitchell-Kernan, Claudia, and Keith T. Kernan. 1977. "Pragmatics of Directive Choice among Children." In *Child Discourse,* ed. S. Ervin-Tripp and C. Mitchell-Kernan, 189–208. New York: Academic Press.

Philips, Susan U. 1980. "Sex Differences and Language." In *Annual Review of Anthropology 9,* ed. Bernard J. Siegel, 523–44. Palo Alto, Calif.: Annual Reviews.

Piaget, Jean. [1932] 1965. *The Moral Judgment of the Child.* New York: Free Press.

Pitcher, Evelyn G., and Lynn A. Schultz. 1983. *Boys and Girls at Play: The Development of Sex Roles.* New York: Praeger.

Sachs, Jacqueline. 1987. "Preschool Boys' and Girls' Language Use in Pretend Play." In *Language, Gender, and Sex in Comparative Perspective,* ed. S. Philips, S. Steele, and C. Tanz, 178–88. Cambridge: Cambridge University Press.

Sacks, Harvey, Emanuel A. Schegloff, and Gail Jefferson. 1974. "A Simplest

Systematics for the Organization of Turn-Taking for Conversation." *Language* 50:696–735.

Schenkein, Jim. 1978. *Studies in the Organization of Conversational Interaction.* New York: Academic Press.

Shuman, Amy. 1986. *Storytelling Rights: The Uses of Oral and Written Texts by Urban Adolescents.* Cambridge: Cambridge University Press.

Stack, Carol. 1974. *All Our Kin: Strategies for Survival in a Black Community.* New York: Harper and Row.

Sutton-Smith, Brian. 1979. "The Play of Girls." In *Becoming Female,* ed. Claire. B. Kopp and Martha Kirkpatrick, 229–57. New York: Plenum.

Thorne, Barrie. 1986. "Girls and Boys Together . . . but Mostly Apart: Gender Arrangements in Elementary School." In *Relationships and Development,* ed. Willard W. Hartup and Zick Rubin, 167–84. Hillsdale, N.J.: Erlbaum.

Thorne, Barrie, and Nancy Henley. 1975. *Language and Sex: Difference and Dominance.* Rowley, Mass.: Newbury House.

Thorne, Barrie, Cheris Kramarae, and Nancy Henley. 1983. *Language, Gender, and Society.* Rowley, Mass.: Newbury House.

Waldrop, Mary F., and Charles F. Halverson. 1975. "Intensive and Extensive Peer Behavior: Longitudinal and Cross-sectional Analyses." *Child Development* 46:19–26.

West, Candace, and Don H. Zimmerman. 1985. "Gender, Language, and Discourse." In *Handbook of Discourse Analysis,* vol. 4, ed. T. A. v. Dijk, 103–24. London: Academic Press.

Zimmerman, Don H., and Candace West, eds.. 1980. *Language and Social Interaction.* Special issue of *Sociological Inquiry* 50.

Women's Aesthetics and
the Quilting Process

In recent years, many scholars, feminists, and artists have begun to examine women's art and experiences in more holistic ways, taking into account, among other things, the role of process in women's aesthetics.[1] They have begun to fashion an interactive approach that calls attention to those features of women's work and aesthetics that have heretofore been overlooked in art history scholarship and largely ignored in studies of material culture. While acknowledging the importance of the artifact, this approach takes into consideration women's perceptions of their art and emphasizes processes involving objects and people, rather than focusing simply upon the products alone.

One scholar who early on advocated such a process-oriented approach to folk art is Michael Owen Jones. He writes, "To treat any work of art as simply an object, without regard for the *processes* of production and consumption, is to fail to understand the meaning for the art or the reasons for the formal, material, and expressive qualities that it exhibits" (1971:102, emphasis mine).

Examining the processes of quilt-making involves looking at these processes in terms of women's lives and work, concentrating on what women say about their work and what it means to them. If, as Fabian and Szombati-Fabian have claimed, "the connection of art to culture is not given but made; . . . not structure but process" (1980:257), then it becomes all the more important to explore the role of process in women's aesthetics and how it fits into the relation between their art and culture.

My approach to this topic was shaped by fieldwork with the Lytton Springs Quilting Club in central Texas.[2] I began the research intending to focus on individual quilt makers and their quilts, but it soon became evident that this focus was too narrow to account for the interaction among club members and the kinds of questions this raised. Working with a group of women added other dimensions to the study. While process is an important component for analysis in any material culture research, it takes on added significance when production is done by a group. In this case, quilting is a social work that depends upon cooperation and a shared aesthetic that is accepted, if not always followed, by the group. Through work with the Lytton Springs Quilting Club, I came to see a quilt not only as a symbolic object but also the quilting process as an expressive form for women. My own experience as participant-observer in the club's quilting sessions thus led me to broaden the scope of my inquiry.

The Lytton Springs Quilting Club developed from the Home Demonstration Club in the early 1950s, although some of its members had been quilting together since the Great Depression. Nearly all of the women learned their quilt-making skills as young girls, although not all of them have made quilts continuously from that time. A few members learned to quilt as adults at the club. They use traditional patterns but also draw ideas from quilts they see featured in magazines, on batting wrappers, in area shows and fabric shops, and from quilt tops sent to them by their customers. Most of the Lytton Springs club members make quilts alone at home in addition to their quilting with the group at its weekly meetings in the Masonic Hall.

The youngest club member is in her midforties, the older ones in their eighties. Most of the older women are widows, all of the other members are married, and the majority have adult children. The members are all Anglos from working- or middle-class backgrounds; several worked outside the home at different points, particularly during World War II. Three members, now retired, pursued careers in teaching, nursing, and the postal service.

Every Tuesday from five to fifteen women, depending upon the weather, members' health, and other obligations, can be found around the quilting frames set up in the Masonic Hall. This two-story frame building across the road from the general store is easily located by visitors and also makes the club highly visible to community residents who pass by or drop in to say hello. From this site, the quilters can monitor traffic on the main road and customers coming and going at the store. As one quilter explained, "We want to be over here, right in the middle of things." And indeed, the quilters are literally and figuratively in the middle of things, playing a central role in the life of the community.

Through their quilting, the women serve their community in various ways. As one member explained, "I think they [the people of Lytton Springs] appreciate our quilts . . . since all of our charities we contribute to receive a nice check yearly, why I think they appreciate it." When the club first began, members only quilted for each other, but soon people outside the club began to engage its quilting services, and customers from all over the United States have sent tops to Lytton Springs to be quilted. This shift to quilting for the public broadened the club's range of transactions and introduced a financial element into its operations. Although the club charges far less than market value for its services, the volume of tops that have been quilted over several decades has resulted in substantial earnings, which the club donates in support of a number of activities, such as the building of a garage for the volunteer fire department and the restoration of the old schoolhouse for use as a community center. In a community of approximately 250 residents, the club's financial resources represent a high proportion of the available funds for such projects.

The quilters are aware that the club's fees are actually low compared with what they could charge for time and labor costs alone, but the club has always charged what members consider a fair price for the work, a price that they know their customers can afford. Members are careful to dissociate themselves from a commercial market, saying they do not want to run a business. The women claim it would be different if they had to support themselves by quilting, but they point out that they are not quilting for the money. By retaining control over the production and management of quilts, quilting, and the resulting capital, the quilters individually and as a group are able to fulfill practical, social, and symbolic needs in ways that might not be possible or accessible in a competitive market. Quilting emerges not only as a creative activity but also as a creative undertaking in community life.[3] The women's skills are respected by the community, and both quilts and quilters are perceived as having positive social value.

While the quilters enjoy a sense of accomplishment upon completion of a quilt, they also talk about how the active doing of quilting provides a sense of satisfaction as well. One woman described her own experience of the quilting process: "I just get in there and get at it and I'm so absorbed in it that just anything could happen around me." She finds it gratifying to be so caught up in an activity that nothing distracts her. Another quilter explained, "It's something to pass off my time. I'm a person, I've got to be doing something, I have worked so all my life and I can't just sit down and hold my hands" (quoted in Shulimson, 1982:13). Some women characterize the activity as "therapeutic and relaxing." All the women say they like "to keep busy," and quilting is one way in which they do that. The western Maryland rug makers that Geraldine Johnson (1985) has studied express similar responses to the weaving process. What sets quilting apart, however, is that it may be done in a group.

Michael Owen Jones has observed that there is "a folk aesthetic in the sense of reactions to traditional and conventional modes of artistic expression generated among members of a group exhibiting shared values and identities" (1971:103). For the Lytton Springs Quilting Club members, this folk aesthetic includes responses to the activity of quilting along with reactions and evaluations of finished quilts.

The members describe their quilting meetings as "just a day of fun," "just gettin' together and bein' with your friends," "a day when you don't have to do nothin'." Quilting brings women together for a common purpose and combines work and play.[4] One member commented, "I do it for pleasure and I don't want it to get down to where it's really work." In this usage, *work* refers to something one has to do, something over which one has little control, something that provides little satisfaction. The women also refer to quilting as work that tires one physically: "Quiltin's hard work. It'll kill ya." Yet the women do not view this work as drudgery. They take satisfaction in it. *Work* is also a term frequently used in evaluating quilting. Asked what makes a good quilt, one quilter replied, "I think the work on it. What I mean, do your work right. Have it smooth and not puckered or, you know, gathered in places." Another talked about how she looks at a quilt: "When you're finished, . . . I can appreciate all the work that goes into it. No matter how it looks, it looks magnificent to me. . . . It's not that important that it's not perfect. I can see that there's a lot of work put into them—all this love."

The women understand that quilting can function both practically and symbolically despite imperfections and inconsistencies. Working with a group of quilters, a woman cannot exert the same kind of control over the quilting process and product that she can working alone at home. Working with the club requires a willingness to compromise.

The group's aesthetic is based on a consensus that encompasses notions of the ideal and the pragmatic. Ideally, quilting consists of tiny, even stitches that go all the way through the three layers of cloth that make up a quilt. The lines of stitching should be spaced closely enough to hold the batt, or filling, in place while complementing the design of the pieced or appliquéd top. Knots in the thread should be hidden between the layers of cloth so that they are not visible on the top or bottom of a quilt. In fact, when the women examine a quilt, they routinely turn it over to look at the stitches from the bottom. One woman talked about her mother's work: "You could turn her quilts over and it was as pretty on the bottom side as it was on the top." Another member agreed, "That's the place where it looks the prettiest, I think."

The ideal of small, uniform stitches is repeated often in the club's discussions around the quilting frame. Just how small a stitch or how many stitches to the inch is not specified. A beginner soon learns that the group aesthetic is not shared equally by all individuals, recognizes various levels of skill, and begins to interpret the collective ideal to suit her own sensibility. If she asks if her quilting is acceptable, she is told she is doing fine, regardless of how her stitches look. She never hears direct criticism, only words of encouragement.

The club accepts differences because it accepts and supports the individuals who exhibit them: the long stitches of a quilter who pushes the group to finish quickly, the wandering stitches of an elderly member who suffers from senility, and the huge, uncertain stitches of a beginner. Even when an older woman is not feeling up to quilting, she may go to the Masonic Hall, if only briefly, to interact with the other women. Her behavior maintains the appearance of control, demonstrates her desire to participate, and permits her to contribute socially, if not materially, to the club's productivity. To reject a woman's quilting would be to deny her this form of community involvement. While a woman's contribution may be small in terms of quilting, her contribution of time, energy, and earning power to the community is considered important no matter what the quality of her quilting performance.

In quilting customers' tops, the women work within certain constraints. These tops provide challenges because the quilters have no control over a top's formal features or its construction. A customer pieces, embroiders, and/or appliqués the top layer of a quilt before it comes to the club. Then the members place the top in a frame over two other layers of cloth, the batting and the back, which are then quilted together. Around the quilting frames, the women discuss customers' tops in terms of patterns, color choices, and quality of work and, in the process, negotiate and reinforce a shared aesthetic for the group.

The following excerpt, taken from a conversation at a quilting club meeting in which the women had two identical tops from the same customer, illustrates this kind of discussion.

RG: This is more gray than it is blue, don't you think?
BS: It's a blue-gray—just like this one.
GC: Why'd she want two alike?
BS: Maybe she's got two beds.
RG: Maybe she's got twin beds.
LR: Not this big.
RG: Well, she wants 'em to hang to the floor.
JI: Does she want them quilted exactly alike?
RG: That's what I'd do.
JI: Maybe she'd like one different.
IG: I don't imagine it'll make any difference to her.

RG: I don't either just as long as she gets them quilted.

—Pause—

RG: This one's not all that hard. Part of it's quilted on both sides and part of it's not. So I don't know what to do.

BS: What?

RG: Oh, these things here.

BS: Well, I'm going to quilt it all the same.

RG: Well, a whole lot of it's quilted on both sides.

BS: Well, yes, that, but then I mean in this white here.

RG: Well, if you're gonna charge a good price for it, you oughta put lots of quiltin' on it.

BS: Quilt it all alike, too.

RG: Yeah. Well, this one is this way here on this side.

—Pause—

RG: Well, it's gonna look peculiar.

IG: This is really kind of a peculiar bunch, wouldn't you say?

RG: I believe so.

GC: Well, when you get this many together, do you think they'd all be alike?

RG: Well, they ought to look to see what's happening.

JS: Well, I thought last week we decided there wasn't enough room here [unintelligible].

RG: Well, it's prettier when it is quilted on both sides.

The discussion begins with a comment about the color of blue in the top, which invites a response with a tag question (don't you think?) and leads into an exchange in which the women elaborate on each other's remarks concerning the maker's reasons for piecing two tops alike. From piecing, the conversation moves on to whether the quilting is also to be the same on both tops and whether that even matters to the customer. The reply that it will not make a difference to the customer may suggest an ambivalent attitude on the part of the quilters toward customers in general, an idea I will return to later. The discussion then shifts to the specific quilting stitches on the top in the frames when one quilter notes variations. In one section of the quilt top, stitching runs on both sides of the seams, while in another, stitching is limited to only one side. Two quilters stress the importance of consistency and uniformity in quilting and bring up the matter of price to support their assertion—the higher the price, the more quilting it should involve. Note the way one woman's use of the word *peculiar* to describe how the top will look is picked up by another and playfully applied to the group of women also, attributing the peculiar differences in the quilting to the peculiarity of the "bunch." A third quilter teases the women by questioning how realistic it is to expect uniformity in a group. As they try to sort out a previous discussion about how to quilt the top uniformly, the woman who raised the topic of

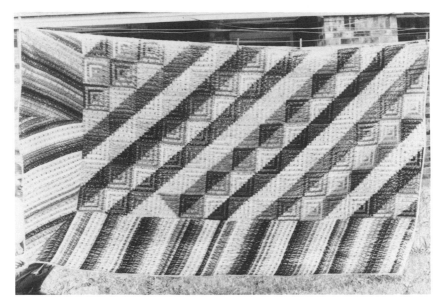

Figure 8.1. Log Cabin Quilt. (Photo by Joyce Ice)

variations states her opinion about which option looks best—quilting on both sides.

Such a conversation is typical because the quilters usually discuss aesthetic choices not in the abstract but in reference to specific tops and their makers. The evaluation of artistic choices and skills within the group is more difficult because of the risk of offending someone. Because many of the tops belong to strangers, the women can comment freely on these tops and assess them without the fear of hurting each other's feelings.

Such was the case when a quilt top arrived from a customer in West Texas, sparking immediate reaction. The log cabin top involved many tiny strips of cloth pieced in alternating light and dark diagonals and no one could imagine ever making such a quilt—it seemed too tedious to the Lytton Springs quilters. They tried to discern what the customer's thoughts and intentions might have been as she was piecing it. In part, her motivation was attributed to the environment: "Out in west Texas, she had to make it pretty [colorful] because it's so ugly out there." Another woman suggested that selection of this pattern had to do with filling time: "She did such a time-consuming pattern because she didn't want to finish too quick. It was all she had to do."

If a quilter knows something about a customer's background or a customer's reason for making the top—that it is for a grandchild's graduation gift or for a wedding present—then that information is shared and discussed with the club. If little is known, the quilters may speculate about what prompted certain color or design choices: "She just used what she had" may be their explanation of the choice of fabrics in a pattern.

While this speculation may be seen as talk that simply helps to pass the time, it also personalizes a quilt by linking it to its maker and placing it in the context of people's lives. In agreeing to quilt a customer's top, the quilters accept a responsibility to that individual. Women's conversations during the quilting process make that obligation real, allowing the quilters to identify a customer, perhaps even to identify with her, and thereby reinforce a connection between her and the club. At the same time, the members assume that a customer who brings a top is willing to accept the club's standards, for, as they say, "if [the customers] don't like the way we quilt, they can take it and do it themselves." The quilters remind each other that no one has ever complained about a quilt, at least not to their knowledge, and express doubt that customers know much about quilting or ever even notice a mistake in their quilts. Thus the club maintains a certain distance and presents a united front against any possible criticism.

As they work, the women may compare a quilt design with similar ones they have done themselves, or if a customer has sent quilt tops to them before, the women may compare the top to others by the same quilt maker. Sometimes a quilt top sparks a memory, as in one session when the women experienced difficulty quilting a top with many uneven, puckered seams. One member recalled her own experience in learning to put together a top: "Mama made me set that son-of-a-gun [four-patch] together fence rows up and down, this-a-way and I want to tell you what. And if I made one little wrinkle in it, she made me take it out—made me so mad, I could've died. I see now where she done right." Her recollection of her mother's instruction about how to avoid this very problem appeals to the authority of tradition in appraising this quilt top and emphasizes to her listeners the importance of careful work.

During the process of working on a quilt top, the quilters sometimes report that their initial perceptions of patterns or colors were altered over the course of several meetings' time. They find that the quilting process has transformed what they considered an ordinary top into a quilt prettier than anyone had anticipated. The log cabin top that elicited ambivalent responses from the club later "kind of grew" on one member after she worked on it for a while, and after several weeks, another quilter stated, "It's a beautiful quilt after you're around it." About this transformation during the quilting process, one woman commented, "I've seen some quilts when they put them in [the frames], you'd think they were horrible, but I never will forget that fan quilt—but it quilted so pretty—one of the prettiest quilts we've done." The common feeling among the women is that "quilting is what makes a quilt. It's always prettier when it's finished than it is when you start with it."

In addition to the actual changes wrought by quilting, this change in the women's perception of the quilt results from the labor expended on it and the careful, close attention this type of work demands over a period of time. Furthermore, the quilters' own aesthetic choices are being incorporated into the overall quilt composition throughout this process, and their discussion of the quilt as they work around the quilting frames serves to "re-frame" it in another perspective.

From discussions about quilts and their makers to recipes, sports, families, and world events, talk in the quilting sessions ranges from the abstract to the commonplace. Topics flow from one to another, moving from a recent death in the community to a television program or a current political issue. With each other in this all-female group, the women articulate their values and concerns through stories, comments, and topic choices.[5] Values are expressed not only in the content of their conversations but also in the structure of interaction within the club. Their conversations, like the club members themselves, follow a participatory model.

It is clear that women value the process as well as the products of quilt-making. When they discuss a quilt as a finished product, they often are talking about process as much as product. Their preference for handmade quilts over machine-made quilts, for example, involves not only aesthetic processes but also social processes that take time to unfold. One quilter stressed the importance of hand-stitching, even if she could do it faster on a sewing machine. A machine can come between the maker and her quilt, but it also comes between quilters because quilting on a sewing machine rules out group participation. Another woman put it in terms of work: "I don't like machine quilts. I think that's the lazy way. Cause I don't think that's what quilts are about."

"What quilts are about" is a process of handwork, of shared work, of social work. As Adolfo Sánchez Vázquez notes, "The similarity between art and labor thus lies in their shared relationship to the human essence; that is, they are both creative activities by means of which man [*sic*] produces objects that express him, that speak for and about him. Therefore, there is no radical opposition between art and work" (1974:63). From an emic perspective, quilting is viewed as practical and satisfying work, and the quilts that result are evaluated first according to the quality of their construction as opposed to their formal properties. Because the quilting process involves individual and group interaction that draws on the women's quilting and verbal skills, the perceptions of a quilt may be modified

Figure 8.2. Members of the Lytton Springs Quilting Club stitching a Lone Star pattern. (Photo by Joyce Ice)

during this process and are influenced at least as much, if not more, by social considerations as by artistic concerns. Through the quilting process, quilts come to externalize a set of aesthetic and social values derived from a shared sensibility. Further analysis of the quilters' behavior and speech reveals additional aspects of their traditional aesthetic.

This case study can only begin to suggest the complex interactions that move between an individual's experiences and the shared identity of women working together in a group. If we want to better understand process and its role in shaping aesthetics, it is clear that we must pay close attention to the actual doing of things—the telling of stories, the weaving of rugs, the making of quilts—and to the talk that is an integral part of the creative enterprise.

Notes

I am indebted to Beverly J. Stoeltje for her comments on earlier versions of this essay and to Judith Shulimson, who began the work with me in Lytton Springs and generously shared her insights. I gratefully acknowledge the unfailing help of the women of the Lytton Springs Quilting Club.

1. Some contextual studies of quilts and their makers have compared the work and the aesthetics of individual women in specific locations (Farb, 1975; McDonald, 1983), while others have investigated quilts as a means for social interaction (Roach, 1985). For more on the Lytton Springs quilters, see my dissertation (Ice, 1984). See also Johnson (1985) on the process of rag rug weaving. For discussions of women's aesthetics, refer to Donovan (1984), Johnson (1982), Nemser (1976), and Showalter (1986).

2. Fieldwork in Lytton Springs was conducted from 1979 to 1981, in the summer of 1982, and periodically since that time. To protect the privacy of individuals, no names are used in this chapter.

3. Several publications resulting from state and regional documentation projects contain articles related to quilts and fund-raising activities. See, for example, Lasansky (1987, 1988); MacDowell and Fitzgerald (1987); Ice and Norris (1989); and Roberson (1988) for cases in Pennsylvania, Michigan, New York, and North Carolina.

4. The concept of work in women's lives and how they regard it is a complex one that relates not only to gender and social issues but also to artistic evaluation and worldview. Unfortunately, space does not permit a fuller exploration here.

5. Sandra Morgen has suggested that women connect political and personal issues in political discussions by using a "vocabulary rich in affect" based upon experience (1983:213).

References Cited

Donovan, Josephine. 1984. "Toward a Women's Poetics." *Tulsa Studies in Women's Literature* 3 (1–2): 99–110.

Fabian, Johannes, and Ilona Szombati-Fabian. 1980. "Folk Art from an Anthropological Perspective." In *Perspectives on American Folk Art,* ed. Ian M. G. Quimby and Scott T. Swank, 247–92. New York: W. W. Norton.

Farb, Joanne. 1975. "Piecin' and Quiltin': Two Quilters in Southwest Arkansas." *Southern Folklore Quarterly* 39 (4): 341–61.

Ice, Joyce Ann. 1984. "Quilting and the Pattern of Relationships in Community Life." Ph.D. diss., University of Texas at Austin.

Ice, Joyce, and Linda Norris, eds. 1989. *Quilted Together: Women, Quilts, and Communities.* Delhi, N.Y.: Delaware County Historical Association.

Johnson, Geraldine Niva. 1982. " 'Plain and Fancy': The Socioeconomics of Blue Ridge Quilts." *Appalachian Journal* 10 (1): 12–35.

———. 1985. *Weaving Rag Rugs: A Women's Craft in Western Maryland.* Knoxville: University of Tennesee Press.

Jones, Michael Owen. 1971. "The Concept of 'Aesthetic' in the Traditional Arts." *Western Folklore* 30 (2): 77–104.

Lasansky, Jeannette. 1987. *Pieced by Mother: Over One Hundred Years of Quiltmaking Traditions.* Lewisburg, Pa.: Oral Traditions Project, Union County Historical Society.

———, ed. 1988. *Pieced by Mother: Symposium Papers.* Lewisburg, Pa.: Oral Traditions Project, Union County Historical Society.

McDonald, Mary Anne. 1983. " 'Which Ever Way I Decide to Do': Afro-American Quilters in Chatham County, North Carolina." Paper presented at the annual meeting of the American Folklore Society, Nashville, Tenn.

MacDowell, Marsha, and Ruth D. Fitzgerald. 1987. *Michigan Quilts: 150 Years of a Textile Tradition.* East Lansing: Michigan State University Museum.

Morgen, Sandra. 1983. "Towards a Politics of 'Feelings': Beyond the Dialectic of Thought and Action." *Women's Studies* 10 (2): 203–23.

Nemser, Cindy. 1976. "Towards a Feminist Sensibility: Contemporary Trends in Women's Art." *The Feminist Art Journal* 5 (2): 19–23.

Roach, Susan. 1985. "The Kinship Quilt: An Ethnographic Semiotic Analysis of a Quilting Bee." In *Women's Folklore, Women's Culture,* ed. Rosan A. Jordan and Susan J. Kalčik, 54–64. Publications of the American Folklore Society, no. 8. Philadelphia: University of Pennsylvania Press.

Roberson, Ruth Haislip, ed. 1988. *North Carolina Quilts.* Chapel Hill: University of North Carolina Press.

Sánchez Vázquez, Adolfo. 1974. *Art and Society: Essays in Marxist Aesthetics.* Translated by Maro Riofrancos. London: Merlin Press.

Showalter, Elaine. 1986. "Piecing and Writing." In *The Poetics of Gender,* ed. Nancy K. Miller, 222–47. New York: Columbia University Press.

Shulimson, Judith A. 1982. "The Quilt as a Visual Metaphor." Paper presented at the annual meeting of the American Folklore Society, Minneapolis.

Reclaiming the Power of the Margins: Gendered Speech in the *Kalevala*

> The central thread or unity of the *Kalevala*-type songs lies in just this point, namely, that they tell how Kaleva's District gradually achieved a prosperity equal to that of North[land] and finally achieved victory over it.
>
> —Elias Lönnrot

The influence of Elias Lönnrot's *Kalevala* on Finnish culture and national identity can hardly be overestimated. The enthusiasm inspired by Lönnrot's creation, which rapidly became accepted as the "Finnish national epic," played a major part in the revival of the Finnish language among the upper classes and the development of a specifically Finnish culture during the nineteenth century and hence in the establishment of a Finnish nation in the twentieth (Wilson, 1976:ix, 3; Branch, 1985:7; Laitinen, 1985:61).[1]

The *Kalevala* was not, however, as its reception and influence might suggest, discovered in its current form among Finnish peasant singers. It is well recognized that Lönnrot himself is responsible for the epic format and the sequencing of individual episodes into the overall narrative. He selected passages, lines, and even individual phrases from a large and varied field collection of shorter folk poetry (narrative, lyric, and ritual) and recombined them according to his own sense of plausibility and narrative logic (Wilson, 1976:41; Salminen and Tarkiainen, 1963:352–54; Honko, 1985:19–20).

Two important aspects of Lönnrot's rationale and motivation are equally well known, but, for lack of a specifically feminist analysis of the work, their import has not been sufficiently appreciated. First, Lönnrot was strongly influenced by Johann Gottfried von Herder's philosophy of national culture, which, as Jennifer Fox has demonstrated, was pervaded with patriarchal notions both implicitly and explicitly detrimental to women (Fox, 1987, and this volume).[2] Second, as the quotation above indicates, Lönnrot organized the poems as he did to emphasize what he had concluded was their common theme: the conflict between and eventual victory of Kalevala (a male-dominated society and the home of the three main male characters) over Pohjola (Northland) (a society controlled by a matriarch, Louhi). When recognized as a story, shaped for nationalist purposes, about how men and men's values and ways of operating compete with and achieve ascendancy over women and women's values and ways of operating, the *Kalevala* surely deserves feminist reconsideration.[3]

In analyzing the *Kalevala* (or indeed any similar reworked and promoted folk text) there are two related but separable issues that deserve attention: first, through what process did it come to exist in this form (and consequently how does it differ from the folk sources) and, second, how has the text functioned since it came into being. In an earlier article I took the first sort of analysis in a feminist direction. By comparing the *Kalevala* as structured by Lönnrot with poems from the folk tradition I noted how he polarized the female characters into good (compatriots and supporters of the men) and bad (foreigners and later opponents of the men) and used the Northland women as the perfidious enemy whom the national fore*fathers* defeat to bring peace and prosperity (Sawin 1988).

Here, in light of the demonstrable historical operation of the *Kalevala* as a text over the past 150 years, I attempt the second type of analysis. In contrast with my previous approach and that of other deconstructionist analysts,[4] I will focus on the story as Lönnrot told it, the text as he left it in 1849, satisfied with his creative process of assembly. I will analyze in particular the verbal actions and interactions of the characters, attending to the variety of speech genres used, their differential accessibility, and the powers they confer. Where it serves to highlight differences between my interpretation and standard readings I will also refer to the folk tradition behind Lönnrot's work and to comparable genres in related bodies of folklore.

Lönnrot's composite epic is particularly susceptible to this kind of reinterpretation. Like the novel in Bakhtin's conception, the *Kalevala* is full of the contesting voices and multiple evaluative accents of earlier speakers, male and female; it is characterized by that "internal dialogism of discourse ... that inevitably accompanies the social, contradictory historical becoming of language" (1981:330). Lönnrot brought together source texts from widely scattered geographical areas and historical periods, texts that had themselves already been reworked repeatedly by folk singers over the years. All these centuries of variation and change were projected into the single plane of Lönnrot's canonical text. The extraordinary complexity of this long process of becoming meant that Lönnrot could not exercise control over all the voices and meanings incorporated into the text that began its remarkable historical life in 1835.

Furthermore, once one is aware of the nationalist ideology that organizes Lönnrot's text and its potential deleterious effect on the representation of women, one is in a position to make an "oppositional reading," systematically challenging evaluations implicit in the text and reassessing productive and destructive actions, good and bad outcomes, in light of feminist values (see Hall, 1980:134). In what follows I am at times exploiting inadvertent inconsistencies (and inadvertent consistencies) in Lönnrot's presentation and arguing for interpretations that the compiler almost surely would not have intended. Nevertheless, these are readings that the text as it exists clearly allows.

What, then, can we make of the *Kalevala* if we take it, as most readers historically have, at face value, as a unified literary narrative? Most readers of the *Kalevala,* even in Finland, and certainly most potential readers anywhere else have had limited access to (and little interest in) the scholarly background and vast body of folk poetry with which one must be acquainted in order to assess critically the differences between Lönnrot's compilation and the folk originals.[5] Furthermore, despite scholarly criticism, the *Kalevala* itself is likely to remain the most enduring and most accessible introduction to this folk poetry (and for non-Finns, to Finnish culture), and it is well worth reading for the beauty and fascination of the poetry.[6] Reading it against the grain, with an eye to women's strengths and accomplishments, enables us to reclaim for women an important part of this heritage.

One particularly evident basis for an oppositional rereading of the *Kalevala* lies in Lönnrot's gender-specific distribution of types of speaking. With one strategic exception, Lönnrot deploys speech roles so that men and women have characteristic styles as different as possible from each other: men get things done with words, while women challenge and obstruct with cryptic questionings. Yet a close look at the workings and effects of these speech forms suggests an alternate reading, one in which women's speech is humane and productive while men's speech, though magically powerful, proves ultimately sterile in human terms and deleterious to the men themselves as well as to the women who oppose them.[7]

While my primary purpose in this essay is to explore the impression a contemporary reader receives from the gender-restricted speaking roles as they are juxtaposed in the text of Lönnrot's epic as we have had it since 1849, the differences between men's and women's speaking are also traceable to the kinds of folk poetry from which each was drawn. In this regard, the techniques of deconstructive, source-analysis scholarship prove quite to my purpose. The source poems for the women's speech belong stylistically and thematically to the "Middle Kalevala" period, distinguishable from both the ancient myth and etiological poems in "Early Kalevala" style, which were composed approximately up to the time of the birth of Christ, and the highly varied legends, ballads, parodies, lyrical epics, and historical narratives of the "Late Kalevala" style, which were influenced by the introduction of Christianity to Finland starting in the twelfth century.[8] The women's style reflects particularly the emphasis on everyday activities, personal relationships, and the kind of familiar though not always friendly dialogue that emerged as predominant features of poetry during the Viking period (A.D.800–1100) (Kuusi, Bosley, and Branch, 1977:50–51). The men's speaking is derived from shamanic charms and poetry about the exploits of shamans. Some scholars also assign this to the Middle Kalevala period, seeing in the competitive interaction of the shamans a pervasive attitude that "the world [was] a battlefield, the hero had to have an opponent—either a rival or an enemy," which they trace to the influence of the "ancient Germans and their descendants" in the early centuries A.D. (Kuusi, Bosley, and Branch, 1977:49). Others argue that these shamanic poems are among the oldest preserved in the *Kalevala* and that "their motifs may even be thousands of years older than the [poems] themselves" (see Pentikäinen, 1989:186).

The three main male figures in the *Kalevala* represent distinct and complementary character types: Väinämöinen is the elderly but powerful sage, Lemminkäinen the unrestrained warrior, Ilmarinen the earnest smith. In Lönnrot's composite, however, they share a distinctive type of speaking. This speech form is most closely identified with Väinämöinen, but his fellow heroes of the Kaleva District also use words to create or transform objects or to vanquish their enemies.

This men's speech is directly and literally effective; through it the will of the speaker is immediately manifested in and impressed upon the world. This power is most obvious in those instances in which a compressed formula, usually "he sang an *x*," reports on the effect of words without inquiring into the specific means: Lemminkäinen "sang . . . a bridge of ice / across the pool of / snow from bank to bank" (26:548–50);

Väinämöinen "started building the boat with wisdom / making the craft with singing" (16:103-4); Ilmarinen "sang his woman [in]to a gull" (38:280).[9] As employed in the course of the narrative, however, the charms and prayers (to Ukko, the old man and thunderer who is chief deity in the ancient pantheon, and to other lesser spirits) are also inevitably effective. The charms appear in situations in which a character is going to accomplish the deed for which the charm was intended, for example, healing, sowing, or protecting himself from enemies. Prayers, though formally distinguishable, are no different in effect because they are so regularly and swiftly granted.[10] When a character prays, "O Old Man, chief god, [do x]," one almost always finds within a few lines an answering formula in which "That Old Man, high creator / god above the clouds, [does x]" (see, e.g., 14:304, 313-14). The speaker has asked for help from a stronger being, but the words of the plea are just as directly powerful as those of a charm or command.

An equally salient feature of the men's forms of speaking is that their power depends upon knowledge, especially knowledge of origins or patterns.[11] Väinämöinen, the "eternal sage," is the most powerful singer. Antero Vipunen, "the old word-hoarder / with great wisdom in his mouth" (17:528-29), is revered even by Väinämöinen for his ability to "s[i]ng Origins in depth / and spells in order / how by their Creator's leave / at the Almighty's command / of itself the sky was born / from the sky water parted / from the water land stretched forth," etc. (17:541-47). When the upstart Joukahainen challenges Väinämöinen's supremacy, the older singer demands, "Tell me that my ears may hear: / what do you know most about / understand above others?" (3:144-46), and later, "Tell me of deep Origins / of eternal things" (3:187-88). Dismissing Joukahainen's recital of practical knowledge—"the perch . . . / in autumn swims in the deep / in summer spawns on dry land" (3:161-63)—and human history—"a fir root first of dwellings / and a stone the first crude pot" (3:209-10)—as mere "Child's wisdom, woman's recall" (3:184), Väinämöinen wins the contest because he was present at the creation of the world and so can describe it (3:235-54) (see Bosley, 1989:xxiii).

Charms and prayers, similarly, bespeak the user's specialized knowledge of culturally defined origins and the supernatural realm. Most of the prayers demonstrate that the speaker understands from which specific supernatural helper he may appropriately and effectively request assistance in particular circumstances. Lemminkäinen's huntsman's charm focuses on invoking (even cajoling) help out of a series of forest spirits whose combined action will set game in his path (14:23ff.); Väinämöinen as sower asks both the "earth-mistress" and the rain-providing Ukko to play their strategic roles to make his grain grow (2:296ff.). When

Väinämöinen gashes his knee with an axe, he rushes to find someone who knows the charm for blood-stanching. The charm itself bespeaks a knowledge of anatomy, telling the blood, "But if you should have a mind / to move more swiftly / then move in the flesh / and in the bones glide! / Inside is better for you / beneath the skin is fairer— / coursing through the veins" (9:353–59), but depends ultimately upon the sage's ability to describe for his healer the origins of the iron that wounded him (9:29–258).

A third notable property of the men's language is that the power of their words is represented as inhering in the words. Such a claim may appear incompatible with the previous one regarding knowledge, and, indeed, the defining line is difficult to draw: is it more accurate to state that the words are an expression of the speaker's powerful knowledge or that the speaker has acquired knowledge of powerful words? The fact that Väinämöinen, unable to complete his boat, goes to Antero Vipunen with the express intent of extracting ship-building charms from him (poem 16) and that Vipunen, as noted above, is called a "word hoarder," argues for the latter interpretation. One should perhaps not take too literally what may be a metaphorical description of shamanic powers. Still, the objectification of words strongly implied here and hinted at elsewhere, the sense that the power of a word derives from the word rather than from the user, significantly distinguishes the men's language from the women's.

Even the fabled beauty of Väinämöinen's singing reinforces rather than contradicts the sense that these words are powerful in themselves. When Väinämöinen finally sings to the music of the harp he has made, the text implies that his performance is beautiful by stressing the power of his singing to make living creatures gather and listen: "the flying birds of the air / gathered upon twigs / and all manner of fishes / crowded on the shore; / the very earthworms / moved to the top of the mould" (44:297–302). And on the pragmatic level, for a folk performer's audience, listening to singing and playing modeled on Väinämöinen's primordial harping, or for the reader of the *Kalevala*'s poetry, the aesthetic effectiveness of the language of the whole serves as an immediately sensible correlate of the described magic power of the eternal singer's words.

In the standard interpretation of the *Kalevala,* the men's ability to control powerful language simply redounds to their collective glory. Yet close examination of the uses to which these putative culture heroes put their power raises troubling questions. The men are sometimes able to create beautiful and beneficial things: Lemminkäinen devises protection against the dangers on his road (poem 26); Väinämöinen sings up a star-laden fir tree and a swift ship (poems 10 and 17). It is difficult to approve these creations fully, however, if one remembers the purposes for which they are designed. Lemminkäinen, rejected as a suitor, is going to attack Northland during the wedding feast. Väinämöinen devises both fir tree and boat as part of an ongoing scheme to trick and exploit his friend Ilmarinen and steal the bride the smith has earned.

While the men's magical creative acts seem positive, many of the transformations that they are able to accomplish actually work against culture and order. Ilmarinen grows disgusted with his wife and turns her into a sea gull, thereby reducing a human being vocal in her criticism of him to a noisy but inarticulate creature (poem 38). Väinämöinen punishes Joukahainen by dissolving each crafted element of the boastful youth's equipment into an analogous natural form: "He sang young Joukahainen . . . / sang his gold-trimmed sleigh / sang it to treetrunks in pools / sang his whip knotted with beads / to reeds on a shore . . . / he sang his gold-hilted sword to lightnings in heaven" (3:301–12). Futhermore, despite their involvement in several warlike expeditions and endemic violence against women, the men enjoy a reputation as relatively peaceful competitors who substitute the power of the word for the power of the sword (William A. Wilson, personal communication, 1987; Bosley, 1989:xliv). Väinämöinen does refuse to "let the sword decide" his dispute with Joukahainen (3:268), but the words he uses instead are not of the calm, persuasive sort brought to mind by the maxim "the pen is mightier than the sword." When Väinämöinen sings his rival deeper and deeper into a swamp, the younger man is in as much danger as if he were engaged in physical combat. Similarly, Ilmarinen's lady, torn to pieces when an angry herdsman transforms her cows into bears and wolves, dies just as horribly as if Kullervo had dismembered her himself: "The wolf rips her face to shreds / the bear yanked her foot sinews / it bit half her calf / broke her heel off her leg bone" (33:215–18). The men do not so much replace weapons with words as turn words into weapons.

Overall, the men's language appears remarkable because it is so directly and obviously effective. Yet in acquiring that unusual capability such speech is also impoverished: it loses those common characteristics that differentiate words from any other brute tool or labor-saving device. Words transformed directly into physical reality are literalized and hardened into a single manifestation; their potential for metaphorical and multiple signification is narrowed, if not relinquished completely. Words that act directly on the world run no risk of misunderstanding or resistance, but neither can they attain the lasting and ramified effect of the command, promise, or persuasive argument that influences the future by changing people's minds. In Hannah Arendt's terms, the men's language devolves into a form of "work," a means of "provid[ing] an 'artificial' world of things" (1958:7) for one's comfort and convenience. The women's speech, in contrast, may be seen as a form of "action," that quintessentially human political activity (1958:8). Action requires courage because, since it works on and through people, its results are never predetermined or controllable (1958:190).

Questions about the value that should be placed on the men's forms of talk are compounded when one considers the women's speech and the verbal interactions between men and women that Lönnrot has engineered in order to represent and justify ultimate male ascendancy. The forms of speaking attributed to the women are even more varied than the men's; they include bridal laments, two riddlelike forms—the posing of impossible tasks and a competition in hypothetical self-transformations[12]—and a kind of persistent questioning that I will call "truth-seeking." Still, all of these forms of talk put the speaker in the position of challenging, obstructing, or resisting the actions and statements of others. Not all the women in the *Kalevala* are enemies of the men. Some are relatives, Kalevans themselves, who support the men and are portrayed in favorable terms, serving as examples of noble womanhood whose presence further condemns by contrast the uncooperative foreign women of Northland (Sawin, 1988:204–7). The Kaleva and Northland women are assigned distinct ways of speaking—I will focus below on one example from each camp—but linkages between their styles partly undermine Lönnrot's attempt to set them against each other. Significantly, Lemminkäinen's mother, the most celebrated of *Kalevala* women, employs powerful speech like the men's (and totally unlike any other woman's) in that tremendously effective scene in which she reassembles the pieces of her son's torn body and restores him to life (poem 15). This is presumably the ultimate expression of motherly love and woman's proper power, the giving of life. Yet note that this scene was almost entirely constructed by Lönnrot out of the charms that he otherwise elected to assign to the men[13] and that in the comparable folk poem featured in the Kuusi, Bosley, and Branch collection this scene ends with Lemminkäinen's mother asking the body, "Will a man still come of you / a new hero be active?" and receiving the answer, "There's no man in the one gone" (1977, 35:258–60).[14]

The other distinctive speech form employed exclusively by Kaleva women is "truth-seeking." In poem 18 of the *Kalevala* Väinämöinen tries to sneak off to Northland in his new boat to steal the bride Ilmarinen had earned there. Annikki, Ilmarinen's sister, spots the old man, demands to know where he is going, and keeps exposing his lies and repeating her question until she gets truthful information that she can pass on to her brother. In poem 15 Lemminkäinen's mother interacts similarly with the mistress of Northland, repeating her question until she finds out where to look for the body of her son, although in this latter case Lönnrot has muddied the water. In the folk originals it is Väinämöinen who sends

Lemminkäinen to his death and whom his mother must petition for information (see KBB 35). By switching genders in this scene, Lönnrot has polarized the women, pitting Lemminkäinen's mother against Louhi, but this form of speaking is fundamentally a tool for women to demand that men tell the truth and share what they know.

While the men's magical speech depends on eternal verities and conventional wisdom, the women gain a measure of power by influencing the distribution of unique, timely information about human motives and deeds. This does not give them the power to change the world at will, but does enable them to respond intelligently to the evolving, sometimes surprising realm of human interaction. Furthermore, the women gain access to the news they want by relying on a knowledge of connections and conventions, even in men's domains, that the men evidently do not expect them to have and by reasoning from that knowledge, comparing current observations with remembered associations. Väinämöinen, dressed in finery and sailing a gorgeous new boat as he goes wooing in Northland, tries to tell Annikki that he is going fishing, hunting, or to war. He finally capitulates when she counters each claim with a shrewd deduction: "Don't tell empty lies, for I / too know about fish spawning! / Differently my father . . . / used to go hunting salmon / trying for sewin: / he had a boatful of nets / a ship full of traps / in it were seines, in it lines / water-bearers on the side / fishing spears under the thwart / long poles in the stern. / Where are you off to, Väinämöinen / roving to, Calm Waters man?" (18:119–32).[15]

It is not entirely clear why the person challenged finally agrees to tell the truth on the third or fourth request, beyond the fact that success on the third attempt has proved a serviceable and satisfying means of ordering oral narratives in Western cultures where three is the usual pattern number. If there is a reason within the logic of the story, it might be that the one interrogated fears losing face if exposed as a persistent liar. Possibly there is some ritualized compulsion to answer after a certain number of demands if the challenger can keep up her nerve, or perhaps the questioner's obstinacy simply wears the questioned one down.[16] In either case, the women's power to get what they want comes from an awareness of how to manipulate and control an interpersonal situation. The men know words of power; the women know how to get control of the power relations inherent in a conversational interaction.

As a component of Lönnrot's narrative, the Kaleva women's action serves to support the men in their conflict with the mistress of Northland. Yet the speech pattern most characteristic of Louhi and her daughter has many of the same features as their Kaleva sisters' truth-seeking: its basic form is a challenge, and it depends upon the speaker's ability to interpret and manage a face-to-face interaction. Where the Kaleva women are direct, however, the Northland women are cryptic. I term their verbal activity "riddling," both because their words require decoding on at least two levels, one pragmatic, one semantic, and because it works on those involved as riddles do, challenging cultural presuppositions and cognitive categories, "deliberate[ly] exploit[ing] . . . incongruities encountered daily in the linguistic and conceptual codes, but generally suppressed to facilitate the necessary illusion of order and security" (McDowell, 1979:110).

Much of the action in the *Kalevala* turns on the men's search for wives. Despite their many skills, magical and otherwise, they find that a woman is the one thing they cannot create for themselves. Ilmarinen's experiment to forge a wife from gold and silver is a pitiable failure (poem 37). All three of the central Kaleva men attempt to woo the maid of the North, daughter of Louhi, and it is in that context that either Louhi or the maid challenges each man to perform apparently impossible tasks. Lönnrot has strung together four separate incidents to create the complex courtship sequence, which makes it a particularly good instance for observing the effects of his opportunistic linking and regularizing. In the first of these scenes, Louhi challenges Ilmarinen to forge the sampo, a magical source of fertility, out of paradoxical materials and promises him the maid for his wife if he succeeds (*Kalevala* 7 and 10; compare KBB 12). In the second, Väinämöinen banters with a young woman—in the originals, the daughter of a nature spirit; in the *Kalevala,* Louhi's daughter—who challenges him to complete impossible tasks (*Kalevala* 8; KBB 6). In the third, concocted by Lönnrot out of totally independent songs about the exploits and failures of a boastful hunter, Louhi poses tasks to Lemminkäinen (*Kalevala* 13–14; compare KBB 53, 54, 35). In the fourth, Ilmarinen and Väinämöinen compete as suitors. Even in the folk poems from which this last section was derived there is often some reference to a previous vow between Ilmarinen and the maid, but her parent, usually a male demon, demands further tasks from the smith before finally consenting to the marriage (*Kalevala* 19; compare KBB 17).

In creating this composite courtship, Lönnrot found a way to accommodate in a single narrative what would otherwise be unrelated or conflicting stories. Yet in so doing he also makes Louhi look dishonest, since she keeps changing the terms of her offer and is willing to entertain other suitors even after Ilmarinen has satisfied her initial request for the sampo. Still, Lönnrot's particular juxtaposition of texts is also susceptible to an alternative reading according to which the women's practice holds tremendous potential for transcending social ills, though that possibility is ultimately squelched by the men's response.

Two key factors encourage such an interpretation. First, Lönnrot has enhanced the assimilation (already partly in evidence in some traditional songs [Kuusi, Bosley, and Branch, 1977:528]) between the common folktale theme of tasks assigned to suitors (Thompson, 1932–36, 4:307, motif H335) and the sexual bantering between lovers in the form of riddles or impossible tasks, familiar from the English riddle ballads (e.g., Child 1, 2, 46, 47).[17] Second, he has set up a situation significantly different from those in the folktales by giving control over the choice of suitors to the bride and her *mother* (rather than to a kingly father)[18] and by assigning each suitor unique tasks peculiarly appropriate to his character and capabilities (rather than the assumed single set of objective tests in which each suitor prior to the hero fails). Thus Lönnrot's story strongly suggests that neither mother nor maid is especially interested in the accomplishment of particular tasks. Rather, both are using them as pragmatic riddles through which they challenge the men to relinquish their image of acquiring a wife as a productive machine "to clean out your hut / and to sweep your floor / rinse your wooden plates / to wash out your cloaks / weave your golden cloak / bake your honey-bread" (3:461–66) and instead to accommodate themselves to what the maid herself wants in a husband.

The women design tasks for each suitor to test what they suspect are each man's unacceptable qualities. Väinämöinen is wealthy, powerful, and influential, but the maid is extremely reluctant to marry him because he is so *old*.[19] The tasks with which she confronts him—to "split a horsehair / with a pointless knife / pull an egg into a knot so that the knot did not show," "peel a stone, / cut fence poles of ice / without a piece breaking off," and "carve a boat / out of bits of my spindle" (8:95–98, 109–11, 124–25)—are significantly akin to those in the English riddle ballads, which Barre Toelken has convincingly interpreted as sexual double entendres that promise "that if the young man succeeds in doing properly the tasks she outlines for him, he will have had his 'Cambric Shirt' in the process" (1966:16).[20] And she introduces these challenges by saying, "I'd consider you a man / I'd reckon you a fellow / if you could" (8:93–95). In short, the maid is challenging Väinämöinen to prove that his sexual abilities have not been affected by his extreme age and that he acknowledges her as a woman with sexual desires that he is able and willing to satisfy.

The old man, however, totally misses the point.[21] In order to respond properly he must first recognize that the maid is asking for a figurative decoding, not a literal performance, and then must interpret what he now knows to be a riddle. Väinämöinen, however, is singularly unsuited to distinguish literal from symbolic uses of language, since his magical verbal powers enable him to perform the tasks literally: "Steady old Väinämöinen / does not fret greatly at that: / he just peeled a stone" (8:113–15). He satisfies the objective terms of the maid's challenge but does not come close to doing what she is *actually* asking of him.[22]

Louhi's challenges to Lemminkäinen, interpreted according to the same model, seem similarly designed to spotlight his deficiencies and to challenge this warrior and man of unrestrained appetite to mend his wanton, violent ways.[23] In light of Lemminkäinen's character, Louhi's request that he capture an elusive, magical elk and the swan that swims on Death's river (mysterious and independent creatures that belong to the margins of the civilized, dominated world) appears as a coded challenge for him to show that he could be gentle with her as yet "unbroken" daughter and that he possesses positive human qualities, such as intelligence and sensitivity. Like Väinämöinen, however, Lemminkäinen interprets the requests literally and approaches the tasks in a predictable way, trying to "ski down" the elk and otherwise outdo the animals at their own specialties, strength and speed. By responding with physicality and violence, he also gives the wrong answer.

Both men are objectively able to accomplish all their stipulated tasks except the last. The maid only avoids being carried away by them because in each case, the result of a prior misdeed (Väinämöinen's violation of an injunction laid upon him by Louhi, Lemminkäinen's grave insult of the Northland herdsman) is suddenly visited upon the man with a fitting *deus ex machina* grossness. Lönnrot, of course, needed to eliminate these alternate suitors somehow, but their literal success and enforced failure highlights Ilmarinen's contrasting approach.

The activities of this final, successful suitor echo a common theme in the suitor-test Märchen, where the hero frequently passes his tests through the intervention of animal helpers who repay a kindness on his part. This suggests that winning the bride is a reward for altruism or for being able to appreciate points of view based on experiences very different from one's own. For example, the youth who listens to the ant king's pleas and prevents his horse from trampling an ant hill later gets the ants' help to sort millet from sand, an impossible task for a human but one for which ants are ideally suited. Ilmarinen's success as a suitor depends similarly on adopting alternative points of view.

This is indicated only indirectly in his initial task, the creation of the sampo, since Ilmarinen appears to do most of the actual work. Still, it is significant that even the smith who hammered out the vault of the sky could not create a sampo for himself prior to Louhi's challenge and that she had to provide the materials. The sampo is made "from a swan's quill tip / a barren cow's milk / a small barley grain / a summer ewe's down" (10:263–66), all of which might also be double entendres alluding to the sexual aspect of fertility. On the literal level, Ilmarinen *forges* the sampo, not out of the kinds of hard materials whose working is cross-culturally men's traditional province but out of the kinds of soft materials from which women make pillows and cloth and food (Sanday, 1981:77–79; Murdock and Provost, 1973:211–12). The sampo itself is an interesting symbolic exchange equivalent for the bride Ilmarinen earns by forging it because it is a limitless source of prosperity and fertility for those who own it. (In its most concrete representations the sampo is described as a magical mill that grinds out grain, salt, and money without having anything fed into it, though at other times it exerts a less determinate, magical influence.) Like women's productive and, especially, reproductive capacities, it has an economic function but eludes definition as simply a commodity and it can be activated only by cooperation between the sexes.

The theme of the benefits of getting outside one's usual perspective is even more clearly illustrated in the case of Ilmarinen's later tasks, Louhi's request that he plow a snake-infested field and capture other dangerous animals. Unlike the other two suitors, whose overwhelming self-confidence led them to misunderstand what was really being asked of them, Ilmarinen professes himself stumped by the riddle tasks. He *is* smart enough, however, to seek the maid's advice and help. He has, in effect, been challenged to use his dangerous and awe-inspiring skills as a smith to support culture, to tame and cultivate and thus make the world safer and more pleasant for human habitation.[24] The maid, understanding the logic of her mother's riddling requests, demonstrates to Ilmarinen how he can use his metal-working skills to create protective armor and other marvelous tools, and he remembers the appropriate charms to clinch the success of their venture.

Ilmarinen commands a specialized technology but does not know how to apply it. The maid (like her mother, who directed Ilmarinen in the forging of the sampo) was raised in a matriarchal culture on the margins of Kaleva society. Thus although she lacks the technical skill, she has a slightly different perspective on the situation that allows her to imagine how one might bend that technology to a new and unforeseen application. When the craftsman is willing to apply his skills according to the maid's directions, they are able together to transcend the limits of the extant culture and to solve what had appeared to be insoluble problems. He thus proves to be the best choice as husband for the maid both in practical terms (as a cooperative helpmate) and in sexual-symbolic terms (as her complement, with whom she can generate new possibilities), and she finally convinces her mother to let her marry him.

Midway through the *Kalevala* one seems to have come to the climax of a romance plot, with attendant jubilation and promise of natural and social renewal (Frye, 1957). This small, but uniquely human, social miracle has been brought about through the exercise of the women's challenging, cryptic speech rather than the men's directly powerful words. The story to this point might serve as a parable about how women's experience of social marginality can be a resource for a society in transition, making the impossible possible by showing that the limits of the conceivable are an artifact of particular sets of conventions, including the assumptions upon which patriarchy rests.

This bright image does not survive for long. The men soon find reasons to kill both the maid of the North and her younger sister, abducted against her will by Ilmarinen. They then claim that Louhi should share the sampo with them, since the brides she had given them in trade turned out to be "defective merchandise" that had to be destroyed. The sampo is the magicosymbolic source of fertility and the literal springhead of food and wealth for Louhi's country. Under most circumstances a demand from some foreign group that you share your natural resources with them amounts to a declaration of war, but in the terms of Lönnrot's logic it is Louhi's resistance that is cast as selfish and irrational. The loss of the sampo at sea (after the men steal it and she attacks their ship to get it back) is also blamed on Louhi alone.

The young women's deaths are emblematic of the men's reassertion of their kind of power. The second daughter protests her abduction by Ilmarinen, attempting to communicate her desire for freedom in metaphorical terms: "If you will not let me go / as a lark I'll soar / hide behind a cloud" (38:172–74). He at first responds hypothetically in kind: "You will not get there / I'll chase you as an eagle" (38:177–78), but later grows irritated and actually sings her into a sea gull to get rid of her.[25] The women have succeeded in their aims by treating social conventions, for example, the sanctioned parental testing of suitors, as a resource to be manipulated and modified. But they have no recourse if the men abrogate the most basic social contracts to listen and negotiate and resort instead to the brute force that their magical power so readily supplies.

The foregoing brief analysis inevitably overgeneralizes, eliding important differences between characters of each gender and giving insufficient attention to fascinating similarities between men's and women's speech. I have certainly not done justice to the variety of speech activity described in the many traditional songs, but that was not my goal. I have attempted, rather, to represent the dominant reading that has been given to the epic (recognizing that in creating a single coherent narrative Lönnrot himself narrowed and polarized the speaking identities of the folk characters) and to propose an alternative, feminist interpretation that this ultimately uncontrollable text equally allows.

The standard, "common-sense" interpretation of the *Kalevala,* easily detectable in scholarly commentary (see Sawin, 1988:202–4), represents only one of the possibilities for evaluation. If, in keeping with the intertwined ideologies of patriarchy and nationalism, one accepts a priori that heroism and magnificent power (extending to violence in the service of a cause) are good things, then it is difficult not to applaud the Kaleva heroes and disparage their opponents. But these are not necessary judgments. A reader who rejects hierarchical ordering and posits as the central values cooperation and enhanced understanding at a realistic human level is likely to see the greatest hope in what the women offer: the possibilities of taking someone else's point of view, getting outside the strictures that one's own cultural assumptions impose, and achieving human-scale "magic" through cooperation.

In Lönnrot's mind, the body of Finnish narrative folk poetry could and should be combined into a single epic because all the poems, together, "tell how Kaleva's District gradually achieved a prosperity equal to that of North[land] and finally achieved victory over it." In creating the *Kalevala* he managed to make the poems tell that story and presumably saw it as a tale of heroic victory in which the nation could rejoice. The reader who understands Lönnrot's influence on the text and recognizes the ongoing effect of nationalist ideology on standard readings may take a different view. Such a reader may instead see the *Kalevala* itself and the metatexts of the compiler's manipulation and the nation's reception as tragedies about a society that prefers to fight with women and then blame them for the violence rather than to learn from the challenges their different experience presents, to welcome and use their skills, or to listen to the solutions provided by their human and humane perspective.

Notes

I gratefully acknowledge the criticism and encouragement provided at various stages of this project by Mary Koske, Jane Marcus, Kenneth D. Pimple, Beverly Stoeltje, David Whisnant, William A. Wilson, and the editors of this volume. Readers should be aware that I am working from English translations of the Finnish texts and with those critical resources available to an English speaker.

1. A sense of distinct Finnish identity among the intelligentsia began to form in the late eighteenth century and was furthered by the transfer of Finland from Swedish to Russian control in 1809 (Honko, 1985:17; Wilson, 1976:26–27). Educated Finns had long spoken Swedish. Lönnrot published a first version of the *Kalevala* in 1835 and an expanded (now standard) edition in 1849. Finnish was

granted official standing as a language for education and government only in the 1860s (Branch, 1985:7).

2. Herder believed that the nation should be modeled after the family in which the father "naturally" and universally holds absolute authority. He also regarded cultural traditions and language, which should serve as the focus of a national identity and the backbone of a proper education, as masculine in their essence, the sole property of the fathers, who would pass them along only to their sons (Fox, 1987:567–68).

3. Most feminist scholarship in Finland has been focused on folk materials rather than the *Kalevala* itself. Other Americans who have taken a feminist approach to the *Kalevala* include Brown (1984) and Van D'Elden (1985). A major recent collection of Finnish feminist folklore studies, entitled *Louhen Sanat* (The Words of Louhi) includes work on folk tales, legends, laments, games, dance, wedding poetry, spells, and funeral traditions (Nenola and Timonen, 1990). Only two of the twenty articles (one by Kirsti Mäkinen on women's role in world creation myths, the other a translation of my 1988 piece) deal specifically with the *Kalevala*. For examples of recent feminist work on Finnish traditional poetry and legend published in English see Nenola-Kallio (1982) and Timonen (1987, 1990). Timonen also, however, contributed a feminist essay on the *Kanteletar* (Lönnrot's collection of women's traditional songs) to Keith Bosley's translation of selections from that text (Bosley, 1990).

4. Väino Kaukonen is famous for his studies of Lönnrot's method of composing the *Kalevala,* in which he traced the provenance of most of the lines (1939, 1945, 1956; see Wilson, 1976:196–97). A more critical practitioner of such approaches is Juha Pentikäinen, who in his recent book details the shamanic religious beliefs that underlie and explain many of the characters' activities in the *Kalevala* (1989, esp. chapter 9).

5. For English speakers who *are* interested in the background of folk poetry, Kuusi, Bosley, and Branch (1977) offer a representative sample of the poems collected from Finnish oral tradition in Finnish and in English translation.

6. See especially the graceful and warm new translation by Keith Bosley (1989).

7. In a fuller understanding of the *Kalevala* and the wider tradition of Finnish folk poetry one may, of course, appreciate the men's powerful language as a reflection of shamanic rituals and invocations to the ancient pantheon of tutelary deities (see Pentikäinen, 1989; Haavio, 1952:234). First, however, it is essential to recognize that *in the context of Lönnrot's composite,* that is, in the story as told by a nationalist presenter for a nineteenth-century and later audience, it is precisely the men's extraordinary verbal powers (imported from an earlier cultural system) that permit them not only to rob, rape, and murder the women but also to ignore and reject what the women have to offer, to the detriment of both.

8. For a concise discussion of the complex processes through which approximate and relative dates have been assigned to Finnish epic poems see Kuusi, Bosley, and Branch (1977:40–61).

9. Keith Bosley provides the following gloss: "*sang:* bewitched. The verb often connotes magic. When its object is a person it is sometimes rendered 'sing at';

when the object is a thing, this is being called into existence" (1989:668). Quotations from the *Kalevala* are from Bosley's translation and will be cited by poem and line number as given therein.

10. Indeed, Lönnrot's treatment elides the classical, Frazerian distinction between charms (magically effective words) and prayers (pleas to a powerful deity).

11. Power conferred by a knowledge of origins is a central feature of the shamanic religion practiced in Finland prior to (and for some centuries concurrent with) Christianity and currently by some Siberian tribes (Pentikäinen 1989:37, 177). Pentikäinen also notes that during the nineteenth century both men and women sang runes of origin related to their specific work duties (1989:114).

12. This kind of competition in metaphor features prominently in a type of dialogue song found in many European folk traditions. The first speaker, a man, declares his intention to possess sexually the woman whom he is addressing. She rebuffs his advances, declaring that to avoid him she will turn herself into a series of creatures or objects. The man responds by describing how he will transform himself so as to stand in the desired relation to each form that she takes. The one English-language example cited by Child ("The Twa Magicians," Child 44) involves a blacksmith and a noblewoman who apparently have magical powers. They begin with verbal bantering but then actually perform the transformations upon themselves, e.g., she becomes a duck, he a drake; she a grey mare, he a gilt saddle upon her back. This may reflect cross-influence from folk tales about a magician's apprentice who escapes from his master through such a series of clever transformations. In most of the songs involving lovers (or potential lovers) the competition remains purely verbal and hypothetical (see Child, 1882–98, 1:399–402).

13. The reconstruction episode has been expanded from 10 lines in the *Proto-Kalevala,* to 289 lines in the 1835 *Old Kalevala,* to 650 lines in the 1849 *Kalevala* (Brown, cited in Van D'Elden, 1985:23).

14. Scholars do not yet agree whether Lemminkäinen's resurrection is really in keeping with Finnish folk tradition. See Alphonso-Karkala (1973) for one view and Pentikäinen (1989:208–11) for a detailed discussion of the debate. Subsequent references to folk poems from the Kuusi, Bosley, and Branch collection (1977) will be indicated with the abbreviation "KBB," followed by the poem number in their listing.

15. See KBB 15, 16, and 17 for examples of folk poems related to those from which Lönnrot drew this segment and also KBB 37:159–91 for a similar segment (one that Lönnrot attributes to Lemminkäinen's mother in poem 28 of the *Kalevala*) in which a mother's questioning induces her son to admit that he has killed a man. In the British ballad "Edward" (Child 13) the mother uses a strikingly similar technique to extract a confession from her son. When she asks about the blood on his coat or sword he claims that he has killed first his hawk, then his greyhound or his horse. Only after the mother counters these explanations with her own observation and reasoning, "haukis bluid was nevir sae reid" (Child 13B, stanza 2, line 1), does he finally admit that he has murdered his brother (or father). Child notes that there is "an exact counterpart" to this ballad in Swedish and very similar ones in Danish and in Finnish (the last probably derived from the Swedish)

(1882–98, 1:167–68). Lönnrot included a version of "The Brother-Slayer" in his collection of lyric songs and ballads (*Kanteletar* iv, Bosley 1990:10) as one of the "later songs" illustrating a type "composed since the Middle Ages, when Scandinavian influences moved in with the older Finnish tradition" (Bosley 1990:7). In the *Kanteletar* ballad the mother simply asks three questions that lead the son to confess his horrid deed. This parallel at least suggests the possible existence in northern European cultures of a concept that women's persistent speech (though often demeaned as gossip or chatter) has special power to force men to reveal truths they would rather keep hidden, especially crimes against their fellows.

16. Kuusi, Bosley, and Branch indicate that the frequent use of dialogue and especially this kind of triplicate questioning are diagnostic features of Viking period poetry, which characteristically downplays supernatural themes and emphasizes individual character and personal relationships (1977:50–51). This suggests that in the original folk poems the woman questioner gets answers by force of will and intelligent playing upon what she knows of her interlocutor rather than by invoking a ritual or magical requirement.

17. In Child 1, 46, and 47 the potential lovers actually pose riddles to each other. In Child 2, however, they challenge each other with impossible tasks—in the familiar American versions: "Tell her to make me a cambric shirt," etc. Child treats these challenges as de facto riddles (1882–98, 1:8), and Barre Toelken analyzes "The Cambric Shirt" on the basis of a "willingness to believe that the impossible-sounding items and situations mentioned in the ballad are true riddles with answers that can be—or could have been—fruitfully sought, recognized, and appreciated by a ballad audience, based on its acquaintance with its own folklore" (1966:7). The interchangeability of task-form and riddle-form is also suggested by Child's C variant of 46, in which the woman demands that Captain Wedderburn "answer questions three" but phrases her "questions" as tasks: "You must get me to my supper a chicken without a bone," etc.

18. Ironically, although the parent whom the suitors approach *is* female in some (though not all) of the source poems, it is Lönnrot who canonized and brought to the attention of the world a situation in which, quite in contrast with Lévi-Strauss's notions regarding the fundamental basis of culture, *women* have control over marriage negotiations rather than being used as valuable objects for men to exchange (Lévi-Strauss, 1969:61–68).

19. At this stage the maid of the North is not explicit about rejecting Väinämöinen because of his age, but later when choosing Ilmarinen, although her mother prefers Väinämöinen, she insists: "I'll not marry Väinö-land's old man / to care for an ancient one: / woe would come from an old one / boredom from someone aged" (18:657–60).

20. Minimally, the image of splitting something with a "knife without a point" suggests sexual intercourse; and in English, at least, "split" has been a slang term for "to copulate" (Partridge, 1961:812). Compare the juxtaposition in the "Scarborough Fair" versions of Child 2 of the images of a "dry well" and a "sickle of leather" (Toelken, 1966:13). The subsequent mention of manipulation of an "egg" recalls the sequence of answers in the "I gave my love a cherry" versions of

Child 46 that suggest the progress of a pregnancy: blossom (= female genitals), egg, ring (compare "cracked in the ring" = no longer a virgin), and baby (Toelken, 1966:3–4). The maid's final request that Väinämöinen transform her spindle (a woman's tool and hence a metaphor for a woman, though simultaneously suggestive of a penis) into a boat (like the shoes tied to the bumper of newlyweds' cars, a partly open vessel symbolizing the vagina) is also not difficult to read as a sexual reference.

21. Väinämöinen dealt similarly with another young woman who was betrothed to him earlier in the epic. Aino drowns herself to escape the marriage, judging the freedom of death better "than to care for an old man / be a dodderer's refuge / one who trips on his stocking / who falls over a dry twig" (4:251–54). She is transformed into a fish, which Väinämöinen catches, but loses again because he does not realize that it is Aino. Pentikäinen suggests that Aino's "metamorphosis into a fish, which symbolizes fertility and womanhood, can perhaps be interpreted psychoanalytically as a girl's changing into a woman," that, "Aino knew immediately that Väinämöinen was not the right man for her, that the old man would not be able to satisfy the woman waking within her, and that he really wanted a servant girl," and that Väinämöinen's nonrecognition of the girl in her fish form proves "that he did not, in fact, recognize the girl's womanhood, and thus would never have been able to satisfy it" (1989:45).

22. Here, as in his previous courting of Aino and in his later warning to other old men against "competing for a maid / with another, younger man" (19:517–18), Väinämöinen appears rather ridiculous. It is clear, however, that—whatever some singers may have thought—Lönnrot did not intentionally burlesque his main character. Of the sage, Lönnrot wrote, "In these runes Väinämöinen is usually spoken of as grave, wise, and full of foresight, working for the good of coming generations, omniscient, powerful in incantation and in music—the hero of Finland. Furthermore, he is called old, although his age alone did not much affect his courting" (quoted in Haavio, 1952:5). In general, scholars have worked to deflect any humorous readings, arguing, for example, that instances of incompetence or human fallibility were the result of "degeneration" of the folk poems over time (Pentikäinen, 1989:48; and see Haavio's uniformly respectful treatment [1952]), although recently Pentikäinen has dared to suggest that "perhaps the old sage pays for the power of his word and his great ability as a conjurer through his impotence" (1989:212). Interestingly, it appears that the description of Väinämöinen's inability to recognize Aino when she comes to him as a fish *was* an intentional attempt by early Christian singers to discredit the pagan hero (Kuusi, Bosley, and Branch, 1977:550) and that Lönnrot included the episode for completeness without understanding its provenance.

23. In the preface to the 1835 *Old Kalevala* Lönnrot describes Lemminkäinen as "wanton, young, arrogant, boastful of his power and knowledge," and explains that "the courtship tasks designated for him at Pohjola cannot, in truth, be clarified, for on another occasion exactly the same tasks are even given to Ilmarinen. I have chosen runes in which it is possible to make a slight distinction between them" (quoted and translated in Pentikäinen, 1989:37). In other words,

Lönnrot himself assigned the tasks to Lemminkäinen and Ilmarinen, and it appears that he made his choices in light of what seemed appropriate to their respective characters. I have consequently felt justified in interpreting the tasks in terms of relatively modern conventional associations—that is, as I assume both Lönnrot and his nineteenth- and twentieth-century readers have or could—rather than trying to find ancient folk analogues.

24. In many societies smiths are treated with a mixture of fear and reverence. Because they are able to control fire and to fashion a natural material, metal ore, into the hardest material known to that society and especially into weapons, smiths are regarded as powerful and dangerous, socially marginal characters who are assumed to have superhuman powers and possibly demonic connections (Talley, 1977:139, 144, 224, 240).

25. The verbal exchange between the second daughter and Ilmarinen demonstrates similarities with a type of dialogue ballad found in many parts of Europe (see Child, 1882–98, 1:399, and the discussion in note 12). The formulaic dialogue in the *Kalevala* is unusual, however, if not unique, in at least three respects: the woman initiates it in response to an actual abduction, rather than a threatened seduction; it combines hypothetical statements with a real transformation; and one participant (significantly, the man) ultimately exercises control over *the other's* transformation, rather than just over his own. In many of these ballads the woman's willingness to engage in verbal play suggests that she is covertly encouraging the suitor's attentions, and in others, although she seriously rejects him at first, she is eventually impressed by his devotion or wittiness. In the *Kalevala,* in contrast, the girl's wish to escape is deadly serious, and because Ilmarinen possesses magic powers she lacks, his descriptions of means of controlling her are grim facts rather than playful expressions of desire.

References Cited

Alphonso-Karkala, John B. 1973. "Woman as Man's Resurrection in Kalevala and Mahabharata." *Indian Literature* 16 (1–2): 70–83.

Arendt, Hannah. 1958. *The Human Condition.* Chicago: University of Chicago Press.

Bakhtin, M. M. 1981. *The Dialogic Imagination.* Translated by Caryl Emerson and Michael Holquist. Austin: University of Texas Press.

Bosley, Keith, trans. 1989. *The Kalevala: An Epic Poem after Oral Tradition by Elias Lönnrot.* Oxford: Oxford University Press.

———, ed. and trans. 1990. *I Will Sing of What I Know: Fifty Lyrics, Ritual Songs, and Ballads from the Kanteletar.* Helsinki: Finnish Literature Society.

Branch, Michael. 1985. "Kalevala: From Myth to Symbol." In *Kalevala 1835–1985: The National Epic of Finland,* 1–8. Books from Finland. Helsinki: Helsinki University Library.

Brown, Marianne Wargelin. 1984. "Demythologizing Lönnrot: The *Kalevala* as Literature." *Ms.*

Child, Francis James, ed. 1882–98. *The English and Scottish Popular Ballads.* Boston: Houghton Mifflin.

Fox, Jennifer C. 1987. "The Creator Gods: Romantic Nationalism and the En-genderment of Women in Folklore." *Journal of American Folklore* 100 (398): 563–72.

Frye, Northrop. 1957. *Anatomy of Criticism.* Princeton: Princeton University Press.

Haavio, Martti. 1952. "Väinämöinen, Eternal Sage." *Folklore Fellows Communications* 144.

Hall, Stuart. 1980. "Encoding/Decoding." In *Culture, Media, Language: Working Papers in Cultural Studies, 1972–1979,* ed. Stuart Hall, Dorothy Hobson, Andrew Lowe, and Paul Willis, 128–38. London: Hutchinson.

Honko, Lauri. 1985. "The Kalevala Process." In *Kalevala 1835–1985: The National Epic of Finland,* 16–23. Books from Finland. Helsinki: Helsinki University Library.

Kaukonen, Väino. 1939. "Vanhan Kalevalan kokoonpano." Part 1. Helsinki: *Suomalaisen Kirjallisuuden Seuran Toimituksia* 213.

———. 1945. "Vanhan Kalevalan kokoonpano." Part 2. Helsinki: *Suomalaisen Kirjallisuuden Seuran Toimituksia* 213.

———. 1956. "Elias Lönnrotin Kalevala toinen painos." Helsinki: *Suomalaisen Kirjallisuuden Seuran Toimituksia* 247.

Kuusi, Matti, Keith Bosley, and Michael Branch. 1977. *Finnish Folk Poetry-Epic: An Anthology in Finnish and English.* Helsinki: Finnish Literature Society.

Laitinen, Kai. 1985. "The Kalevala and Finnish Literature." In *Kalevala 1835–1985: The National Epic of Finland,* ed. Books from Finland, 61–64. Helsinki: Helsinki University Library.

Lévi-Strauss, Claude. [1949] 1969. *The Elementary Structures of Kinship.* Translated by J. H. Bell, J. R. von Sturmer, and Rodney Needham. Edited by Rodney Needham. Boston: Beacon Press.

McDowell, John Holmes. 1979. *Children's Riddling.* Bloomington: Indiana University Press.

Magoun, Francis Peabody, Jr., ed. and trans. 1963. *The Kalevala or Poems of the Kaleva District, Compiled by Elias Lönnrot.* Cambridge, Mass.: Harvard University Press.

Murdock, George P., and Caterina Provost. 1973. "Factors in the Division of Labor by Sex: A Cross-cultural Analysis." *Ethnology* 12:203–25.

Nenola, Aili, and Senni Timonen, ed. 1990. *Louhen sanat: kirjoituksia kansanperinteen naisista.* Helsinki: Suomalaisen Kirjallisuuden Seura.

Nenola-Kallio, Aili. 1982. "Studies in Ingrian Laments." *Folklore Fellows Communications* 234.

Partridge, Eric, ed. 1961. *A Dictionary of Slang and Unconventional English.* London: Routledge and Kegan Paul.

Pentikäinen, Juha Y. [1987] 1989. *Kalevala Mythology.* Translated and edited by Ritva Poom. Bloomington: Indiana University Press.

Salminen, Väinö W., and Viljo Tarkiainen. 1963. *The Kalevala.* Appendix 1b in

The Kalevala or Poems of the Kaleva District, Compiled by Elias Lönnrot, ed. and trans. Francis Peabody Magoun, Jr. Cambridge, Mass.: Harvard University Press. Originally published in *Iso Tietosanakirja,* 2d ed., vol. 5, col. 1141–55. Helsinki, 1933.

Sanday, Peggy Reeves. 1981. *Female Power and Male Dominance: On the Origins of Sexual Inequality.* Cambridge: Cambridge University Press.

Sawin, Patricia E. 1988. "Lönnrot's Brainchildren: The Representation of Women in Finland's *Kalevala.*" *Journal of Folklore Research* 25 (3):187–217.

Talley, Jeannine Elizabeth. 1977. "The Blacksmith: A Study in Technology, Myth and Folklore." Ph.D. diss., University of California at Los Angeles.

Thompson, Stith. 1932–36. *Motif-Index of Folk-Literature.* 6 vols. Indiana University Studies, nos. 96–101. Bloomington: Indiana University.

Timonen, Senni. 1987. "The Cult of the Virgin Mary in Karelian Popular Tradition." *Acta Byzantica Fennica* 3:101–19.

———. 1990. "Women's Experience as Expressed in their Oral Poems." Paper presented at the annual meeting of the American Folklore Society, Oakland, Calif.

Toelken, Barre. 1966. "Riddles Wisely Expounded." *Western Folklore* 25:1–16.

Van D'Elden, Stephanie Cain. 1985. "Women in the World of the *Kalevala.*" Paper presented at Finnfest, Hancock, Mich.

Wilson, William A. 1976. *Folklore and Nationalism in Modern Finland.* Bloomington: Indiana University Press.

Ancient Egyptian Women and the Sky Goddess Nut

Modern scholarship acknowledges that every people and culture has its folklore, traditional materials, which serves, among other functions, to amuse, educate, validate, and maintain conformity in relation to that particular culture (Bascom, 1965:290–96). Interpreting folklore raises many questions, however, and commentators find a particular challenge in trying to understand a culture through its narrative forms such as myths and tales. As a result, an ever-increasing body of scholarship on the meaning of myths and tales has appeared over the millennia—for such interpretation had begun at least by the middle of the first millennium B.C.E.[1] (Honko, 1984:44–46)—which includes interpretations ranging from the allegorical to the psychoanalytic to the sociological and many more.[2] One approach asserts that the folklore reflects its people in something like a one-to-one correspondence (Honko, 1984:47). Observers have questioned, however, "the extent to which folklore . . . is a mirror of (a people's) culture and incorporates details of ceremonies, institutions and technology as well as the expression of beliefs and attitudes" (Bascom, 1965:284). Nevertheless, some recent commentators in the field of women's studies have used the one-to-one correspondence in seeking to understand the origins of the position of women in various cultures. For instance, in the early chapters of *Female Power and Male Dominance,* Peggy Reeves Sanday establishes "a congruence between the gender of a people's creator god(s), their orientation to the creative forces of nature, and the secular expression of male and female power" (1981:6). And the historian Gerda Lerner states, "If we applied Sanday's generalizations, which are derived from the study of contemporary primitive people, backward in time, we should expect to find major economic and social changes to occur prior to or about the time in which we find evidence of the change in creation stories in the societies of the Ancient Near East" (1986:146).

Egypt is one of the ancient Near Eastern societies to which Lerner refers, and it is one that would appear to be an excellent candidate for the approach that argues that a myth reflects its society. This is the case especially for women's studies because of the common understanding that the women of Ancient Egypt enjoyed rights equal to those of its men[3] in concert with the presence of several significant goddesses, among them the cosmogonic[4] sky goddess Nut. Using what Wendy Doniger O'Flaherty, a scholar of Sanskrit Indian mythology, has termed the "tool-box" approach (1980:3–14), which employs a range of different theories[5] about the meaning of myth to elicit the maximum understanding of the material, I will examine very briefly both the common beliefs about ancient Egyptian women and about Nut.[6] In some measure, the argument serves as a partial refutation of the myth-as-mirror-of-culture theory as presented by Sanday (1981) and especially by Lerner (1986), since it demonstrates that a one-to-one correspondence or cause and effect relationship between the position of ancient Egyptian women and the status and role of the cosmogonic Nut does not stand up under scrutiny.

As already noted, some commentators in the first millennium B.C.E. attempted to interpret and understand other peoples, one of which was the ancient Egyptians, through their myths. In the fifth century B.C.E., the Greek historian Herodotus wrote that the Egyptians "made all their customs and laws of a kind contrary for the most part to those of all other men. Among them, the women buy and sell, the men abide at home and weave; . . . Men carry burdens on their head, women on their shoulders" (2:35). In the first century B.C.E., seeking to explain the why of this "strange" behavior, Diodorus Siculus, another Greek, wrote:

> The Egyptians also made a law . . . permitting men to marry their sisters, this being due to the success attained by (the goddess) Isis in this respect; for she had married her brother Osiris, and upon his death, having taken a vow never to marry another man, she both avenged the murder of her husband and reigned all her days over the land with complete respect for the laws, and, in a word, became the cause of more and greater blessings to all men than any other. It is for these reasons, in fact, that it was ordained that the queen should have greater power and honour than the king and that among private persons the wife should enjoy authority over her husband, the husbands agreeing in the marriage contract that they will be obedient in all things to their wives. (1.27.1–2)

Clearly Diodorus felt that the status of Egyptian women was based on the actions of their deities, that is, that the culture mirrored the myth,[7] and both he and Herodotus were impressed with the sharp divergence of Egyptian behavior from that with which they were acquainted in their contemporary Greek worlds (Pomeroy, 1975:78). In their times, ancient Greeks cloistered their women and definitely treated them as second-class people, not even having the rights of citizens (Pomeroy, 1984:45–47). Because of this background, one can view the Greek historians' comments, probably correctly, as exaggerations or overstatements about reality, but at the same time one must give credence to their observations that there was something distinctive about the Egyptian women they encountered. But what were these differences and, Diodorus notwithstanding, why did they arise?

In addressing these questions, some very real problems come to light. For one, Herodotus and Diodorus wrote respectively near and at the end of the decline of what had once been a magnificent civilization with a very long history. In Herodotus's time, the third quarter of the fifth century B.C.E., the Persians controlled Egypt, and when Diodorus wrote, the land was under the rule of the Ptolemies, the Greek heirs of Alexander the Great who conquered the world in the third quarter of the fourth century B.C.E. Thus one should be wary of taking these men's observations and projecting them back over the nearly three millennia of history that preceded them, since the cultural values, beliefs, and practices would have changed and developed during this long span of time. And along with concern about the biases of the Greek historians, one must be alert to the biases of modern views and commentary as well.

To meet these concerns, one must obviously go directly to Egyptian sources themselves, but this action too is problematical, for the materials available for study are far more numerous from later periods than from earlier times, and also climatic effects and conditions of preservation affected these materials differently in different parts of the country. For example, the drier areas of southern Egypt tended to be more conducive to preservation than the wetter lands of the northern Delta area with its higher water table.

Bearing these caveats in mind, the investigator may begin to ask how the materials portray women during Egypt's long history. Again, one must exercise caution for, as in any culture, women in Egypt ranged from the very privileged, such as queens and nobility, to the very poor, and one would expect to find many more materials deriving from the former than from the latter. In fact, generally the materials about the lower classes are available merely as appendages to materials focusing on the elite and then in idealized form.[8] Again, because of the time span involved, one must be alert to and have respect for historical processes and change.

One of the most revealing circumstances about the status of ancient

Egyptian women lies in the fact that several of them actually ruled the land, something which sets this civilization apart from other contemporary cultures. The most notable ruling queen was Hatshepsut, the female king of the eighteenth dynasty who ruled in the second quarter of the fifteenth century B.C.E.[9] She truly ruled, promoting activities such as trading expeditions and extensive building, as would any powerful king, even portraying herself as such with the ceremonial beard and male dress kilt (Hayes, 1959:94–95, figs. 51, 52), but she was not the only woman who ruled. Twosre at the end of the nineteenth dynasty and Nefrusobk at the end of the twelfth dynasty also ruled the land, and there is reason to think that two first dynasty queens, Neith-Hetep and Meret-Neith, did so too (Seipel, 1980:14, 35). In fact, Meret-Neith had a tomb at Abydos, the ancient royal cemetery in southern Egypt, comparable in size to, and set among those of, contemporaneous male rulers.[10]

Although not so clearly an independent ruler as the preceding women, another famous and powerful royal woman was Nefertiti, the wife and queen of the so-called "heretic" King Akhenaton, ruler during the third quarter of the fourteenth century B.C.E., who is known to many because of her beautiful bust in the Egyptian Museum in Berlin. Much debate rages over the exact influence that this woman had on the rule of her husband,[11] though there is no question that various representations depict her in typical royal poses such as the head-smiting scenes so characteristic of kings (Redford, 1984:138). As a strong ruling power either with or behind her husband, she inherited the legacy from earlier queens in the same eighteenth dynasty who also exercised great power relative to the throne, e.g. Ahhotep I and Ahmose Nefertari.[12] Thus while such occurrences were rare, women could actually rule in ancient Egypt. This fact was noted by the third-century B.C.E. Egyptian priest Manetho in his *Aegyptiaca (Epitome)* when he wrote that in the second dynasty the king Binothris/Biophis, probably Ninetjer, the third king of the dynasty, "decided that women might hold the kingly office" (Fr. 8–10). They also could exercise strong influence on their ruling husbands.

Two major questions arise from the presence of strong and ruling queens. First, did equality truly exist when only a handful of women, probably five,[13] ruled during the periods of native rule, while virtually countless men ruled?[14] And second, how did women reach this position and what supported and justified them in such a high place? A partial response lies in circumstances, for each queen seems originally to have stepped into a breach in the male succession, ruling at least initially as regent for an underage male heir or as queen regnant when the dynasty lacked an obvious male heir. These situations tended to happen coincidentally with times of political disturbance or government disorder. None save Hatshepsut ruled for more than a year or two, and none save Hatshepsut made much of an impact. It is also important to note that many epithets carried by various queens, both ruling and nonruling, described them in relation to the king,[15] but no reciprocal epithets were borne by the king. Thus while a queen could be *mwt nsw,* "mother of the king," no king was **it ḥmt nsw,*[16] "father of the queen." Furthermore, she was designated most often as *ḥmt nsw,* literally "wife of the king," while the king was *nsw,* "king," or occasionally by means of the feminine form of a word normally used for the king, e.g., *ity.t* (queen) from *ity* (king). Thus it appears that in fact males did dominate the kingship, but females were not totally excluded and indeed actually participated both directly and indirectly at different times.

Not surprisingly this mixed picture of the respective roles of the king and the queen appears in iconographic representations[17] of royalty. An excellent example is available in the comparison of two portrayals of royal couples dating from the Old Kingdom in the fourth dynasty, ca. 2575 to 2465 B.C.E. The first example is a broken statue of Djedef-Re, the third king of the dynasty (2528–2520 B.C.E.), with his queen, Khenitit-n-ka, the latter in very small size, squatting with her arm about his lower left leg (Smith, 1949:32, fig. 10). In contrast, the sixth king of the same dynasty, Menkaure (Mycerinus [2490–2472 B.C.E.]), the builder of the smallest of the three great pyramids at Giza, is portrayed standing shoulder to shoulder beside his queen, Khamerernebty, she with her arm about his waist (Aldred, 1965:111, ill. 110). The difference is striking, even without knowledge of the Egyptian convention of depicting the most important person or persons in a scene as very large and all others much smaller (Schäfer, 1974:231–32). The first example suggests a sharply divergent importance between the king and his queen, while the second shows an equality not even hinted at in the first. Nevertheless, these two modes of presentation of the royal couple "existed side by side without conflict" (Aldred, 1965:114–15).

Lest a question arise that this mixed picture was limited to the Old Kingdom, it is important to note that Nefertari, the beloved wife of Ramesses II of the nineteenth dynasty in the New Kingdom (1290–1223 B.C.E.), appears in both modes. The king's colossi at Abu Simbel show the huge king accompanied by considerably smaller forms of his wife and children at his feet (Freed, 1987:66–67), and yet he honored this same queen with one of the most beautiful tombs in the Valley of the Queens (Hornung, 1983:52), the mortuary area for royal spouses in the period. The existence of the Valley of the Queens speaks to the honoring of queens in general as they, like their husbands, were entombed in special areas. Nevertheless at this time, as earlier, the central figure was the king, not the queen. What the queen had, she had through the king.

Among nonroyal women of the middle and upper classes much the same pattern prevails. Nonroyal Old Kingdom pair statues depict the same equality seen in the pair portraying Menkaure and his queen (cf. Smith, 1949:plates 25c, 25f, 26g), and yet various contemporaneous wall reliefs and sculptures also show the woman as much smaller than her husband (cf. Lange and Hirmer, 1957:plate 74; Smith, 1949:plate 221). During the New Kingdom, paintings and reliefs on the walls of nonroyal tombs often present the husband and wife as equal in size, usually with the wife shown seated or standing behind her husband. Since the tombs are most often his, that she appears the same size suggests at least companionship and possibly an equal status. Furthermore, although artistic convention depicts the woman behind the man, she is actually right beside him (Schäfer, 1974:172), thus affirming the companionship.[18]

A few of the paintings also tell the modern observer other information about women in this period. For instance, some funerary depictions from the New Kingdom and earlier show scribal paraphernalia under the chairs of women, replicating the portrayals of male scribes, a highly respected group. Since the materials shown under the chair in funerary depictions represent items closely associated with the deceased during their lifetimes, one can be sure that some women actually were literate (Bryan, 1984:17–32). These New Kingdom women were not unique, however, for at least one woman from the sixth dynasty apparently acted as vizier,[19] that is, as the king's deputy ruler (rather like a prime minister), a job requiring literacy, and others acted as administrators for both personal estates and in larger offices as well (Théodoridès, 1975:289).

Written documents show that women of all periods had various legal rights upon which they could and did act, though there was not a written body of laws in ancient Egypt. For instance, a document from the Old Kingdom states that a man willed a plot of land to his wife, while another tells of a man who disposed of land for the benefit of his wife and sons (Allam, 1989:124).[20] It also appears that Egyptian women of the New Kingdom had the same rights of inheritance as men, and one New Kingdom document reports that a woman successfully sued for her heritage following her husband's death (James, 1984:95–96). A woman was entitled to one-third of her husband's estate on his death, and she could inherit from her father just as did her male siblings. She also could serve as executor for an estate (B. Lesko, 1987:22). Furthermore, a woman's dowry was hers should her marriage result in divorce, and there existed marriage contracts to govern this and other possible eventualities (Théodoridès, 1975:284; Pestman, 1961).

That these legal rights existed within real relationships shows on the mortuary stela[21] of the butler Merer of Edfu, dating from the twenty-first century B.C.E., where he refers to his "beloved wife, who shares (his) estate" (Lichtheim, 1973:87), conveying a sense of caring and harmony. This sense of concern for the woman, like women's legal rights, has antecedents in the older periods. In a text from the late sixth dynasty, ca. 2200 B.C.E., the vizier Ptahhotep instructs his son:[22]

> If you prosper, found your house,
> And love your wife ardently,[23]
> Fill her stomach, clothe her back.
> The unguent soothes her body.
> Gladden her heart as long as you live,
> She is a fertile field for her lord.
> (Ptah. 325–30).

He suggests the need to please her; in return she will provide him with richness, which means children according to most interpreters. Ptahhotep continues:

> You should not reprove her (or)
> Keep her from power (or) restrain her—
> Her eye is her storm when she looks about her—
> This assures she stays in your house.
> (Ptah. 331–35)

Both sections counsel the preservation of harmony, peace, and an intact household. Unspoken but implied by Ptahhotep is the sense that a beleaguered or crossed woman not only could, but would, leave her husband. Nowhere does there appear the command that a man make his wife submit to or obey him (B. Lesko, 1987:29–30). The woman was truly *nbt hwt,* "mistress of the house," and was respected as such.

In a New Kingdom instructional text, Any, a minor government official, gives advice to his son that shows the same kind of respect:

> Do not control your wife in her house,
> When you know she is efficient;
> . . . .
> Let your eye observe in silence,
> Then you recognize her skill;
> It is joy when your hand is with her.
> (Lichtheim, 1976:143)

Any also advises his son to care for and support his mother, the person who cared for and nourished him when he was an infant and incontinent (Lichtheim, 1976:141).

It is important to note, however, that each of these counsels is presented by or to a man in terms of his needs and pleasures, not those of the woman, even though in them she is respected. In fact, Any observes that "a woman is asked about her husband, (while) a man is asked about his rank" (Lichtheim, 1976:140). This statement, clearly defining nonroyal women in relation to men, recalls the many epithets of queens that related them to the king.

Considering that the largest number of texts from this culture, as from nearly all ancient cultures, were written by men, one can expect concern for the man's situation to be paramount, and yet one wonders what a man meant to a woman in the course of her daily life and marriage. Lacking similar texts from women, it is a hard question to answer. That they took pleasure in men, however, does find expression in the corpus of love songs dating to the late New Kingdom, some of which reflect a woman's hand as she speaks of her lover and her delight in him.[24] Nevertheless, modern researchers must take very seriously the definition of women in texts in terms of their relationships with men.

From this brief survey, it is clear that in the world of ancient Egypt, women were respected and had a certain independence, but their position was not as extreme as the Greek commentators asserted. The latter reflected the contrast of the Egyptian culture with their own as much as objective observation. Something similar is also the case with Diodorus's attribution of women's status to Isis's actions, for Isis, while dominant during the Greek period, did not hold such a status in the earliest periods of Egyptian history (Hollis, 1989b, 1990).

As it happens, however, Egypt was distinctive among its neighboring cultures in having in its mythology a cosmogonic sky goddess, Nut. This situation represents a sharp contrast with the sky gods of Egypt's neighbors, e.g., Baal, Marduk, Zeus, and YHWH,[25] and should lead, following Sanday's and Lerner's reflective theories, to just the kind of behaviors described by Herodotus and Diodorus.

In her cosmogonic role Nut, *Nwt,* fills a very defined and significant place in the creation and maintenance of the Egyptian cosmos. Her importance is eminently clear from her presence and actions in the Pyramid Texts—the earliest religious texts, written on the walls of the pyramids beginning about 2350 B.C.E.—texts in which she is clearly the dominant goddess.[26] In these texts, she and her husband Geb represent respectively sky and earth, the reverse of what is the case in Canaan, Mesopotamia, and Greece. The historian of religions Mircea Eliade, referring to the feminine nature of the sky, incorrectly dismissed her anomalous presence as "a chance of grammar" (Eliade, 1958:242, 1975:365). For one thing, Nut is not the only female sky deity in Egypt since Hathor also fills this role (see Hollis, 1989a), although Nut is the only formally cosmogonic one. Furthermore, the situation can hardly be accidental considering that in the language of the ancient Egyptians, the various words for earth are usually masculine and those for sky are generally feminine (see L. Lesko, 1991:117–18; Silverman, 1991:34; Hornung, 1982:68; te Velde, 1977:163).

The most common Egyptian word for sky is *pt,* and although at times the two words, *pt* and the goddess's name *nwt,* may appear to be interchangeable (Erman and Grapow, 1982, 1:491.8; 2:214.15), in fact, generally they are not. Nut, perceived largely as the night sky,[27] appears in an organic activity, namely bearing the gods,[28] rather than as the static, lifeless, heavenly roof of the world structure that is the usual portrayal of the sky (Kurth, 1981:535–38nn6–7). This activity makes her more than a simple personification of the sky.

As bearer of the gods, Nut fits mythically into the so-called Heliopolitan theology, a theology originating with the priests in the northern Egyptian town of Heliopolis (cf. Gardiner, 1961:84; L. Lesko, 1991:91–92). In this scheme, Nut and her husband Geb are the children of Shu and Tefnut, the primordial parents, and grandchildren of Atum, the primordial creator.[29] Nut and Geb are also the parents of four active, noncosmogonic gods, Osiris, Isis, Seth, and Nephthys, and the grandparents of Horus, the son of Osiris and Isis. Horus appears as the ruling king on earth, while his father, Osiris, is the deceased king who rules as king of the underworld. In a slightly different genealogy, also Heliopolitan in origin, Nut is the mother of the so-called epagomenal[30] gods: Osiris, Horus, Seth, Isis, and Nephthys, born on the five extracalendrical days of the year (Sethe, 1908–10:2, §1961c). Here again Osiris and Horus are respectively the deceased king/king of the underworld and the living king.

In both genealogies, Nut is intricately bound up with the royal house of Egypt, most especially with the deceased ruler. It is she who receives Osiris in the sky as his mother, a sharp contrast to the more usual reception of the deceased by mother earth, as appears in many other cultures (Eliade, 1959:140–41). For instance, in the earliest pyramid with Pyramid Texts, the deceased king is assured that "the embrace of your mother Nut will enfold you" (Sethe, 1908–10:1, §208b) and, in a text from a later pyramid, that "she has embraced you in her name of 'Coffin' and you have been brought to her in her name of 'Tomb'" (Sethe, 1908–10:1, §616d-f). The tomb and the coffin were, of course, actually those places, the localities in which the remains of the deceased were placed. It must be understood, however, that even as "coffin" and "tomb," Nut was not envisioned as an earth-related deity, as are many mother goddesses, but rather as the embracing protector *in the sky,* as a third Pyramid Text attests: "Sothis has caused [the king] to fly up to the sky in the company of [his] brethren the gods, Nut the great has uncovered her arms for [him]" (Sethe, 1908–10:1, §459*b-c*). Yet another statement shows her as the heavenly goal to which the deceased king aspired, declaring: "You have set this king as an imperishable star who is in you" (Sethe, 1908–10:1, §782*e*). Certainly there is no question that Nut was an active sky deity, playing a very significant role in assisting the king to achieve life among the gods, embracing him as a star in the sky in the role of his mother.

As the night sky, Nut also swallowed the stars, sometimes withholding them from view for lengthy periods of time.[31] One tale relates that this action evoked the wrath of her husband-brother Geb, necessitating the forcible separation of the pair by their father, Shu (Parker and Neugebauer, 1960:1, 67–68). This narrative represents the Egyptian version of the separation of the earth and sky by force, an act of creation.[32]

Correspondingly Nut bore the stars on a regular basis, including the brightest star, the sun-god Re, giving birth to him daily. Thus, it is not surprising to find the king seeking to be identified with the sun in his search for eternal rebirth and life. Again a text from one of the pyramids describes the situation. In it, the king is commanded: "Sit on the throne of Re that you may give orders to the gods, because you are Re who came forth from Nut who bears Re daily, and she bears [you] daily like Re" (Sethe, 1908–10:2, §1688*a-c*). The same image appears iconographically in royal tombs of the New Kingdom where the sun is shown being swallowed by Nut in the evening, traversing through her body at night, to be born again at dawn. It also appears, although less elaborately, on coffin lids, where it serves to emphasize Nut's age-old role as the coffin, a role in which she literally embraces the deceased.

It is especially in her relation to the sun that it is possible to see at least one reason why the Egyptians had a sky goddess. Egypt was and is a country dominated by sun—even today rain is rare, and it is accepted that although pharaonic times may have been marginally wetter than modern times (Butzer, 1976:26), rain was very much a rarity then as well. It is not surprising, therefore, to find in a land where the daily rebirth of the sun was a given, where there was little rain, and where water came from the ground, i.e., the caverns from which the Nile and its annual flood with its fertile topsoil appeared to originate, that a sky goddess and an earth god fulfilled the same functions as those deities portrayed in the more usual configuration of a sky god who gives water and an earth goddess who gives growth. That is to say, the sky goddess Nut, mother of the sun, provided one of the essentials of life, namely the daily rebirth of the sun, and the earth god Geb provided the other, namely water, semen if you will (cf. te Velde, 1977:163). Numerous mythological papyri depict their relationship, including the impregnation of Nut by Geb and the separation of the pair by their father Shu. One might suppose that the need for the daily rebirth of the constellations, clearly a female function in nature, contributed to, or even demanded, the existence of a cosmogonic sky goddess. Finally it is necessary to note one other implication of Nut's activity: she is de facto the regulator of the passage of days and nights, the movement of the sun and stars, therefore of time, a function normally established in the ancient world by male deities, e.g., Marduk of Babylon (Pritchard, 1969:67–68, 501) and YHWH of ancient Israel (Gen. 1:14–19).[33]

An examination of the worship and ritual of this goddess shows that her cult was relatively modest. She had few priests and fewer sanctuaries, although she is known to have received food offerings in her mortuary role and to have been presented the sacred menat necklace in a ritual scene (Kurth, 1981:538). The minimality of cultic practice demonstrates her distance from the living people, both as the night sky and as a mortuary deity.[34] In fact, her appearance in third-millennium B.C.E. Egypt perhaps reflects more the powerful priesthood at Heliopolis (Gardiner, 1961:84) than a belief emanating from the people.

Finally, despite Nut's importance in the cosmogonic configuration and her dominance as a goddess in the most ancient mortuary texts, she is neither the oldest nor cultically the most significant of the goddesses. Two more ancient goddesses, Neith, who predominates in the very earliest periods and demonstrates aspects of a primordial creator (Hollis, 1987a), and Hathor, who rose to prominence in the last half of the third millennium B.C.E. (Hollis, 1988, 1989a, 1989b), were far more central to everyday life than Nut, and they both had cults with numerous attendant personnel (Galvin, 1981). In addition, that certain evidence of the existence of Nut is unknown before her appearance in the Pyramid Texts (Hollis, 1987b), added to her few sanctuaries and almost nonexistent priesthood, suggests that despite her position in the sky, she could not have influenced directly the position of women in the formative years of this culture, as, for instance, during the time of the reigning queens Meret-Neith and Neith-Hetep during the first dynasty.[35] Her distance from the living people in contrast with the centrality of Neith and Hathor suggests that these latter two deities would be the more likely candidates to have affected women in some way. Since, however, neither Neith nor

Hathor fits into the neat cosmogonic role filled by Nut during the time of the native dynasts,[36] it is clear that a congruence of ancient Egypt's creator deities with the expression of female and male power postulated by Sanday and built upon by Lerner does not withstand scrutiny such as given it here, and thus one concludes that ancient Egypt's folklore/ mythology questionably serves as a mirror of its culture.

Although one cannot validate a one-to-one correspondence between the practices of the ancient Egyptians and its expressed mythology, the theory has proved useful as a challenge not only to examine the relationship but also to look at the component parts, studies which are continuing. Much work remains to be done, not only making use of the tools of feminist discourse and literary criticism but also those of feminist anthropology and archaeology of ancient cultures (cf. Meyers, 1988, 1989) as well as in analyzing the growth and interrelationships of Egyptian myths.

Notes

An earlier version of this essay appeared in 1987 in the *Journal of American Folklore* 100 (398): 496–503. My thanks to Bruce Jackson for his editorial suggestions pertinent to its inclusion in that volume. The present essay represents a thorough reworking of the earlier paper, reflecting both the incisive comments of my coeditors and outside readers and my research instigated by and done since the earliest version was presented in 1986 at the annual meeting of the American Folklore Society in Baltimore.

1. The abbreviations B.C.E. and C.E. stand for, respectively, "before the common era" and "common era," which replace the older abbreviations B.C., "before Christ," and A.D., "anno Domini."

2. For delineation and discussion of the different approaches, see Honko (1984:41–61), Cohen (1969:337–53), Doty (1986:chap. 2), and Kirk (1974:chaps. 1, 3, and 4).

3. For example, see Desroches-Noblecourt (1986:276–78), Théodoridès (1975:280), B. Lesko (1987:intro.), and Wenig (1969:11).

4. *Cosmogonic* means having to do with the creation of the cosmos, the universe.

5. See the references in note 2 for some of the possibilities.

6. The study of the women of ancient Egypt is in its infancy and has scarcely been affected by the tools of modern feminist scholarship. Such is also the case for the goddesses, although some of them, most notably Isis and to a lesser degree Hathor, have been the subject of major monographs. Even in these cases, however, the resources of modern feminist scholarship have not been used.

7. The apparent difference between the approach contending that a culture

mirrors its myth and a myth mirrors its culture revolves around the commentator's perception of the origin of a myth: did the myth precede the people and their practices or did the people construct the myth and then treat it as "other," having objective power? While at least some myths reflect the encounter with the ineffable "other," the expression of this "other" is idiosyncratic. Thus a discussion of origins, while fascinating, falls outside the scope of this chapter.

8. On this point see the essays by H. G. Fischer, William A. Ward, and G. Robins in B. Lesko (1989) and Fischer (1989a). In two recent articles, John Baines has begun to explore the "ordinary" people of ancient Egypt, at least in relation to religion, a topic very little addressed in previous scholarship (1987, 1991).

9. According to Baines and Málek (1984:32), her dates were 1473–1458 B.C.E. See also note 13.

10. W. F. Flinders Petrie (1900) viewed Meret-Neith as a male ruler. See his frontispiece.

11. See especially the implications found in the temples of this queen, which Donald B. Redford and his archaeological team have excavated and studied (1984).

12. Leonard Lesko (1986) argues that three tales from the post-Akhenaton Egypt, i.e., the later New Kingdom, reflected a negative attitude toward queens as a reaction to these strong queens.

13. The use of the equivocal words *probably* and *possibly* reflects the gaps in certainty about historical facts for ancient Egypt. For instance, many dates are far from certain, and the same applies to the rulers in particular time periods as well, especially periods of general governmental upheaval and distress.

14. The numbers are truly in question but range upward of 144 native Egyptian dynasts (Baines and Málek, 1984:32–33).

15. See Troy (1986:app. A and B).

16. Among ancient Near Eastern scholars, it is customary to put an asterisk before an unattested word or phrase to show its hypothetical or speculative nature.

17. *Iconographic* refers to pictorial in every sense, sculpture, painting, and relief. It is important to note that art did not exist simply for the sake of art in ancient Egypt, but rather all representations served a purpose other than literal imagery.

18. See Fischer (1989a) for a detailed discussion.

19. See Théodoridès (1975:289); see also Fischer (1976:74).

20. See Fischer (1989a, 1989b) for more discussion.

21. A stela is a commemorative slab or upright stone celebrating the deceased.

22. I have translated this and the following reference to Ptahhotep from the hieroglyphic text published by Zába (1956). The last line, the subject of much heated discussion, has parallels within the Arabic world. A convenient translation of the whole text may be found in Lichtheim (1973:61–80), specifically p. 69.

23. What I have translated as "ardently" means, literally, "with blistering."

24. See Lichtheim (1976:182–84, stanzas 2, 4, 6; 190–91, numbers 7 and 8).

25. Baal, Marduk, Zeus, and YHWH come respectively from Canaan, Mesopo-

tamia (Babylon), Greece, and the Hebrew people. Canaan was what is now the Israelite-Palestinian area and refers to the land in the second and first millennia B.C.E., and Mesopotamia was present-day Iraq. YHWH, the Tetragrammaton, refers to the proper name of the Israelites' deity.

26. A count of the references in the Pyramid Texts to the most important goddesses reveals that Nut appears ninety-nine times, Isis eighty-two, Nephthys sixty-six (fifty-seven of Isis's and Nephthys's appearances are as a pair in parallel actions), Neith seven, and Hathor three.

27. Her role as the night sky emphasizes her cosmogonic nature, for in this and neighboring cultures, the creation began in XAOΣ, chaos, which is infinite darkness, nether abyss.

28. In the Coffin Texts, the corpus of mortuary texts from the Middle Kingdom, she is named "the one who bears the gods" (Buck, 1935–61:7, 120e). I have translated this text from the hieroglyphic as I have also done for those cited as "Sethe."

29. Atum or Atum-Re is usually presented iconographically as male but like all Egyptian primordial creators, whether shown as male or female, is defined by androgynous epithets, e.g. "father of fathers, mother of mothers" (Westendorf, 1976:634).

30. *Epagomenal* is intercalary, used especially, although not solely, in relation to these particular gods in this particular culture.

31. One can relate this observation to the absence from view at different times of particular stars and constellations due, as modern astronomy has shown, to the earth's rotation.

32. See Eliade (1958:241), for other examples, and Numazawa (1953), for a general discussion. For further discussion of this concept specific to ancient Egypt, see te Velde (1977).

33. To date, scholars have neglected to give serious consideration to this aspect of her being.

34. Her distance might lead a student of comparative religions, especially those of classical and ancient Near Eastern cultures, to ask if Nut could be identified with Mircea Eliade's *deus otiosus* (1963:93–98) or Frank Moore Cross's "olden gods" (1976). In each case, the cosmogonic gods so characterized either withdrew to the sky or were killed by succeeding generations, thus leaving their creations to be ruled by other (younger) deities. Given Nut's persistent presence as the sky and her continuing significance in the mortuary realm, to define her as an otiose or olden deity appears inappropriate despite the minimality of priests, cults, and temples. Nevertheless, since Cross suggests that the funerary cult of the (dead) Hermopolitan Ogdoad (another set of ancient Egyptian creator deities) is the exception that proves the point (1976:332), an examination of the possible presence of otiose or "olden" deities in Egypt presents a challenging topic for further study. For the beginning of such a discussion, see Hollis (1992).

35. On this problem, see Hollis (1989b).

36. Although certain names connected with Neith in the earliest history

of Egypt hint at cosmogonic activity by her, she did not appear as an explicitly cosmogonic deity until the Ptolemaic period, in the last years of Egyptian history.

References Cited

Aldred, Cyril. 1965. *Egypt to the End of the Old Kingdom.* London: Thames and Hudson.

Allam, Schafik. 1989. "Women as Owners of Immovables in Pharaonic Egypt." In *Women's Earliest Records from Ancient Egypt and Western Asia,* ed. Barbara S. Lesko, 123–35. Atlanta, Ga.: Scholars Press.

Baines, John. 1987. "Practical Religion and Piety." *Journal of Egyptian Archaeology.* 73:79–98.

———. 1991. "Society, Morality, and Religious Practice." In *Religion in Ancient Egypt: Gods, Myths, and Personal Practice,* ed. Byron E. Shafer, 123–200. Ithaca: Cornell University Press.

Baines, John, and Jaromír Málek. 1984. *Atlas of Ancient Egypt.* New York: Facts on File.

Bascom, William R. 1965. "Four Functions of Folklore." In *The Study of Folklore,* ed. Alan Dundes, 279–98. Englewood Cliffs, N.J.: Prentice Hall. Originally published in *Journal of American Folklore* 67 (1954): 333–49.

Bryan, Betsy M. 1984. "Evidence for Female Literacy from Theban Tombs of the New Kingdom." *Bulletin of the Egyptological Seminar* 6:17–32.

Buck, Adriaan de. 1935–61. *The Egyptian Coffin Texts.* 7 vols. Chicago: University of Chicago.

Butzer, Karl W. 1976. *Early Hydraulic Civilization in Egypt.* Chicago: University of Chicago Press.

Cohen, Percy S. 1969. "Theories of Myth." *Man* 4:337–53.

Cross, Frank Moore. 1976. "The 'Olden Gods' in Ancient Near Eastern Creation Myths." In *Magnalia Dei: The Mighty Acts of God, Essays in the Bible and Archaeology in Memory of G. Ernest Wright,* ed. Frank Moore Cross, Werner E. Lemke, and Patrick D. Miller, Jr., 329–38. Garden City, N.Y.: Doubleday.

Desroches-Noblecourt, Christiane. 1986. *La femme au temps des pharaons.* Paris: Stock/Laurence Pernoud.

Diodorus Siculus (Diodorus of Sicily). 1968. *Library of History 1.* Books 1–2. Translated by C. H. Oldfather. Loeb Classical Library, no. 279. Cambridge, Mass.: Harvard University Press.

Doty, William G. 1986. *Mythography: The Study of Myths and Rituals.* Tuscaloosa: University of Alabama Press.

Dundes, Alan, ed. 1984. *Sacred Narrative: Readings in the Theory of Myth.* Berkeley: University of California Press.

Eliade, Mircea. 1958. *Patterns in Comparative Religion.* Translated by Rosemary Sheed. New York: Sheed and Ward.

———. 1959. *The Sacred and the Profane: The Nature of Religion.* Translated by Willard R. Trask. New York: Harcourt Brace.

———. 1963. *Myth and Reality.* Translated by William R. Trask. New York: Harper Colophon Books.

———. 1975. *Myths, Rites, Symbols: A Mircea Eliade Reader.* Vol. 2, ed. Wendell C. Beane and William G. Doty. New York: Harper Colophon Books.

Erman, Adolf, and Hermann Grapow. 1982. *Wörterbuch der aegyptischen Sprache.* 4th ed. 5 vols. Berlin: Akademie-Verlag.

Fischer, Henry George. 1976. *Egyptian Studies I: Varia.* New York: Metropolitan Museum of Art.

———. 1989a. *Egyptian Women of the Old Kingdom and of the Heracleopolitan Period.* New York: Metropolitan Museum of Art.

———. 1989b. "Women in the Old Kingdom and the Heracleopolitan Period." In *Women's Earliest Records from Ancient Egypt and Western Asia,* ed. Barbara S. Lesko, 5–24. Atlanta, Ga.: Scholars Press.

Freed, Rita. 1987. *Ramesses the Great: An Exhibition in the City of Memphis.* Memphis: City of Memphis, Tenn.

Galvin, Marianne. 1981. *The Priestesses of Hathor in the Old Kingdom and the First Intermediate Period.* Ann Arbor, Mich.: UMI.

Gardiner, Sir Alan. 1961. *Egypt of the Pharaohs.* New York: Oxford University Press.

Hayes, William C. 1959. *The Scepter of Egypt: A Background for the Study of the Egyptian Antiquities in the Metropolitan Museum of Art. Part II: The Hyksos Period and the New Kingdom (1675–1080 B.C.).* New York: Metropolitan Museum of Art.

Herodotus. 1975. *Histories.* Books 1–2. Translated by A. D. Godley. Loeb Classical Library, no. 117. Cambridge, Mass.: Harvard University Press.

Hollis, Susan Tower. 1987a. "The Goddess Neith in Ancient Egypt through the End·of the Third Millennium B.C." Paper presented at the annual meeting of the American Academy of Religion, Boston, Mass.

———. 1987b. "Nut in the Pyramid Texts." Paper presented at the annual meeting of the American Research Center in Egypt, Memphis, Tenn.

———. 1988. "Neith: Bees, Beetles, and the Red Crown in the Third Millennium B.C." Paper presented at the annual meeting of the American Research Center in Egypt, Chicago, Ill.

———. 1989a. "Neith, Hathor, and the Queen in the Third Millennium B.C.E.. Egypt." Paper presented at the annual meeting of the American Research Center in Egypt, Philadelphia, Pa.

———. 1989b. "The Roles of Two Third Millennium BCE Egyptian Goddesses: Hathor and Isis." Paper presented at the annual meeting of the Society of Biblical Literature, Anaheim, Calif.

———. 1990. "Isis until the End of the Old Kingdom." Paper presented at the annual meeting of the American Research Center in Egypt, Berkeley, Calif.

———. 1992. "Otiose Deities and the Ancient Egyptian Pantheon." Paper presented at the annual meeting of the American Research Center in Egypt, Seattle, Wash.

Honko, Lauri. 1984. "The Problem of Defining Myth." In *Sacred Narrative: Readings in the Theory of Myth,* ed. Alan Dundes, 41–61. Berkeley: University of California Press. Originally published in *The Myth of the State,* ed. Haralds Biezias, 7–19. Stockholm: Almqvist and Wiksell Förlag.

Hornung, Erik. 1982. *Conceptions of God in Ancient Egypt: The One and the Many.* Translated by John Baines. Ithaca, N.Y.: Cornell University Press.

———. 1983. *Tal der Könige: Die Ruhestätte der Pharaonen.* Zürich: Artemis Verlag.

James, T. G. H. 1984. *Pharaoh's People.* Chicago: University of Chicago Press.

Kirk, G. S. 1974. *The Nature of Greek Myths.* New York: Penguin.

Kurth, Dieter. 1981. "Nut." *Lexikon der Ägyptologie,* vol. 4:535–41. Wiesbaden: Otto Harrassowitz.

Lange, K., and M. Hirmer. 1957. *Egypt: Architecture, Sculpture, Painting in Three Thousand Years.* 2d ed. Translated by R. H. Boothroyd. London: Phaidon Press.

Lerner, Gerda. 1986. *The Creation of Patriarchy.* New York: Oxford University Press.

Lesko, Barbara. 1987. *The Remarkable Women of Ancient Egypt.* 2d ed. Providence, R.I.: B. C. Scribe.

———, ed. 1989. *Women's Earliest Records from Ancient Egypt and Western Asia.* Atlanta, Ga.: Scholars Press.

Lesko, Leonard H. 1986. "Three Late Egyptian Stories Reconsidered." In *Egyptological Studies in Honor of Richard A. Parker,* ed. Leonard H. Lesko, 98–103. Hanover: University Press of New England for Brown University Press.

———. 1991. "Ancient Egyptian Cosmogonies and Cosmology." In *Religion in Ancient Egypt: Gods, Myths, and Personal Practice,* ed. Byron E. Shafer, 88–122. New York: Cornell.

Lichtheim, Miriam. 1973. *Ancient Egyptian Literature: A Book of Readings.* Vol. 1, *The Old and Middle Kingdoms.* Berkeley: University of California Press.

———. 1976. *Ancient Egyptian Literature: A Book of Readings.* Vol. 2, *The New Kingdom.* Berkeley: University of California Press.

Manetho. 1971. *Aegyptiaca (Epitome).* Translated by W. G. Waddell and F. E. Robbins. Loeb Classical Library, no. 350. Cambridge, Mass.: Harvard University Press, 1971.

Meyers, Carol. 1988. *Discovering Eve: Ancient Israelite Women in Context.* New York: Oxford.

———. 1989. "Women and the Domestic Economy of Early Israel." In *Women's Earliest Records from Ancient Egypt and Western Asia,* ed. Barbara S. Lesko, 265–78. Atlanta, Ga.: Scholars Press.

Numazawa, K. 1953. "The Cultural-Historical Background of Mythos on the Separation of Sky and Earth." *Scientia* 1:28–35. Reprinted in *Sacred Narrative: Readings in the Theory of Myth,* ed. Alan Dundes, 182–92. Berkeley: University of California Press, 1984.

O'Flaherty, Wendy Doniger. 1980. *Women, Androgynes, and Other Mythical Beasts.* Chicago: University of Chicago Press.

Parker, R., and O. Neugebauer, eds. and trans. 1960. *Egyptian Astronomical Texts.* Vol. 1. Providence, R.I.: Brown University Press.

Pestman, P. 1961. *Marriage and Matrimonial Property in Ancient Egypt.* Leiden: E. J. Brill.

Petrie, William M. Flinders. 1900. *The Royal Tombs of the Earliest Dynasties.* Vol. 1. London: Egyptian Exploration Society.

Pomeroy, Sarah B. 1975. *Goddesses, Whores, Wives, and Slaves: Women in Classical Antiquity.* New York: Schocken Books.

————. 1984. *Women in Hellenistic Egypt from Alexander to Cleopatra.* New York: Schocken Books.

Pritchard, James, ed. 1969. *Ancient Near Eastern Texts Relating to the Old Testament.* 3d ed. Princeton, N.J.: Princeton University Press.

Redford, Donald B. 1984. *Akhenaten, the Heretic King.* Princeton: Princeton University Press.

Robins, Gay. 1989. "Some Images of Women in the New Kingdom Art and Literature." In *Women's Earliest Records from Ancient Egypt and Western Asia,* ed. Barbara S. Lesko. 105–16. Atlanta, Ga.: Scholars Press.

Sanday, Peggy Reeves. 1981. *Female Power and Male Dominance: On the Origins of Sexual Inequality.* Cambridge: Cambridge University Press.

Schäfer, Heinrich. 1974. *Principles of Egyptian Art.* Translated by John Baines. Edited by Emma Brunner-Traut and John Baines. London: Clarendon Press.

Seipel, Wilfried. 1978. "Königsmutter." In *Lexikon der Ägyptologie,* vol. 3:538–40. Wiesbaden: Otto Harrassowitz.

————. 1980. "Untersuchungen zu den ägyptischen Köninginnen der Frühzeit und des alten Reiches: Quellen und historische Einordnung." Ph.D. diss, Universität Hamburg.

Sethe, Kurt. 1908–10. *Die altägyptischen Pyramidentexten.* 2 vols. Hildesheim: Georg Olms Verlagsbuchhandlung.

Shafer, Byron E., ed. 1991. *Religion in Ancient Egypt: Gods, Myths, and Personal Practice.* Ithaca: Cornell University Press.

Silverman, David P. 1991. "Divinity and Deities in Ancient Egypt." In *Religion in Ancient Egypt: Gods, Myths, and Personal Practice,* ed. Byron E. Shafer, 7–87. Ithaca: Cornell University Press.

Smith, William Stevenson. 1949. *A History of Egyptian Sculpture and Painting in the Old Kingdom.* 2d ed. Boston: Museum of Fine Arts.

te Velde, H. 1977. "The Theme of the Separation of Heaven and Earth in Egyptian Mythology." *Studia Aegyptiaca* 3:161–70.

Théodoridès, Aristide. 1975. "Frau." In *Lexikon der Ägyptologie,* vol. 2:280–95. Wiesbaden: Otto Harrassowitz.

Troy, Lana. 1986. *Patterns of Queenship in Ancient Egyptian Myth and History.* Uppsala Studies in Ancient Mediterranean and Near Eastern Civilizations, no. 14. Uppsala: Acta Universitatis Upsaliensis.

Ward, William A. 1989. "Non-royal Women and their Occupations in the Middle Kingdom." In *Women's Earliest Records from Ancient Egypt and Western Asia,* ed. Barbara S. Lesko, 33–43. Atlanta, Ga: Scholars Press.

Wenig, Steffen. 1969. *The Woman in Egyptian Art.* Translated by B. Fischer. New York: McGraw-Hill.

Westendorf, Wolfhart. 1976. "Götter, Androgyne." *Lexikon der Ägyptologie,* vol. 2:633–35. Wiesbaden: Otto Harrassowitz.

Zába, Zbynek. 1956. *Les maximes de Ptahhotep.* Prague: Éditions de l'Académie Tchécoslovaque des Sciences.

Women, Reproduction, and Religion in Western Puebloan Society

Ethnographers who have written about Western Puebloan religion have focused almost exclusively on the ritual activities of men, implying that women have no significant role to play in religious practice (Benedict, 1935; Bunzel, 1932; Cushing, 1896; Parsons, 1936, 1939; Stevenson, 1904; Voth, 1905). Even though many of these early ethnographers were women, they were trained in an anthropological tradition that gave precedence to the ritual activities of men. I maintain, however, that although Western Puebloan women are seldom physical participants in the formal religious rituals, they are central to the ideological basis of this religion. This centrality of women is underscored by the ritual behavior of the men, which is imitative of the reproductive power of the women. Using evidence from the historical record as well as from contemporary ethnographies and my own fieldwork, I will examine the powerful role women exert in Western Puebloan society in general and in religious life in particular (Bunzel, 1972; Englander, 1977; Fewkes, 1906; Parsons, 1919; Schlegel, 1977, 1979; Titiev, 1944). By *Western Puebloan* I refer to the Hopi in Arizona and the Zuni in New Mexico (fig. 11.1). I will focus primarily on the time period prior to World War II, when there was greater cultural continuity and less change due to acculturation than in the present. I will, however, also point out the directions gender interactions are taking today.

The anthropologist Alice Schlegel has suggested that reproduction is the dominant theme of Western Puebloan society because the ideological focus of this culture is life; warlike aggression is viewed as a highly

Figure 11.1. View of Zuni Pueblo looking southeast, showing waffle gardens in the distance and squash and corn drying on the rooftops. (Photograph by John K. Hillers, 1879. Courtesy of the Smithsonian Institution, National Anthropological Archives, Neg. No. 2301-B–2)

undesirable characteristic, either as a community focus or an individual personality trait (1977:262). Life in this sense refers to the birth of many children (female reproduction) and also to the growth of the crops that support life (male reproduction, based on the model of female reproduction). Reproduction then is the key metaphor of Western Puebloan life—indeed, the central request of the ritual prayers is for increase, a term that encompasses the bearing of children and the growth of the crops. Women are crucial to this model because of their two primary responsibilities—both actual and symbolic—described as "producing life" and "feeding." It is a biased perspective that states that the role of women in religious practice is insignificant because they do not participate publicly. Overt participation is hardly necessary in a cultural group for whom the overall model of religion is the reproductive power of women. Furthermore, the extremely important but "unofficial" role of women in religious practice has been overlooked entirely. For the Western Puebloans, the private pilgrimages of the women to fertility shrines is as crucial a focus of religion as the public rain dances performed by the men so that there will be rain for the crops

Figure 11.2. "Zunis imitating dance of the 'Yebitchai' gods of the Navaho" (original caption to photograph). (Photograph by Matilda C. Stevenson, 1896–98. Courtesy of the Smithsonian Institution, National Anthropological Archives, Neg. No. 2356-B)

(fig. 11.2). At these shrines the women pray to have many children or sometimes express the particular desire to have a girl or boy. Thus there is a link for both women and men with fertility—the women bear children and the men grow the crops. Frequently, however, the Western Puebloans regard the fertility of the women as more potent and direct than that of the men. When Alice Schlegel asked Hopi women, "Who are the most important, women or men?" the most common reply was "We are, because we are the mothers." Some women added that men, too, were important, because they were messengers to the gods (Schlegel, 1977:245). Women and men I talked with at Zuni made similar remarks about the relative significance of women and men—both carry out important but different roles that are equivalent in status and value. Such commentary suggests that the importance of men lies in their role as intermediaries while women are directly responsible for reproduction. As I will show, reproduction is a life metaphor that is suffused throughout women's work—it is this metaphor that underlies all aspects of religious practice and then delineates these roles in other aspects of community life.

Religion

Men are the principal actors in the formal religious sphere of village life and, until recently, were responsible for growing corn and other crops (often in fields that were controlled by the female heads of households). Agriculture was the mainstay of life for the Puebloans and their ancestors, and the major function of religious practice was to ensure rain for the crops. Thus the main responsibility of the men could be described as that of giving life to the corn. It must be added, however, that the Western Puebloans believe that all crops spring from the womb of Mother Earth. The Hopi even avoid the use of steel plows in the spring because that might disturb the pregnancy of Mother Earth (Toelken, 1976:14). The men who tend the crops, then, act more as intermediaries and caretakers than as primary engenderers. They plant the seed in the body of Mother Earth, but, according to tradition, that seed was first given to the Puebloans by the Corn Maidens. Even though agriculture has ceased to be so critical to Puebloan subsistence, the central purpose of religion is still the request for increase: whether it be rain for the crops, many children, a long life, or increased sales of jewelry (Young, 1985:8). In formal religious practice this increase is attained by symbolic imitative acts through which the men seek to accrue to themselves the reproductive powers associated with the women.

Significantly, these rituals are enacted in the *kiva* (fig. 11.3), the underground circular chamber that, in itself, is symbolic of the womb of Mother Earth who gave birth to the people back in the time of the beginning (Englander, 1977). Most kivas contain a *sipapu,* a hole dug near the center of the kiva symbolizing the opening through which the people passed in the myth time when they emerged from the womb of mother earth to the earth's surface on which they live today (Prudden, 1914:33–58). At a certain point in these rituals, the religious leader sprinkles the *kachinas* (masked god personators) with sacred cornmeal (ground by women); this act, explicitly imitative of women's role as feeders, is described by the Puebloans as "feeding" the kachinas.

Although women do not take direct part in these "official" religious enactments, they do participate in religion in an informal but significant way, performing tasks that only women may perform: they grind the sacred cornmeal—the symbol of natural and spiritual life—which is an essential component of all Puebloan rituals (fig. 11.4); they provide the food that nourishes the participants in the ceremonies; they feed cornmeal to the sacred masks; and in a purely private act they create their own personal prayers by painting certain designs on their pottery.[1] Some of this pottery is used to hold the sacred cornmeal necessary to ritual

Figure 11.3. Casa Rinconada, Chaco Canyon, New Mexico. Built by the Anasazi about A.D. 1100, Casa Rinconada is a great kiva aligned along the cardinal directions. Many of the Puebloan kivas are similar in shape and purpose. (Photograph by Ray A. Williamson, 1977)

activities—the designs the women paint on these pots are efficacious in bringing rain. Barbara Tedlock has suggested that Zuni women play an important role in the creation of the rain dance songs, sung by the men, that are the main focus of the summer rain dances (personal communication, 1981). Further, although women do not gather in the kivas, they plaster the walls when the structures are completed, as they plaster the walls of all new buildings; sometimes they leave their "signature" by plastering their handprints on the roof beams. Such a signature serves as a metonymic image that enables the women to be copresent with the ritual activities carried on by the men in the kivas. As one of my male Zuni colleagues said, "We look up and see the handprints and are reminded of our mothers, wives, and daughters."

The central role of women in Western Puebloan religion is further underscored by the number of the most important personages in the pantheon of deities that are female. The specific powers and attributes of these deities reflect the importance of women as feeders and producers of life. At Zuni, since women do not belong to the Kachina Societies, the roles of these female beings in ritual drama are enacted by men. As in the example discussed above, female beings are thus copresent with male

Figure 11.4. Two Zuni women grinding wheat (using implements and following procedures that are similar to those involved in grinding corn). (Photograph by A. C. Vroman, 1899. Courtesy of the Smithsonian Institution, National Anthropological Archives, Neg. No. 2259)

beings in the ritual and frequently play significant roles as the progenitors of life and wisdom. But women themselves do not take part, because participation in the rituals would entail a crossing over from their proper sphere of activity into an area that is considered inappropriate and potentially harmful.[2] Certainly there is danger involved in ritual activity. The Zuni say that men may be suffocated by the kachina masks if they are not thinking good thoughts during the ceremony. Furthermore, since the Western Puebloans believe that one *becomes* the god when one dons the mask—as opposed to merely *representing* the god—the men who wear the masks and costumes of the female deities experience, while the ritual is enacted, aspects of femaleness. This, too, has been associated by my Zuni colleagues with enhancing the request for rain for the crops.

Both the Hopi and Zuni revere a being described as "Mother of the Gods," who plays a primary role in the ceremony during which young boys are initiated into the Kachina, or masked gods, Society. In one act of the ritual drama that comprises this initiation, puppets representing the fierce Horned Water Serpent knock over imitation fields of corn. Then the Mother of the Gods appears. She suckles the Horned Water Serpent puppets and offers them sacred corn meal from a tray that she carries (fig. 11.5)—an act of propitiation that serves to quell the antagonism of the serpents toward the young corn plants (Young, 1987:133). At the conclusion of the ceremony, members of the Kachina Society gather the corn plants and distribute them to the women and young girls who comprise part of the audience for the initiation ritual. This ceremony emphasizes the symbolic role of women as feeders and producers of life. Nevertheless, the Western Puebloans place a significant restriction on certain women's attendance at this ritual drama. They do not allow pregnant women to attend the puppetry performances that involve the Horned Water Serpent; nor do they permit any women to touch any part of the puppets that represent this mythical being. Perhaps these special conditions arise from the Horned Water Serpent's association with agricultural fertility, which imbues it with power that is more germane to the domain of men than of women (Young, 1987:146n3). The Hopi say that if pregnant women do attend the Water Serpent dance the fetus will swell up (Fewkes, 1900:627n). A male Hopi colleague of mine has suggested that because pregnant women's fertility is without question, it is unnecessary, or even involves the accretion of too much power, for them to be present at such ceremonies. This commentary underscores the idea that such female presence would entail a redundancy of power. Still, this implies a certain type of danger as well. According to the Puebloan principle of balance, one must never try to invoke or exercise too much power.[3]

Among the Hopi, the kachina doll representing the Mother of the Gods is the first image presented to newborn babies (Wright, 1977:56). Her mouth is turned up in a perpetual smile and her cheeks are red disks. In her right hand she carries a gourd of water and frequently in her left an ear of corn or a tray of cornmeal. Thus, from the moment of birth the image of reproduction is presented to both boys and girls as the *first* and most meaningful image they will encounter.

Female kachinas also symbolize the importance of women in the economic life of the village. According to the Hopi, the wife of the Sun Father is the Goddess of Hard Substances, that is, turquoise in particular or wealth in general (Voth, 1905:1–9). This seems appropriate in a society in which all wealth is passed on through the female line.

Both the Hopi and Zuni pantheons include a goddess known as Salt Old Woman—an extremely important personage who brings rain as well as salt (Bunzel, 1932:1035). The Zuni kachina of Salt Old Woman carries a feathered staff with which she pulls down the rain clouds. According to Zuni legend this goddess once lived close to the village and afforded people salt, which was an important mainstay of Zuni foodways. When she was not treated with due reverence, Salt Old Woman became angry and left the pueblo to settle at a lake over forty miles away. Certain lopsided boulders mark her angry path. Now the people must travel this

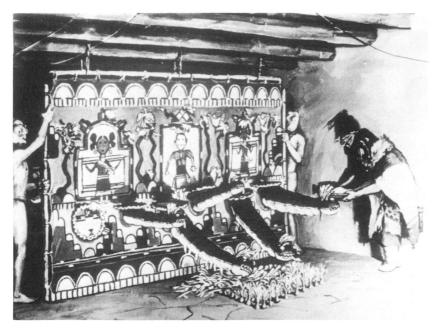

Figure 11.5. *Hahai Wuhti* (Mother of the Gods) offering cornmeal to Horned Water Serpent puppets during a ritual at the Hopi Pueblo of Walpi. (Drawing by M. Wright Gill, 1900. Courtesy of the Smithsonian Institution, National Anthropological Archives, Neg. No. 1813-C)

distance, often in a pilgrimage undertaken on foot, to reach her. They perform elaborate ceremonies to make up for their early disrespect before they may return to Zuni with salt.

As mentioned earlier, the Seven Corn Maidens are crucial to Zuni life and ceremonialism. It is they who first gave the people corn seed, which they created by rubbing off bits of their own skin. For the Zuni, corn is symbolic of life itself. The Corn Maidens are represented in Zuni ritual by corn ears in the colors of the six directions plus the center.[4] According to one Zuni legend, back in the time of the beginning, after the Corn Maidens gave the people corn seed, they rose from the earth and became the seven stars of the Big Dipper. The Zuni word for this constellation means "seven ones," and the Zuni first plant corn in the spring by the light of the seven stars, which at that time rise bright overhead (Cushing, 1896:392; Young and Williamson, 1981:183–84, 191).

Although Western Puebloan women are not official members of the Kachina Society, they are quite likely to be initiated into any one of the medicine societies and thus have access to esoteric healing knowledge.

The healing knowledge of women is regarded by the Zuni as an extension of their reproductive roles—they both produce life as child bearers and sustain life as feeders and healers. With the exception of this female membership in the medicine societies, formal membership in the religious societies is the male domain because its focus is the reproduction of the crops; women do not need to participate in this formal religion because their reproductive powers are evident in the birth of children and their family and community duties do not involve agriculture per se. In contrast, men carry out their various religious activities because they lack the natural ability of fecundity with which women are born. Access to the Kachina Society thus repairs male deficits rather than excluding females. Furthermore, until recently, even though the men grew the crops, they turned over the corn they had harvested to the authority of the women, who, in another act of "feeding," distributed it as they saw fit among their kin networks.

Household

The overall importance of reproduction as a crucial factor in Western Puebloan life can be seen in the way in which the authority and responsibilities of women and men are perceived in community affairs as well as in the formal practice of religion. Women have authority in the domestic sphere; they describe their major tasks in this arena as "producing life" and "feeding." This domestic authority of women is strengthened by economic and social factors: it is especially significant that women own the houses, all of the household goods (until recently this included cars), and frequently the fields as well. Western Puebloan society is matrilocal and matrilineal—inheritance of material goods and clan membership is passed along through the female line, and the newly married couple lives with the bride's family; the groom works under the direction of the bride's father in the clan-allotted fields and is subject to the ultimate authority of the bride's mother. If the bride is not the eldest daughter of the family, her husband must eventually build her a house of her own (Schlegel, 1977:247). The woman generally initiates the marriage proposal, perhaps partly because she is aware that she needs a man to work in the fields of her clan and also because the primary role of women is to produce children. When she takes cornmeal to the groom's household, it is described as "paying for him" (Schlegel, 1977:248). The Western Puebloans sum up the female domestic authority in these words: "A man's place is outside the house" (Schlegel, 1977:247). It is not surprising then that the men spend much of their leisure time in the kivas—private places that women enter only on very special ritual occasions. In the kivas the men chat and work on the

Figure 11.6. Zuni men in one of the ceremonial rooms working on ritual paraphernalia. (Photograph by Matilda C. Stevenson, 1896–98. Courtesy of the Smithsonian Institution, National Anthropological Archives, Neg. No. 2360)

religious paraphernalia (fig. 11.6). Furthermore, the crowded living conditions (a desirable characteristic of domestic life to the Puebloans) render the household anything but private. The most private places are those frequented by men—the kivas and the shrine areas in lands around the village proper where women and children rarely venture. Thus the dichotomy male : female :: public : private :: powerful : powerless, prevalent until recently in anthropological writings on gender interactions (Ortner, 1974:67–87; Rosaldo, 1974: 7–42), does not pertain among the Western Puebloans. Both sexes are perceived to have power in different, but equal and complementary, realms.

Unlike the woman, the man in Western Puebloan society must divide his duties between two social units (Schlegel, 1977:248). As a father and a husband, he owes his labor and care to his wife's household. He also owes allegiance to his mother's household and clan. As a child of his mother's clan, he is expected to take part in clan matters, especially the participation in ceremonies and the determination of land usage. All religious positions are inherited through the clan (determined matrilineally), and religious leaders are expected to train clan mates as successors.

Women, however, are responsible only to their own households. In the estimation of the community they have fulfilled their role as adults once they have married and given birth to children, particularly daughters (Schlegel, 1977:249). Through their power of fertility they have produced life. From this point on their primary role is to sustain physical life through feeding their family and others and to maintain spiritual life through feeding sacred objects. Women also nourish the spirits of the dead, the kachinas who have the power to bring rain. At meals, the matriarch of the family in which someone has recently died sets aside portions of food, which she later burns in the fire or gives to her eldest son to put in the Zuni River—an act that is described as "feeding the dead."

According to Alice Schlegel, the difference between the Hopi and most other matrilineal societies is that "the mother's brother is not the kinsman who receives the greatest respect. Rather, it is the *mowi,* or female in-law, the wife of a son, brother, or mother's brother" (1977:251). Men and women address and refer to the *mowi* throughout her lifetime only by this term, which connotes extreme respect and deference as well as an element of power and danger. The Hopi believe that using her given name might subject one to great harm. In no other circumstance, kinship or otherwise, does a name taboo operate. The explanation the Hopi men offer for this practice is that "she cooks for us [while her wedding robes are being woven] and brings food when she comes to visit" (Schlegel, 1977:251). Although Schlegel describes this belief as an "example of the high value placed upon women as feeders" (1977: 241), I suggest that even though this explanation constitutes the overt reason given by men for using this deferential title, there is a covert reason operating as well. Since the example given relates to the time of marriage, the respect accorded the female in-law may include her value as a feeder, but it also refers to her potential powers of fertility—powers so efficacious that the men seek to achieve them by imitation in their task of caring for the crops and executing the religious duties that are aimed at producing rainfall.

Community

While female authority is generally limited to the household, women often "unofficially" influence the community activities of the men. After all, they own the houses in which the men live and do not hesitate to make their own opinions known at every opportunity. They rarely need to exert this unofficial veto, however, because on the whole, community activities are carried out to benefit men and women. For example, women are quite vocal in tribal meetings that are held frequently to discuss matters that affect the entire community, such as land and water usage, tourism, education, and so on. Everyone is given a voice at such meetings, which are democratic in principle and practice—community consensus is the desired result. Still, after the conclusion of such meetings I have often heard the Zuni comment on the insight of particular tribal members; various tribal matriarchs usually outnumber the men in receiving such praise.

Household and community are to a large extent separate areas of activity, but the Western Puebloans do not regard them as two separate domains (Schlegel, 1977:252). The village is patterned after the model of the house; so to understand male and female roles in the community, one must understand the metaphoric nature of the idea of the house. The house plays both an actual and symbolic part in Western Puebloan life. Not only does it shelter the individual but it situates that person in a specific place, providing safety both in daily life and in the land of the dead. People, animals, and all other living beings have houses. The only time one is without a house is during the four-day journey from the land of the living to the land of the dead. This is a time of extreme danger, and the relatives of the deceased one bend their thoughts and energies toward helping this spirit safely reach the house/village where the dead reside.

Complementing this symbolic idea of the house is the actual structure into which every Western Puebloan person is born. As stated earlier, women remain in their mother's house, and their husbands join them there. These places, where familial activities occur, are under the primary authority of the women, and here men play a secondary role.

Just as each individual has an actual and symbolic house, so does each clan. The actual clan house belongs to the leading family of that clan, the family to which the Clan Mother and her brother, the Clan "Big Uncle," belong (Schlegel, 1977:253). The Clan Mother plays a central nurturing role in this house, for it is her duty to feed cornmeal to the sacred masks and in other ways care for the clan-owned ceremonial property. Thus, although the Clan Mother does not publicly participate in the sacred rain dances, she has a crucial part in the ongoing cycle of ceremonial activities. Indeed, one may not assume that women know nothing about the ceremonies enacted by the male clan members. They are a primary audience—at Zuni, only the matrons of the tribe sit in the plaza where the kachina personators dance and sing. Frequently they tape-record the songs and listen to them in their houses throughout the week. But not only do they watch and listen, they also gain knowledge of rituals through tending the sacred paraphernalia used in the ceremonies. While conducting fieldwork at Zuni, I often had the experience of talking to one of the male family members about ceremonial matters only to have him turn to the matriarch of the household and ask her the same questions so that he could give me the correct answer. Although the activities of women are significant in the actual clan house—because clan membership is determined matrilineally and the Clan Mother carries out special duties—both women and men participate in the Clan House as a symbolic structure. In this sense the Clan House is the focus and unifying factor of all clan activities, and authority here is exercised jointly by the Clan Mother and Big Uncle.

Contemporary Situation

Western Puebloan society is being changed by the introduction of a cash economy, the reduction of time spent in subsistence agriculture, and new attitudes toward fertility. With the advent of the cash economy the men are less willing to turn cash—the product of their labor—over to the women. Women are entering the extratribal labor market and no longer spend the many hours grinding corn; they use machine-ground meal instead. Birth control methods are becoming more widely accepted, and the younger women tend to favor small families. Women are also beginning to be elected to the formerly all-male Tribal Council.[5] Furthermore, the impact of ideas and imagery from Anglo-American and other cultural groups is certainly evident (for example, the Czechoslovakian shawls that have become a sign of female "Zuniness"—see fig. 11.7—or the inclusion of Wonder Woman on a young girl's birthday cake—see fig. 11.8). I maintain, however, that the Zuni retain a stable "cultural core" that has remained largely unaffected by such superficial elements. Thus changes in the subsistence, domestic, and political activities of women and men do not reflect a change in the overall ideology of Western Puebloan life—reproduction is still the controlling metaphor, expressed particularly in the role of women as feeders and nourishers, those who produce and maintain life.

A secular example of the continuing importance of women as bearers of Zuni culture is the practice, during the Zuni Tribal Fair, of choosing a teenage girl to be Miss Zuni. Miss Zuni not only takes part in intratribal events but also represents the Zuni tribe at various pan-Indian cultural events. This example also illustrates the Zuni ability to incorporate elements from mainstream society without essentially changing the core of their own tribal life. Significantly, Miss Zuni is chosen not for her beauty but for her knowledge of Zuni culture. She must prepare a traditional meal for the judges (made up of respected female and male tribal elders), answer questions concerning the history and present situation of the tribe, demonstrate fluency in the Zuni language, and appear in traditional Zuni dress. In a culture so strongly matriarchal, it is significant that the young women are submitted to such a test—thus ensuring that the culture will be passed on (Young, 1982:46).

Figure 11.7. Miss Zuni being crowned during the Zuni Tribal Fair. (Photograph by M. Jane Young, 1981)

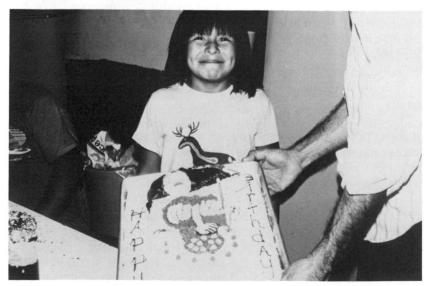

Figure 11.8. Arlene Sheyka celebrates her birthday with a "Wonder Woman" cake, Zuni, New Mexico. (Photograph by M. Jane Young, 1984)

Although their daily activities have undergone change, the symbolic roles of women and men have changed very little. Agriculture is no longer a central means of subsistence, but the rain dances continue. The request for rain for the crops has come to symbolize a request for *increase* in general—many children, a long life, even the sale of much jewelry and pottery. Women and men are still powerful actors in promoting and sustaining this ideology, which is based on the principles of balance and equality. In a culture that focuses on reproduction and life, neither women nor men are regarded as dominated or dominating. Both are seen as partners operating in an interdependent manner to keep the heart of the village, the essential core of tribal life, alive and strong.

Notes

An earlier version of this essay appeared in 1987 in the *Journal of American Folklore* 100 (398): 436–45. I am grateful to Bruce Jackson for his editorial suggestions for that article and am also thankful to Marilyn Englander, Susan Hollis, Elaine Jahner, Linda Pershing, Suzanne Seriff, and Kay Turner for further comments and suggestions. I acknowledge a scholarly debt to Alice Schlegel, whose excellent work on gender roles at Hopi has contributed significantly to my own research. I am particularly grateful to my colleagues at the Pueblos of Hopi and Zuni for their commentary on this essay; I especially thank the families of Arlen Sheyka and Augustine Panteah for their hospitality and support during my various periods of fieldwork. The National Anthropological Archives of the Smithsonian Institution has kindly given me permission to reprint photographs from their collections here. Ray Williamson generously sent me one of his photographs of the great kiva at Casa Rinconada, the Zuni Tribal Fair Committee has allowed me to use reprints of publicity photographs I took for them in the summer of 1981, and Arlene Sheyka (and her parents) have agreed that her picture could be used in this article.

1. Zuni women do not take direct part in the Kachina Society, nor do they enter the kivas except on special occasions when they are invited to attend certain rituals, such as the initiation of young boys into the Kachina Society, as audience members (Bunzel, 1932:975–80). On the other hand, although Hopi women do not personate kachinas, they do participate in village-wide ceremonies that involve unmasked dancers. There are three women's ceremonial societies at Hopi that have their own special rites, but these societies are not "of equivalent importance" to those of the men (Frigout, 1979:565). Like the Zuni women, Hopi women enter the men's kivas on special occasions, but not as primary participants in the enacted rituals. Ceremonies conducted in the kivas constitute the most private part of Pueblo religion. Such ceremonies become public (although clearly still

sacred) when they are enacted outside of the kivas in the plazas of the various Pueblo villages.

2. I have discussed the fact that women do not personate kachinas with both Zuni women and men; their responses indicate that the role of the kachinas is primarily to bring rain for the crops and thus involves the male sphere of activity. The concern of women, on the other hand, is with child-bearing and nurturing. The Zuni regard these as equally important, but separate, domains. Those I talked with frequently stated that it would be dangerous for women to attempt to participate in the Kachina Societies and also redundant, since the role of women as reproducers is already well established. If men were to attempt to participate in the women's sphere, a similar situation of redundancy would not pertain. Although such action is frowned on, men can choose not to participate in the kachina rituals, but they cannot take on the primary area of women's power and responsibility—giving birth. The redundancy of female power is discussed explicitly by the Zuni, and, as explained in note 3, both males and females in Pueblo society avoid evoking too much power. Implicit in these examples, however, is the notion that such redundancy is dangerous, because it would threaten the equilibrium, or desired balance, which is a central focus of Zuni religion.

3. The use of fetishes (carved or natural animal figures of particular birds, mammals, and reptiles in which the spirit of that being is believed to reside) of the Beast Gods in hunting provides a good example of this avoidance of evoking too much power. Because the Beast Gods are all predators, the Zuni believe that their images have great power in bringing success in the hunt, and nearly everyone at Zuni has fetishes of these beings. The potency of the fetishes is derived by analogy from the efficacy that their animal counterparts have in the "natural" world, so each fetish has greatest power with respect to the particular game animals that are its prey. Thus, a hunter takes with him only the fetish that has the most power over the game he wishes to hunt. Mountain lion, for example, has power over deer; eagle has power over rabbits. I asked a number of men who were known for their hunting ability, particularly in earlier days when game was more prevalent, whether they would ever take more than one fetish with them at a time. They replied that they would not do so because too many fetishes at once were dangerous and that it would be greedy and inappropriate to hunt for more than one type of game at one time. They added that the necessary rituals employed in hunting are specific to certain types of prey and "it would not be right" to combine these rituals.

4. Animals (the Zuni Beast Gods) and colors are part of this six-directional scheme that is linked to the summer and winter solstice sunrise and sunset positions (northeast, northwest, southwest, southeast) as well as to the above and the below. This network of cultural symbolism includes the yellow mountain lion of the northeast, the blue bear of the northwest, the red badger of the southwest, the white wolf of the southeast, the speckled or all-colored eagle of the zenith, and the black mole of the nadir. Sometimes Knife-Wing (the mythic being with wings and tail of knives) rather than the eagle is associated with the zenith. In certain situations, depending on the ritual circumstances, the cardinal rather than the

semicardinal directions are employed. For further discussion of the importance of the number six in Zuni cultural symbolism, see Young (1988:101–7).

5. Prior to the Spanish Entrada (A.D.1540), "official" Pueblo governance was carried out by the religious leaders, in particular, the war chiefs and war captains. In the seventeenth century, in accordance with their own governing practices, the Spaniards created a division between sacred and secular realms by instituting Tribal Councils (governor, lieutenant governor, and council members) for all of the Pueblo groups except Hopi to oversee all nonreligious matters (see, for example, Eggan, 1979:230–32). Since religion and daily life are intimately connected among the Puebloans this rather arbitrary division has been a constant source of friction. Until recently, the Pueblo Tribal Councils were comprised of men, but women are now being elected to the formal governing body. A number of scholars of early American history have suggested that throughout the "New World," Europeans established the patriarchal forms of control with which they were familiar (see especially Leacock, 1980:25–42). This practice of establishing a European model was followed even with such obviously matriarchal tribes as the Montagnais-Naskapi, so drastically altering their sociocultural pattern that later colonizers perceived only patriarchal institutions (Leacock, 1980:25–42). Of course, such attempts to change the role and status of women is endemic to situations of colonization (Etienne and Leacock, 1980).

References Cited

Benedict, Ruth. 1935. *Zuni Mythology*. Columbia University Contributions to Anthropology, no. 21. New York: Columbia University Press.

Bunzel, Ruth L. 1932. "Introduction to Zuñi Ceremonialism, Zuñi Origin Myths, Zuñi Ritual Poetry, Zuñi Katchinas: An Analytical Study." In *Bureau of American Ethnology Annual Report,* vol. 47:467–1086. Washington, D.C.: GPO.

———. [1929] 1972. *The Pueblo Potter: A Study of Creative Imagination in Primitive Art.* New York: Dover.

Cushing, Frank H. 1896. "Outlines of Zuñi Creation Myths." In *Bureau of American Ethnology Annual Report,* vol. 13:321–447. Washington, D.C.: GPO.

Eggan, Fred. 1979. "Pueblos: Introduction." In *Handbook of North American Indians.* Vol. 9, *Southwest,* ed. Alfonso Ortiz, 224–35. Washington, D.C.: GPO.

Englander, Marilyn. 1977. "Women's Roles and Prehistoric Kivas in Anasazi Society." Ms.

Etienne, Mona, and Eleanor Leacock, eds. 1980. *Women and Colonization: Anthropological Perspectives.* New York: Praeger.

Fewkes, J. Walter. 1900. "A Theatrical Performance at Walpi." In *Proceedings of the Washington Academy of Sciences,* vol. 2:605–29. Washington, D.C.: GPO.

———. 1906. "Hopi Shrines near the East Mesa, Arizona." *American Anthropologist* 8 (2): 346–75.

Frigout, Arlette, 1979. "Hopi Ceremonial Organization." In *Handbook of North American Indians*. Vol. 9, *Southwest,* ed. Alfonso Ortiz, 564–76. Washington, D.C.: GPO.

Leacock, Eleanor. 1980. "Montagnais Women and the Jesuit Program for Colonization." In *Women and Colonization: Anthropological Perspectives,* ed. Mona Etienne and Eleanor Leacock, 25–42. New York: Praeger.

Ortner, Sherry B. 1974. "Is Female to Male as Nature Is to Culture?" In *Woman, Culture, and Society,* ed. Michelle Zimbalist Rosaldo and Louise Lamphere, 67–87. Stanford: Stanford University Press.

Parsons, Elsie Clews. 1919. "Mothers and Children at Zuñi, New Mexico." *Man* 19:168–73.

———. ed., 1936. *Hopi Journal of Alexander M. Stephen.* 2 vols. Columbia University Contributions to Anthropology, no. 23. New York: Columbia University Press.

———. 1939. *Pueblo Indian Religion.* Chicago: University of Chicago Press.

Prudden, T. Mitchell. 1914. "The Circular Kivas of Small Ruins in the San Juan Watershed." *American Anthropologist* 16:33–58.

Rosaldo, Michelle Zimbalist. 1974. "Woman, Culture, and Society: A Theoretical Overview." In *Woman, Culture, and Society,* ed. Michelle Zimbalist Rosaldo and Louise Lamphere, 17–42. Stanford: Stanford University Press.

Schlegel, Alice. 1977. "Male and Female in Hopi Thought and Action." In *Sexual Stratification: A Cross-cultural View,* ed. Alice Schlegel, 245–69. New York: Columbia University Press.

———. 1979. "Sexual Antagonism among the Sexually Egalitarian Hopi." *Ethos* 7:124–41.

Stevenson, Matilda C. 1904. "The Zuñi Indians: Their Mythology, Esoteric Fraternities, and Ceremonies." In *Bureau of American Ethnology Report,* vol. 23:3–634. Washington, D.C.: GPO.

Titiev, Mischa. 1944. *Old Oraibi: A Study of Hopi Indians of Third Mesa.* Papers of the Peabody Museum of American Archaeology and Ethnology, vol. 22, no. 1. Cambridge, Mass.: Peabody Museum.

Toelken, J. Barre. 1976. "Seeing with a Native Eye: How Many Sheep Will It Hold?" In *Seeing with a Native Eye: Essays on Native American Religion,* ed. W. H. Capps, 9–24. New York: Harper and Row.

Voth, H. R. 1905. *The Traditions of the Hopi.* Field Columbian Museum Publication no. 96, Anthropological Series, vol. 8. Chicago: Field Columbian Museum.

Wright, Barton. 1977. *Hopi Kachinas.* Flagstaff: Northland Press.

Young, M. Jane. 1982. " 'We Were Going to Have a Barbeque, but the Cow Ran Away': Production, Form, and Function of the Zuni Tribal Fair." *Southwest Folklore* 5:42–48.

———. 1985. "Images of Power and the Power of Images: The Significance of Rock Art for Contemporary Zunis." *Journal of American Folklore* 98 (387): 3–48.

———. 1987. "Humor and Anti-humor in Western Puebloan Puppetry Performances." In *Humor and Comedy in Puppetry: Celebration in Popular Culture,* ed. Dina Sherzer and Joel Sherzer, 127–50. Bowling Green, Ohio: Popular Press.

———. 1988. *Signs from the Ancestors: Zuni Cultural Symbolism and Perceptions of Rock Art.* Albuquerque: University of New Mexico Press.

Young, M. Jane, and Ray A. Williamson. 1981. "Ethnoastronomy: The Zuni Case." In *Archaeoastronomy in the Americas,* ed. Ray A. Williamson, 183–91. Los Altos, Calif.: Ballena Press.

Peasant Grandmother, Hunting Helpmate, Silent Wife: Women and Text in Gascon Tall Tales

The themes of ethnicity, modernity, sexuality, and gender, frequently embodied in female subjects, structure many of the tales told in the Moncrabeau Liars' Festival in southwestern France. The verbal excess needed for good lies, which are evaluated by their weight in salt, frequently moves contest participants to recount tales about the excessive sexuality of human and animal protagonists. The contest theme of exaggerated sexuality is inspired as well by a goat, the totemic symbol of the festival and of the village. The very name of the village festival site, *Moncrabeau,* means "mountain of goats" in Gascon, the regional language.

There is a complex metaphor at work between goats as animals that like salt and the saltiness of the tales told in the course of the contest. In French particularly obscene narratives are said to be salty (*histoires salées*). While goats are associated with the devil and the evil eye, their association with sexuality is more important for this discussion. Like rabbits, goats are considered to be sexually overactive. Goats may also be symbols of socially inappropriate human sexuality (Herzfeld, 1984:445), and in this region of southwestern France the sign of the cuckold is a pair of goat horns. Consequently, the framing metaphor of salt and goats gives rise to tales about sexuality in various guises, both overt and latent. In this regard the contemporary Moncrabeau Liars' Festival tales parallel the historical genre of the medieval fabliaux in which animal and human sexuality is ever present (Bloch, 1986; White, 1982).

The object of the Moncrabeau liars' competition is to tell the best, or saltiest, lie. The fifteen to twenty contestants, most of them men, are residents of neighboring villages and towns. Some come from adjoining departments, and a few come from as far away as the environs of Paris. The contestants are requested to submit their tales in writing several weeks before their actual performance. This allows the jury to censor inappropriate tales and help determine good ones before the public judging. However, not all participants take this preliminary step, and each year's competition includes at least three to four individuals whose tales are heard for the first time in performance.

Although the majority of the liars' festival narrators are men, several women have participated within the last ten years, and in 1979 and 1984 the contest winners were women.[1] The few female narrators who perform break with social and speech conventions, for in rural southern France women occupy the private domain of home for the most part and therefore do not participate in the economy of the speech community in public settings (see the discussion of women's space in a Provençal village in Reiter, 1975; for comparative perspectives, see also Ortner, 1974, and Jordan and Kalčik, 1985:xii-xiii). Adult women's verbal communications take place primarily with other relatives and neighbors within the home, at the market, and in the course of errands. Women do not have access to the public spaces of male sociability of the café or the political meeting. The women contestants are therefore in a minority and must negotiate their relationship to a mixed audience concerning sexuality and gender (both theirs' and their female protagonists'), central themes in the tales told by the male contestants.[2]

In examining women's narratives from a male performance event, I will focus on whether the content of tales told by women differs from tales told by men, particularly in the representation of female protagonists, and how female narrators treat sexuality. Despite recent Marxist criticism that regards "images of women" studies as reductionist in ignoring the discourses of race and class and in assuming a unified female subject (Kaplan, quoted in Greene and Kahn, 1985:148, and Moi, 1985:45), I find this to be a valid approach. I will show that the narrators often juxtapose female subjects with other social categories, such as class and ethnicity, to transmit complex messages about the region's traditional identity.

The Performance Event: The Moncrabeau Liars' Festival

The origins of the Moncrabeau Liars' Festival lie in the eighteenth century, although this is difficult to pinpoint (see Thomas's historical account, 1977:24–30). The festival reemerged at times during the last two centuries when regional Gascon identity had been consciously recreated and promoted: in the nineteenth century, during the period of Romantic nationalism, in the twentieth century, during the post–World War II years, and, most recently, after 1968. Catering both to a local and foreign audience, this celebration of local pride is paralleled by similar festivals held throughout rural France during the summer. Gascon identity is celebrated through regional foods, available for sale during the festival, while the themes of rurality, tradition, and ethnicity, present in the contestants' narratives, help to valorize peasants over technocrats, rural over urban life, and Gascons over eastern Europeans or more distant "others."

The Moncrabeau Liars' Festival is held on the first Sunday of August in a small village located in the southwestern department of the Lot-et-Garonne. It draws its audience from Moncrabeau and neighboring towns and villages, as well as northern France, Belgium, the Netherlands, and Germany, whose tourists come for their summer holiday. In addition, every four years a delegation from the town of Namur in southern Belgium attends the fête. Moncrabeau has been linked with Namur since 1946, for Namur also has a liars' festival in which the tall tale is often told in Walloon, the regional language of southern Belgium. The judges and some performers, typically the reigning king, may travel from one contest to the other. The judges include the members of the Belgian Académie des Molons, who preside over the Namur fête, and their Gascon counterparts, the members of the Moncrabeau Liars' Club.[3]

The afternoon liars' competition is the high point of a day that begins with a morning performance of folkloric dances by a village group that is followed by a lunch of regional specialties. The contest takes place over a period of several hours and has a brief intermission in midafternoon. The narrators sit together in a semicircular row directly behind the jury on the village square, facing the stone liars' armchair, dated 1748, the presumed beginning of the event. The contestants are called at random, and the host identifies them by their village and department of origin. The candidates must go forth and swear to tell only the truth before the president of the Moncrabeau Liars' Club. Each one must then climb up on the liars' armchair and kiss the wall above it before sitting down on the chair to begin a five- to ten-minute narrative performance. The narrator speaks into a microphone while facing a predominantly adult audience of some three to four hundred people, who sit on chairs and bleachers in a semicircle surrounding the open stage area. The jury of men and women dressed in splendid Renaissance-style velvet robes, village residents who comprise the Moncrabeau Liars' Club, give each tale its due in salt, weighed on a scale carried about by two children dressed as pages.

At the end of the narrative performances, just before the contest winner is announced, a drawing is held from the numbered ticket stubs allowing entrance into the fête, and prizes are awarded. Many of the prizes come from the displays of locally made foods and spirits, which their makers sell throughout the village during the festivities. Symbolically, the most important prize is a kid goat, drawn last and which the winner may take away live or slaughtered. After awarding the goat prize, the contest participants' names are then called out, from last to first place, along with the corresponding weights of their tales in grams of salt. The heaviest tale wins and its author is crowned king or queen of the liars and carried about the village in an animated procession preceded by the festival mascot.

Gender, Genre, and Performance

Many folklorists view the tall tale as a male genre. In terms of content, the tall tale often involves outstanding hunting and fishing exploits undertaken by men. These and elements from the classical tall-tale repertoire documented in other areas are present in the texts of the Moncrabeau Liars' Festival and include exaggerations of nature, such as an unusually large animal, fish, or crop found in hunting, fishing, or farming; physiological acts against nature, such as abnormal ingestion or elimination of liquids; and unnatural social relations, such as incestuous ones with relatives or with misfits and outsiders (Thompson, 1955–58, motifs X1100–1560; Randolph, 1951). Many of the tales involve dupery and tricks—of men by women, of upper classes by lower classes, and of outsiders by insiders (for similar qualities in an expressive genre of a different time period, the medieval French fabliaux, see White, 1982).

In terms of performance, the tall tale has been documented in public settings such as liars' benches, cafés, and ethnic festivals, all of which are dominated by men. Farrer reflects this view in her preface to *Women and Folklore* when she suggests that the legitimate genre of the tall tale is the province of men, while the nonlegitimate genre of exaggeration is its female corollary (1975:xvi). Farrer maps genre against gender and performance setting—the tall tale is a marked male genre of public performance, whereas exaggeration within conversational discourse is an unmarked female genre limited to private interactions in domestic settings. Recent folklore studies continue to use this public-private distinction to qualify women's traditions and performances (Jordan and de Caro, 1985; Jordan and Kalčik, 1985).

In addition to content and performance setting, language also marks the Moncrabeau Liars' Festival with respect to gender. Gascon, the Romance-based language of southwestern France, was spoken throughout the region into the early decades of the twentieth century. However, as French took over as the dominant language, Gascon acquired the specialized function of the language of jokes and, more specifically, that of *couillonnades,* or dirty jokes, told by men. Each year at least one or two such tales in the liars' festival are told partially or wholly in Gascon by male narrators. In contrast, the few female narrators tell their tales in French.

The Moncrabeau Liars' Festival tales—performed orally but frequently written down by their individual creators—lend themselves to several kinds of analysis. Their written form allows critics to use literary techniques in examining content and authorial intention, an aspect that cannot be treated in the collectively authored texts typically studied by folklorists. The oral delivery of the tales encourages perspectives from folklore and theater in examining performance. Literary and performance analysis complement one another in arriving at interpretations.

Rather than texts reflecting a unified and discrete meaning of "the author," reader-response criticism has revealed that multiple significations emerge through active engagement between reader and text, a process in which the subjectivity of the reader necessarily figures (Abel, 1982; Suleiman and Crosman, 1980). That is, texts are systems of signs that *construct* meaning rather than reflect it, inscribing simultaneously the subjectivity of speaker and reader (Kaplan, 1985:161). In the Moncrabeau Liars' Festival, multiple significations emerge through active engagement between listeners, narrators, and the performed texts. In the following discussion I note how the subjectivity of the female narrators is inscribed in their texts and performances.

The analysis is based on written sources consulted during fieldwork in southwestern France in 1981–82 (Amicale des Conteurs de Gascogne, 1982) as well as on the transcriptions of the thirty-three tales recited in the 1984 and 1987 festivals.[4] In 1984 I was a member of the audience; in 1987 I was a member of the audience as well as the only woman contestant. I will analyze three texts performed by women, two from the 1984 contest and one from the 1979 contest, and I will offer a fourth text by a male narrator from the 1984 contest as counterpoint. This fourth tale deals with similar themes and is also representative of an antifemale tone present in many of the men's texts.

The Women's Texts

The first tale is derived from a collection of French and Gascon writings by local authors that is sold at regional tale-telling events (Amicale des Conteurs de Gascogne, 1982). Entitled "Grandmother and the Rabbit-Eggs," it was recited by a twenty-two-year-old young woman nurse in 1979 and resulted in conferral of the title queen of the liars for the first time since the contest's revival in 1972. The narrator began her ode to the strength and wisdom of peasant grandmothers by apologizing that she was no La Fontaine. She manipulated both realistic details and a positive stereotype in her text. Its heroine is a prototypical regional symbol: *Menine,* the Gascon term for grandmother. Ethnic identity is marked by region and class through the simple food items that *Menine* consumes in the tale: country bread, some garlic, and red wine. Her positive qualities, grounded in the peasant world, are enumerated: she is wise, clever, economical, hardworking, and supremely capable as she takes care of the hearth fire, the cooking, the garden, the poultry yard, and larger animals, such as the cattle and the hog. *Menine*'s maternal role is emphasized in her caring for the barnyard animals as tenderly as for her children and grandchildren.

In the first half of the tale, conformity to cultural conventions in work and social roles[5] contributes to the image of the heroine as the "authentic Gascon woman," to quote the narrator's characterization. The audience hears that the traditional Gascon world, embodied in an idealized female ancestor, is best. This rural world is explicitly contrasted with the other one of modern technologies, as when the heroine refuses to heat by oil and sticks with her traditional local source, firewood. There is a more subtle message about relations between the Western world and the Middle East when a reference is made to the oil embargo of the late 1970s:

> Mais faute de pétrole, technocrates en détresse,
> Imitez la mémé, retrouvez sa sagesse
> Copiez sur son bon sens, vous serez étonnés.

> But due to a lack of oil, technocrats in need,
> Imitate Granny, find her wisdom,
> Copy her good sense, you'll be amazed.
> (Amicale des Conteurs de Gascogne, 1982:4)

Common to many of the Gascon tales is the valuing of the Western world over the Middle East, seen as an economic competitor. Here the female subject resists encroachment of the outside world by using a local traditional resource.

Despite this initially positive image of traditional Gascon culture, in the second half of the tale the peasant grandmother is forced to follow the new ways of progress, which include giving prepackaged food to barnyard animals in place of traditional grain. The heroine reluctantly acquiesces, but in so doing she makes a mistake because she cannot read the labels and contents of the packages. Instead of food she gives her rabbits a medicine, the antiwormer intended for hogs. Her mistake results in the rabbits' death. The second mistake occurs sometime later when the old woman gives her new rabbits the wrong food again, this time the prepackaged food intended for the laying hens. This mistake arises because the grandmother has mixed up the food for the two kinds of animals, which share a common pen, instead of the separate pens typical of a traditional farm. This innovation in living quarters had been introduced by the young male master of the farm, who, in his idealistic move back to nature, wanted the animals to profit from "pure air and blue skies." The result is that the rabbits lay two eggs. This represents an example of a classic folkloric motif, a rabbit transformed into another animal (Thompson, 1955–58, motif D413).

The two mistakes, which reflect the female protagonist's inability to abandon traditional ways and adopt modern practices as well as the appropriation of farm women's work of caring for barnyard animals, are summarized in the closing lines of the tale. The subjectivity of the narrator, who is a nurse, is evident as she projects her own work world and its concerns with life and death into her text. Thus she contrasts the natural processes of human procreation characteristic of the traditional rural world, implicitly identified with women, with their potential destruction by technologies such as the atom bomb, which are part of the modern world, implicitly identified with men. After outlining the negative consequences of the modern technologies of prepackaged food, central heating, and bombs, the young woman narrator concludes by comparing the Gascon rural world with the negative space of the city:

> Cette histoire est rurale ne vous en gaussez pas
> Car sur les boulevards que n'arrive-t-il pas?

> This story is rural, don't laugh at it,
> Because on the boulevards what doesn't happen?
> (Amicale des Conteurs de Gascogne, 1982:7)

In other words, what is rural is most authentic, while the boulevards of the city, home to the cabaret and the murky underworld of urban life, can only be host to dangerous excess.[6]

At one level, in this tale the Gascon rural world of tradition is positively valued over the French urban one of modern technologies, which in recent years has transformed peasant life. The commentary on larger social processes present in this and other narrative texts from the festival may therefore be read as a mode of resistance. Technological changes occurred most dramatically in Gascony in the immediate post–World War II period, when small-scale farming was transformed by mechanization and redistribution of landholdings, due largely to the influx of French ex-colonists from the former territories in North Africa. Many narratives in the liars' festival reflect an ongoing concern with the ultimate destruction of peasant cultures. This is no easy matter of cultural assimilation, but a problematic and dramatic one.

In this text, rurality, tradition, and ethnicity, embodied within a maternal figure, confront modernization. Regional Gascon culture is engendered in a female subject by a female narrator in a positive affirmation as grandma knows best. Her positive affirmation is a minority view in comparison with many of the other texts told by men, in which female characters typically represent the region in negative terms, often through their excessive sexuality. However, the largely positive image of the Gascon grandmother contains a certain element of pathos, for the current generation, typified by the young male head of household, has different ideas about how to run a farm. In the new order of things, the peasant grandmother's place and work roles are uncertain.

The other text to gain its teller the title of queen of the Moncrabeau Liars' Festival was recited in the 1984 contest and was told by a woman in her late fifties who is a resident of the village. Her origin tale, a popular subgenre with narrators, purported to explain the history of the relationship between Moncrabeau and Namur, seen through the positive consequences of the sexuality of the liars' festival mascot. The tale's main protagonist was a billy goat won in a drawing at the Moncrabeau Liars' Festival by a vacationing Belgian couple. The goat happened to have the same name as the village. As a young kid, he was able to speak in good French (Thompson, 1955–58, motif B211.12). His adoptive parents brought him back to Belgium, where he grew up in a human family. Upon reaching sexual maturity, he was so successful in his amours that his adoptive father decided to market the goat's sperm commercially. The mass marketing of the Gascon-born Moncrabeau's sperm is explained as the origin of artificial insemination, a practice common throughout present-day rural France. At a critical point when it appears that Moncrabeau will exhaust himself from his amorous travails, he is revived by a good swig of Armagnac, a regional brandy specific to southwestern France. This remedy, proposed by the goat's adoptive mother, is what her spouse used to counter his own impotence. Moncrabeau's successful production of sperm and its commercialization leads to the uniting of the two countries in friendship and in a political and economic exchange pact. In a celebration of life, a genetic natural link underscores the relationship between the Gascon village of Moncrabeau and the Belgian town of Namur.

In this tale the woman narrator appropriated the male genre of the tall tale and the most potent symbol of the fête, the goat. Although she dared to talk about the billy goat's sexuality, she lessened the impact by using a motherly voice through which she underscored her own conventional social role in the course of her recitation. She began by describing the young goat in maternal and familial terms, as if talking about a child. Later her tone changed to bawdiness when she turned to the goat's sexuality and that of its human adoptive parents. But she discreetly apologized before finally mentioning the term *artificial insemination*. Then, upon catching a glimpse of her little grandson in the crowd, the narrator paused in her recitation and announced that she would say no more about this term. She returned to her tale and concluded with a lyrical description of the new economic partnership between Belgium and France.

This second festival queen's tale is not merely a playful narrative about animal sexuality, for larger social concerns emerge. The technology imposed on the rural world this time is artificial insemination. The region is positively valued through its native son's sperm and the local beverage of Armagnac brandy, which revives the billy goat, while relations between France and Belgium, a fellow EEC member, are encouraged. As in the first tale, the underlying theme concerns Gascon ethnic identity, although here it is displaced onto southern Belgium. If the region is empowered through a strong maternal human figure in the first narrative, here it is empowered through a rampant male animal sexuality that is efficiently harnessed into biological reproduction. Male virility is lauded by the middle-aged female narrator, whose explicit identification with her own role as grandmother in the course of her performance played up her maternity and downplayed her sexuality. As an older married woman, she had the license to talk about sexuality, which she combined with the themes of rurality and ethnicity to positively encode Gascon identity.

The next text was also performed by a female resident of the village of Moncrabeau; it took seventh out of fourteen places in the 1984 festival. However, its narrator, a single young woman, was subject to social conventions regarding sexuality, unlike her predecessor, and so fared less well in the judging of her tale. Following Dell Hymes ("The 'Wife' Who 'Goes Out' like a Man," [1968]), one might subtitle this tale "The 'Woman' Who 'Went Out Hunting' like a Woman/Man," for the narrative was structured around gender confusion. It began with a number of realistic details, as the action was situated during the fall grape harvest, a time for hunting wood pigeons in southwestern France. The tale was thus ethnically localized through a leisure activity associated with Gascon men. Speaking in the first person, the young woman narrator explained how the female protagonist reluctantly accompanied her male cousin on a hunting expedition. She would replace his hunting dog, he told her, and so would help fetch any game that he killed. As she was about to urinate behind a bush, her cousin went off and took aim at a flock of starlings. In contrast with her cousin, who relied on the force of gunshot to hunt, the heroine succeeded at finding game by merely tapping around with a big stick. First she caught a garter snake and then a hare, which she clubbed (Thompson, 1955–58, motif N620ff). The two cousins returned home with the woman's hare, not bothering to pick up the dead starlings that the man had shot down. In the meantime, the garter snake got away.

An initial reading of this tale might suggest that its teller merely manipulated and reinforced negative stereotypes of men as hunters and women as gatherers and helpmates. Yet the text is subversive on a number of levels. To suggest that a man and woman—here a pair of cousins, taboo sexual partners—go together on a hunting expedition does not follow social conventions. Typically three to four men hunt together, accompanied only by their dogs. Furthermore, the two cousins go by themselves and leave for their expedition in the afternoon after a hunters' meal, when in fact normal practice would be to leave early in the morning. If psychoanalytic perspectives are applied to the text, it can be argued that a woman enters an extrasocial space, the woods, with a close male relative, a taboo sexual partner. She finds her first phallic symbol, a garter snake, which she puts into her receptacle, a hunting bag. She finds a hare after tapping and hitting something hard, which she also puts into her hunting bag.

In other words, a male story is retold in which the female protagonist/narrator is herself ambiguously implicated. The listener is left puzzled—is the narrator, who maintained first-person voice throughout the prose recitation, really the protagonist, and if so, how is she implicated? Is she subverting a male approach to hunting that relies on shooting game? It is a strange hunt indeed, for her cousin shoots at a flock of semidomestic birds, starlings, rather than game. The initial image of woman as helpmate, which the narrator underscored at one point by observing, "I was only a girl," is distorted on two occasions in the tale: first, when she goes to urinate in the woods, a motif frequently used by male narrators (although she goes behind a bush); and second, when she finds the hare, which she overpowers by stunning it. The underlying motifs point to a tabooed set of relations and a complex chain of sexual innuendo. The public tellingly expressed its disapproval by its silence throughout the performance and laughed only when the narrator played on a negative stereotype in the beginning, when she/the protagonist agreed to fetch game in place of the hunting dog. As Radner and Lanser note in their discussion of coding strategies that mask or reveal messages about women's experience, here trivialization of woman as helpmate reinforces the very ideology it critiques (1987:423).

Although the tale fell flat at the end and so could not get a real laugh from the audience, there is another explanation for its lack of success with the judges and public. It was too subversive in its performance by a young woman, both in her appropriating the male genre of the hunting story (*histoire de chasse*) and in treating it through ambiguous gender identity. The subversiveness of the tale was heightened through the collapsing of content and performance boundaries, with the result that the audience could not tell if the narrator was indeed the subject of the tale. This tale is more than an exaggeration about game caught in an exceptional manner, a typical tall-tale motif and in that sense an obvious lie. It also contains elements of the scatological and the sexual, organizing metaphors of the contest.

These three texts from the Moncrabeau Liars' Festival told by women reflect a diversity of voice, theme, and intention. Rather than speaking directly, female performers' voices in the first two tales of rhymed verse are filtered through the authorial/narrator's voice. The celebration of the region and a traditional way of life through positive stereotypes of a human or animal subject, practiced by these women narrators, is exploited by other male tellers, however, and so is not unique to female performers. In contrast, the third woman's narrative is actively subversive through its appropriation of the male genre of the hunting tale. It provides a critique of negative stereotypical images of women as passive helpmates by presenting a split female subject, a supposedly passive heroine who acts like a man in the tale. The critique is structured by references to the scatological (urinating), the violent (clubbing a hare), and the sexual (putting the garter snake in the hunting bag), taboo subjects for a single young woman narrator in the public festival setting.

A Man's Tale

The final text contains a male performer's manipulation of negative gender and ethnic stereotypes. Its narrator was a retired post office employee from a nearby village and a regular participant in regional story-telling events. The tale took fifth out of fourteen places in the 1984 festival. It relates to the preceding women's texts on several grounds—like tale one, it focuses on the rural world, this time negatively portrayed through human and animal characters; like tale two, it focuses on the village totem, this time engendered as a female goat; like tales two and three, it focuses on the body, with sexuality ever present. The man's tale juxtaposes the health problems of a peasant woman, the wife of the male peasant protagonist, with those of the couple's female goat. The habitually talkative peasant wife is narratively silent from beginning to end (Thompson, 1955–58, motif D2072.053). The first image of her, a negative stereotype, is of a woman who has talked so much that she has lost her voice.[7]

The peasant husband therefore calls in a doctor who is a former veterinarian. Conveniently, the physician's training enables him to look after both the man's wife and the female goat. After examining the woman from head to toe and from front to back, the doctor turns to the goat, who can no longer digest because she is pregnant. Sexuality is evoked when the doctor observes that he can still smell the billy goat's presence (Thompson, 1955–58, motif A2416.1; see Bakhtin, 1984:chap. 6). The doctor then prescribes two different medications, one for the wife, the other for the goat. The peasant responds by asking if he can't get reimbursed for his goat's medical expenses by filing its case with social security under his wife's name. The doctor at first reacts indignantly and asks the peasant if he thinks he is in an Arab emirate and can thereby cheat the national security system by bending the rules; but eventually he agrees to his client's request. After cheating the social security system, the peasant is swindled in turn. Somehow the medicines get mixed up, and, by the end of the tale, the goat talks and the wife chews cud. In a Bakhtinian inversion of orifices, the active sexuality of the female animal subject, the goat, leads positively to biological reproduction and human speech, whereas the excessive speech of the female human subject, the peasant wife, leads negatively to animal-like digestion and silence, or social death.

The subjectivity of the narrator and the tale's male protagonist must be examined. In his closing moral coda, the narrator mixes the level of content with that of performance. His moral states: "savoir guérir ou mentir, il faut choisir" ("you have to choose between knowing how to cure or to lie"). As in the previous hunting tale told by a young woman, the male narrator of this mixed medicines tale superimposed the performance frame onto the narrative itself, for the curing occurs by the protagonist, while both the protagonist and narrator can lie. The origin of the mistake that leads to the lie is unclear. Has the doctor mixed up the medicines, has the peasant mixed up the medicines in administering them, or has the common name on the medical prescription led to the confusion? If the mistake comes from the doctor in his writing of the prescription, this is a satire of the medical profession that harkens back to the Renaissance and is evident in the writings of Rabelais (Bakhtin, 1984:179–80). If the peasant has mixed up the medicine unintentionally, he comes across as an illiterate country bumpkin. If he has acted intentionally, he has worked to keep the woman silenced. The confusion over who perpetrates the mix-up has consequences for interpretation and intention. Either way, men keep women in their place. This tale also contains a commentary on the rural world as it first came into contact with the national bureaucracy through social security, which was instituted in France in the mid–1930s. It suggests that peasants accept medical care more readily for their animals than for themselves.[8]

Conclusion

To assess the content of the tales and the performance strategies of the narrators in the Moncrabeau Liars' Festival, one must not forget that textual production is "a highly complex, 'over-determined' process with many different and conflicting literary and non-literary determinants (historical, political, social, ideological, institutional, generic, psychological and so on)" (Moi, 1985:45). If it is no longer necessary to prove that certain literary forms reflect social conditions, one may return to accounting for descriptive aspects. To conclude I will briefly address the role of performance, historical moment, ideological currents, and psychological effect in the liars' festival.

In a sense the performance frame of the liars' festival and generic conventions and motifs give *all* narrators, male and female, license to overturn social and sexual conventions (Bauman, 1986:20). However, the tales do not reveal a direct reversal or inversion of social roles, as Sarah Melhado White (1982) has shown for medieval fabliaux and Natalie Z. Davis (1975) has demonstrated for festive behavior in early modern France. Instead, these contemporary Gascon tall tales appear to parallel a different genre of French verbal art, that of the proverb, in reproducing social conventions rather than calling them into question (Segalen, 1976:77). This results in different consequences according to the gender of the performer.

By reproducing social conventions, female narrators can strategically express their ambivalence about performing in a male event while simultaneously representing positive images of women. This was brought home to me on a personal level in the 1987 festival. When offered the chance to participate, I found myself caught in the same dilemma as my female predecessors. I knew perfectly well what kind of story would be favorably received by the judges and audience, yet I felt constrained to present an uncontroversial tale, since I wanted to return to the area for further research. One young woman friend was horrified to hear that I was going to the liars' festival and warned me that its bad reputation would do me great harm. Two older women friends noted approvingly that I had managed to create an amusing story without resorting to licentiousness. Falling back on women's role as nurturer, I composed a tale that recounted how I had returned back home to run a restaurant in my native Gascony after having first made my fortune in America. My lie, which took fourth out of fifteen places, described various American regional culinary specialties so convincingly that several members of the audience came up to me after the contest was over to discover when I served these foods. I had counted on the audience's and judges' ability to detect my true social identity as that of an American, evidenced by my accent and detailed discussion of American culinary geography. Therefore I could not possibly be a native-born Gascon, as I had claimed during my recitation. My nuances of reversed social identity were overshadowed, however, by the perceived absence of motifs of exaggeration or sexuality, which function as overt indexes of tall tales. Thus the audience and judges chose to accept my tale as true. The next day, as they cleaned up the stage area, I spoke with several male members of the liars' club about the lack of women contestants that year. The men vaguely remembered that several women had participated in the past, but they clearly saw the contest as a male event.

The male narrators who comprise the majority of the contest participants typically present negative stereotypes of women in their texts. Men have less at stake in reproducing these negative images than do their female counterparts. In their tales the men can project fears about women's powers, particularly with respect to sexuality and reproduction. Female protagonists appear in traditional social roles as silent wives and helpmates. In terms of sexuality, they appear as unwilling or overwilling lovers in some cases, controlled through the eroticized violence of their male partners. In other instances female protagonists negatively type the region through their sexuality with outsiders, for example, or without distinction, as prostitutes. Thus the region is engendered regularly by male narrators through female subjects whose sexuality renders the region's traditional identity vulnerable.[9]

Power inequities in gender, class, and ethnic relations are played out through the bodies of women protagonists in other tales told by male narrators in the 1984 and 1987 performances, as the following plot summaries reveal. Thus Joan of Arc is both an innocent virgin and an astute Gascon businesswoman who manages to save herself from prostitution by arranging a deal with the historic enemy, the Burgundians who sided with England in the Hundred Years' War between France and England. A highly eligible rich Norman landowner's daughter is married off to an impoverished simpleton who physically abuses her. The virgin shepherdess heroine of a pastoral is raped and then consents to marry her violator. The breast milk of a Russian wet nurse nun turns into yogurt while she dances the waltz at the Hapsburg court and is subsequently distributed commercially under the Dannon yogurt label. These absurd combinations are based on incongruities that arise from the juxtaposition of opposing qualities or elements embedded within cultural images of women. The resulting dissonance is meant to provide humorous effect. In these latter instances, sexuality and bodily functions, often combined with reproduction in absurd and surreal ways, endangers the female subjects of the tales more than it empowers them. Only when excessive sexuality is matched up with ethnicity, as a metaphorical extension of the region's strength, for example, does it become an acceptable subject for women narrators. The 1984 festival queen adopted this strategy in her choice of a male animal subject to symbolize the village and the region.

Yet stereotypes—of gender, ethnicity, and class—are not unique to the liars' festival, for they underlie a range of historical and contemporary narrative genres and performances. Thus, in the popular culture of the Renaissance blazons of rhymed verse based on stereotypes of a village, region, or nation functioned to praise or denigrate (Bakhtin, 1984:428). Ethnic jokes and festivals are other obvious instances in which stereotypes of various ethnic and racial groups prevail (see Miller, 1977).[10] In addition to praising or denigrating certain social groups, in the Moncrabeau context stereotypes signal the generic frame to the audience and prepare it for the exaggerations they are about to hear. But why even tell tales based on gender stereotypes in the late twentieth century, at a moment when women's conventional social roles have been so called into question? One might consider whether celebrations such as the liars' festival arise when the cultural identity and economy of the region are most in crisis, reflected here in the concerns about the process of modernization. Does playing upon gender and ethnic stereotypes in a village fête reassure narrators and audience of their identity in a changing social world?[11] Furthermore, since the tales are told in rather quick succession, can the audience really decode their complex messages?

In his study of the medieval fabliaux R. Howard Bloch has noted that many scholars view the genre as the ultimate natural text, simplistically "reflecting" the world and incapable of theoretical analysis (1986:6). It might be argued that the contemporary tales discussed here are equally "natural texts," focused as they are on human and animal sexuality and the rural world. However, their treatment of technological change and displacement of cultures; of gender, class, and ethnic relations; of political relations between western and eastern Europe and the Middle East; and the rewriting/reinvention of history make them heterogeneous and complex textual constructions. Whether guided by conscious or unconscious intentions, the liars' festival tales represent power inequities in gender, ethnic, and class relations through the body social. Although similar relations have been analyzed in other narrative genres (see Marin, 1986; White, 1982), they have become marked in French expressive culture as ethnically Gascon through the Moncrabeau fête.

Notes

I wish to acknowledge the Wenner-Gren Foundation for Anthropological Research, the Fulbright Commission, and the Sigma Xi Society for funding the initial fieldwork from 1981 through 1982. The 1987 fieldwork was funded through a grant from the Institute for the Arts and Humanistic Studies of the Pennsylvania State University. I have retained the real names of places. Thanks go to Nathalie Chevrin for her extensive help on transcriptions of the 1987 festival and cultural decoding of the 1984 and 1987 performances; to Joan Gross, Stephanie Kane, Janet Roesler, and Monìque Yaari for their critical comments on an earlier draft of this essay; and to Anne-Marie Lallement and Jacqueline Rogers for their help with the translations. An earlier version of this work appeared in 1987 in the *Journal of American Folklore* 100 (398): 504–27, edited by Bruce Jackson, whom I thank for editorial assistance.

1. Initially, out of feminist conviction, I wanted to find that women narrators in the Moncrabeau Liars' Festival were subversives, mavericks in a domain that was not their own. To a degree this is correct, for the women's presence reflects their historical role as transmitters of Gascon oral literature, which lasted well into the nineteenth century and was documented by Bladé (1967), a folklorist who made extensive collections of Gascon oral literature. In the midnineteenth century, inspired by Romantic nationalism, folk literature became appropriated by male amateur folklorists who printed it to make this material available to a larger public. From the twentieth century on, the editors of such collections were men, and with the revival of regional expressive culture in the sixties and seventies, so, too, were the performers in public festivals.

2. Dégh's study of two elderly Hungarian women in Gary, Indiana, documents obscene anecdotes that alternate with jokes and witch stories in the women's repertoires (1985:10, 15–16). Dégh notes that both women surpass the usual amount of obscenity that occurs in the jokes and the talk of old peasant women. Both favor discussing sexual affairs, including their own past erotic experiences, which they project to the present (23). The two women are most at ease telling obscene anecdotes to each other on the telephone, their usual channel of communication. When Mrs. Kovács told a string of dirty jokes to people in the church hall during a bingo party break, she was bemusedly praised by male members of the audience, but chastised by the minister for her performance (15). Dégh's study suggests female joke tellers' preference for domestic settings and a female audience when telling obscene anecdotes. This is borne out by Mitchell's comparative survey of male and female joke tellers undertaken at Colorado State University in the early seventies, which showed that females told their lowest percentage of obscene jokes to members of the opposite sex. When females told jokes to males, humorous jests based on ethnic stereotypes in Polish jokes predominated (1985:184). Mitchell notes that while the *number* of obscene jokes men told to men was higher than the number of obscene jokes they told to women, the *percentage* of obscene jokes they told to women was almost exactly the same as the percentage of obscene jokes they told to men (181). Thus

men do not hesitate to tell obscene jokes to single or mixed audiences, while women do.

3. In its costumes and ceremonies, the Moncrabeau Liars' Club parallels other local groups, such as gastronomic societies. These societies, whose members consist primarily of male village residents, function to express local pride, heightened on ceremonial occasions that celebrate the founding of the society or a significant element of the village or region's identity.

4. The tales cannot be readily categorized by genre or mode of composition. Most are recited orally from memory; some are read from the handwritten copies of their authors. Many are recited in couplets of rhymed verse, a form popular with other local poets; others are moral prose tales. Most of the festival texts are recited in French; a few are recited in Gascon. The increased use of French reflects accommodations to tourists and the generation of local young adults in the audience who do not know Gascon.

5. In her vast study of marriage, love, and women in a different genre of verbal art, that of French proverbs, Segalen observes a positive image of old age in which the domestic activities and functions of women are greatly valued (1976:55).

6. This parallels the conclusions of Barbé (1983) in her study of folktales printed in Gascon almanacs published between 1890 and 1930. Barbé shows that in the folktales published between 1915 and 1930 the city is a dangerous place where French rather than Gascon is spoken, peasant migrants seek the entertainment of socialist cabarets, and the mass culture of radio and newspaper threatens the local traditions of oral networks of information and communication.

7. This is not just a gender stereotype, however, but an ethnic one, for both Gascon men and women are said to be big talkers and therefore potentially excellent liars. The relation between voice and positive or negative characterizations has been addressed by several scholars of gender relations in oral and written literature. Segalen notes the prevalence of associations between talkativeness and indiscretion in negative characterizations of women in French proverbs (1975a, 1975b, 1976:56). Bottigheimer notes that women characters never get to center stage and use direct speech. Instead, they are narratively silent in Grimms' fairy tales (1987:52).

8. The encounter between a peasant and a doctor, who represents the medical knowledge of another modernizing world, is a theme common to narratives that appear in regional almanacs in the first three decades of this century. Typically, peasants find themselves on the losing end in such encounters. For further discussion, see Barbé (1983).

9. The contemporary Gascon tales are part of a broader picture concerning representation of women in genres of verbal art in French and other cultural settings. In the French context, Segalen finds that proverbs underscore the importance of endogamy in the choice of marital partners, while outsiders are a threat to the social order. Women who choose husbands beyond the borders of local space are seen as immoral and even as prostitutes (1976:65). In their analyses of Grimms' fairy tales, both Bottigheimer (1987) and Tatar (1987) discuss representation of female protagonists with respect to narrative voice and social roles.

Bottigheimer links female characters' powerlessness with lack of a voice, with gradual or prolonged loss of speech (1987:52–53, 72–77). Tatar shows how female protagonists are humiliated victims of powerful men or excessively proud individuals whose position is diminished through their own transformation (1987:116–18, 133). For Tatar's discussion of female ogrelike characters, including cooks, stepmothers, witches, and mothers-in-law, see chapter 6 (1987:137–55).

10. Stereotypical representations of ethnic and racial groups occur in the liars' festival tales, where certain ethnic and racial groups remain distant and subordinate to the dominating Gascons. At times these stereotypes are intertwined with those of women. For further discussion, see Mark (1991a, 1991b).

11. In her study of indigenous tribal politics of the Emberá in the Panama Darién jungle (1986), Kane investigates the significance of the representation of women as traditional, exemplified in women's dress and their performance of animal dances. Kane finds that Emberá women's purity and traditionalism is reconstructed and reframed to legitimate an emerging political structure dominated by men, a structure that articulates with a national one in which men's dominance is even more strongly rooted (7). Gender and the role of women figure prominently as domains of male control when indigeneous social systems are under threat.

References Cited

Abel, Elizabeth, ed. 1982. *Writing and Sexual Difference.* Chicago: University of Chicago Press.

Amicale des Conteurs de Gascogne, eds. 1982. *Lous dou Parsan: Contes, Menteries, Poésies.* Sauboires, France: Centre Rural d'Aide aux Associations du Bas Armagnac.

Bakhtin, Mikhail M. [1968] 1984. *Rabelais and His World.* Translated by Helene Iswolsky. Bloomington: Indiana University Press.

Barbé, Colette. 1983. "La littérature populaire gasconne dans les almanachs gersois de la fin du XIXe siècle à 1940." Ph.D. diss., Ecole Pratique des Hautes Etudes en Sciences Sociales, Paris.

Bauman, Richard. 1986. *Story, Performance, and Event: Contextual Studies of Oral Narrative.* Cambridge: Cambridge University Press.

Bladé, Jean-François. [1885] 1967. *Contes populaires de la Gascogne.* 3 vols. Paris: Maisonneuve et Larose.

Bloch, R. Howard. 1986. *The Scandal of the Fabliaux.* Chicago: University of Chicago Press.

Bottigheimer, Ruth B. 1987. *Grimms' Bad Girls and Bold Boys: The Moral and Social Vision of the Tales.* New Haven: Yale University Press.

Davis, Natalie Z. 1975. "Women on Top." In *Society and Culture in Early Modern France,* 124–51. Stanford: Stanford University Press.

Dégh, Linda. 1985. "Dial a Story, Dial an Audience: Two Rural Women Narrators in an Urban Setting." In *Women's Folklore, Women's Culture,* ed. Rosan

Jordan and Susan J. Kalčik, 3–25. Philadelphia: University of Pennsylvania Press.

Farrer, Claire R. 1975. *Women and Folklore.* Austin: University of Texas Press.

Greene, Gayle, and Coppélia Kahn, eds. 1985. *Making a Difference: Feminist Literary Criticism.* London: Methuen.

Herzfeld, Michael. 1984. "The Horns of the Mediterraneanist Dilemma." *American Ethnologist* 11 (3): 439–54.

Hymes, Dell. 1968. "The 'Wife' Who 'Goes Out' Like a Man: Reinterpretation of a Clackamas Chinook Myth." *Social Science Information* 7 (3): 173–99.

Jordan, Rosan, and F. A. de Caro. 1985. "Women and the Study of Folklore." *Signs* 11 (3): 500–518.

Jordan, Rosan A., and Susan J. Kalčik, eds. 1985. *Women's Folklore, Women's Culture.* Philadelphia: University of Pennsylvania Press.

Kane, Stephanie. 1986. "Cultural Representations of Women and the New Politics of the Emberá." Paper presented at the annual meeting of the American Anthropological Association, Philadelphia, Pa.

Kaplan, Cora. 1985. "Pandora's Box: Subjectivity, Class, and Sexuality in Socialist Feminist Criticism." In *Making a Difference: Feminist Literary Criticism,* ed. Gayle Greene and Coppélia Kahn, 146–76. London: Methuen.

Marin, Louis. 1986. *La parole mangée et autres essais théologico-politiques.* Paris: Méridiens Klincksieck.

Mark, Vera. 1991a. "Cultural Pastiches: Intertextualities in the Moncrabeau Liars' Festival Narratives." *Cultural Anthropology* 6 (1): 193–211.

———. 1991b. "Représentations de l'Ethnicité dans une Fête Gasconne." *Ethnologie française.* 21 (1): 28–41.

Miller, Edward K. 1977. "The Use of Stereotypes in Inter-ethnic Joking as a Means of Communication." *Folklore Annual* 7–8:28–42.

Mitchell, Carol. 1985. "Some Differences in Male and Female Joke-Telling." In *Women's Folklore, Women's Culture.* ed. Rosan Jordan and Susan J. Kalčik, 163–86. Philadelphia: University of Pennsylvania Press.

Moi, Toril. 1985. *Sexual/Textual Politics.* London: Methuen.

Ortner, Sherry. 1974. "Is Female to Male as Nature Is to Culture?" In *Woman, Culture, and Society,* ed. Michelle Zimbalist Rosaldo and Louise Lamphere, 67–87. Stanford: Stanford University Press.

Radner, Joan N., and Susan S. Lanser. 1987. "The Feminist Voice: Strategies of Coding in Folklore and Literature." *Journal of American Folklore* 100 (398): 412–25.

Randolph, Vance. 1951. *We Always Lie to Strangers.* New York: Columbia University Press.

Reiter, Rayna. 1975. "Men and Women in the South of France." In *Toward an Anthropology of Women,* ed. Rayna Reiter, 252–82. New York: Monthly Review Press.

Segalen, Martine. 1975a. "Le mariage, l'amour et les femmes dans les proverbes populaires français." *Ethnologie française* 5 (1–4): 119–62.

————. 1975b. "Le mariage et la femme dans les proverbes du sud de la France." *Annales du Midi* 87 (123): 265–88.

————. 1976. "Le mariage, l'amour et les femmes dans les proverbes populaires français (fin)." *Ethnologie française* 6 (1): 33–88.

Suleiman, Susan R., and Inge Crosman, eds. 1980. *The Reader in the Text: Essays on Audience and Interpretation.* Princeton: Princeton University Press.

Tatar, Maria. 1987. *The Hard Facts of the Grimms' Fairy Tales.* Princeton: Princeton University Press.

Thomas, Gerald. 1977. *The Tall Tale and Philippe d'Alcripe: An Analysis of the Tall Tale Genre with Particular Reference to Philippe d'Alcripe's "La Nouvelle Fabrique des Excellents Traits de Vérité."* Memorial University of Newfoundland Folklore and Language Publication Series, no. 1. Publications of the American Folklore Society Bibliographical and Special Series, vol. 29. St. Johns, Newfoundland: Department of Folklore, Memorial University of Newfoundland.

Thompson, Stith. 1955–58. *Motif-Index of Folk-Literature.* 6 vols. Bloomington: Indiana University Press.

White, Sarah Melhado. 1982. "Sexual Language and Human Conflict in Old French Fabliaux." *Comparative Studies in Society and History* 24 (1): 185–210.

Access to the Pulpit: Reproductive Images and Maternal Strategies of the Pentecostal Female Pastor

In her introduction to a special issue of *American Quarterly* devoted to women and religion, Janet Wilson James points out that "an exploration of women's part in the history of religion soon encounters two constants: women usually outnumber men; men exercise the authority" (1978:579). James goes on to point out, however, that the "shock waves of the sixties" have weakened the "familiar authority structures," and women are flooding the religious scene, searching out the "liberating promises of scripture to revise theologies," contending for the "right to be ordained and to exercise sacerdotal authority" (1978:579; cf. Behnke, 1982). Intrigued by the significant number of Pentecostal female preachers I had located in both southern Indiana and central Missouri in 1983–86, a phenomenon that seemed to fly in the face of the tenets of this male-dominated religion, I set out to examine James's contention in terms of Pentecostalism. My study of female preachers in the Pentecostal faith does not illustrate how women have weakened authority structures or sought the "liberating promises of scripture to revise theologies." This study challenges the contention that men always exercise the authority, but ironically, it in no way demonstrates that a large number of women consciously or overtly strive for "liberating promises" or support efforts toward a "new theology" or a "new ethics." Rather, it is the strong connection these women maintain with conservative religion and patriarchal constructs that enables them to acquire the position of power and authority in a church as pastor and provides the means for them to maintain that position.

Firmly entrenched in Pentecostalism, as practiced by whites in southern Indiana,[1] is the tension between the religiously inscribed inferiority of women who are expected to be submissive to men and the belief in individual equality before God in terms of salvation. The traditional belief in the inferiority of women is based on an interpretation of the biblical story of the garden of Eden, an interpretation that insists on Eve's transgression and her subsequent seduction of Adam to join in her disobedience to God's direct orders. Pauline directives to the Christian church have remained the clear directives of God for this denomination, stemming from "the fall": "Let your women keep silence in the church: for it is not permitted for them to speak: but they ought to be subject, as also the Law saith. And if they will learn any thing, let them ask their husbands at home: for it is a shame for a woman to speak in the church" (1 Cor. 14:34–35). And later, Paul writes to Timothy, "Let the women learn in silence with all subjection: I permit not a woman to teach, neither to usurp authority over the man, but to be in silence" (1 Tim. 2:11–12).

While it certainly seems clear enough in the verses quoted above that Paul insists on silence for women, he also confuses the issue when he says, "But every woman that prayeth or prophecieth bareheaded, dishonoreth her head" (1 Cor. 11:3–5).[2] Given the scriptural foundation for the muted subjection of women in Christian religions, how is it, then, that women in the strictly conservative Pentecostal religion come to be selected for the chief post of church pastor, and images are most salient in their attempts to authenticate both their religious power and their church authority? By firmly basing their role as preacher and pastor within the frameworks that support a traditional and spiritual religiosity, one closely aligned with nineteenth-century notions of religion as part of the woman's sphere and maintained close to hearth and home, these female pastors are able to gain power and authority through already established female attributes (Welter, 1976). The maternal and reproductive images they convey as religious strategies serve to strip their presence behind the pulpit of its most threatening aspects.

Most important to the congregations that have a female as pastor is the perception of that woman as "mother" to the congregation. When group members are asked to say why they think a particular woman is a good pastor, they often answer: "She takes good care of us" or "She's just like a mother; she cares for everybody." Female pastors themselves recognize the importance of acting out the role of symbolic mother to their congregations:

> Women have a special gift of compassion, don't you think? A real caring, loving compassion. Maybe it's because God made us mothers, you know.

We know how to comfort our babies, you know, when they're little, and they need attention. And I think it's a special love God puts into the heart of a mother, and gives her such tender love for her family, and then, naturally, why couldn't he use that tender love that he put there to begin with, you know, he made the mamas. He made the mamas, you know, and he put that love in their hearts to be mamas, and so it is a special love, so why can't he use that love out of a woman to relate to the people that need encouragement from him? I believe it's that motherly quality of love that God puts in a mother to bring up that baby . . . a motherly love. And I believe the people can feel that—that goes along with this guy I worked for, even though he didn't believe in women preachers, he did say to me, "I believe that ladies can have more compassion to minister than the men do."[3] (Sister Pat Roberts, Centerville, Missouri)

I think a woman has more of a tendency to mother the people than lead them as a shepherd. And it's hard [for a man] to follow a woman pastor [i.e. be the next pastor] because they don't take a firm stand on things. It's more or less "Yes, honey, I understand," you know, like that. (Sister Alma Cotton, Smithville, Missouri)

God told me, "I've chosen you. I've put you in the furnace of affliction that others can identify with you." Because I had prayed, "Lord, give me compassion. Like you feel compassion for people." And you can't feel that with people unless you've gone through what they have. Unless you can walk in their shoes. But I'll tell you one thing, here's one preacher that will sit and listen when somebody is read to, needs somebody to listen. I've been told a number of times, "Sister, I believe it's because you're a mother. I feel a compassion that I don't feel in men." (Sister Anna Walters, Centerville, Missouri)

These statements are filled with the implications of what a "mother" is likely to do for her "children." Several of these female pastors speak of their congregation members as their "babes in Christ," especially new converts who have just joined their churches. Traditional "motherly" images include caring, compassion, empathy, the ability to be a good listener, cheerfulness, understanding, loving, and comforting; most of these capabilities are offered as positive attributes of the female pastor and are often offered in contradistinction to the attributes of many male pastors, who are more often characterized as fine leaders or strict disciplinarians who "lead them as a shepherd." This characterization of female pastors certainly reflects Carol Gilligan's suggestions that women are more inclined toward care and community (1982; cf. Ortner, 1974).

To complement the image of the female pastor as the "mother" of the church, the women know that in addition to mothering the congregation, they must be biological mothers as well. The sermons of the women in this study are filled with references to their own children, to the raising of their children, to the family as a unifying image. Adrienne Rich, in her examination of motherhood, focuses upon society's need for women to be mothers: "Women who refuse to become mothers are not merely emotionally suspect, but are dangerous. Not only do they refuse to continue the species; they also deprive society of its emotional leaven—the suffering of the mother" (1977:164). An unmarried woman, rejecting the life of wife and mother, would pose a serious threat to the equilibrium of a socially conservative congregation. A female pastor's own maternal experience becomes weighted and must be foregrounded to minimize the danger that her elevated position in the church be perceived as a rejection of (what is perceived to be) her "natural" role as wife and mother. The following remarks from female pastors reflect the importance of this image of them first as wives, mothers, and caretakers, and only secondarily as pastors. These quotes are equally full of disclaimers about their own ambitions for the pulpit; the tradition of women placing the responsibility with God for calling them into the ministry can be traced back to medieval female visionaries whose instructions to write down their spiritual experiences came directly from God and were often met with resistance from the women themselves.[4]

> When my own kids were little, I'd hold two kids and preach, you know. They'd be crying without me, you know, so I'd hold them and preach. I've always said I've got more sermons over the ironing board and the dishpan than I ever did on my knees. (Sister Ruth Hatley, Murray, Missouri)

> I've had to prove all of these years that a woman can be called into the ministry. And I've kept loving the people even when they criticized me and telling them, "Look, this wasn't my choice." I've stood in front of the mirror lots of times and said, "God, are you sure you know what you're doing?" I'm a wife. I'm a mother. I didn't ask for this.
> (Sister Anna Walters, Centerville, Missouri)

> Two or three months [after being saved] that's when I began to feel it [the call to preach], but I didn't let on, you know, I didn't know what it was. Really, the most I felt it was, like, when I was home alone, just me and the Lord. Like when I'd be at home with, just reading my Bible, and you know, maybe the babies playing or something at my feet. I enjoy what I'm doing. I enjoy just what God's made me do. I enjoy being a lady. I enjoy being a wife, a mother, a grandma. I just love it. (Sister Pat Roberts, Centerville, Missouri)

In light of the mothering capacities of female pastors, it seems no coincidence that almost every woman I interviewed had an invalid mother of her own.[5] In nearly every case, these women had to take on the duty of mothering their siblings at a very young age, often forfeiting their own education and aspirations to care for an ailing mother and carry the responsibilities of the household. Sister Mary did not finish high school until she was an adult: "See, when I was a sophomore, right before I was called to preach, when I was fifteen, my mother got real sick and she miscarried, had a stillborn baby. And I had to quit school, because I was the oldest." Anna's story of how she had to quit school and care for her family similarly illustrates how she developed her virtuous maternal inclinations at such an early age. Her success as a young "mother" to her siblings served as a test, perhaps, of her strength and stamina, one that prepared her well for another extraordinary "test," the call to preach.

> When I was nine years old, my mother's health began to fail, and when I was almost ten, my mother gave birth to my youngest brother, Danny Joe, and she later had pneumonia and took strong medicine, and her heart began to bother her. So more and more responsibility fell upon my shoulders. I had to learn to cook, and Mama would tell me to put a dash of this, a pinch of that, and this is how I cooked for the family when Mama was bedfast. My responsibilities grew, and it was very difficult to care for a bedfast mother and five younger brothers and sisters. And I helped my dad and two older brothers milk and do usual chores on the farm. There was water to carry, and I would heat it on the wood cookstove to wash clothes for the family. The night before I would pick up chips and bring in dry corncobs. They made it easy to start a good hot fire in the morning. My dad felt he didn't have a good start for his day if he didn't have biscuits and gravy along with his ham or bacon and eggs. At night I would light the coal oil lamp and turn out the electric lights, and while everybody else slept, many times I've rubbed my mother's back; she never had a bedsore in all of her time of being bedfast. This was a nervous strain upon young shoulders. She was in and out of the hospital so much before she died at the age of thirty-seven years.

Sister Anna does not remind us, in this portion of her narrative, that she was born with severe scoliosis of the spine. Doctors tried to get her family to take her to St. Louis for surgery and remedial treatment, but the family's finances and their unfamiliarity with urban centers prevented them from seeking the help that young Anna needed. A local doctor warned her family that she would never be able to carry or deliver children of her own. Yet, Anna sensed the importance of her own maternity and denied the doctors the last word on that matter.

> I prayed and prayed to get pregnant. I just pleaded with the Lord. And I lost my first one. But—I don't know, maybe it's stubbornness, God has given me a lot of something—God has give me a lot of determination and willpower. I have three now. They fixed a support, and I would go and they

would adjust that support every month, then, for me to carry my children. But, God was so good to me during the time that I carried them. I was suffering so bad during the time I was carrying my children and each time, of course, it spread the spine more and crippled me a little more—but God was so good to me [by allowing her to become pregnant and carry the children].

The female pastor is expected to be tough. She must possess stamina and display the fierce, tenacious tendencies of a mother likely to protect her young. Many of the women speak of the determination God gave them to survive the hardships of being a female preacher. They speak of the criticism, heartaches, and ostracism they have encountered both in their families and in the community. The accounts they give of their experiences sound very much alike. When asked about women as preachers, Sister Mabel Adams answered: "I've thought all right, then, I thought he could make a woman preach if she wanted to, if he wanted her to. I've told them they didn't hire me and they sure couldn't fire me.[6] God called me, God sent me, and I'm here!" Similarly, Sister Ruth Hatley recalls that there have been moves to oust her from her post, but she says: "They did not hire me and they can't fire me. So, I got God to answer to. I've got a determination that I am not going to give up. When God has something for us to do, he means for us to do it." This image of the women as tough and hardy, able to withstand the threats of both men and devils, can be readily reconciled if considered within the imagery of ferocity of the "natural" mother, strong enough to protect her own children and her position.

Within the religious community female pastors have clear directives: they must be compassionate, caring, loving mothers for their congregations, and it will be most beneficial if they are biological mothers as well. As pastor of a church, a woman's strength in that capacity will lie in her ability to apply all the maternal aspects of her female being to the care and guidance of her symbolic family, her "babes in Christ." Much of what the women preach about is, I believe, firmly entrenched in this same maternal imagery. Gilligan's thesis that women's perspective is more inclined toward connection and community is also reflected in the rhetoric of women preachers (1982). The most common foci of women's sermons are variations on the themes of "total sacrifice" and a sharpened concern with "making it into heaven," no matter how godly a life one has lived; for women, anyway, the concern seems to hang in the air.[7] The reunion of the family—both biological and religious—in the community of heaven as an extension of this latter theme seems to be an excellent illustration of Gilligan's hypothesis. Sister Anna, for example, in an interpretation of a

Bible verse, uses a particularly striking image of heaven as a low-slung balcony, just out of sight of earthlings, where our families who have gone on before us watch us and wait for us to join them:

> [Reading] "Likewise, I say unto you,
> There is joy in the presence of the angels of God
> Over one sinner that repenteth."
> I believe that that simply means this:
> All those people in heaven
> There in the presence of angels and the presence of God
> They rejoice.
> I believe that a precious Mom and Dad
> Who have prayed long and fervent
> And hard
> For unsaved children
> I tell you, I believe,
> Even though they went on home to their reward
> And they didn't see those children saved,
> I want to tell you something,
> I believe when that one, that child,
> Bows on their knees to God
> That that Mom and Dad
> Rejoice in heaven.
> I believe over the balcony of heaven this morning
> If one soul in this congregation this morning
> Repents of sin
> They know it and they rejoice
> In the presence of angels.[8]

These women must be loving and tough, but they must deny that they have or seek equal footing with men. The "mother" of the church must not be confused with or made the equivalent of what the "father" of a church might be. This is due largely to the maintenance of a strict hierarchical power structure in the home and in the community, a hierarchy that is expected to prevail in the religious context as well, even with a female at the helm. The forceful role of men in the homes, recognized by the believers as God-given and prescribed by the Bible, is mirrored in the context of the religion: even when a woman is the pastor much of the organization of the service is determined by males, and the governing body of the church is made up of male deacons. The women know that their position must not suggest an attempt to usurp the divinely authorized authority of men.

It's been a real barrier, of criticism, because they've used the scripture that the women keep silent in the church, and so on. But I usually tell them, it's usually a man, I've never found a woman being critical—they've never spoken to me, now, they might have, in their hearts, but never said anything—but it's usually a man and I'll tell them, "If you men will do what god wants you to do, we women won't have to." And that usually hushes them. (Sister Alma Cotton, Smithville, Missouri)

The scriptural directives that insist on female silence in the churches are not taken lightly by either the women or the men in the congregation. Pentecostals take the Bible to be literal truth (although interpretation is, of course, evident at times even to them), and Paul is quite clear on the issue of women speaking out in church. Most men would, in both theory and practice, agree with the following clergyman's assessment:

They [female ministers] are handmaidens. They should wait upon the [male] ministers of the church. A handmaiden to Christ. A woman's got no right. She is over the house. She is not over a man. A man is over the woman and Christ is over the man, over the church. Now, she's got a place in the church as a Sunday School teacher or maybe as advising to the women. But she can't stand up in that pulpit and tell people what to do because that makes her over the man and that's not according to God's word. (Brother William Bird, Bedford, Indiana)

Women most often justify their position behind the pulpit by agreeing that they are merely "handmaidens of the Lord," going about the business of saving souls in these the "last days." They point to Joel's prophecy in the Old Testament, which is repeated by Paul in Acts 9:16 and 17, after a group of both men and women experienced speaking in tongues together. The scriptures read: "And it shall come to pass afterward, that I will pour out my spirit upon all flesh; and your sons and your daughters shall prophesy, your old men shall dream dreams, your young men shall see visions; And also upon the servants and upon the handmaids in those days will I pour out my spirit" (Joel 2:28, 29). The implied authority given in these verses to women to "prophesy" is repeated by female preachers as evidence of their own right to speak in church. Yet, the women know their use of ritual disclaimers will act to remove from the situation some of its threatening potential. The women are most accommodating.

The following was spoken from the pulpit by the female co-pastor of a fairly large congregation: "I always present myself as a handmaiden of the Lord. Let the men take the part of the ministry and the government of the church because they are the head. The Bible clearly says we are the weaker vessel. Relax, I don't call myself a preacher. Let the men do that; it's all right. But you have got to give me the right to be a handmaiden of the Lord and he has poured out his spirit unto me, and he has called me into his work, and I'm here" (Sister Wanda Nelson, Taft, Indiana). While a male minister may offer similar disclaimers, such as "I'm only a mouth-piece of the Lord" or "The sermon you are about to hear comes to you directly from God and not from me," such a disclaimer does not have to justify his presence in the pulpit, it only has to serve to indicate his meekness. Like the disclaimers of the women, his speech acts to place responsibility for the message on God, rather than on the person speaking.

Interestingly, the Bible verses that are being interpreted to allow women to speak in the religious arena are verses that give voice to "your daughters" and to "servants and handmaidens." It is understandable, I think, that the women focus on the term *handmaiden* rather than on the term *daughter* to justify their role as pastors. Referring to themselves as "handmaidens of the Lord" acknowledges both their servant status and their subservience to God and men. Most of their ritual disclaimers downplay their own abilities and acknowledge that some people may be more comfortable if they distinguish between women "preaching" and women "teaching": "Well, I kinda hope you all aren't expecting too much. Now, I want you to know that I never thought about these things on my own. I prayed and the Lord revealed these things to me. I have not got that much sense in my head. I'm not intelligent. Now, this may be kinda like teaching, I don't know. You know, sometimes it's kinda hard to preach, but maybe a mixture of both, preaching and teaching" (Sister Connie Morton, Hinkson, Indiana).

The pressure to acquiesce to societal notions of propriety for women is stronger on a female pastor than it is on a female itinerant preacher who does not have her own home congregation but travels from church to church. This is evidenced by the different preaching styles of women pastors and women preachers: women pastors are more subdued in their presentation style and much more vocal about their personal concern for the individual members of their congregations (see Lawless, 1988b). Traveling female evangelists, on the other hand, are much more likely to be energetic behind the pulpit and adopt a preaching style that is more like that of a male preacher, largely because they will not have to answer to the concerns of the congregation the next day. A traveling female preacher does not have a position of power and authority in a church, thus she does not have to be so careful to protect that position. While the women applaud their own tenacity and determination to survive all criticism, males in the congregation might agree with this man: "I don't believe in women preachers. God didn't have any. He told the men to go out and preach the gospel. He never told a woman to do that. Lord told his disciples, 'I send you amongst wolves.' Now, do you think I'd send my wife out amongst a bunch of heathens? Sinners don't care what they do. They'll string you out. They don't care" (Brother William Bird, Bedford,

Indiana). Yet, Sister Anna denies this point of view and sees herself as fearless and paints that image of herself in her narratives. She believes the "hard hearts" against her are a direct influence of Satan; yet, she illustrates her bravado against a Satan who might approach her directly:

> I've felt it right in this room with me. Some time ago when I was in bed, it woke me up. His presence was so strong that it woke me. And I knew—I felt that same eerie cold darkness there that I recognized as Satan. And so I said, "Devil, in the name of Jesus, get out of here! Leave me alone." And I literally felt him go. I went back to sleep. He woke me up for the third time. Finally, the third time, I said, "All right, devil, I am tired of you. I need my rest. You get out of here, leave me alone. I am going to put this Bible under my arm. And I'm going to sleep on the promises of God and you're not coming back in here to bother me anymore." And with that, I reached over and got the Bible and laid it under my arm. And I went back to sleep.

Strong maternal and reproductive images help us to understand how a woman functions within the role of pastor more than they aid us in understanding how she got there in the first place. To understand that, we must probe much deeper into the various levels of human mythology—both the mythology of male/female characteristics and the prevailing religious mythology as well. In addition, we must ground our analysis in an understanding of southern Pentecostalism (see Lawless, 1988a).

Barbara Welter has argued that during the nineteenth century a "feminization" of American religion developed because the conceptions of sex-role divisions of labor stipulated that men were out doing the "important business" and religion became categorized as an "expendable institution," one that eventually became the property of the "weaker members of society which . . . generally meant women." This reallocation of religion to the women's sphere determined that it came "more domesticated, more emotional, more soft and accommodating—in a word, more 'feminine'" (1976:84). Welter notes, of course, that the authority of religion did not become "feminized" at all; rather, the churches were filled with women who were subject to male control. With the rise of camp-meeting and revival religions, she found the language to be "sexual in its imagery," urging the (largely female) penitents to "stop struggling and allow yourself to be swept up in his love." She suggests this language was familiar to women:

> Whether in the divine or human order, woman was constantly urged to be swept away by a torrent of energy, not to rely on her own strength which was useless, to sink into the arms of Jesus, to become absorbed and assimilated by the Divine Will—the kind of physical sensations which a woman expected to receive and did receive in the course of conversion. "A

trembling of the limbs," "a thrill from my toes to my head," "wave after wave of feeling," are examples of female reaction to the experience of "divine penetration." (1976:93)

The father/husband who generated this experience through the male pastor or preacher was a jealous God and a demanding one. He expected full submission and obedience to his will. Should he be angered, he would "cast out" his "children" without relent. In time, however, camp-meeting religion's emphasis on religious emotionalism, spirit possession, and a personal relationship with Jesus for all participants, female or male, eventually led to the emergence of twentieth-century Pentecostalism. From camp-meeting religion to Pentecostalism, the large number of women involved saw Jesus as friend and helper, mediator between not only the religious women and their earthly life and problems but, to some degree, the mediator between the women and an awesome, fearful Father God. Jesus was the husband their own husbands could never be: kind, loving, sympathetic, empathetic, and merciful; furthermore, he was available to them through the Holy Ghost and spirit possession. And it was in the enthusiastic revival and camp-meeting services that women came to realize and execute their own spiritual power. Dickson Bruce, in his examination of camp-meeting religion from 1800 to 1845, tells us: "The major operations of the churches were dominated by men, who had all the ecclesiastical authority. Only at the height of excitement in a camp-meeting could women come to share in the leadership of frontier religious activities" (1974:76). That this was unusual and potentially disruptive is borne out by Bruce's continued comments: "Given the usual position of women in the religious organizations and in plain-folk society, their behavior here [the conversation "pen," analogous to a spirit-filled altar-call in Pentecostal services] constituted a significant reversal of status, for those who were normally expected to take a subordinate role in life were here enabled to take control of a situation. Not only were the structures of the meeting—which replicated the social structure—purposefully negated, but for a time they were turned upside down" (1974:86–87).

To help us understand how religious fervor, spirit possession, and emotionalism have been closely aligned with the female religious experience, it may be helpful to note the perceived differences between male and female characteristics and tendencies prevalent in the nineteenth century, as outlined by such scholars as Barbara Welter and Sherry Ortner. The dichotomous model offered by these and other scholars suggests that the female arena came to be associated closely with the home, hearth, and religion—spheres connected in the thinking of the time with woman's "natural" reproductive and mothering capacities. In contrast, the male was associated with an arena defined as more "cultural," one associated with work and politics and centered outside the home. According to this point of view, perceptions of men and women, their affinities, and their roles in society may arise from distinctions based on broad stereotypes that identify man as the hunter/provider and woman as the procreator/nurturer. The various aspects of these polarities in terms of male/female spheres and attributes include culture/nature, public/private, active/passive, dominant/submissive, producers/reproducers, and rational/spiritual.

Certainly, in the years since the publication of Rosaldo and Lamphere's ground-breaking work, *Women, Culture, and Society,* which included Ortner's essay outlining this nature/culture duality, the dichotomous model has been challenged, with arguments suggesting it is too simplistic, overgeneralized, and suggests a cross-cultural homogeneity that simply does not exist. Janet Sharistanian specifically addresses the evolution of thinking about the public/domestic dichotomy and reports that arguments against the model—or reinterpretations of it—usually focus on its cross-cultural limitations, its inability to account for transhistorical variation and change, and its insensitivity to considerations of race and class (1986:4, also 1987). Yet, Sharistanian asserts that the "domestic/public paradigm continues to be of value, when it is given precise definition and tested by a specific context" (1986:7). It is in this spirit that we can find the public/private dichotomy applicable to the specific lives of Pentecostals in the Upland South, as well as in other sociocultural arenas where patriarchy reigns and where thinking and behavior clearly delineate specific roles and spheres for women and men based on what is "proper" for a woman (domestic) and what is "proper" for a man (public). In the areas where I have done my fieldwork, in southern Indiana and in Missouri, specifically, the male-dominated hierarchy in homes and religion persists, and these rural people are suspicious of and stand rigidly against change. Here it is appropriate for men to "go out" and get jobs (usually employment done in conjunction with farming) and work in the public arena, while the women are expected to stay at home with the children. It is a matter of intense pride that a man can say his wife "doesn't have to work." If she finds she must work to help lighten the financial burdens, this is often perceived as sad and unfortunate, perhaps even pointing to the failure of the husband to provide for his family. As Bruce suggests, the social hierarchy is replicated in the structural composition of the religious beliefs and services. Not only is the pulpit generally reserved for men, who are in a direct line from God to Jesus to Man, but many staunch believers still quote the Pauline directives that direct women to be silent in the churches.

The maternal and reproductive imagery discussed in this essay derives from a culturally based perception of the woman's "natural" role as mother and nurturer. Because of the various fluid emissions that naturally flow from the woman's body (such as blood and milk), her cycle of menses, her ability to carry a child until she bears it, childbirth itself, and her perceived maternal instincts to nurture and protect the child, the female is both consciously and unconsciously seen to exist in a state that is closer to nature than to the world of men (see Douglas, 1966). This "natural" world in which the woman operates has been relegated by men to the domestic sphere because the home is assumed to be the seat of the family, the reproductive lair, the safe haven for the rearing of the children, the escape for the husband. Mother and children are safely ensconced in the private sphere of the home while the male goes out into the cultural and political arena. While we may not appreciate this picture, it does accurately reflect a way of life for most of the Pentecostals in this study.

How then did women during and following the camp-meeting era find ways for spiritual and religious expression within the services? In religious terms, woman's "closer-to-nature" nature was closely aligned with her spiritual nature, which gave her easier access to spirits and religious ecstasy (of course, in other eras, this perceived feminine nature allowed her to consort with devils and demons). While it was easy to say women were simpler, less complicated, more childlike, and therefore more likely to succumb to emotionalism and interactions with spirits, their spiritual powers were, nonetheless, respected and even encouraged. As Bruce points out, it was a woman's access to spiritual power that could lead to "control of a situation," as is the case in women's testimonies that are so long and elaborate, they actually serve to dominate the church services (see Lawless, 1983b).

While it is true that males have argued that their arena is the more important and sophisticated, they have, nevertheless, never lost sight of the importance of female spiritual power and reproductive capacity. In an insightful article on the roots of patriarchy, Azizah al-Hibri has further suggested an important connection between reproduction and immortality, posting that the awe men feel about women's ability to reproduce themselves is intensified by the notion that her progeny actual serve to immortalize her. Males, on the other hand, suffer a bit of a crisis when they realize that they cannot bear their own progeny. Certainly men have claimed the seed of the life force and attempted to hyperbolize their reproductive participation, but in the end, they can only call their ideas, their books, and their technological products the "babies" they have "labored" over. But the bottom line, according to al-Hibri, is that they can only produce not reproduce (1983).

Man's inability to come to grips with the seat of female power, in sexual, spiritual, and reproductive terms, underlies the seemingly contradictory stance males have taken toward the hearth and home and toward women and religion. The image of woman as a dangerous temptress, powerful and capable of controlling men, has its counterpart, of course, in woman as mother and faithful wife, protector of the family, the hearth and home, the upright advocate of Christian morals and ethics. This is not a new nor unique notion, of course. Writing about the Puritans, Mary Dunn comments that "feminine virtue became a family affair. Indeed, it is through the family that the Christian community would be preserved. To be a good woman is to be a good Christian" (1978:594). By relegating woman to the domestic sphere and by claiming dominance over that sphere, men have attempted to render it, and the women in it, ineffectual and unimportant; yet, relegating morality and even salvation to the sphere of women enhances women's status. Welter, examining the attitudes of males toward wife and mother, found that women came to embody all the values men profess to hold so dear—family, home, purity, and piety. She proposes that as the world became more and more unstable, "true womanhood" became the one stable element (1976).

Spiritual power, as opposed to church authority, is permitted the woman because it does not detract from her natural feminine delicacy; it makes her, in fact, even lovelier by stressing her attributes of holiness and encouraging her to maintain her position in the home and remain submissive to her husband. Woman is held to be stronger only in her defense against the evils of the world and in her ability to give birth and raise children; she was often held up as perfect. Woman, dressed in holiness garments, told she was pure and selfless, was given the responsibility of rearing the children and maintaining piety. She ran the risk of becoming a self-fulfilling prophecy. Of course, this image of woman also denies, ignores, and defeats woman's sexual powers, while still allowing for the deep-seated notion of woman as sin incarnate but under control.

During the great revivals of the eighteenth and nineteenth centuries, spiritual fervor swept the country, and women were noted to have participated in great swelling numbers (Bruce, 1974). Mary Ryan makes a connection between women's religious roles and the rise of American revivalism and enthusiastic religion: "At the time of the first [documented] revival [in New York, 1814], women constituted 70% of the church population. The mother, in other words, firmly planted the families' religious root on the frontier" (1978:602–24). Even today, women dominate in numbers in Pentecostal churches and persist in their conviction that the secular and the sacred are to remain separate worlds. My own fieldwork has consistently indicated that the moral and spiritual aspects, which may be recognized as religious concerns, remain within the women's sphere, closely associated with home and hearth and with the rearing of offspring. In southern Indiana, for example, very few men attended the churches I observed with the exception of a male pastor (if that was the case) and older men.[9] When I asked men why there were more women attending the services, they were often embarrassed and contended that religion was a bit "sissy," especially in the small churches where emotionalism, tongue-speaking, and shouting was the norm. The men perceived this to be female behavior. Women, on the other hand, expressed great love for the church services and the opportunity to see the other women in their immediate geographical community. They often hugged and kissed one another in greeting and departure, talked at length both before and after service, and claimed the women in the church were their "sisters." Their strong devotion and dedication to things religious directly affected the perception of women as the protectors of the spiritual realm. On the other hand, it was noticeable that male religious leaders were often more inclined to move the church into a more public, political, and secular arena. As religious leaders seek to become community powers, their authority often crosses various public and political boundaries. This move into the public, secularized arena is a move that is resisted by many staunchly conservative Pentecostals in this country, both women and men.

How does all of this help us to understand how women might come to have the power and authority of the pastorate of a Pentecostal congregation? The answer lies in the recognition that Pentecostalism has resisted secularization, largely because its constituents are more comfortable within the spiritual world of traditional religion than they are in the secular world (see Clements, 1974). The central concerns of Pentecostalism rest firmly in the sacred, spiritual realm, one that rejects outright the secular world and all the evil it is perceived to hold. All aspects of "the world," as they refer to any arena not connected with the spiritual/religious world, are shunned and perceived as sinful, evil, uncontrolled, and inspired by Satan (see Lawless, 1983a). Humans are safe, they believe, only within the confines of the religious world. Ironically, the power a woman is able to utilize in her quest for the pulpit and in her procurement of religious authority stems from the most conservative, traditional roots of this twentieth-century American denomination. If a woman can assure her conservative congregation that she will keep the religion closely connected to the spiritual realm and the family-based community, as far away from the secular as is realistically possible, then she has a better chance of gaining the pastorate than a man who may be perceived as more likely to take the church toward undesired intersections with the secular world. The female pastor's disregard for the public arena and her inclination toward the home and family represent the aspects of life her congregation holds most dear. By making a clear commitment to the sacred/religious realm and by pronouncing her intention and ability to keep the church within the domestic/spiritual sphere, she can win their confidence. And, further, if she "mothers" the congregation, cares for them, nurtures them, empathizes with them, counsels them, and can pray their souls into heaven, then they are all that much more likely to allow her to serve as their pastor. It is, after all, her ability to confer with God's spirit that has made her a spiritual being; therefore, she must utilize this perception of her natural/spiritual powers in order to assume a position of authority within the church. She is, they recognize, a spiritual being who can reproduce herself; she is close to nature and close to God and his spirits. Unleashed, her power becomes contradictory, even dangerous, but employed for the guidance and nurturance of men's and women's souls it might prove beneficial. At least for this conservative religion, the risk is worth taking. Her guidance in the spiritual world becomes a reality, especially as opposed to a dreaded move toward secularization and the evils the world has to offer.

Anna Walters and her sister Pentecostal pastors do not represent a flood of women "searching out the liberating promises of scripture to revise theologies," nor are they taking great strides toward a "new theology" or a "new ethics." Within the context of their lives, such a stance would be counterproductive. These women are not liberated from the prejudices and restrictions that hamper other women in this conservative milieu, but they are liberated from the standard script of cloistered wife and mother. The penalties can be high, however, for they must also be "superwomen." The young woman who contemplates being a pastor must also be a wife and mother, and she must extol the virtues of those capacities at every opportunity. She must demonstrate her "motherly" nature, exclaim her delight in being a wife and mother, her joy in her children and her home. She must deny her sexuality, and she must acknowledge her inferior status as woman and submit herself to all men. Yet, she can extol her spiritual power and utilize her reproductive and maternal capacities as strategies to strengthen her position. The role is complex, full of pitfalls and possible infractions. The female pastor must balance her life carefully—a move too far in any direction could alter the balance of sacred and domestic power.

Notes

I began fieldwork on Pentecostal women in southern Indiana in 1978 and began researching women preachers in Missouri in 1983. My work has been supported by the University of Missouri in the form of two research council grants, a summer research grant, and a semester's leave. Fieldwork in 1986 was supported by a National Endowment for the Humanities Research Fellowship. A shorter version of this essay was delivered at the American Folklore Society meeting in 1987 and subsequently appeared also in 1987 in the *Journal of American Folklore* 100 (398): 467–79. A longer version of this material was also developed in my book *Handmaidens of the Lord: Pentecostal Women Preachers and Traditional Religion.*

1. Scholars familiar with traditional African American religion in this country and the role of women often note significant differences with this Anglo-American religious tradition and female pastors.

2. Bible citations are from the King James Version, the only standard version accepted by all of the Pentecostal churches included in this study.

3. Most of the interviews with the women in this study were conducted in 1984 and 1985. The tapes are housed in my personal archives at the University of Missouri, Columbia. All names of people and places have been changed to protect their privacy.

4. See, for example, Petroff (1986), especially her introduction (3–59).

5. I am particularly intrigued with the notion of these mothers being "in-valid" for their daughters, noting the historical correlation of femaleness, illness, and "invalidity" in the early years of this century.

6. Both of these women claim that their churches "did not hire me" and "cannot fire me." In truth, some of these small rural congregations do not actually "hire" a pastor. The process is rather loose at times. Ministers do not have to attend seminary or gain official documentation of their status except from the state in order to marry and bury people. Persons who feel a call from God to preach may make the rounds from church to church preaching only when the opportunity arises for several years before becoming established as the pastor of a church. They must be selected, in essence, by the congregation, but often there is no money involved, so the women may be technically correct in asserting the congregation "didn't hire" them and "cannot fire" them. I suspect these strong statements also reflect a shared opinion by the congregations and the pastors that *God* calls one to preach and that, in reality, God hires and God fires and that is not the prerogative of the congregation members.

7. While the women in this study have seen my descriptions and interpretations of their lives and their preaching and, in general, approve of my conclusions, they do not agree with my interpretation of this particular point. Even though I can point out to them (and they, of course, already know this) that a considerable number of their sermons come back to a concern with "making it into heaven," they do not agree that this is an indication that they are, in fact, fearful of getting into the gates of heaven themselves. My own interpretation suggests that the predominance of this image stems from their own ambivalence about their role in

the religion and their public role in the church. I do not make this suggestion lightly or without attention to their point of view; rather, I think it is possible that the concern may be there in an unconscious way and is revealed in their religious rhetoric and language. Neither of these foci of sermons is gender-specific; that is, one would find sermons on total sacrifice and making it into heaven in male sermons as well. The particular ways these topics are developed in the sermons of women, however, do suggest a female perspective. The themes of Pentecostal women's sermons have been examined in more detail in my book *Handmaidens of the Lord*. I have also continued my thinking on this issue in two recently published articles (1991, 1992)

8. This sermon by Sister Anna Brock Walters can be found in its entirety in the appendix of *Handmaidens of the Lord,* 171–88.

9. It is my contention that the men come back to church later in life because they have agreed all along with the tenets of the faith and believe it is important to "get right with God" before it is too late. Most often during their middle-aged years, however, they were more likely to drop off their wives and children at church and go to town until time to pick them up; I have even known men who will sit in the car and wait for their family through the entire church service.

References Cited

al-Hibri, Azizah. 1983. "Reproduction, Mothering, and the Origins of Patriarchy." In *Mothering: Essays in Feminist Theory,* ed. Joyce Trebilcot, 81–93. Totowa, N.J.: Rowman and Allanheld.

Behnke, Donna. 1982. *Religious Issues in Nineteenth Century Feminism.* New York: Whitsom.

Bruce, Dickson. 1974. *And They All Sang Hallelujah: Plain-Folk Camp-Meeting Religion, 1800–1845.* Knoxville: University of Tennessee Press.

Clements, William. 1974. "The American Folk Church." Ph.D. diss., Indiana University.

Douglas, Mary. 1966. *Purity and Danger: An Analysis of the Concepts of Pollution and Taboo.* London: Routledge and Kegan Paul.

Dunn, Mary M. 1978. "Saints and Sisters: Congregational and Quaker Women in the Early Colonial Period." *American Quarterly* 30:582–602.

Gilligan, Carol. 1982. *In a Different Voice: Psychological Theory and Women's Development.* Cambridge: Harvard University Press.

James, Janet Wilson. 1978. "Women and Religion: An Introduction." *American Quarterly* 30:579–81.

Lawless, Elaine J. 1983a. "Brothers and Sisters: Pentecostals as a Folk Group." *Western Folklore* 43:85–104.

———. 1983b. "Shouting for the Lord: The Power of Women's Speech in the Pentecostal Service." *Journal of American Folklore* 96 (382): 434–59.

———. 1988a. *God's Peculiar People: Women's Voices and Folk Tradition in a Pentecostal Church.* Lexington: University Press of Kentucky.

———. 1988b. *Handmaidens of the Lord: Pentecostal Women Preachers and Tradi-

tional Religion. Publications of the American Folklore Society, n.s., no. 9. Philadelphia: University of Pennsylvania Press.

———. 1991. "Women's Life Stories and Reciprocal Ethnography as Feminist and Emergent." *Journal of Folklore Research* 28, no. 1 (Fall): 35–61.

———. 1992. " 'I Was Afraid Someone like You . . . an Outsider . . . Would Misunderstand': Negotiating Interpretive Differences between Ethnographers and Subjects." *Journal of American Folklore* 105 (417): 302–15.

Ortner, Sherry, 1974. "Is Female to Male as Nature Is to Culture?" In *Woman, Culture, and Society,* ed. Michelle Zimbalist Rosaldo and Louise Lamphere, 67–87. Stanford: Stanford University Press.

Petroff, Elizabeth Alvilda. 1986. *Medieval Women's Visionary Literature*. New York: Oxford University Press.

Rich, Adrienne. 1977. *Of Woman Born: Motherhood as Experience and Institution.* New York: Bantam Books.

Rosaldo, Michelle Zimbalist, and Louise Lamphere, eds. 1974. *Woman, Culture, and Society.* Stanford: Stanford University Press.

Ryan, Mary. 1978. "A Women's Awakening: Evangelical Religion and the Families of Utica, N.Y., 1800–1840." *American Quarterly* 30:602–24.

Sharistanian, Janet, ed. 1986. *Gender, Ideology, and Action: Historical Perspectives on Women's Public Lives.* Westport, Conn: Greenwood Press.

———. 1987. *Beyond the Public/Domestic Dichotomy: Contemporary Perspectives on Women's Public Lives.* New York: Greenwood Press.

Welter, Barbara. 1976. *Dimity Convictions: The American Woman in the Nineteenth Century.* Athens: Ohio University Press.

PART THREE

Carol Mitchell

Feminist Lenses and Female Folklore

In Part 3, the five studies focus on topics that have not traditionally been included within the purview of folklore, and they continue the never-finished process of showing women's culture as an important part of human culture. The authors cross traditional disciplinary and genre lines, bringing them together to help us perceive well-known activities such as housework, birthing, needlework, cartoons, and personal narratives in new ways.

As I read these essays I was reminded of a pair of metaphors that we use when discussing how our cultures teach us to perceive the world in certain ways: cultural lenses and cultural blinders. And I appreciated the ways in which each of these essays helps us to modify those cultural lenses or take off certain cultural blinders. For example, Judith Levin's essay helps us to take off some of our blinders about housework, while Robbie E. Davis-Floyd uses the lens of ritual to expand our awareness of the way in which technology is glorified even in the natural process of giving birth, and Elaine K. Miller shows how our stereotypes of women act as distorting lenses through which we see not only women but also cartoons about one particular woman.

Too often folklore scholarship continues to retain its patriarchal blinders. Despite the risk of making one recent study seem too important, a perfect example of "an intellectual history" that almost completely omits contemporary women and their ideas is Simon J. Bronner's *American Folklore Studies: An Intellectual History.* For Bronner contemporary feminist studies of folklore are completely invisible. As a matter of fact he seems unable to see the scholars themselves if they are contemporary women (as a brief look at his index will show). The scholars omitted include such well-known women as Linda Dégh, Rayna Green, Zora Neale Hurston, Rosan Jordan, Barbara Kirshenblatt-Gimblett, Katherine Luomala, Joan Radner, Ellen Stekert, Kay Stone, Beverly Stoeltje, and Marta Weigle, just to name a few, while comparable or lesser-known men are included. For feminist folklorists the title of his last chapter, "Folklore in an Era of Communication," seems incredibly ironic, since clearly there is no communication between him and women folklorists, whether those women are feminists or not. While Bronner certainly does not represent all male folklorists, his example shows the need for modified cultural lenses in folklore scholarship. Perhaps the cultural lenses metaphors are not the ones we need here, but rather metaphors of blindness and helping the blind to see. Certainly he still wears the cultural blinders of the patriarchy in his discussion of contemporary folkloristics. Women's studies in general, and this book in particular, are concerned with eliminating distortions in our cultural lenses, with reviewing our culture from new angles, and in taking off our cultural blinders in the study of women's folk culture that forms such an important part of human culture.

Judith Levin makes a convincing argument for folklorists to begin studying housework in her essay. Occupational folklorists have not studied housework because it has not been considered work. She discusses folklorists' ambivalence toward housework, not only whether or not it is work but also women scholars' ambivalence toward this work because of the way it binds women to the house and to stereotypical images of women. Her discussion of a process-oriented aesthetic rather than a product-oriented one vividly points out how our cultural lens has become a blinder in looking at the aesthetic sensibilities of the nondominant groups in our society—women in this example. And her discussion of the film *Clotheslines* demonstrates how some women have incorporated their aesthetic and creative senses into doing laundry. Levin's essay, like Linda Pershing's essay, shows the importance of process and context in the study of women's folklore as do several of the essays in Parts 1 and 2.

Robbie E. Davis-Floyd shows us how the birth process itself has become a ritual celebrating technology rather than the naturalness of giving birth, and by this means she shows us how the technocratic model of birth limits and dehumanizes not only the mother but also the doctors and nurses in attendance. Because birthing is not generally understood as a ritual since it is not self-consciously so, we have not thought about and analyzed what is being expressed and taught in this ritual—a marvelous example of how blind we are about so many aspects of our society. It has only been since the emergence of the women's movement and its new cultural lenses that we have begun to analyze the process of giving birth in this society. Prior to this analysis, mothers might have been unhappy with their doctors, nurses, and hospitals, but they were individual voices of protest. With the women's movement those voices have begun to come together, and as Davis-Floyd points out, the technocratic model is under attack in the birthplace: feminists, natural childbirth activists, childbirth educators, humanistic obstetricians and nurses, midwives, and consumers are joining forces to invert the core value system underlying this model, seeking to eliminate patriarchy, and to place science, technology, and institutions at the service of birthing women and their families, instead of the other way around. But as she also notes there are forces pushing the doctors back toward the technological model of birthing, and it is not yet clear whether or not the more humanistic model will prevail. In this essay Davis-Floyd stretches the usual boundaries of folklore in the direction of unconscious ritual and cultural paradigms. In addition, she, along with Levin and Young and Lawless, previously, shows the complexity of how our images of public/private and culture/nature issues affect women's lives.

Linda Pershing has written an almost poetic essay on The Peace Ribbon in which she discusses not only traditional women's needlework and its contemporary use in creating a fifteen mile-long "ribbon" as a means of working for peace but she also discusses the way in which some feminist scholars have used the metaphors of needlework to describe the very work that feminist scholars are doing. Quoting Jane Marcus, she says, "Preserving the fabric of history is the same job as mending the family's jackets and sweaters." But Pershing points out that it is more than just "mending" the social fabric that needs to be done, for there are flaws in the total structure of the social fabric that must be modified.

In her essay, Pershing weaves together the comments of some of the women who worked on The Ribbon and her own analysis of what this needlework and political stance meant to them and what traditional women's culture contributes to the larger human culture of which women's culture is a part. The focus on the values and "images of relationship, wholeness, and relatedness" become a reaffirmation of often-undervalued ideals in our society, which so often emphasizes individuality, specialization, and competition, for the process and aesthetics of making The Ribbon is more important than the evaluation of the product, The Ribbon, itself.

In her essay Marilynn J. Phillips illustrates the need for studies about all kinds of women. She shows us how stereotyping women into categories such as sex object, child, and victim projects images that are even more problematic for disabled women, in part because many feminists have continued to view disabled women through those traditional and stereo-typical lenses. Like Pershing, Phillips weaves together disabled women's personal narratives with her own analysis in such a way that she helps us to modify our images of reality to include the disabled. More than any of the other writers in this part Phillips is directly discussing our cultural lenses, for she says, "how do members of a society decipher the culturally coded disabled body and what meaning do they derive from these physiological texts?" Thus she makes us more aware that most of us, when seeing a disabled person, see not just the particular kind of disability but also a whole series of qualities, such as asexuality, weakness, or dependence, that have nothing to do with the person we see but rather are products of our cultural assumptions or lenses. Phillips, like Davis-Floyd, discusses how technology can dehumanize women, but she tends to focus on the positive aspects of the technology of prostheses.

Elaine Miller discusses some interesting questions about stereotypes or images of women and their use in cartoons in her chapter. While the subject of the images of women in folklore has been a major category for the study of women and folklore, Miller moves into the area of popular culture. By using a number of oral jokes along with cartoons she illustrates how closely connected is the imagery of women in folklore and popular culture. In her discussion she points out that the fact that Geraldine Ferraro is a woman was more important to the cartoonists than were her views on political issues. Miller shows that even when cartoonists wished to be supportive of Ferraro as a vice-presidential candidate, the traditional imagery of women available for them to use created an ambiguous message. As folklorists have noted before, humor is often ambiguous and open to different interpretations depending upon the attitudes of the audiences. Beyond this, her essay also calls into question our values and what we value in a president or vice-president.

These studies illustrate some of the new directions for folklore studies that feminist approaches can offer. From housework to childbirth to needlework to body images to cartoons, these studies open our eyes to a few of the kinds of women and activities in which women are involved that are modifying the lenses through which we view human culture. No doubt we will begin to see new studies of family folklore as it varies in our diverse forms of families including not only extended and nuclear families but also single-parent families and homosexual families and other groupings that may become recognized as fulfilling family functions. And to the extent that all scholarship is political, this more complete picture of human life will change the lives of women and men of the future, for in changing the cultural lenses that bring our world into focus, we necessarily change our responses to that world.

In the final analysis, all scholarship is political for it reflects an unconscious as well as a conscious ideology. In the kinds of questions scholarship chooses to ask and in its conclusions, scholarship reinforces existing cultural lenses and ideologies and/or creates new ones. Each ideology has its own cultural lenses that help us in our study of the world, but it also creates its own cultural blinders that limit us in what we see and what we choose to study. Western patriarchal ideology has created cultural lenses that emphasize males, hierarchy, dualism, and linear/logical ways of knowing, and the cultural lenses of the patriarchy have been very useful in analyzing certain facets of our world. But these lenses have also blinded us to other facets of that world (see Griffin, 1978; Keller, 1985; Keohane, Rosaldo, and Gelpi, 1982; Stimpson, 1978). Feminist scholarship, in conjunction with the women's movement, is helping us to create new lenses for viewing that world with an emphasis on females, egalitarianism, and multiplicity (see Eisler, 1987; Lerner, 1986), and the recognition of other ways of knowing, such as emotional and spiritual ways of knowing (see Belenky, et al., 1986; Hall, 1976). Women's studies has helped to make us conscious that patriarchy has been an unconscious ideology, not just a mode of social organization.

Feminists have been and need to continue to be conscious that we are creating a new ideology, and we have been apprehensive of the blindness that any ideology can create. We are studying women's altars, women's jokes, women's needlework, women's talk, and women's values, not just because they are intrinsically interesting (though certainly they are just as intrinsically interesting as men's cultural practices), but also because they validate women's lives, including our lives as scholars. But women's studies scholarship, as helpful as it is in giving us new lenses with which to view our world, will also have its own set of cultural blinders.

Perhaps what is most important for us to realize is that these new truths we are learning are not The Truth (see Spelman, 1988). This realization will help us to value the many truths that come from our varied approaches to knowledge (see Hawkesworth, 1989): the interpretations of oral narratives or games or rituals that are inspired by the various disciplines such as history, psychology, philosophy, and comparative religion or the interpretations that are influenced by scholars' various nationality, ethnic, racial, and religious lenses (see Harding, 1987; Cruikshank, 1982). Too often the lenses of Western patriarchy, in part because of its hierarchical worldview, have caused us to expect one Right Answer, one Objective Truth, and those lenses have blinded us to the truths of the nondominant groups within our society and within the world.

We also need to become more aware of the truths that come from ways of knowing that are other than the linear/logical model of knowing. Linear/logical knowing has made our science and technology possible, but it has also blinded us to the values of our emotions, our spirituality, and our physicality, and at least in part because of this, we do not have the values that will help us to use our science and technology for the benefit of all rather than for the benefit of the few. We have ignored the interconnectedness of the world in our emphasis on logic and hierarchy, such that we are creating technologies that are destroying our very environment (see Merchant, 1983). And we have ignored the interconnectedness of our ways of knowing by believing that we can think logically without understanding and while ignoring our emotional, spiritual, and physical ways of knowing (see Belenky, et al., 1986; Hall, 1976; Rose, 1983). Recent right- and left-brain studies are a logical/linear way of approaching the idea that there are various ways of knowing, but these studies do not help us much in actually "knowing" in other modes. Eventually, we must recognize that knowing is an integrated process and that what we think we know logically can be either reinforced or denied by emotional and spiritual and physical knowing. All of these ways of knowing are useful in their particular realms, but they are also interconnected with each other, and the denial of one or more of these modes of knowing can lead to distortions in our perceptions of and dealings with the world.

The focus on contexts of folklore, the processes involved in the production of folklore artifacts, and the personal narratives and reactions to folklore found in many of the essays in this volume indicate the feminist scholars' recognition that emotional reactions to and emotional ways of knowing or interpreting the world are important in understanding the artifacts of folklore. Yet the word *emotion* is rarely used or valued in folklorists' or others' scholarly discussions, for scholarship has generally, even in these postmodern times, seen emotions as fuzzy, inexact, feminine, and suspect when analyzing almost any aspect of culture. Furthermore, we are not yet clear on exactly what the ramifications of various ways of knowing are. We know that needlework or playing the piano involve physical ways of knowing, but how does that affect our images or cultural lenses through which we see and participate in our society? We assign the study of emotions to psychology and teach many courses describing the emotions, but in the academy we teach no courses in how to love or how to use our emotional reactions to scholarly analysis and ideas in a complementary way to our logical analysis of culture. Until we recognize and study these other ways of knowing in the same detail as we have recognized and studied logic, we will be unable to fully integrate them into our analyses. The studies in this volume involving context, process, personal narrative, and stereotype are all steps in expanding our ways of knowing and widening the lenses through which we view our culture and ourselves.

I would like to conclude with Marlene Mackie's version of the folktale "The Emperor's New Clothes" that can be read as a traditional warning about cultural blinders that keep us from knowing the obvious.

> There once lived an Emperor with a serious sartorial obsession. For reasons that need not concern us, he acquired a new suit fashioned from invisible

material and paraded about the street stark naked. The townsmen encouraged the Emperor's performance. "What a splendid design! What glorious colors!" "But the Emperor has nothing on at all!" cried several brave women. Some of the onlookers suddenly realized they were viewing not the Emperor's magnificent new suit, but his private parts. However, their dissident voices were drowned out by loud groans and hoots of laughter. The people with the deviant perspective (mostly women) stood confused on the margins of the assembly. Should they slip inconspicuously into the crowd? To this day, the Emperor prances about naked whenever he likes. The dissidents discuss their objections among themselves. Whenever they try to share their views with the townspeople, the latter say, "There, there, my dears," to avoid hurting their feelings. (1988:1)

To this Maya Angelou's warning might be added, "Be careful when a naked person offers you a shirt" (1989).

References

Angelou, Maya. 1989. Performance at Colorado State University, Sept. 16.

Belenky, Mary F., Blythe M. Clinchy, Nancy R. Goldberger, and Jill M. Tarule. 1986. *Women's Ways of Knowing: The Development of Self, Voice, and Mind.* New York: Basic Books.

Bronner, Simon J. 1986. *American Folklore Studies: An Intellectual History.* Lawrence: University Press of Kansas.

Cruikshank, Margaret, ed. 1982. *Lesbian Studies: Present and Future.* Old Westbury, N.Y.: Feminist Press.

Eisler, Riane. 1987. *The Chalice and the Blade.* New York: Harper and Row.

Griffin, Susan. 1978. *Woman and Nature: The Roaring inside Her.* New York: Harper and Row.

Hall, Edward. 1976. *Beyond Culture.* Garden City, N.Y.: Anchor.

Harding, Sandra, ed. 1987. *Feminism and Methodology.* Bloomington: Indiana University Press.

Hawkesworth, Mary E. 1989. "Knowers, Knowing, Known: Feminist Theory and Claims of Truth." *Signs* 14:533–57.

Keller, Evelyn Fox. 1985. *Reflections on Gender and Science.* New Haven: Yale University Press.

Keohane, Nannerl O., Michelle Z. Rosaldo, and Barbara C. Gelpi, eds. 1982. *Feminist Theory and a Critique of Ideology.* Chicago: University of Chicago Press.

Lerner, Gerda. 1986. *The Creation of Patriarchy.* New York: Oxford University Press.

Mackie, Marlene. 1988. "Sexism in Sociological Research." In *Gender Bias in Scholarship: The Pervasive Prejudice,* ed. Winnifred Tomm and Gordon Hamilton. Waterloo, Ontario: Wilfrid Laurier University Press.

Merchant, Carolyn. 1983. *The Death of Nature: Women, Ecology, and the Scientific Revolution.* New York: Harper and Row.

Rose, Hilary. 1983. "Hand, Brain, and Heart: A Feminist Epistemology for the Natural Sciences." *Signs* 9:73–90.
Spelman, Elizabeth V. 1988. *Inessential Woman: Problems of Exclusion in Feminist Thought.* Boston: Beacon.
Stimpson, Catharine R., ed. 1978. *Women, Science, and Society.* Special issue of *Signs* 4.
Weedon, Chris. 1987. *Feminist Practice and Poststructuralist Theory.* Oxford: Basil Blackwell.

Why Folklorists Should Study Housework

The study of housework has received a great deal of scholarly attention in recent years, very little of it from folklorists. Collections of folk beliefs and practices frequently contain chapters of "domestic" or "household" lore and customs, and song collections sometimes include a version of "The Housewife's Lament," "Washing Day," "A Woman's Work Is Never Done," or one of the many songs about the grumpy farmer who exchanges tasks with his wife, but housework remains largely absent from the work of contemporary "performance-centered" folklorists. It seldom appears in the places one might expect to find it, namely in discussion of the folklore of families, women, or occupations. I will argue here that housework can better be understood if studied with modern folkloric approaches and with the folklorist's eye for the meaningful patterns of everyday life, but, additionally, that the issues raised by a folkloric study of housework contribute to folklore theories and methods.

Folklore's neglect of housework is surely part of its general neglect of women's activities, yet even with the current interest in women's lore, and after the study of housework began to receive attention in other disciplines, folklorists have avoided it. To understand how and why a folklorist would study housework, it is useful first to understand how and why housework has fallen through folklore's disciplinary and theoretical cracks. The explanation is revealing both in what it demonstrates about housework and in what it demonstrates about folklore.

One problem in studying housework is that the term itself is so ambiguous. People generally agree that it refers to tasks that someone, often a woman, does around a house, but there is little consensus about what these tasks are. *Housework* may refer to a very limited number of housecleaning tasks or it may refer to everything a woman does in her house and so merge with categories such as housewifery, housekeeping, or "women's work." It may or may not be used to describe the paid household work one does in someone else's house. Many people (but not all) agree that housework refers to usual and repeated tasks rather than to ones that are unusual or unique: sweeping or vacuuming is more likely to be called housework than is laying a carpet or painting a room. It may or may not be thought to include child care, cooking, shopping, laundry, sewing, cleaning, and so on, depending not only on which tasks someone does but on which ones count as housework rather than as something else. When I queried a freshman writing class on the subject—a class consisting primarily of older, married students—one man explained to me that the work his wife does around the house is housework, but when he does the same tasks they are called "chores," a more gender-neutral term. In this instance, it is not the task alone that makes something housework, but also the gender of the person performing the task. None of the other students made this distinction, but neither did they agree about what is included in the category. So, even without moving out of the English language—or out of a single college classroom in Philadelphia— someone studying housework has a definitional problem.

The problem of defining housework is based in part on changes in the household and in the work that men and women do there. Ruth Schwartz Cowan (1983) points out that the term *housewife* is far older than *housework*. The Oxford English Dictionary's earliest citation for *housewife* is 1225. *Housework* does not even appear in the original OED, and its supplement does not list a citation for it before 1841 (in England—the earliest in the United States is 1871). Cowan is just one of the many feminist historians and sociologists who have studied the historical development of modern housework and housewifery. The studies expand on the ideas of Veblen (1934), E. P. Thompson (1966), and others who analyzed the effects of the industrial revolution on the household and family. Although these studies tend to overgeneralize the historical change, they do have some validity, at least for the middle class. The history is helpful in understanding modern attitudes toward housework, since these attitudes continue to affect how (or if) housework is studied.

The social historians of housework point out that for centuries the household was the center of production, with both men and women contributing directly to the physical and economic well-being of the family. Women's work usually included dishwashing and cooking (or the supervision of the people responsible for these tasks), but women also were likely to be responsible for the weaving of cloth and the making of clothes; they might also be responsible for the care of the sheep whose wool they spun, for the care of other domestic animals, or for work in the fields. Industrialization changed this by moving much of the productive work—the actual making or growing of things—away from the home. Beginning in the early nineteenth century, the middle-class housewife's role was redefined in ways that later filtered into working class life. She became a consumer and procurer of material goods, but also, increasingly, the producer and conserver of more ephemeral and ideologically laden ones, such as morality and spirituality (and, later still, mental health). This change in household roles was, of course, codified into the doctrine of separate spheres, which explicitly defined the home as a private, female-dominated, nonproductive sphere, distinct from the male world of work.

Household technology gradually improved during that time, at least for the middle and upper classes, but feminist historians note that while the growing availability of ready-made clothing, store-bought food, running water, and electrical appliances made the housewife's work less physically strenuous, changing ideology and changing standards of cleanliness and child supervision—as well as the disappearance of household servants for the middle class—resulted in the housewife's never actually having more free time. Although a clothes washer made doing laundry easier, it also meant that clothes were washed more often. According to this view, housework today consists of the tasks left over when the real productive work such as making clothing and churning butter was industrialized out of the house, but these leftovers were restructured such that housework remains—unnecessarily—a full-time job (see, for example, de Beauvoir, 1961; Friedan, 1964; Ehrenreich and English, 1978; Strasser, 1982; Cowan, 1983).

When considering this argument, it is necessary to remember that even when women's work in the home was productive, it was not necessarily a source of pleasure nor of prestige. The work was often back-breaking, and women were still likely to be economically dependent (Davidson, 1982; Juster, 1979; Matthews, 1987). But if we look at the way modern housework is generally characterized, we will see that the characterization reflects the historical changes historians describe. When men or women, feminist or not, object to housework, they generally object to it for similar reasons. The following constellation of objections is the most common:

1. Housework seldom produces a concrete product.
2. Housework is endless. De Beauvoir says it is "consumable work."
3. Housework is often done in isolation from other adults, though it is likely to be interrupted by children's demands.
4. Housework—at least in one's own house—is unpaid.
5. For all of the above reasons, housework is often not considered to be work at all.

This is a portrait of housework as trivial, repetitive, and invisible—one sees it only if it is not done—and as requiring little creativity from the people who do it.

Given this dominant characterization of housework, it is not surprising that folklorists have neglected to study it. Because housework done in one's own home is unpaid and (reputedly) done in isolation, and, especially, because its status as "work" is disputed, it does not appear to be an appropriate study for occupational folklorists. Feminist folklorists are mostly likely to have established it as an area of study because of their interest in discovering "women's genres" and genres that exist in the private domain (Jordan and Kalčik, 1985:ix) and in calling attention to and revaluing women's "mundane" activities (Weigle, 1982:chap. 7); but the movement to study women's folklore began in the context of the feminism of the 1970s and, as such, was characterized by the same condemnation of housework that characterized the feminist historical and sociological writings of that period. The feminist movement intended to free women from the home and to allow them to pursue other careers. Feminist folklorists couldn't very well argue that housework was creative and traditional, because that argument was the very one used to argue that women's place was in the home (e.g., McGinley, 1960; Andelin, 1975). It is worth noting that the first "women and folklore" panels at the 1973 American Folklore Society meetings were originally to be titled "World View from the Mop Bucket" (Farrer, 1986:viii). But the mop bucket was not something upon which the participants wanted to lavish attention; it was something to be gotten away from. When I talk about housework now, many women folklorists find it a compelling topic and speak at length about the rules and practices for housework with which they were raised, but some of them add that they feel guilty speaking about the subject with such interest: professional women are not "supposed" to be interested in housework.

A Celebration of Family Folklore suggests another reason why housework and folklore have remained estranged. When the authors write of family customs, they say: "Many [of the activities families do] are just ordinary household necessities—washing dishes, cleaning house, eating breakfast. The shared activities we call customs generally extend beyond everyday necessities" (Zeitlin, Kotkin, and Baker, 1982:162). They add that "even day-to-day housework can become 'ritualized' when adorned with expressive activities," a wording suggesting that housework itself is not an expressive activity and that only "adornment" would make it so. The anthropologist Mary Douglas, on the other hand, insists "we must treat the spring millinery and spring cleaning in our towns as renewal rites which focus and control experience as much as Swazi first fruit rituals"

(1984:68). For her the work itself is important; for many folklorists, it is the "adornment" that makes the work worthy of study. This bias toward art and toward play is one for which occupational folklorists have already been criticized and which some have begun to correct. Abrahams notes that "if worker lore is collected it tends to be that generated while playing at work" and suggests studying "the lore which arises from the social dimension of work itself or from the workers as they group themselves outside of the actual work situation" (1978:20). McCarl goes one step further, studying the work itself, rather than just the lore about the work (1985). But the bias toward play and art still cause the family folklorists to overlook housework as an expressive activity that takes place in families.

Finally, if we look at how modern folklorists define their area of study and look at the common characterization of housework, we will realize that *folklore* and *housework* are defined almost as opposites. In the past and in Europe—in situations where folklore had been defined as the speech, beliefs, or activities of a particular group of people called "folk"—the folklore of housework was collected. Now folklore is defined as the study of expressive, creative, traditional, skilled cultural performances, usually ones that create a product (although the product might be as intangible as a story). Housework is characterized as trivial, mindlessly repetitive, invisible, productless, and isolated (de Beauvoir, 1961; Friedan, 1964, among others). Furthermore, many of the feminist writings on housework have emphasized the similarities in the way women do housework and in the problems they face, so cultural differences have been obscured for the purpose of making political statements. Considered in these terms, it is not surprising that quilting and cooking are studied, but that sweeping and dishwashing are not.

Although, as I have shown, folklorists studying the lore of occupations, women, and families have had reasons not to study housework, it remains a topic that could fruitfully be studied by them. For example, contrasting the folklore of a factory production line worker and that of a full-time housewife may raise useful questions about the relationship between work situation and folklore. Production line workers suffer from problems such as too much supervision, too little variety in tasks, too few interruptions (such that breaks become an essential part of work culture), too little worker commitment to, or knowledge of, the product, and trouble getting time to pass. The problems of a full-time housewife with children are likely to be almost the opposite. She may feel she has too little structure to her day, too many separate tasks to perform, too many interruptions, an overinvestment in her product (a clean house, happy and successful children), and not enough time to accomplish her work. Presumably the folklore developed by these groups will reflect the different problems they face. Housework also presents an obvious area of study for people study-ing women's folklore or gender-based folklore. Given that, generally speaking, women have been responsible for housework and housewifery (or at least for the activities now called by these names) for a very long time, it would be surprising indeed if there was not folklore of housework. Moreover, given the current definitions of folklore, I believe that we should, as I have already suggested, study the folklore of housework itself and not just as a source of verbal traditions about it.

What makes housework a possible topic for folklorists is, in part, the very definitional problem to which I alluded in the beginning of this essay. If "housework" meant exactly the same thing to everyone and if the various tasks were done in the same way by everyone, there would be nothing to study. It is because housework consists of culturally defined and variable tasks, techniques, and attitudes that one can ask what is shared and what is specific to an individual, neighborhood, region, ethnic group, family, generation, class, or gender. Faced with the various tasks, what do people make of them? What do they elaborate, omit, enjoy, dislike? What *matters*? Even when people define housework as including roughly the same group of tasks, their understanding of why, how (by what method, with what technology), when, by whom, how thoroughly, and how often the tasks need to be accomplished is likely to vary. The social, emotional, and associational meanings of the tasks are not the same for all people who perform them.

So, to begin with, it is not possible to start with a rigid notion of what housework consists of in a particular community. One can begin by asking about "housework," "housekeeping," "household chores," "house-wifery," or "*faccende di casa*" (activities or matters of the house)—but eventually it will be necessary to do a taxonomy of the phrases used by one's informants and the relationship between the phrases and the tasks they include. Someone who went into the home of my male student who did only "chores" and asked "who does the housework here?" might well misunderstand the answer.

Some of how one might begin to approach the folklore of housework can be learned from current approaches to occupational lore. One of contemporary folklore's strengths is its ability to understand the ways in which both tradition and creativity permeate the ordinary activities through which individuals and groups constitute themselves. Michael Owen Jones's interest in the "feeling for form" (an idea borrowed from Boas) is a good example of this. Believing creativity to be innate and universal, he looks for evidence of it in occupations that, like housework, have been consid-ered repetitive and unskilled, requiring—and allowing—little creativity or intelligence. In "A Feeling for Form, as Illustrated by People at Work"

(1980), Jones writes of people doing jobs, often monotonous jobs, who derive aesthetic satisfaction from some aspect of those jobs by finding or creating rhythms in the work or by otherwise manipulating the work in playful ways. The strength of this approach is that it broadens the definition of *aesthetic* beyond its use in the fine arts to include those senses not acknowledged by Western aesthetics—smell, touch, and taste—and also a sense of bodily rhythms and patterning, of getting into a "groove" with a task or a machine. It is, on the whole, a less product-oriented aesthetic, one that values not only the thing created but the worker's sense of creation, of transcendence, of mastery. It is a performance-oriented study of occupation. The approach encourages us to see meaningful patterns in situations like the factory assembly line—and in housework—where creativity and control have otherwise been ignored, and it suggests that people are able to maintain their creativity in the face of mechanization and standardization.

The limitation of the approach—a tendency to romanticize boring and culturally devalued work by overemphasizing the aesthetic components of it—and the implications of that limitation for the study of housework are evident when his findings are compared with those of the filmmaker Roberta Cantow. Cantow, without knowing Jones's work, took a similar approach to his in her film *Clotheslines,* and, while the effect of the film is lyrical rather than analytic—she juxtaposes images and her informants' voices but does not comment overtly on either—Cantow provides excellent insight into the folklore of laundry. In the film women talk about doing the wash, a task most of them loathe. All of them, however, enjoy and elaborate some aspect of the process or the product. One woman enjoys only being done with it, but she ties ribbons around the stacks of clean linens and takes great pride in the appearance of her linen closet. She says her visitors admire it too. Several of the women Cantow interviewed like hanging the wash out to dry and demonstrate a "feeling for form." They find it aesthetically pleasing to hang wash in the sun, to smell the clean clothes, and to hang similar colors or items together to make patterns. The film's footage of clotheslines, urban and rural, show them to be very beautiful indeed. One might argue that it is Cantow's filmmaking that makes them beautiful, but this is belied by the experience of the film's viewers, many of whom find themselves admiring the artistry of the clotheslines they see around them.

The women in the film also speak of the social and communicative aspects of laundry and of clotheslines. One woman says she feels linked to all other women when hanging wash; another associates it with her mother. Additionally, much of what the women say suggests that the clothesline itself is a form of communication and that its messages can be read by neighbors. It is clear that the women with whom Cantow spoke care when the wash is hung, whether it is clean enough, and whether it is hung correctly. Some tell stories of being taught these things as children or as young married women. These are matters of importance: hanging wash at the wrong time or hanging the wrong wash—black lace underwear, for example—can damage a woman's reputation.

The critical difference between the information presented in the film and that presented by Jones and some of the occupational folklorists who follow his lead is that Cantow situates the aesthetic and enjoyable components of the work in the context of other components of the work and in the women's lives. It seems fine to recognize and appreciate the clothesline as an art form. Feminist folklorists have talked about discovering women's genres, and the clothesline is one that's been overlooked. However, most of the women in the film really do hate laundry. It has been the most hated of all household tasks for many generations and is the source of the once-common expression "Blue Monday," Monday, of course, being the traditional wash day in England and the United States. So a feminist folklorist does not want to romanticize laundry or any other aspect of housework. Cantow's film denies the women neither their artistry nor their pain.

A folklorist studying housework must consider not only the expressive culture surrounding the work but also, following McCarl's lead, the work itself and the meaning of that work within a particular culture. One necessary question concerns the relationship between the expressive aspects of tasks and the functional ones. Hanging wash can itself be a way of communicating—or a situation that allows for verbal communication, which some people call "clotheslining" (Farrer, 1986:xx)—but primarily it is a way to dry clothes and one that may or may not be a choice among alternatives such as using one's own clothes dryer, going to a laundromat, hanging the clothes on bushes to dry, or sending them out to be laundered. Sometimes changes in technology mean that something that was once instrumental or functional is now symbolic or expressive, as when women doing laundry insist on washing the white clothes before the colored ones, a holdover from the time when the clothes would have all soaked in succession in the same water. Then, doing the white clothes first was necessary to avoid discoloring them with dyes or dirt from the other clothes; now it is simply a matter of what feels right or, perhaps, of doing the job as one was taught.

One must also consider that how or when or by whom or with what technology a task is performed may communicate information the person performing the task does not intend. A clothesline may communicate information about the people who use it simply by its existence. In one area, it shows that—or if—the housewife is doing what she ought to be doing, but in some well-to-do American communities the presence of a clothesline would cause an uproar because of the belief that clotheslines make a neighborhood look "lower class." In Italy, on the other hand, the idea that a clothesline was something to be ashamed of would be much less likely to arise. Even in major cities and in homes or hotels that possess extremely "hi-tech" washing machines, laundry is hung out to dry (just as rugs are hung out windows to be beaten and aired) because air is important. One hangs wash outside not just to take the water out of it, but to let something into it. In the same way, one "changes the air" in one's house each day by opening the windows and speaks of the food local to one's region as identifiably from that region "because of the air" (Laura Meland Flanagan, personal communication).

I elaborated somewhat on the subject of laundry both because it is a job most people characterize as housework and because the clothesline is more visibly and obviously social than many parts of housework. Another major area of housework, house cleaning, is also social in a different way, in that it produces a product that can be (and often is) evaluated by one's community or even people from outside one's community.

Mary Douglas further says, "In chasing dirt, in papering, decorating, tidying, we are . . . positively reordering our environment, making it conform to an idea" (1984:68). While many people would not characterize papering or decorating as housework, the statement raises two important points that are helpful in studying housework. One is that housework is indeed connected to an "idea," the idea of what a house is supposed to look like. This links the study of housework to the study of vernacular architecture and to issues of cultural aesthetics, which also involve the question of what a living space is supposed to look like. The other is that while the majority of people to whom I have spoken recognize a distinction between "chasing dirt" and "tidying," some value tidiness more; others, cleanliness. Others value both equally—or neither very much. Additionally, people seem often to differentiate between "dirty dirt" ("crud") and dust. Different degrees of cleanliness and tidiness are required by different people, and different degrees at different times. Visits from an old friend, an in-law, a potential buyer, or "the cleaning lady" may require different amounts of preparation, and these different standards are sometimes reflected in the verbal folklore about housework. Explaining her family's housekeeping habits to me, one women told me a joke she had read in *Reader's Digest* about a woman who cleans her house for a visit from her sister who lives out of town. The following day, the mother is due to arrive, and the woman starts cleaning again, explaining to her bewildered sister, "That was sister clean; now I have to get it mother clean." Other housecleaning patterns are based on times of the week or year. Traditionally, for example, the Sabbath day requires a clean house (as well as clean clothes and a clean body), regardless of who is present. Christmas requires an especially thorough housecleaning in some places; in others, big spring and fall cleanings take place. Additionally, different rooms of the house may require different degrees of neatness or cleanliness. In some houses, one standard is maintained in the more public spaces (the living and dining rooms), which must be kept ready for visitors, while standards for bedrooms can be more relaxed; in others, the entire house must be kept pristine at all times, and children are forbidden even to sit on their beds.

Other questions one might ask about housecleaning, as for other parts of housework, concern the ways people speak about or evaluate each other's performance within a community or between communities. The Norwegians, for example, say of a particularly clean and tidy home that it is "licked," and the image is that of a mother animal licking her young (Gullestad, 1984:105). A book on Australian slang says that a messy room might be described as "a fowl-yard on Christmas day, with all the chooks drunk" (Keesing, 1982:93). The difference between calling balls of dust "slut's wool" and calling them "dust kittens" may imply a different attitude toward them—one might feel kindly to something called a "dust kitten," but surely never toward "slut's wool." What is the acceptable range of variation for cleanliness or tidiness, and what are the consequences of exceeding these at either extreme? (Might a child be forbidden to play in a friend's house because it is "too dirty"? Would a house kept spotlessly clean and tidy at all times be admired or thought "sterile"?) What is a clean house (or a dirty one) thought to *mean* in the culture? The Anglo-Saxon middle class believed "cleanliness is next to godliness," which associates cleanliness with morality, but the woman who told me why Italians do not like clothes dryers suggested that Mediterranean peoples value cleanliness as part of their household aesthetic: a house must be clean to be beautiful.

Another category of questions concerns the relationship between process and product, or methods and results. Does it matter to an individual or group how a task is done or does only the result matter? Often individuals have a pattern or rhythm for how and when to accomplish certain tasks. Patterns become automatic and free in the mind; they also break big jobs into smaller parts. They impose order on the work and thus mitigate against the "endlessness" that so many people complain of in doing housework. They also may be fun. But, these patterns seem to be symbolically as well as functionally important to people, especially to women. Once, as part of an American Folklore Society meeting about housework, I read out a set of directions for ironing a shirt: iron the sleeve, then the cuff (inside, then out); then the other sleeve, cuff (inside, out); then the yoke, collar back, collar top; front band inside, front band outside (working from buttonhole band to button band). After my presentation, one woman folklorist came rushing up to tell me that my directions were in the wrong order, and she told me the "right" way. I do not think that this same woman would have told a singer that his or her version of a ballad was the wrong one.

Often, one's ideas about the "right" way to do housework stem from what one was raised with, though certainly people do not all do housework the way their parents did. A folklorist studying housework must ask where and from whom various practices or beliefs have been learned. Individuals may be raised with family and community traditions for doing housework as portrayed in advertisements, by home economics teachers, and by advice columns in magazines—or as managed by a new housemate or spouse—and the ways in which they negotiate differences and accept or reject proposed changes will show which parts of the learned patterns are most important. One can also ask how housework is taught—by verbal teaching, by example, through games or threats—and to whom. Many of the differences I have encountered in the ways men and women do housework are based on the women having been taught traditional methods of performing tasks—and having a commitment to those methods —while the men were not. Some of the women I have spoken with have argued about whether one is supposed to sweep a room first or dust it first, a difference of opinion based on conflicting interpretations of the old saying "dust settles," but only a man has told me that he dusts by flapping a piece of cardboard over the furniture to blow the dust on the floor "because you have to vacuum anyway."

A rich and diverse folklore of housework exists and should be studied. Its existence does not prove that people like doing housework, though certainly some do, but, rather, that cultural differences and human creativity permeate our lives in unexpected ways. The focus of feminist studies of housework has often been on the way housework oppresses women, on what housework has done to women, as it were. Without at all wanting to detract from feminist efforts to make housework something other than "women's work," I want to suggest that we must look more carefully at what people—men and women—have made of housework.

References Cited

Abrahams, Roger D. 1978. "Towards a Sociological Theory of Folklore: Performing Services." In *Working Americans: Contemporary Approaches to Occupa-*

tional Folklore, ed. Robert H. Byington, 19–42. Smithsonian Folklife Studies, no. 3. Washington, D.C.: Smithsonian Institution Press.

Andelin, Helen B. [1965] 1975. *Fascinating Womanhood.* Rev. ed. New York: Bantam.

Cantow, Roberta, dir. 1981. *Clotheslines.* Buffalo Rose Productions.

Cowan, Ruth Schwartz. 1983. *More Work for Mother: The Ironies of Household Technology from the Open Hearth to the Microwave.* New York: Basic Books.

Davidson, Caroline. 1982. *A Woman's Work Is Never Done: A History of Housework in the British Isles, 1620–1950.* London: Chatto and Windus.

de Beauvoir, Simone. [1953] 1961. *The Second Sex.* New York: Bantam.

Douglas, Mary. [1966] 1984. *Purity and Danger: An Analysis of Concepts of Pollution and Taboo.* London: Ark.

Ehrenreich, Barbara, and Deidre English. 1978. *For Her Own Good: 150 Years of the Experts' Advice to Women.* Garden City: Doubleday.

Farrer, Claire R., ed. 1986. *Women and Folklore: Images and Genres.* Prospect Heights, Ill.: Waveland Press.

Friedan, Betty. 1964. *The Feminine Mystique.* New York: Dell.

Gullestad, Marianne. 1984. *Kitchen-Table Society.* Oslo: Universitetsforiaget.

Jones, Michael Owen. 1980. "A Feeling for Form, as Illustrated by People at Work." In *Folklore on Two Continents,* ed. Nikolai Burlakoff and Carl Lindahl, 260–69. Bloomington, Ind.: Trickster Press.

Jordan, Rosan A., and Susan Kalčik. 1985. *Women's Folklore, Women's Culture.* Philadelphia: University of Pennsylvania Press.

Juster, Norton. 1979. *So Sweet to Labor: Rural Women in America, 1865–1895.* New York: Viking.

Keesing, Nancy. 1982. *Lily on the Dustbin: Slang of Australian Women and Families.* Victoria, Australia: Penguin.

McCarl, Robert. 1985. *The District of Columbia Fire Fighters' Project: A Case Study in Occupational Folklife.* Washington, D.C.: Smithsonian Institution Press.

McGinley, Phyllis. 1960. *Sixpence in Her Shoe.* New York: Dell.

Matthews, Glenna. 1987. *"Just a Housewife": The Rise and Fall of Domesticity in America.* New York: Oxford.

Strasser, Susan. 1982. *Never Done: A History of American Housework.* New York: Pantheon.

Thompson, E. P. 1966. *The Making of the English Working Class.* New York: Vintage.

Veblen, Thorstein. [1899] 1934. *The Theory of the Leisure Class: An Economic Study of Institutions.* New York: New American Library.

Weigle, Marta. 1982. *Soldiers and Spinsters: Women and Mythology.* Albuquerque: University of New Mexico Press.

Zeitlin, Steven, Amy J. Kotkin, and Holly Cutting Baker. 1982. *A Celebration of American Family Folklore.* New York: Pantheon.

The Technocratic Model of Birth

"But is the hospital necessary at all?" demanded a young woman of her obstetrician friend. "Why not bring the baby at home?"

"What would you do if your automobile broke down on a country road?" the doctor countered with another question.

"Try and fix it," said the modern chaffeuse.

"And if you couldn't?"

"Have it hauled to the nearest garage."

"Exactly. Where the trained mechanics and their necessary tools are," agreed the doctor. "It's the same with the hospital. I can do my best work—and the best we must have in medicine all the time—not in some cramped little apartment or private home, but where I have the proper facilities and trained helpers. If anything goes wrong, I have all known aids to meet your emergency."

—*Century Illustrated Magazine,* Feb. 1926

Anybody in obstetrics who shows a human interest in patients is not respected. What *is* respected is interest in machines.

—Rick Walters, M.D.

Why is a birthing woman like a broken-down car, and whence comes this mechanistic emphasis in obstetrics?

For the past eight years, I have been researching the sociocultural implications of the obstetrical "management" of birth in American society.[1] This research has led me to conclude that both of these questions have the same answer: since the early 1900s, birth in the United States has been increasingly conducted under a set of beliefs, a paradigm, which I believe is most appropriately called "the technocratic model of birth."[2] I use the word *paradigm* here in the sense of both a conceptual model of and a template for reality. Such a template can only mold reality to fit its conceptual contours when these contours are specifically and consistently delineated and enacted through ritual. In this essay I will attempt to explicate the basic tenets of this paradigm, to hint at its historical roots, to demonstrate how it is both delineated and enacted through the rituals of hospital birth, and to consider its sociocultural and folkloristic implications.

Data for this article were obtained through interviews with one hundred mothers and many obstetricians, midwives, and nurses in Chattanooga, Tennessee, Austin, Texas, and elsewhere in the United States. Their names, wherever used, have been changed to protect their privacy. The majority of the people in my study were middle-class, mainstream American citizens. I was seeking to understand the processes at work in childbirth as it is experienced, not by any particular minority, but by the majority of American women, regardless of ethnicity. Although my study included few women from lower socioeconomic groups, I can say with certainty that the technocratic model analyzed here is applied even more intensively to the poor than to the women I interviewed, for middle-class women who pay for private obstetricians can afford to have some choice in their birthways, while poor women who must go through hospital clinics simply have to take what society chooses to give them (Lazarus, 1987; Scully, 1980; Shaw, 1974).

The birth process as it is lived out in contemporary American society constitutes an initiatory rite of passage for nascent mothers (Davis-Floyd, 1992).[3] Rites of passage are accomplished through ritual. A ritual may be defined as a patterned, repetitive, and symbolic enactment of a cultural belief or value. Such enactments may be *both* ritual and instrumental or rational-technical (Leach, 1979; Moore and Myerhoff, 1977:15). In my analysis of hospital birth I shall show that the obstetrical routines applied to the "management" of normal birth are also transformative rituals that carry and communicate meaning above and beyond their instrumental ends.

Ritual works by sending messages through symbols to those who perform and those who receive or observe it. The message contained in a symbol will often be experienced holistically through the body and the emotions, not decoded analytically by the intellect, so that no conceptual distance exists between message and recipient and the recipient cannot consciously choose to accept or reject the symbol's message. Thus the ultimate effect of the repetitive series of symbolic messages sent through ritual can be extremely powerful, acting to map the model of reality presented by the ritual onto the individual belief and value system of the recipient, thereby aligning the individual cognitive system with that of the larger society (Munn, 1973:606). Below, I will demonstrate how routine obstetrical procedures, the rituals of hospital birth, can work to map a technocratic view of reality onto the birthing woman's orientation to her labor experience, thereby aligning her individual belief and value system with that of American society.

But first, I must point out that my interviewees did not constitute an identifiable "folk group," except insofar as they are all participants in "American culture." The technologically oriented belief system within which most of them gave birth can be considered a folk model only under an expansive definition of folklore—one that stresses not its artistic/aesthetic dimensions (Kirshenblatt-Gimblett, 1988) but its expression of the underlying paradigms of a given group. In this country, the term *folklore* has usually been used to identify the expressive forms of smaller subgroups within the dominant society. But in Germany and Finland, primary countries of origin for the field of folklore scholarship, the original motivation behind the search for "folklore" was the conceptual unification of the country as a whole. Active performance and propagation of this folklore was consciously encouraged by the governments of those two countries as a means of first creating and then enacting a mythic reality model in which the emergent nations could find their conceptual grounding and sense of national identity.

In the United States today our sense of national identity is grounded in our technology. The technocratic model of birth is not the "folk model" of a small subgroup but part of the larger technocratic model of reality that forms a conceptual cornerstone of American society. The rituals of hospital birth enact and transmit this model in ways that affect every American woman, no matter what her ethnicity or small-group affiliation.

Those scholars who identify as folklore the expressive forms of small-scale, low-technology societies still balk at applying the same logic to the expressive forms of large, complex, high-technology societies like that of the contemporary United States. Concomitantly, the medical profession convinced the public seven decades ago that moving birth into the hospital represented the de-ritualization of what had heretofore been a primitive process, managed by backward midwives and laden with "folkloristic" superstition and taboo. I submit, however, that American society is no less dependent upon ritual (a traditional expressive form that folklorists have long claimed as part of their purview) than any other society. On the contrary, our exaggerated dependence on technology and our accompanying fear of natural processes has led to the "re-ritualization" of birth under the technocratic model in a manner more elaborate than anything heretofore known in the cultural world. When a society's dominant reality model is tacit, largely outside of conscious awareness, as is the technocratic model, its rituals need to be even more intensely elaborated than those enacting explicit belief systems (such as Catholicism), for it is only through ritual and symbol that such tacit models are transmitted. The cross-cultural ethnographic literature on childbirth yields nothing to compare with the number and intensity of symbolic interventions in the birth process developed by the physicians of Western society to enact and transmit its technocratic model.

The Technocratic Model and American Obstetrics

Because the belief system of a culture is enacted through ritual (McManus, 1979; Wallace, 1966), an analysis of ritual may lead directly to an understanding of that belief system. Analyses of the rituals of modern biomedicine (Fox, 1957; Henslin and Biggs, 1971; Miner, 1975; Parsons, 1951) reveal that it forms a microcosm of American society that encapsulates its core value system, a condensed world in which our society's deepest beliefs stand out in high relief against their cultural background. American biomedical cures are based on science, effected by technology, and carried out in bureaucratic institutions founded on principles of patriarchy and the supremacy of the institution over the individual. These core values of science, technology, patriarchy, and institutions are derived from the technocratic model of reality on which our society is increasingly based.

As Carolyn Merchant demonstrates in *The Death of Nature,* this model, originally developed in the 1600s by Descartes, Bacon, Hobbes, and others, assumed that the universe is mechanistic, following predictable laws that those enlightened enough to free themselves from the limitations of medieval superstition could discover through science and manipulate through technology to decrease their dependence on nature:

> These philosophers transformed the body of the world and its female soul . . . into a mechanism of inert matter in motion. The resultant corpse was a mechanical system of dead corpuscles, set into motion by the Creator, so that each obeyed the law of inertia and moved only by external contact with another moving body. . . . Because nature was now viewed as a system of dead, inert particles moved by external, rather than inherent forces, the mechanical framework itself could legitimate the manipulation of nature. (1983:193)

In this model the metaphor for the human body is a machine:

> The application of a technological model to the human body can be traced back to Rene Descartes's concept of mind-body dualism. . . . The Cartesian model of the body-as-machine operates to make the physician a technician, or mechanic. The body breaks down and needs repair; it can be repaired in the hospital as a car is in the shop; once fixed, a person can be returned to the community. The earliest models in medicine were largely mechanical; later models worked more with chemistry, and newer, more sophisticated medical writing describes computer-like programming, but the basic point remains the same. Problems in the body are technical problems requiring

technical solutions, whether it is a mechanical repair, a chemical rebalancing, or a "debugging" of the system. (Rothman, 1982:34)

After my stepfather's recent heart attack, a cardiologist gave me an update on this metaphor of the body-as-machine: "Don't worry about him! Just think of it this way—he's like an old Cadillac that has broken down and needs repair. He's in the shop now, and we'll have him just as good as new in no time. We're the best Cadillac repairmen in town!"

As it was developed in the seventeenth century, the practical utility of this metaphor of the body-as-machine lay in its conceptual divorce of body from soul and in the subsequent removal of the body from the purview of religion so it could be opened up to scientific investigation. At that time in history, the dominant Catholic belief system of Western Europe held that women were inferior to men—closer to nature, with less-developed minds, and little or no spirituality (Ehrenreich and English, 1973; Kramer and Sprenger, 1982). Consequently, the men who established the idea of the body-as-machine also firmly established the male body as the prototype of this machine. Insofar as it deviated from the male standard, the female body was regarded as abnormal, inherently defective, and dangerously under the influence of nature, which, due to its unpredictability and its occasional monstrosities, was itself regarded as inherently defective and in need of constant manipulation by man (Merchant, 1983:2). The demise of the midwife and the rise of the male-attended, mechanically manipulated birth followed close on the heels of the wide cultural acceptance of the metaphor of the body-as-machine in the West and the accompanying acceptance of the metaphor of the female body as a defective machine—a metaphor that eventually formed the philosophical foundation of modern obstetrics. Obstetrics was thus enjoined by its own conceptual origins to develop tools and technologies for the manipulation and improvement of the inherently defective and therefore anomalous and dangerous process of birth:

> In order to acquire a more perfect idea of the art, [the male midwife] ought to perform with his own hands upon proper machines, contrived to convey a just notion of all the difficulties to be met with in every kind of labour; by which means he will learn how to use the forceps and crotchets with more dexterity, be accustomed to the turning of children, and consequently, be more capable of acquitting himself in troublesome cases. (Smellie, 1756:44)

> It is a common experience among obstetrical practitioners that there is an increasing gestational pathology and a more frequent call for art, in supplementing inefficient forces of nature in her effort to accomplish normal delivery. (Ritter, 1919:531)

The rising science of obstetrics ultimately accomplished this goal by adopting the model of the assembly-line production of goods—the template by which most of the technological wonders of modern society were being produced—as its base metaphor for hospital birth. In accordance with this metaphor, a woman's reproductive tract is treated like a birthing machine by skilled technicians working under semiflexible timetables to meet production and quality control demands:

> We shave 'em, we prep 'em, we hook 'em up to the IV and administer sedation. We deliver the baby, it goes to the nursery and the mother goes to her room. There's no room for niceties around here. We just move 'em right on through. It's hard not to see it like an assembly line. (fourth-year resident)

The hospital itself is a highly sophisticated technological factory (the more technology the hospital has to offer, the better it is considered to be). As an institution it constitutes a more significant social unit than the individual or the family, so the birth process should conform more to institutional than personal needs. As one physician put it: "There was a set, established routine for doing things, usually for the convenience of the doctors and nurses, and the laboring woman was someone you worked around, rather than with." This tenet of the technocratic model— that the institution is a more significant social unit than the individual—will not be found in obstetrical texts, yet is taught by example after example of the interactional patterns of hospital births (Jordan, 1980; Scully, 1980; Shaw, 1974). For example, Jordan describes how pitocin (a synthetic hormone used to speed labor) is often administered in the hospital when the delivery-room team shows up gowned and gloved and ready for action, yet the woman's labor slows down. The team members stand around awkwardly until someone finally says, "Let's get this show on the road!" (1980:44).

The most desirable end product of the birth process is the new social member, the baby; the new mother is a secondary by-product: "It was what we all were trained to always go after—the perfect baby. That's what we were trained to produce. The quality of the mother's experience—we rarely thought about that. Everything we did was to get that perfect baby" (thirty-eight-year-old male obstetrician).

This focus on the production of the "perfect baby" is a fairly recent development, a direct result of the combination of the technocratic emphasis on the baby-as-product with the new technologies available to assess fetal quality. Amniocentesis, ultrasonography, "antepartum fetal heart 'stress' and 'non-stress' tests . . . and intrapartum surveillance of fetal heart action, uterine contractions, and physiochemical properties of fetal blood"

(Pritchard and MacDonald, 1980:329) are but a few of these new technologies:

> The number of tools the obstetrician can employ to address the needs of the fetus increases each year. We are of the view that this is the most exciting of times to be an obstetrician. Who would have dreamed, even a few years ago, that we could serve the fetus as physician? (Pritchard and MacDonald, 1980:vii)

The conceptual separation of mother and child basic to the technocratic model of birth parallels the Cartesian doctrine of mind-body separation. This separation is given tangible expression after birth as well as when the baby is placed in a plastic bassinet in the nursery for four hours of "observation" before being returned to the mother; in this way, society demonstrates conceptual ownership of its product.[4] The mother's womb is replaced not by her arms but by the plastic womb of culture (which, comfortably or uncomfortably, cradles us all). As Shaw points out, this separation of mother and child is intensified after birth by the assignment of a separate doctor, the pediatrician, to the child (1974:94). This idea of the baby as separate, as the product of a mechanical process, is a very important metaphor for women because it implies that men can ultimately become the producers of that product (as they already are the producers of most of Western society's technological wonders), and indeed it is in that direction that reproductive technologies are headed (Corea, 1985), as we will briefly investigate in the conclusion.

The Enactment and Transmission of the Technocratic Model through the Rituals of Hospital Birth

Hospital delivery as a whole may be seen as a ritual enactment of this technocratic model of birth. Once labor has begun, a variety of "standard procedures" will be brought into play to mold the labor process into conformity with technological standards. These various interventions may be performed by obstetrical personnel at different intervals over a time period that varies with the length of the woman's labor and the degree to which it conforms to hospital standards. The less conformity the labor exhibits, the greater the number of procedures that will be applied to bring it into conformity. These interventions, aimed at producing the "perfect baby," are thus not only instrumental acts but also symbols that convey the core values of American society to women and their attendants as they go through the rite of passage called birth. Through these procedures the natural process of birth is deconstructed into identifiable segments, then reconstructed as a mechanical process.

Birth is thereby made to appear to confirm, instead of to challenge, the technocratic model of reality upon which our society is based.

Shortly after entry into the hospital, the laboring woman will be symbolically stripped of her individuality, her autonomy, and her sexuality as she is "prepped"—a multistep procedure in which she is separated from her partner, her clothes are removed, she is dressed in a hospital gown and tagged with an ID bracelet, her pubic hair is shaved or clipped (conceptually returning her body to a state of childishness), and she may be ritually cleansed with an enema.[5] Now marked as institutional property, she may be reunited with her partner and put to bed. Her access to food will be limited or prohibited, and an intravenous needle will be inserted in her hand or arm. Symbolically speaking, the IV constitutes her umbilical cord to the hospital, signifying her now-total dependence on the institution for her life, telling her not that she gives life but rather that the *institution* does.

The laboring woman's cervix will be checked for degree of dilation at least once every two hours and sometimes more often. If dilation is not progressing in conformity with standard labor charts, pitocin will be added to the intravenous solution to speed her labor (60 percent of the women in my study were given pitocin, or "pitted"). This "labor augmentation" indicates to the woman that her machine is defective, since it is not producing on schedule, in conformity with production timetables (labor time charts). The administration of analgesia and/or anesthesia (which almost all of the hospital birthers in my study received, in various forms) further demonstrates to her the mechanicity of her labor; epidural anesthesia, which can numb a woman from the chest down, produces an especially clear physiological separation of her mind from the body-machine that produces the baby. This message is intensified by the external electronic fetal monitor, attached to her body by large belts strapped around her waist to monitor the strength of her contractions and the baby's heartbeat. An obstetrical resident commented, "The vision of the needle travelling across the paper, making a blip with each heartbeat, [is] hypnotic, often giving one the illusion that the machines are keeping the baby's heart beating" (Harrison, 1982:90). The internal monitor, attached through electrodes to the baby's scalp, communicates the additional message that the baby-as-hospital-product is in potential danger from the inherent defectiveness of the mother's birthing machine.

If we stop a moment now to see in our mind's eye the images that a laboring woman will be experiencing—herself in a steel bed, in a hospital gown, staring up at an IV pole, bag, and cord on one side and a big whirring machine on the other and down at two huge belts encircling her waist, wires coming out of her vagina, and steel bars, we can see that her entire visual field is conveying one overwhelming perceptual message about our culture's deepest values and beliefs—technology is supreme, and you are utterly dependent on it and on the institutions and individuals who control and dispense it:

> At Doctor's Hospital I attached the woman to the monitor, and after that no one looked at her any more. Held in place by the leads around her abdomen and coming out of her vagina, the woman looked over at the TV-like screen displaying the heartbeat tracings. No one held the woman's hand. Childbirth had become a science. (Harrison, 1982:91)

These routine procedures speak as eloquently to the obstetrical personnel who perform the procedures as to the women who receive them; the more physicians, medical students, and nurses see birth "managed" in this way, and the more they themselves actively "manage" birth this way, the stronger will be their belief that birth *must* be managed this way: "Why don't I do home births? Are you kidding? By the time I got out of residency, you couldn't get me *near* a birth without five fetal monitors right there and three anesthesiologists standing by" (female obstetrician, one year in practice).

As the moment of birth approaches there is an intensification of the ritual actions performed on the woman. She is transferred to a delivery room, placed in the lithotomy position, covered with sterile sheets, and doused with antiseptic, and an episiotomy is cut to widen her vaginal opening. These procedures cumulatively make the birthing woman's body the stage on which the drama of society's production of its new member is played out, with the obstetrician as both the director and the star (Shaw, 1974:84). The lithotomy position, in which the woman lies with her legs elevated in stirrups and her buttocks at the very edge of the delivery table, completes the process of her symbolic inversion from autonomy and privacy to dependence and complete exposure, expressing and reinforcing her powerlessness and the power of society (as evidenced by its representative, the obstetrician) at the supreme moment of her own individual transformation. The sterile sheets with which she is draped from neck to foot enforce the clear delineation of category boundaries, graphically illustrating to the woman that her baby, society's product, is pure and clean and must be protected from the inherent uncleanness of her body.

The delineation of basic social categories is furthered by the episiotomy, which conveys to the birthing woman the value and importance of the straight line—one of the most fundamental markers of our separation from nature (because it does not occur in nature). Of equal significance, the episiotomy transforms even the most natural of childbirths into a surgical procedure; routinizing it has proven to be an effective means of justifying the medicalization of birth. (Estimates of episiotomy rates in first-time mothers [primagravides] range from 50–90 percent; large teaching hospitals often have primagravida rates above 90 percent. Multigravida rates are estimated at 25–30 percent. In contrast, in the Netherlands episiotomies are preformed in only 8 percent of births [Thacker and Banta, 1983].)

The obstetrician instructs the mother on how to push, catching the baby and announcing its sex, then hands the baby to a nurse, who promptly baptizes "it" through the technological rituals of inspection, testing, bathing, wrapping, and the administration of a vitamin K shot and antibiotic eye drops. Thus properly enculturated, the newborn is handed to the mother to "bond" for a short amount of time (society gives the mother the baby), after which the nurse takes the baby to the nursery (the baby really belongs to society). The obstetrician then caps off the messages of the mother's mechanicity by extracting her placenta if it does not come out quickly on its own, sewing up the episiotomy, and ordering more pitocin to help her uterus contract back down. Finally the new mother, now properly "dubbed" as such through her technological annointings, will be cleaned up and transferred to a hospital bed.

These routine obstetrical procedures work cumulatively to map the technocratic model of birth onto the birthing woman's orientation to her labor experience, thereby producing a "coherent symmetry" (Munn, 1973:593) between her belief system and that of society. Diana experienced this process as follows:

> As soon as I got hooked up to the monitor, all everyone did was stare at it. The nurses didn't even look at me any more when they came into the room—they went straight to the monitor. I got the weirdest feeling that *it* was having the baby, not me.

Diana's statement illustrates the successful progression of conceptual fusion between her perceptions of her birth experience and the technocratic model. So thoroughly was this model "mapped onto" Diana's experience that she began to *feel* that the machine itself was having her baby and that she was a mere onlooker. (Soon after the monitor was in place, Diana requested a cesarean section, stating that there was "no more point in trying.")

Merry's internalization of one of the basic tenets of the technocratic model—the defectiveness of the female body—is observable in the following excerpt from her written birth story:

> It seemed as though my uterus had suddenly tired! When the nurses in attendance noted a contraction building on the recorder, they instructed me

to begin pushing, not waiting for the *urge* to push, so that by the time the urge pervaded, I invariably had no strength remaining, but was left gasping, dizzy, and diaphoretic. The vertigo so alarmed me that I became reluctant to push firmly for any length of time, for fear that I would pass out. I felt suddenly depressed by the fact that labor, which had progressed so uneventfully up to this point, had now become unproductive.

Merry does not say "the nurses had me pushing too soon," but "my uterus had suddenly tired" and labor "had now become unproductive." These responses reflect a basic tenet of the technocratic model of birth—when something goes wrong, it is the woman's fault:

Yesterday on rounds I saw a baby with a cut on its face and the mother said, "My uterus was so thinned that when they cut into it for the section, the baby's face got cut." The patient is always blamed in medicine. The doctors don't make mistakes. "Your uterus is too thin," not "We cut too deeply." "We had to take the baby" (meaning forceps or cesarean), instead of "The medicine we gave you interfered with your ability to give birth." (Harrison, 1982:174)

The obstetrical procedures briefly described above fully satisfy the criteria for ritual: they are patterned and repetitive; they are symbolic, communicating messages through the body and the emotions; and they are enactments of our culture's deepest beliefs about the necessity for cultural control of natural processes, the untrustworthiness of nature, and the associated defectiveness of the female body. They also reinforce the validity of patriarchy, the superiority of science and technology, and the importance of institutions and machines. Furthermore, these procedures are transformative in intent—they attempt to contain and control the inherently transformative natural process of birth and to transform the birthing woman into a mother in the full social sense of the word—that is, into a woman who has internalized the core values of American society: one who believes in science, relies on technology (and on those in charge of ordering/operating it), recognizes her inferiority (either consciously or unconsciously), and so at some level accepts the principles of patriarchy. Such a woman will tend to conform to society's dictates and meet the demands of its institutions and will raise her children to do the same. These birth rituals also transform the resident who is taught to do birth in no other way into the obstetrician who performs them as a matter of course: "No—they were never questioned. Preps, enemas, shaves, episiotomies—we just did all that; no one ever questioned it" (Dr. Stanley Hall).

Of course, there are many variations on this theme. Many younger doctors are dropping preps and enemas from their standard orders (although several complained to me that the nurses, also strongly socialized into the

technocratic model, frequently administer them anyway). Increasing numbers of women opt for delivery in the birthing suite or the LDR (labor-
delivery-recovery room), where they can wear their own clothes, do
without the IV, walk around during labor, and where the options of
side-lying, squatting, or even standing for birth are increasingly available.
(That many of the procedures analyzed above can be instrumentally
omitted underscores my point that they are rituals.) Yet in spite of these
concessions to consumer demand for more "natural" birth, a basic pattern of consistent high-technological intervention remains: most hospitals
now *require* at least periodic electronic monitoring of all laboring women;
analgesias, pitocin, and epidurals are widely and commonly administered;
in spite of decades of research that clearly demonstrate its severe physiological detriments (Johnstone, Abaedmagd, and Harouny, 1987; McKay
and Mahan, 1984), the lithotomy position is *still* the most commonly
used position for birth; and nearly one in four American women will be
delivered by cesarean section. Thus, while some of the medicalization of
birth drops away, the use of the most powerful signifiers of the woman's
dependence on science and technology intensifies.

Obstetrics, unlike other medical specialties, does not deal with true
pathology in the majority of cases it treats: most pregnant women are not
sick. It is, therefore, uniquely vulnerable to the challenges to its dominant
paradigm presented by the natural childbirth and holistic health movements,
for these movements rest their cases on that very issue—the inherent
wellness of the pregnant woman versus the paradoxical insistence of
obstetrics on conceptualizing her as ill and on managing her body as if it
were a defective machine. Over the past two decades, childbirth activists
and younger doctors aware of this paradox have succeeded in increasing
the number of birthing options available to women. Thus obstetrics is no
longer as reliable as it once was in the straightforward transmission and
perpetuation of American society's core value system. To deal with this
challenge, our society has gone outside the medical system, using the
combined forces of its legal and business systems to keep obstetricians in
line.

Over 70 percent of all American obstetricians have been sued, more
than in any other specialty (Easterbrook, 1987). Malpractice insurance
premiums in obstetrics began their dramatic rise in 1973, just at the time
when the natural childbirth movement was beginning to pose a major
threat to the obstetrical paradigm. A common cultural response to this
type of threat is to step up the performance of the rituals designed to
preserve and transmit the reality model under attack (Douglas, 1973:32;
Vogt, 1976:198). Consequently, the explosion of humanistic and holistic
options that challenge the conceptual hegemony of the technocratic

model has been paralleled by a stepping up of ritual performance in the form of a dramatic rise in the use of the fetal monitor (from initial marketing in the sixties to near-universal hospital use today ["Every Woman," 1982]), accompanied by a concurrent rise in the cesarean rate, from 5 percent in 1965 to almost 25 percent nationwide today (Taffel, et al., 1991), reaching 50 percent in many teaching hospitals. Although technically not a routine obstetrical procedure, the cesarean section is well on its way to becoming routine.[6] A number of studies have shown that increased monitoring leads to increased performance of cesareans (Banta and Thacker, 1979; Haverkamp and Orleans, 1983; Young, 1982:110). These dramatic increases in the ritual use of machines in labor and in the ritual performance of the ultimately technological birth, delivery "from above," are at least partially attributable to the coercive pressure brought to bear on obstetricians by the pervasive threat of lawsuit.

In their quest for the perfect babies and safe births they feel they are owed under the technocratic paradigm, most women sue because of the underuse of technology, not because of its overuse. Most obstetricians interviewed perceived electronic monitoring as a means of self-protection and confirmed that they are far more likely to perform a cesarean than not if the monitor indicates potential problems, because they know that the risk of losing a lawsuit is lower if they cleave to the strict interpretation of the technocratic model; if they try a more humanistic approach—that is, if they try to be innovative, less technocratic, and more receptive to the woman's needs and desires, they place themselves at greater risk. As one obstetrician put it:

> Certainly I've changed the way I practice since malpractice became an issue. I do more C-sections—that's the major thing. And more and more tests to cover myself. More expensive stuff. We don't do risky things that women ask for—we're very conservative in our approach to everything. . . . In 1970 before all this came up, my C-section rate was around 4 percent. It has gradually climbed every year since then. In 1985 it was 16 percent, then in 1986 it was 23 percent.

These legal and financial deterrents to radical change powerfully constrain our medical system, in effect forcing it to reflect and to actively perpetuate the core value and belief system of American society as a whole. From this perspective, the malpractice situation emerges as society's effort to keep its representatives, the obstetricians, from reneging on their responsibility for imbuing birthing women with the basic tenets of the technocratic model of reality. Purely economic analyses of the malpractice situation lose sight of the deeper cultural truth: the money goes where the values lie.

From a more personal perspective, the value of careful adherence to form in ritual must be appreciated to understand the powerful appeal the repetitive patterning of obstetrical procedures has for obstetrical personnel. Moore and Myerhoff observe that order and exaggerated precision in performance, which set ritual apart from other modes of social interaction, serve to impute "permanence and legitimacy to what are actually evanescent cultural constructs" (1977:8). This establishment of a sense of "permanence and legitimacy" is particularly important in the performance of obstetrical procedures because of the limited power the obstetrician's technocratic model actually imparts over the events of birth.

Although through ritual a culture may do its best to make the world appear to fit its belief system, divergent realities will occasionally perforate the culture's protective filter of categories and threaten to upset the whole conceptual system. Thus obstetricians and nurses, who have experienced the agony and confusion of maternal or fetal death or the miracle of a healthy birth when all indications were to the contrary, know at some level that ultimate power over birth is beyond them and may well fear that knowledge. In such circumstances, humans use ritual as a means of giving themselves the courage to carry on (Malinowski, 1954). Through its careful adherence to form, ritual mediates between cognition and chaos by appearing to restructure reality. The format for performing standard obstetrical procedures provides a strong sense of cultural order imposed on and superior to the chaos of nature:

> "In honest-to-God natural conditions," [the obstetrician] says [to the students observing the delivery he is performing], "babies were *sometimes* born without tearing the perineum and without an episiotomy, but without artificial things like anesthesia and episiotomy, the muscle is torn apart and if it is not cut, it is usually not repaired. Even today, if there is no episiotomy and repair, those women quite often develop a retocoele and a relaxed vaginal floor. This is what I call the saggy, baggy bottom." Laughter by the students. A student nurse asks if exercise doesn't help strengthen the perineum. . . . "No, exercises may be for the birds, but they're not for bottoms. . . . When the woman is bearing down, the leveator muscles of the perineum contract too. This means the baby is caught between the diaphragm and the perineum. Consequently, anesthesia and episiotomy will reduce the pressure on the head and, hopefully, produce more Republicans." More laughter from the students. (Shaw, 1974:90)

To say that obstetrical procedures are "performed" is true both in the sense that they are done and in the sense that they can be "acted" and "staged," as is evident in the quotation above. Such ordered, acted, and stylized techniques serve to deflect questioning of the efficacy of the underlying beliefs and forestall the presentation of alternative points of view (Moore and Myerhoff, 1977:7) by the medical and nursing students as they undergo the process of their own socialization into the technocratic model.[7] This model has internal logic and consistency; once these medical initiates have absorbed its basic tenets, including, as we see above, the notions of the defectiveness of nature and the female body and the superiority of the technocratic approach, they will come to perceive all the other aspects of the obstetrical management of birth as reasonable and right. Thus the system becomes tautological, and its self-perpetuation is assured.

Women's Rites: The Politics of Birth

"In a traditional philosophical opposition," writes Jacques Derrida, "we have not a peaceful coexistence of facing terms but a violent hierarchy. One of the terms dominates the other (axiologically, logically, etc.) and occupies the commanding position" (1981:56–57). The feminist scholar Hélène Cixous states that the man/woman opposition may well be *the* paradigmatic opposition in Western discourse (1975:116–19). Certainly, it was *the* fundamental opposition of the Roman Catholic Church (Ehrenreich and English, 1973; Merchant, 1983), which held conceptual hegemony over western Europe for over five hundred years and from which we moderns have inherited a pervasive legacy of symbolic thinking—a legacy of which we are generally unaware. Although the advent of the Protestant Reformation and the scientific and industrial revolutions undermined Catholic religious hegemony in the West, none of these events had any fundamental effect on the cultural articulation of this male/female opposition. Inherent in this opposition, as in our entire social discourse, is a "violent hierarchy" in which the value-laden male dominates the devalued female.

Shifting needs in our society enable women to work in a man's world, sometimes for equal pay, but no matter how early in life a woman begins her career, nor how successful she is, she will still be living and working under the constraints of her conceptual denial by the technocratic model of reality. Based as it is on a fundamental assumption of her physiological inferiority to men, that model guarantees her continued psychological disempowerment by the everyday constructs of the culture-at-large and her alienation both from political power *and* from the physiological attributes of womanhood.

It came as a shock to me, then, to discover that fully seventy (70 percent) of the women in my study expressed varying degrees of contentment with their technocratic births. As I explored the reasons behind this finding, I came to realize that the technocratic rituals of hospital birth, in spite of the philosophy that underlies them, do of course provide the same sense of order, security, and power to birthing women as they do to physicians and nurses. Moreover, that philosophy itself is not so alien to today's women as I had imagined. Although forty-two of these seventy women did enter the hospital with the expressed intention of "doing natural childbirth," this philosophical goal faded in importance as labor progressed—or "failed to."[8] As these women gradually became convinced of the defectiveness of their birthing machines or of the birth process, they came to interpret the interventions they experienced as appropriate (albeit sometimes unpleasant) and so clearly stated that they "did not mind" or felt "okay with" or "good about" the technological births they ended up with. The other twenty-eight entered the hospital already convinced that the way of technology was better than the way of nature. They wanted technological births to begin with and were generally satisfied with the ones they got. I consistently found that such women, who generally wish to live within American society's dominant core value system, will feel *slighted* if their births are not technocratically marked by the procedures that they themselves view as ritually appropriate:

> My husband and I got to the hospital, and we thought they would take care of everything. We thought that we would do our breathing, and they would do the rest. I kept sending him out to ask them to give me some Demerol, to check me—anything—but they were short-staffed and they just ignored me until the shift changed in the morning. (Sarah Morrison)

Because the technocratic model of birth encapsulates the core values of the wider culture, in many ways it offers to postmodern women the opportunity to further integrate themselves with that wider culture. The technocratic model itself replaced an earlier and narrower paradigm of birth that still retains a certain symbolic force—a paradigm that today's women still have many reasons for wishing to escape. In the 1800s in the United States, a woman's place was in the home, and motherhood was the central defining feature of a woman's life. Her primary duties were childbearing, nursing, and child-rearing. As American society switched from an agricultural to an industrial basis and the nuclear family replaced the extended family, increasing numbers of women found good reason to wish to define themselves in broader terms.

In *Lying-In: A History of Childbirth in America,* Dorothy Wertz and Richard Wertz describe the process by which many women began to seek hospital birth because of the freedom it provided from their regular household work cycles. Hand-in-hand with this freedom went a redefinition of the roles of women in American society. For accompanying this shift in birthplace was a shift in society's definition of women's bodies, reflecting a cultural reconstruction of femininity and the female role. As long as women gave birth exclusively in the home, that home remained their exclusive domain, excluding them by definition from participation in the wider world and its challenges. To reconceptualize birth as a mechanical process best handled by trained technicians and machines was to remove its feminine mystique, and in so doing, to remove the mystique from the feminine. When separated from the biological "earthiness" that had so long kept them down, women were able to be freer than they had been for countless centuries in the West, finally given license to seek equal opportunity with men in the nonbiological arena of the workplace.

By the early 1900s, women were rejecting both the rituals of confinement and the accompanying exclusive definition of their lives by maternity. The first maternity clothes appeared in 1904; hospital birth was on the rise, and the next step in women's liberation from the home was the appearance and spread of bottle-feeding. As one mother put it to her daughter in a novel written in 1936, "The bottle was the battle cry of my generation" (quoted in Wertz and Wertz, 1989:150). Moreover, women themselves campaigned for the acceptance in America of scopolamine-induced "twilight sleep" as further means of freeing themselves from what they were increasingly beginning to perceive as enslavement to their biological processes.[9] Pursuing this trend to its logical conclusion, it should come as no surprise that many of today's postmodern women would wish to identify with their earthy biological selves and the confines of the domestic realm even less than their turn-of-the-century sisters who paved the way for them.

Unlike these historical sisters, to whom adequate contraception was unavailable, most of the women in my study chose to have only one or two children and placed a great deal of emphasis on being present to the experience of giving birth. While the total personal obliteration of a scopolamine birth would have been anathema to all of them, many nevertheless did seek a high degree of detachment from the biology of birth through epidural anesthesia. Joanne put it this way:

> Even though I'm a woman, I'm unsuited for delivering . . . and I couldn't nurse. . . . I just look like a woman, but none of the other parts function like a mother. I don't have the need or the desire to be biological. . . . I've never really been able to understand women who want to watch the birthing process in a mirror—just, you know, I'm not, that's not—I'd rather see the finished product than the manufacturing process.

Joanne, like many others in my study, preferred epidural anesthesia for both of her cesarean births, as it allowed her to be intellectually and emotionally present, while physically detached:

> [I liked that because] I didn't feel like I had dropped down into a biological being. . . . I'm not real fond of things that remind me I'm a biological creature—I prefer to think and be an intellectual emotional person, so you know, it was sort of my giving in to biology to go through all this.

Such attitudes, increasingly common especially among professional women, have generated what many childbirth practitioners are calling the "epidural epidemic" of the nineties. (60 percent of the women in my study, and 80 percent of the women in a study by Sargent and Stark [1987], received epidurals.) As the epidural numbs the birthing woman, eliminating the pain of childbirth, it also graphically demonstrates to her through her lived experience the truth of the Cartesian maxim that mind and body are separate, that the biological realm can be completely cut off from the realms of the intellect and the emotions.[10] The epidural is thus the perfect technocratic tool, serving the interests of both the technocratic model (by transmitting it) and of the women giving birth under that model, who usually find that they benefit most not from rejecting that model but from using it to their own perceived advantage:

> When I got there, I was probably about five centimeters, and they said, "Uh, I'm not sure we have time," and I said, "I want the epidural. We must go ahead and do it right now!" So, we had an epidural. (Beth)

> Ultimately the decision to have the epidural and the cesarean while I was in labor was mine. I told my doctor I'd had enough of this labor business and I'd like to . . . get it over with. So he whisked me off to the delivery room and we did it. (Elaine)

While the majority of women in my study, like Joanne, Beth, and Elaine, found some degree of empowerment in technocratic conformity, fifteen (15 percent) successfully avoided conceptual fusion with the technocratic model by adhering to and achieving their goals of "natural childbirth" in the hospital. In contrast with the majority, these fifteen women were personally empowered by their resistance to the technocratic model. They tended to view technology as a resource that they could choose to utilize or ignore and often consciously subverted their socialization processes by replacing technocratic symbols with self-empowering alternatives (e.g., their own clothes and food, perineal massage instead of episiotomy):

> The maternity room sent somebody down with a wheelchair. I didn't have any need for a wheelchair, so we piled all of the luggage into it and wheeled it up to the floor. (Patricia)

> Giving birth was really satisfying. . . . I felt incredibly powerful and absolutely delighted. I felt that I knew exactly what was happening. . . . My perception of it was that I was in charge and these other people were my assistants. (Teresa)

In contrast, nine (9 percent) of my interviewees entered the hospital believing strongly in the benefits of natural childbirth and in their ability to give birth naturally, but came out feeling "beat to death," "like a failure," "totally disempowered" by the highly technocratic births they ended up with. The messages of helplessness and defectiveness that they received from these births engendered considerable conflict between the self-images they previously held and those they internalized in the hospital:

> After the birth I felt just miserable, agonizingly miserable. When I was relating to the baby, I was totally happy—I was so thrilled with her. But all the rest of the time I felt so sad—gray around the edges . . . and ashamed. I felt so *ashamed* of myself for . . . not being able to do it. . . . And I had so many questions that I started to read some more. More and more. And I started to admit to myself that I felt humiliated by my birth. And then when I realized that I probably hadn't even needed a cesarean, I started to realize that I felt raped, and violated somehow, in some really fundamental way. And then I got angry. (Elise)

When I began this research, I nurtured the illusion that women like Elise would be in the majority. I thought women everywhere would be rising up in resistance to their technocratic treatment. But I found, to summarize, that twenty-eight women did not want anything to do with natural childbirth, and forty-two, while initially giving what apparently was lip service to the ideal of natural childbirth, quickly and easily adapted to technocratic interventions, expressing no resistance to or resentment of those interventions.[11] Only twenty-four women out of a sample of one hundred actually succeeded at "natural childbirth" or were distressed when they did not succeed. This low number of women deeply committed to the philosophy of natural childbirth is quite representative of the fate in the nineties of the natural childbirth movement of the seventies and eighties—much of its force has been redirected (some would say subverted and co-opted [Rothman, 1982]) from educating women to resist technocratic birth into educating women to feel comfortable with and even empowered by birth under the technocratic paradigm. Many childbirth educators, who used to make it a point to serve as a primary counteracting force to technocratic socialization, are finding that there is no longer much reason to rail against technocratic abuses in their classes.[12] (The cover on a recent childbirth education magazine asks plaintively, "Have epidurals made childbirth education obsolete?" [Simchak, 1991].)

Opposition to technocratic birth has thus become much more polarized than before. Women who seek true alternatives to the technocratic model, finding them generally unavailable in the hospital,[13] often choose to give birth in midwife-attended free-standing birth centers[14] or at home.[15]

The Holistic Alternative

Six of the women in my study (6 percent) gave birth at home. The alternative paradigm these women adopted is based on systems theory and offers a holistic, integrated approach to childbirth as well as to daily life—an approach that stresses the inherent trustworthiness of the female body, communication and oneness between mother and child and within the family, and self-responsibility (Davis-Floyd, 1986, 1992; Rothman, 1982; Star, 1986). Tara illustrates one aspect of their systemic view:

> Pain? It's part of the whole experience. In this society, we try not to experience pain. We take lots of drugs, I mean legal things. And I feel that's why a lot of people get into other forms of drug abuse.... Even though during labor I remember feeling it was almost unbearable, it never entered my mind to wish I had "something for the pain." ... I wanted the pain to stop, but not because somebody gave me something. I guess part of it is ... the wonderful physical and emotional stuff that is going on at the same time as the pain. If you took drugs for the pain, you would change all the rest of it, too.

These home birthers sought not a return to the "motherhood as defining feature" paradigm of the nineteenth century but an expanded vision of womanhood that encompasses both the gains achieved in the workplace under the technocratic model and a renewed sense of the value of the feminine. As one woman put it, "It's a spiral, not a circle. We're not going backwards to 'women's domain,' but forward, to a space where *all* our attributes can be celebrated."

In technocratic reality, not only are mother and baby viewed as separate, but the best interests of each are often perceived as conflicting. In such circumstances, the mother's emotional needs and desires are almost always subordinated to the medical interpretation of the best interests of the baby as the all-important product of this "manufacturing process." Thus, individuals operating under this paradigm often criticize home birthers as "selfish" and "irresponsible" for putting their own desires above their baby's needs. But under the holistic paradigm held by these home birthers, just as mother and baby form part of one integral and indivisible unit until birth, so the safety of the baby and the emotional needs of the mother are also one. The safest birth for the baby will be the one that provides the most nurturing environment for the mother. Said Tara: "The bottom line was that I felt safer [at home] and I think that's what it boils down to for most people. That's why it didn't seem unusual to me. It seemed strange to me that people feel safer with the drugs and that type of thing because I'm just not that way." Elizabeth said, "My safest place is my bed. That's where I feel the most protected and the most nurtured. And so I knew that was where I had to give birth." And Ryla noted: "I got criticized for choosing a home birth, for not considering the safety of the baby. But that's exactly what I *was* considering! How could it possibly serve my baby for me to give birth in a place that causes my whole body to tense up in anxiety as soon as I walk in the door?"

According to the technocratic model, the uterus is an involuntary muscle and labor proceeds mechanically in response to hormonal signals. Proponents of the holistic model see the uterus as a responsive part of the whole, and therefore believe that the best labor care will involve attention to the mother's emotional and spiritual desires, as well as her physical needs. The difference between these two approaches is clearly illustrated by the responses of a physician and a lay midwife to the stopped labor of a client. The physician said, "It was obvious that she needed some pitocin, so I ordered it," and the midwife said, "It was obvious that she needed some rest, so she went to sleep, and we went home." Here is Susan's story:

> Nikki [the midwife] kind of got worried about it towards the afternoon. Because it just kept going on and nothing was changing. And she took me to the shower and said, "Just stay in there till the hot water goes away." And Ira went with me to massage me and try to get everything relaxed. And then Nikki asked my friend Diane, "What's the deal with Susan, what's going on? Is she . . . stressed out about work?" And Diane said, "Well, yeah, I think she's afraid to have the baby . . . [that] she's not going to be able to go back to her job and all that." So when I came back out . . . Nikki started in on me about it. She said, "Right now your job is not important. What you have to do right now is have this baby. This baby is important." And I just burst into tears and was screaming at her and started crying and I could feel everything when I started crying just relax. It all went out of me and then my water broke and we had a baby in thirty minutes. Just like that.

The Technocratic Model and the Future

Our cultural attachment to the technocratic model is profound, for in our technology we see the promise for our society of eventual transcendence of both our physical and our earthly limitations (already we build humanlike robots, freeze bodies in cryogenic suspension, and design space stations).

In the cultural arena of birth, the technocratic model's emphasis on mechanicity, separation, and control over nature potentiates various sorts of futuristic behavioral extremes. These include, among many others: court-ordered cesareans—cases in which the mother refuses to have a cesarean, but is forced to do so by the courts against her will (Irwin and Jordan, 1987; Shearer, 1989); surrogacy—a contractual arrangement in which the womb of one woman is rented to incubate someone else's child (Sault, 1989); sex preselection—using various techniques to try to ensure that the baby will be a boy or a girl, using amniocentesis to determine which it is, and then aborting if it isn't the desired sex; and genetic engineering—altering genes to select for certain desired traits or eliminate undesirable ones. (It is worth remembering that such futuristic reproductive technologies are envisioned, invented, and "chosen" in a sociocultural context that values *them* more than the female bodies they act upon.) How far can this trend carry us? The February 1989 issue of *Life* magazine's cover story, "The Future and You," predicts "Birth without Women":

> By the late 21st century, childbirth may not involve carrying at all—just an occasional visit to an incubator. There the fetus will be gestating in an artificial uterus under conditions simulated to recreate the mother's breathing patterns, her laughter and even her moments of emotional stress. (1989:55)

The paradigm that makes such futuristic options seem not only possible but also *desirable* presents real dangers to those who conceptually oppose it and act on their convictions. Across the country, would-be home birthers and the lay midwives who attend them report harassment and sometimes prosecution by the medical and legal establishment, as do women who attempt to refuse obstetrical interventions, including court-ordered cesareans. Such interventions are often ordered because the technocratic paradigm grants no legitimacy to women who value their own "inner knowing" more than technologically obtained information about what is "safe":

> In a 1981 Georgia case, doctors told the court there was a 99% chance of fetal death and a 50% chance of maternal death unless a scheduled Cesarean section was performed, since two ultrasounds indicated a complete placenta praevia [a potentially life-threatening situation in which the placenta lies under the baby, blocking the entrance to the birth canal]. The mother steadfastly believed in her ability to give birth safely. After the court order was granted, a third ultrasound showed no praevia at all. Either the placenta had moved late in pregnancy or the ultrasound machine had been wrong. (Shearer, 1989:7)

In contrast to the futuristic scenarios of technocracy, home birther Tara's vision for the future makes an explicit connection between the ecological principles of the environmental movement and home birth:

> How do we change this trend toward more drugs for birth, more machines? I think it starts with the way we raise our kids. I think the environmental movement could help as much as anything. . . . It encourages us to love Mother Earth and to teach our children—boys and girls—to be emotional, feeling, and caring. The environmental movement can help us to change our sex-role stereotypes. Men have been moving in that direction, but society has not been very accepting. There is a passion and emotion that comes out in the environmental movement that both men and women feel and accept as good. And that will influence birth. It will take both parents seeing things differently to change birth. As men open up to their emotional, caring selves, they will begin to feel strongly about natural birth. Mother Earth has historically been seen as feminine. If we get back to caring about the Earth, being caretakers, it would be difficult not to translate that into other parts of our lives. Sooner or later people will ask themselves how they can give birth drugged and hooked up to machines, when they are trying to stop treating their own Mother Earth that way.

Extremes, on both ends of the spectrum, play an important role in defining the outer edges of the possible and the imagined. Most especially, those at the extreme of conceptual opposition to a society's hegemonic paradigm—the radical fringe—create much more room for growth and change within that society than would exist without them. How much more technocratic might hospital birth look if no one in this country believed that mother and baby are one, that there is an inner knowing that can be tapped, that fulfilling the emotional needs of the mother is the best approach to the health of the child?

Because the technocratic paradigm *is* hegemonic, pervading medical practice and guiding almost all reproductive research, no middle-class woman who gives birth at home can fail to be aware that she is battling almost overwhelming social forces that would drive her to the hospital. The home birthers in my study who espouse the holistic model do so in direct and very conscious opposition to the dominant technocratic model. They represent the fewer than 1 percent of American women who choose to give birth at home. I suggest that the importance to American society of this tiny percentage of alternative model women is tremendous, for they are holding open a giant conceptual space in which women and their babies can find metaphorical room to be more than mechanistic antagonists. Home birthers I have interviewed use rich metaphors to describe pregnancy, labor, and birth that work to humanize, personalize, feminize, and naturalize the processes of procreation. They speak of mothers and babies as unified energy fields, complementary coparticipants in the creative mysteries, entrained and joyous dancers in the rhythms and harmonies of life. They talk of labor as a river, as the ebb and flow of ocean waves, as ripened fruit falling in its own good time.

Home birthers in the United States are an endangered species. (As part of a fund-raising effort, a group of local lay midwives is selling T-shirts with whales painted on the front; the caption underneath reads "Save the Midwives!") Should they cease to exist, the options available in American society for thinking about and treating pregnancy, birth, and the female body would sharply decrease, and our society would be enormously impoverished. Should they thrive, we will continue to be enriched by their alternative visions.

As feminists, we fight for the right to make our bodies our own, to metaphorize, care for, and technocratize as we please. The intensifying quest of many postmodern women for distance from female biology leads inevitably to the following question: As women increasingly break out of the confines of the biological domain of motherhood, will/should our culture still define that domain as primarily belonging to women? What do we want? As we move into the twenty-first century, will the options opened to us by our technology leave equal conceptual room for the women who want to *be* their bodies as well as for the women for whom the body is only a tool? As researchers like Ehrenreich and English (1973), Corea (1985), Rothman (1982, 1989), and Spallone (1989) have shown, the patriarchy has been and is only too willing to relieve us of the necessity of our uniquely female biological processes. To what extent do we desire to give up those processes that since the beginning of the species have defined us as women in order to compete with men on their terms and succeed? In the new society we are making, will the home birthers and home schoolers, the goddesses and the Earth Mothers have equal opportunity to live out their choices alongside those who want to schedule their cesareans and those who want their babies incubated in a test tube?

Because the birth process forms the nexus of nature and society, the way a culture handles birth will point "as sharply as an arrowhead to its key values" (Kitzinger, 1980:115). Any changes in these values and in the model of reality that underlies them will thus be both reflected in and effected by changes in the way that culture ritualizes birth. The existence of core value options is of critical importance for the future directions our society will take; changes in the hegemonic values transmitted through birth could profoundly alter those directions. In times of rapid change such as these, a society's adaptive capacity lies in its conceptual diversity just as surely as in its genetic diversity. As the natural childbirth movement of the seventies and eighties has been largely co-opted and subsumed into the service of technocratic hegemony, so the holistic models of lay midwives and home birthers could be completely overrun by the technocratic paradigm. I believe that it is the responsibility of feminist scholars everywhere to track the cultural treatment of birth, to register the disappearance of old options and the opening of new ones, and to work to make us all aware of their implications for the kind of culture that future generations of our society will acquire through the ritualization of birth.

Notes

I wish to express my appreciation to M. Jane Young, Linda Pershing, and Susan Hollis for their hard work and for the endless patience it has taken to see this volume through to publication and to Bruce Jackson for his excellent editorial assistance on the first version of this essay. An earlier version of this essay appeared in 1987 in the *Journal of American Folklore* 100 (398): 93–101.

1. The full results of this research appear in Davis-Floyd (1992).
2. In this version of this work I have used *technocratic* rather than *technological* because the former more fully expresses not only the technological but also the highly bureaucratic and autocratic dimensions of the reality model I am delineating. *Webster's New Collegiate Dictionary* (1979) defines *technocracy* as "management of society by technical experts."
3. My interview questions were primarily focused on first births.
4. In most hospitals the scientific rationale for this standard separation period involves the need to keep the baby warm and to monitor its condition. According to one obstetrician, this routine separation of mother and child was instituted during the period of the routine use of scopolamine for labor and birth, when the mother was quite literally unable to care for her baby for some time after its delivery. Routine continuance of the separation period today reflects both past precedent and current events—many mothers are still too anesthetized after their births to care well for their babies, and it is a fact of institutional life that nurses have to process a good deal of paperwork concerning the baby, which they are best equipped to do in the nursery. However, mothers who give birth in birthing rooms are allowed to keep their babies with them continually; because standard sterile procedures are not used in these birthing rooms, these babies are considered "contaminated" and therefore are not allowed in the nursery.
5. The underlying justification for the symbolic interpretations summarized here can be found in Davis-Floyd (1992). Portions of this analysis appear in Davis-Floyd (1987, 1988, 1989).
6. In my ongoing interviews with new mothers and childbirth practitioners, I have recently noticed a new trend. Obstetricians are under intense pressure to reduce the cesarean rate, so in lieu of cesareans, they are increasingly resorting to reliance on epidurals, large episiotomies, and forceps. The last three women I have

interviewed were delivered in this manner; they all said proudly, "I didn't have to have a cesarean!"

7. Detailed analysis of obstetrical training as an initiatory rite of passage appears in Davis-Floyd (1987).

8. "Failure to progress" is a catch-all diagnosis in obstetrics, applied when women's labors "fail" to conform to standardized labor time charts. Such a diagnosis usually leads first to the administration of pitocin to speed labor and then to the performance of a cesarean section.

9. Ironically, scopolamine, which reduced the birthing woman to an animalistic state (but then erased all events from her memory), was quickly co-opted by the medical profession into providing the rationale for claiming complete control of the birth process. This drug, once a symbol of women's liberation from the pain of childbirth, became for the childbirth activists of the seventies and eighties a symbol of women's subjugation to the medical profession. Even its replacement by the epidural is symbolic: the calm, controlled "awake and aware" Lamaze mother with the epidural fits the picture of birthing reality painted by the technocratic model far better than the "scoped-out" screaming "wild animal" of the fifties.

10. Physiological advantages of the epidural include pain relief that leaves the woman alert and aware throughout labor with small risk to the baby. Disadvantages include an increased incidence of cesarean section, forceps delivery, and urinary tract infection (from the urinary catheterization that must be done every few hours); dependence on others for basic physical needs because the woman must stay in bed with her head slightly elevated; constant electronic fetal monitoring; and frequent blood pressure monitoring. The result of an epidural, thus, is the elimination of the possibility of the activities a woman herself can do to facilitate labor and delivery: using a comfortable upright position, changing position frequently, emptying her bladder often, and walking (which greatly facilitates the effectiveness of contractions and cervical dilation) (Simchak, 1991:16).

11. Close examination of the birth narratives of these forty-two women reveals that prior to entering the hospital, their belief systems showed a relatively high degree of correspondence with the technocratic model (Davis-Floyd, 1992:chap. 5). Intensive socialization into a paradigm that one already more or less agrees with is certainly less painful a procedure than socialization into a paradigm radically different from one's own.

12. It is still possible to find childbirth educators in most cities who are truly committed to teaching the philosophy and methods of natural childbirth. Most notably, instructors trained in the Bradley method tend to take an uncompromising stance: "In the Bradley method, when we say successful outcome, we mean a totally unmedicated, drug-free natural childbirth without routine medical intervention, that enables the woman to exercise all her choices in birthing and give her baby the best possible start in life. And we expect this over 90% of the time" (McCutcheon-Rosegg, 1984:8). In this technocratic age, it is fascinating to note that this expectation has consistently been fulfilled in over 90 percent of the birth experiences of over 4,000 low- and high-risk couples taught the Bradley method

by American Academy of Husband-Coached Childbirth founders Jay Hathaway and Margie Hathaway.

13. Alternative birthing centers within hospitals became widespread in the eighties. Although in their homelike and cozy appearance they seem to offer the best of both worlds, in most hospitals few of the women who start out in such centers actually end up giving birth there, as most labors do not conform closely enough to technocratic standards to be allowed to remain in the ABC.

14. A recent study of 11,814 births in free-standing birth centers (Rooks, et al., 1989) showed clearly that the physical lack of connection to a hospital is accompanied by a conceptual lack of connection to the technocratic model. Births in such centers tended to be intervention-free, with outstanding outcomes: the Cesarean rate was 4.4 percent and the perinatal death rate was 1.3/1000 (the national average is 10/1000).

15. Available statistics indicate that midwife-attended planned home birth is safer than hospital birth. A brief summary of the U.S. (Marimikel Penn, personal correspondence; Sullivan and Weitz, 1988) and Canadian (Kenneth C. Johnson, personal correspondence) midwifery data I have collected on home birth shows that cesarean rates are consistently around 4 percent; hospital transfer rates range from 8 to 11 percent; perinatal mortality rates range from 1 to 3/1000. (Maternal mortality is almost nonexistent in planned home birth.) In further summary, I quote a recent study from Holland on far larger numbers than are generally available: "The PNMR [perinatal mortality rate] was higher for doctors in hospital (18.9/1000 [83,351 births]) than for doctors at home (4.5/1000 [21,653 births]), which was in turn higher than for midwives in hospital (2.1/1000 [34,874 births]) than for midwives at home (1.0/1000 [44,676 births]). . . . [These results show] that care by obstetricians is not only incapable, save in exceptional cases, of reducing predicted risk, but even that it actually provokes and adds to the dangers. . . . [They confirm] that midwives, practising their skills in human relations and without sophisticated technological aids, are the most effective guardians of childbirth and that the emotional security of a familiar setting, the home, makes a greater contribution to safety than does the equipment in hospital to facilitate obstetric interventions in cases of emergency" (Tew, 1990:267). For a more detailed discussion of the relative safety of home versus hospital birth, see Davis-Floyd (1992:chap. 4).

References Cited

Banta, H. Davis, and Stephen B. Thacker, 1979. *Costs and Benefits of Electronic Fetal Monitoring: A Review of the Literature.* U.S. Dept. of Health, Education, and Welfare, National Center for Health Services Research, DHEW Publication No. (PHS) 79–3245. Washington, D.C.: GPO.

"Birth without Women." 1989. *Life,* Feb., 54.

Cixous, Hélène. 1975. "Sorties." In *La jeune nee,* ed. Catherine Clements and Hèléne Cixous, 114–425. Paris: Union Generale de Editions.

Corea, Gena. 1980. "The Cesarean Epidemic." *Mother Jones,* July, 28–35.

———. 1985. *The Mother Machine: Reproductive Technologies from Artificial Insemination to Artificial Wombs.* New York: Harper and Row.

Davis-Floyd, Robbie E. 1986. "Afterword: The Cultural Context of Changing Childbirth." In *The Healing Power of Birth,* ed. Rima Star, 121–35. Austin, Tex.: Star Publishing.

———. 1987. "Obstetric Training as a Rite of Passage." In *Obstetrics in the United States: Woman, Physician, and Society,* ed. Robert A. Hahn. Special issue of *Medical Anthropology Quarterly* 1 (3): 288–318.

———. 1988. "Birth as an American Rite of Passage." In *Childbirth in America: Anthropological Perspectives,* ed. Karen Michaelson, 153–72. Beacon Hill, Mass.: Bergin and Garvey.

———. 1989. "Ritual in the Hospital: Giving Birth the American Way." In *Anthropology: Contemporary Perspectives,* ed. David Hunter and Phillip Whitten. Boston: Little, Brown.

———. 1990. "The Role of Obstetrical Rituals in the Resolution of Cultural Anomaly." *Social Science and Medicine* 31 (2): 175–89.

———. 1992. *Birth as an American Rite of Passage.* Berkeley: University of California Press.

Derrida, Jacques. [1972] 1981. *Positions: Three Interviews on Marxism, Psychoanalysis, and Deconstruction.* Chicago: University of Chicago Press.

Douglas, Mary. 1973. *Natural Symbols: Explorations in Cosmology.* New York: Vintage Books.

Easterbrook, Gregg. 1987. "The Revolution in Medicine." *Time,* 26 Jan., 40–74.

Ehrenreich, Barbara, and Deirdre English. 1973. *Witches, Midwives, and Nurses: A History of Women Healers.* Old Westbury, N.Y.: Feminist Press.

"Every Woman Probably Should Be Monitored during Labor." *Ob/Gyn News* 17 (20): 1.

Fox, Renee. 1957. "Training for Uncertainty." In *The Student Physician: Introductory Studies in the Sociology of Medical Education,* ed. Robert K. Merton, George G. Reader, and Patricia L. Kendall. Cambridge: Harvard University Press.

Harrison, Michelle. 1982. *A Woman in Residence.* New York: Random House.

Haverkamp, Alert D., and Miriam Orleans. 1983. "An Assessment of Electronic Fetal Monitoring." In *Obstetrical Intervention and Technology in the 1980s,* ed. Diony Young, 115–34. New York: Haworth Press.

Henslin, J., and M. Biggs. 1971. "Dramaturgical Desexualization: the Sociology of the Vaginal Exam." In *Studies in the Sociology of Sex,* ed. J. Henslin, 243–72. New York: Appleton-Century-Crofts.

Inch, Sally. 1984. *Birth-Rights.* New York: Pantheon.

Irwin, Susan, and Brigitte Jordan. 1987. "Knowledge, Practice, and Power: Court-Ordered Cesarean Sections." *Medical Anthropology Quarterly* 1 (3): 319–34.

Johnstone, F. D., M. S. Abaedmagd, and A. K. Harouny. 1987. "Maternal Posture in Second Stage and Fetal Acid Base Status." *British Journal of Obstetrics and Gynaecology* 94:753–57.

Jordan, Brigitte. 1980. *Birth in Four Cultures.* Montreal: Eden Press.

Kirshenblatt-Gimblett, Barbara. 1988. "Mistaken Dichotomies." *Journal of American Folklore* 101 (400): 140–55.

Kitzinger, Sheila. 1980. *Women as Mothers: How They See Themselves in Different Cultures.* New York: Vintage.

Kramer, Heinrich, and Jacob Sprenger. [1486] 1972. "Excerpts from the *Malleus Maleficarum (The Hammer of Witches)."* In *Witchcraft in Europe, 1100–1700: A Documentary History,* ed. Alan C. Kors and Edward Peters, 113–89. Philadelphia: University of Pennsylvania Press.

Lazarus, Ellen D. 1987. "Poor Women, Poor Outcomes: Social Class and Reproductive Health." In *Childbirth in America: Anthropological Perspectives,* ed. Karen Michaelson, 39–54. Beacon Hill, Mass.: Bergin and Garvey.

Leach, Edmund. [1966] 1979. "Ritualization in Man in Relation to Conceptual and Social Development." In *Reader in Comparative Religion,* ed. William A. Lessa and Evon Z. Vogt. 4th ed., 229–33. New York: Harper and Row.

McCutcheon-Rosegg, Susan, with Peter Rosegg. 1984. *Natural Childbirth the Bradley Way.* New York: E. P. Dutton.

McKay, Susan, and Charles Mahan. 1984. "Laboring Patients Need More Freedom to Move." *Contemporary Ob/Gyn* (July): 119.

McManus, John. 1979. "Ritual and Human Social Cognition." In *The Spectrum of Ritual: A Biogenetic Structural Analysis,* ed. Eugene d'Aquili, Charles D. Laughlin, and John McManus, 216–48. New York: Columbia University Press.

Malinowski, Bronislaw. [1925] 1954. "Magic, Science, and Religion." In *Magic, Science, and Religion and Other Essays,* 17–87. New York: Doubleday/Anchor.

Merchant, Carolyn. 1983. *The Death of Nature: Women, Ecology, and the Scientific Revolution.* San Francisco: Harper and Row.

Miner, Horace. [1956] 1975. "Body Ritual among the Nacirema." In *The Nacirema: Readings on American Culture,* ed. James P. Spradley and Michael A. Rynkiewich, 10–13. Boston: Little, Brown.

Moore, Sally Falk, and Barbara Myerhoff, eds. 1977. *Secular Ritual.* Assen, the Netherlands: Van Gorcum.

Munn, Nancy D. 1973. "Symbolism in a Ritual Context: Aspects of Symbolic Action." In *Handbook of Social and Cultural Anthropology,* ed. John J. Honigmann, 579–611. Chapel Hill: Rand McNally.

Parsons, Talcott. 1951. *The Social System.* Glencoe, Ill.: Free Press.

Pritchard, Jack A., and Paul C. MacDonald. 1980. *Williams Obstetrics.* 16th ed. New York: Appleton-Century-Crofts.

Ritter, C. A. 1919. "Why Pre-natal Care?" *American Journal of Gynecology* 70:531.

Rooks, Judith P., Norma L. Weatherby, Eunice K. M. Ernst, Susan Stapleton, David Rosen, and Allan Rosenfield. 1989. "Outcomes of Care in Birth Centers: The National Birth Center Study." *New England Journal of Medicine* 321:1804–11.

Rothman, Barbara Katz. 1982. *In Labor: Women and Power in the Birthplace.* New York: Norton. Reprinted as *Giving Birth: Alternatives in Childbirth.* New York: Penguin Books, 1985.

———. 1989. *Recreating Motherhood: Ideology and Technology in Patriarchal Society*. New York: W. W. Norton.

Sargent, Carolyn, and Nancy Stark. 1989. "Childbirth Education and Childbirth Models: Parental Perspectives on Control, Anesthesia, and Technological Intervention in the Birth Process." *Medical Anthropology Quarterly* 3 (1): 36–51.

Sault, Nicole. 1989. "Surrogate Mothers and Spiritual Mothers: Cultural Definitions of Parenthood and the Body in Two Cultures." Paper presented at the annual meeting of the American Anthropological Association, Washington, D.C.

Scully, Diana. 1980. *Men Who Control Women's Health: The Miseducation of Obstetrician-Gynecologists*. Boston: Houghton-Mifflin.

Shaw, Nancy Stoller. 1974. *Forced Labor: Maternity Care in the United States*. New York: Pergamon Press.

Shearer, Beth. 1989. "Forced Cesareans: The Case of the Disappearing Mothers." *International Journal of Childbirth Education* 4 (1): 7–10.

Simchak, Marjorie. 1991. "Has Epidural Anesthesia Made Childbirth Education Obsolete?" *Childbirth Instructor* 1 (3): 14–18.

Smellie, William. 1756. *A Treatise on the Theory and Practice of Midwifery*. 3d ed. London: D. Wilson and T. Durham.

Spallone, Patricia. 1989. *Beyond Conception: The New Politics of Reproduction*. Granby, Mass.: Bergin and Garvey.

Star, Rima Beth. 1986. *The Healing Power of Birth*. Austin, Tex.: Star Publishing.

Sullivan, Deborah, and Rose Weitz. 1988. *Labor Pains: Modern Midwives and Home Birth*. New Haven: Yale University Press.

Taffel, Selma, Paul Placek, Mary Moien, and Carol Kosary. 1991. "1989 U.S. Cesarean Section Rate Studies." *Birth* 18 (2): 73–78.

Thacker, Stephen B., and H. David Banta. 1983. "Benefits and Risks of Episiotomy." In *Obstetrical Intervention and Technology in the 80s,* ed. Diony Young, 161–78. New York: Haworth Press.

Tev, Marjorie. 1990. *Safer Childbirth: A Critical History of Maternity Care*. New York: Routledge, Chapman, and Hall.

Vogt, Evon Z. 1976. *Tortillas for the Gods: A Symbolic Analysis of Zinacanteco Rituals*. Cambridge: Harvard University Press.

Wallace, Anthony F. C. 1966. *Religion: An Anthropological View*. New York: Random House.

Wertz, Richard W., and Dorothy C. Wertz. 1989. *Lying-In: A History of Childbirth in America*. 2d ed. New York: Free Press.

Young, Diony. 1982. *Changing Childbirth*. Rochester, N.Y.: Childbirth Graphics.

Peace Work out of Piecework: Feminist Needlework Metaphors and The Ribbon around the Pentagon

I want you to imagine; I want you to shut your eyes . . . and imagine that the bomb is going to land here in ten minutes. I want you to shut your eyes and think. What are you going to do now? Where will you go? Where are your children? Where is your family? Those that you love? What do you value the most about your life? Think of the spring and the flowers and the planet. Don't forget.

— Helen Caldicott, 1980 Gandhi Peace Prize Recipient

Justine Merritt is a sixty-nine-year-old former high school teacher who learned needlework from her grandmother and mother. As we talked together she often stitched, pausing with her needle poised in midair while she considered difficult questions, as though her mind and her embroidery were symbiotically fused. Merritt used to teach classes entitled "Embroidered Memories" to other women, encouraging them to reflect on important events in their lives by symbolically representing them on fabric.[1] A converted Catholic who has become increasingly concerned about the nuclear arms race, Merritt first got the idea for The Ribbon during an Ignacian retreat in 1982, when she sought spiritual direction concerning what she should do next in her life. Shortly before the retreat Merritt had seen Judy Chicago's exhibit "The Dinner Party" and was impressed by the lavish needlework that embellished the placemats and runners in the show and by the efforts of a large group of women who had worked together to make it happen.[2] Soon after the retreat she articulated, first in her journal and then in talking with family members, the idea of making an immense ribbon of decorated fabric to tie around the Pentagon as a ceremonial plea for peace. Merritt intentionally chose the Pentagon, rather than, for example, the United Nations Building or the Soviet embassy, because she saw it "as a symbol of my nation's violence, and of my own" (Lark Books Staff and Philbin, 1985:11).

She began working on a yard-long panel, creating a rainbow collage of embroidered names that took over seven hundred hours to complete. The names represented people—what Merritt said she most treasured in life—or, as later became the theme for The Ribbon and the subject of each individual panel, "what I cannot bear to think of as lost forever in a nuclear war." She invited family and friends to join her in making panels of decorated fabric. Pieces of ribbon were sewn to the corners of each panel so that they could be tied together to form one long banner. Merritt sent out fliers to the people on her Christmas card list, the idea spread by word-of-mouth and through informal networks, and soon people from across the country were sewing panels to contribute to the project—using embroidery, quilting, appliqué, knitting, batik, and many other fabric arts.

Among a group of her closest women friends in Denver a plan emerged to encircle the Pentagon on August 4, 1985, to commemorate the fortieth anniversary of the atomic bombing of Hiroshima and Nagasaki. From the spring of 1982 until the summer of 1985 the idea continued to spread until the project received local and national media coverage, usually as "human interest" rather than news stories. Church Women United, a national ecumenical organization of religious women, adopted The Ribbon as an official project and publicized it widely in their newsletters. A grass-roots organizational structure was established, and volunteers (almost entirely women) gradually came forward in each state to coordinate the project.[3] Initially the Denver organizers estimated that they would need a little over a mile of panels to encircle the Pentagon, with perhaps one thousand people to hold them for the tying ceremony. No one knows the exact number of participants, but on August 4 there were about fifteen miles of ribbons and over twenty thousand people present—enough so that they wove around not only the Pentagon, but also the Capitol Building and the Lincoln and Washington Memorials.

With only the theme and the dimensions as their guidelines, panel makers used a vast range of motifs and a seemingly endless variety of fabrics in their segments (figs. 16.1–2). There were butterflies, family portraits, and abstract designs made out of everything from gold lamé to favorite socks and baby bibs. One panel asks the question "Will they be the only survivors?" and shows a giant cockroach with rhinestone eyes and corduroy wings. Thousands of panels depict children: tiny handprints outlined in stitchery, photos encased in calico frames, a cloth rendition of a doorjamb embroidered with the dates and heights of several youngsters. Although some panels were made by men, children, families, or community groups, survey data indicate that the overwhelming majority, possibly over 90 percent, were created by women.[4]

The imagery is startling and compelling. Think of it—a ribbon around the Pentagon—lengths of colorful fabric stitched by women and ceremonially wrapped around an impenetrable, stone building that symbolizes the nation's military might. My attention has focused on discerning what these women hoped to accomplish with such a project and understanding why it was done in just this way.

Processual Concerns in Making The Ribbon

Several months after the ceremony I began my research by interviewing twelve women panel makers. Three of them lived in Austin, Texas. The other nine were organizers of the event: eight from Denver and one from Arlington, Virginia. Like Ribbon participants more generally, they were predominately white and middle- or upper middle-class women. Among the twelve, ten of them were white, one African American, and one Hispanic. Nine were middle or upper middle class, and three were working class or without steady sources of income.[5]

I soon discovered that for Merritt, and for the other participants I interviewed, the making of Ribbon panels became an affirmation of life and an act of self-actualization and empowerment, choosing to create a thing of beauty and value in the face of despair over the possibility of future annihilation. Indicative of the emphasis in the eighties on self-realization rather than its collective effect, many organizers described The Ribbon as a vague type of social action without linking it to any specific agenda for political change. Mary Frances Jaster, a close friend of Merritt's who became the national coordinator for the project, explained that the purpose of The Ribbon was "to help people get in touch with their fears and their hopes; to get in touch with their fears of nuclear destruction and get in touch with their hopes for life." This heightened perception of the importance of personal self-realization and its expression may have been related to the race and class identities of the panel makers and organizers. But it also was related to the perception on the part of many U.S. women that their views and actions have little actual effect on established governmental processes. Unexpectedly, I found that few of the participants I interviewed believed The Ribbon would make a significant or identifiable impact on U.S. military or nuclear policy.[6] In characterizing the project, Jaster was comfortable with Merritt's notion that The Ribbon represented "a profound moment in history," but she did not see the

Figure 16.1. Ribbon panels, each 18 inches high by 36 inches long with strips of ribbon sewn to the corners so that the panels can be tied together. *Top:* "Our Brightest Memories," the Henshaw Family, Wakefield, Mass. The bird is fashioned out of a handkerchief, and underneath is embroidered "wedding handkerchief." Below the nightgown are the tiny embroidered words "Craig and Elizabeth's baby nightgown." This panel contains hand and machine appliqué and embroidery on a hot-pink cotton background. *Bottom:* "Save Us Too," Jacquie Porter, Cape Cod, Mass. This panel has exquisitely hand-embroidered birds and the background is hand-quilted. Typed on a piece of pellon stitched to the back of the panel is the following explanation: "We moved here to Brewster, Cape Cod, Mass. from Maryland five years ago when my husband retired from teaching. I have found it the ideal place to indulge my life-long love of birds. The seasons change and move with the migrations of the hawks and warblers, the arrivals and departures of the wintering waterfowl and summering shore birds. Flocks of bob white quail come to my feeders and the pine trees are alive with

goldfinches, titmice and chickadees. I watch the birds on the beaches and in my garden and I embroider them in my livingroom. I cannot imagine the sadness of a world without them, and I chose birds from different habitats to convey their peaceful encirclement of our Earth." (Photo by Linda Pershing)

Figure 16.2 *Top:* "World without End," Yellowstone Valley Quilters' Guild of Billings Montana. This panel has " 'World without End' pattern symbolizes our hope for world peace" cross-stitched on beige muslin. The surrounding blocks in the panel are quilted. The guild used hand appliqué, quilting, and cross-stitch. *Bottom:* "Looking out of a Window," Lois Lounsbery, Ithaca, N.Y. The panel was made with machine appliqué and embroidery. The panel maker describes herself on the back as a "piano teacher and mother of Adam (Age 10)." Adam's photograph is stitched into the book depicted in the panel. (Photo by Linda Pershing)

project as "a challenge to 'the powers that be.' " Reflecting on this, she commented:

> It might seem contradictory to say it's a profound moment in history and not a challenge to "the powers that be," but I think the impact of The Ribbon is more on individuals, and individuals touching individuals, rather than on powers, on the people who have the power. But I do think that if enough individuals are touched, eventually "the powers that be" could be challenged by that. But I don't think the event in Washington is going to change anybody's minds on voting they're going to do in Congress or anything like that.

Like Jaster, some participants spoke of The Ribbon as just a beginning, recognizing that it takes time and continued work to change the minds of policymakers. No one I interviewed seemed surprised, for example, by press reports that on the day of the ceremony President Reagan left the White House for Camp David in a helicopter, after which his aides stated that from the air he "never noticed" The Ribbon that virtually encircled the entire Mall area of Washington, D.C.[7] As Mary Beard, an Austin panel maker, put it: "I don't think it had any effect. . . . I really don't think it has had; I have not felt or seen or read or had any indication that it had an impact. I think that government, as the entity, thought it was a real nice, beautiful thing that happened that all these women were walking around with very nice banners, and they had to provide a lot of security guards, and it was just a real pain in the neck. That's really it."

However, ambiguity or negative feeling about The Ribbon's impact on governmental decision makers did not appear to dampen participants' enthusiasm about the project. Anne Long of Austin, Texas, described her decision to participate as a matter of conscience. For her, participation was significant and pleasurable because it combined making a political statement and doing needlework with two close friends:

> But I also felt that even if only a few people did this, it was very worthwhile, because, let's face it, if ever there's another nuclear war, the world's just going to be destroyed! And if there is anything left, I don't think the quality of life will be worth very much. I personally would not care to survive. And I'm totally against all the weapons build-up and paranoia that's going on right now about our so-called enemies. And I felt that, well, this banner I'm doing is part of a large project, and it may make no difference because peaceful demonstrations are often not as dramatically received by the press or reported like protests that are more violent. I still felt I must participate. And, of course, I love Ari and Mary and the fact that they were involved in it, too. I felt that the three of us can really make something that will be very nice.

Mary Beard, who was the most pessimistic about the tangible effects of The Ribbon, spoke of her involvement as a significant, transformative event in her life, providing an opportunity to express her political concerns using a medium that felt familiar and comfortable to her. When I asked Beard what made her decide to participate in The Ribbon, she responded:

> I guess it was the old antiwar feelings comin' out, that I, at the time in 1965 and '69—when Vietnam was really hot and heavy—I had just graduated from high school and gotten married, then had several friends who were killed during the Vietnam War, several friends now who are still suffering problems from the Vietnam War, and [I] really wanted to get out and be antinuke, an antiwar protester, but didn't have the nerve and the guts to do it. And [I] was never the hippie type, you know, pretty conservative, and this was my ability now, you know, a long time later—twenty years later—to finally say something that I didn't have the nerve to say then.

Despite their indifference to or pessimism about the political effects of The Ribbon, participants I interviewed conveyed the feeling that what they had done nonetheless mattered, that their work on the panels was significant to them and to others in their lives, that they would do it again. In fact, some of them are still working on panels or starting on new ones, even though the official ceremony has long since passed.[8] Here I found a simultaneous expression of excitement about participation in the project and reservation about its results. I suggest that one way of making sense of this tension is the development of an analytical framework that recognizes a greater interest in process than product.

In The Ribbon, the process involved the methods and means of communication—the actual making of panels and the creation of an emergent ritual—which were emphasized more than the product and its effects, particularly the ramifications for governmental policy. What these women valued was not just the potential results—the completed Ribbon and its impact on the attitudes of the American public and, more specifically, on legislators—but the experiences involved in the process of participation itself. The remainder of this essay is an examination of two feminist needlework metaphors that can facilitate a fuller understanding of the participants' concerns with process over product. First, I explore a metaphor suggested in the work of the literary critic Jane Marcus, comparing her notion of "invisible mending" to The Peace Ribbon in order to better understand various processual aspects of the project. Subsequently, using Marcus's ideas as a springboard for further development, I offer a needlework metaphor of my own creation, arguing that there is a need to account for the simultaneous elements of social conformity and critique that are evident in The Ribbon.

Trends in Needlework Research Conducted by Folklorists

While the study of women's folklore and the development of feminist folklore theory have, in general, been much-neglected areas of inquiry, this has been particularly the case within material culture research (Limón and Young, 1986:449–54). Indeed, a 1986 review article on women and the study of folklore, written by two folklorists, reinforces this oversight, noting (mistakenly) that English-speaking folklorists have only directed their attention to material culture "in the last two decades" (Jordan and de Caro, 1986:500).[9]

One area of material culture research that has been slighted by folklorists is women's traditional needlework, weaving, and other fabric arts. To date the majority of U.S. folklore research on needlework has focused on quilting, but even with regard to quilting—perhaps the best known of the American needle arts—there is a decided denigration of its significance by many folklore scholars, as though enough had already been written on this centuries-old and widely variable practice. In fact, only four articles that have quilts or quilting as their primary subject have appeared in the *Journal of American Folklore* during the last century (Bergen, 1892; Parsons, 1919; Gayton, 1945; Hammond, 1986). Outside this journal, quilt researchers have offered a variety of fascinating observations on the quilting process, including a focus on the ways in which quilts can reflect the personalities of their makers (Clarke, 1976), quilts as keys to individual life histories (Cooper and Buferd, 1977), quilts as expressions of racial and ethnic identity (Vlach, 1978), the significance of contextual analysis in understanding the meaning of quilts to their makers (Ice and Shulimson, 1979), and the linkages between verbal and visual modes of communication within quilting bees (Roach, 1985). A number of insightful analyses of women's needlework have also appeared in doctoral dissertations, which are, as yet, unpublished (Ice, 1984; Roach, 1986; Weidlich, 1986). Much of the recent revival of scholarly interest in quilting has focused on the ways in which it has served as a metaphor for women's creativity and the maintenance of community.[10] However, with the exception of quilting, research conducted within the academic community on the many other varieties of needlework—including embroidery, lace-making, knitting, tatting, drawnwork, cross-stitch, and crochet—is still in its formative stages.[11] These needle arts also deserve additional attention by folklorists and may provide fresh insights into women's expressive behavior. For example, in her study of embroidery, art historian Rozsika Parker (1984) demonstrates the ways in which this form of needlework—and this could be expanded to include many other fabric arts—has become indissolubly associated with popular notions of femininity. The investigation of other types of fabric art will, no doubt, lead to similarly insightful findings on women's expressive behavior.

In general, when folklorists have studied women's needle arts, along with many other types of material culture, it has been with a focus on their formal features, such as size, design, texture, materials of composition, and technique. However, recent attention to processual dynamics in the study of material culture has been encouraged within folklore studies by the development and influence of performance theory and its attention to social behavioral processes (e.g., Paredes and Bauman, 1972; Bauman, 1975, 1986). With the advent of performance-centered approaches, which have as their primary concern the behavior, activity, and creative communicative processes of expression, many folklore scholars have moved away from analysis of the folk object as an end in itself and toward the study of people's behavior in interacting with objects. With this new focus there is a recent concern for the people who create and use objects and for how they behave in relation to those objects within a specific sociohistorical setting (Limón and Young, 1986:453). This newer orientation has as its goal the better understanding of how people relate to and manipulate objects in order to express themselves, their notions of identity, and their personal and cultural values (see Bronner, 1983, 1986; Jones, 1980; Sherzer and Sherzer, 1976).

Feminist Needlework Metaphors as Interpretive Frameworks

Outside of folklore studies, women's traditional needlework, weaving, and sewing recently have provided feminist authors a source of metaphorical imagery that they have used in their analyses of women's cultural practices. Much of this writing focuses on the literary depiction of needlework and its processual aspects—how the needlework is done—and on the ways in which these processes parallel women's experiences and values (see, for example, Morgan, 1982; Piercy, 1980; Radner and Lanser, 1987; Showalter, 1986; Walker, 1973). Metaphors, in which one kind of item or idea is used in place of another to suggest a likeness or similarity between them, frequently are invoked to make conceptual connections between two conventionally unrelated items. For feminist authors, needlework metaphors frequently are intended to demonstrate the inherent connectedness (and integrational nature) of seemingly disparate aspects of women's experiences. Believing, as art critic Lucy Lippard has contended, that "the quilt has become the prime visual metaphor for women's lives, for women's culture" (1983:32), these authors explore quilting as a potential "root metaphor" that can illuminate new ways of understanding women's lives (see V. Turner, 1974:23–59).

In her essay "Piecing and Writing," for example, Elaine Showalter compares the quilting and writing of U.S. women in the last two centuries, noting metaphorical relationships between women's needles and their pens (1986:224). As a literary critic, Showalter finds distinctive characteristics (e.g., repetition, fragmentation, creativity that emerges out of scarcity) in the process of quilting that reflect women's experiences as they often are similarly expressed in literature. She even argues that not only do women's material creations parallel women's writing but also that piecing, patchwork, and quilting have had tangible effects on the structures, genres, themes, and meaning of U.S. women's literature. This is a fascinating reversal of the more common attempt to understand objects as "texts." Here Showalter proposes that rather than using literary or linguistic models to analyze material culture, the study of objects can inform textual or verbal analysis. Her analysis, and others like it, offers a key to understanding processual concerns in women's culture, attempting to demonstrate that how the needlework is done can provide clues to interpreting women's lives, aesthetics, and values.

Jane Marcus describes a sewing technique called "invisible mending" that her mother and aunt did in the forties and fifties at their garment shop in Boston. In an autobiographical article, Marcus likens her own work to the invisible mending done by women in repairing damaged clothing so that the holes and tears in the cloth were imperceptible. "Invisible mending," she writes, "an extremely delicate and meticulous kind of darning, the mending of moth holes and cigarette burns, is exactly like the skill I have tried to develop as a writer and historian" (1984:381). Significantly, Marcus notes that it is the *invisibility* of the stitches that marks their cultural value: "Invisible mending is delicate, necessary, skilled labor, mending and preserving the fabric of society. The measure of a woman's skill is the degree to which the work *can't* be seen" (1984:388, emphasis mine).

The invisibility of the stitches parallels the way that The Ribbon event was organized. On the surface, both are expressions of the desire to avoid disruption and transgression. The Washington, D.C., ceremony was characterized by the "invisible" work of women, when invisibility is marked by a nonconfrontational approach, using a medium traditionally associated with women. When contrasted with the stiff cardboard placards on sticks often carried by protesters or the heavy metal chains that peace activists sometimes use to link themselves to gates and edifices, the medium for The Ribbon was soft, malleable, and stereotypically feminine. Interestingly, it was one of the few male members of The Ribbon board of directors who took on the task of responding to the hate mail received by the project, a job that necessitated dealing with a more confrontational style of interaction. Merritt repeatedly described The Ribbon as "a *gentle reminder* [rather than a "strong protest" or a "bold statement"] to the nation that we love the earth and all its people" (1985b:11, emphasis mine). Denver organizers such as Mary Frances Jaster even objected to the use of the word *demonstration* to describe The Ribbon. In her letter to the Internal Revenue Service, which was responsible for awarding tax-exempt status to the project, she wrote:

> You have asked whether these sew-ins are "demonstrations against nuclear war." Certainly, the gatherings are intended to express a horror of nuclear war. In addition, however, the gatherings, like all our activities, are intended to help ourselves and others come to terms with our fears of nuclear war and to translate those fears into an affirmation of life and all that we cherish. We dislike the term "demonstration" because it connotes confrontation and violence. Our gatherings are intended to be non-confrontational, non-violent, quiet and prayerful. (July 13, 1984)

In negotiating permits for the ceremony and applying for nonprofit status, the organizers articulated their desire to "keep the gathering quiet, prayerful and contemplative," promising that The Ribbon would "encircle the outer perimeter of the Pentagon grounds" and "not touch the building itself," and that the ceremony would not "block ingress and egress to the Pentagon" (Ribbon National Headquarters to the Internal Revenue Service, July 13, 1984). From the beginning, the Denver organizers decided to strictly adhere to all legal statutes pertaining to public demonstrations; they discouraged any form of civil disobedience.

One Denver organizer, Alice Coleman, contrasted The Ribbon to other peace demonstrations, noting, "When you demonstrate, it's usually a form, almost, of fighting, and this was such a loving expression. It was demonstrating without hostility. You were making a statement, but there was this love." Many aspects of the project design were intended to encourage the participation of people who did not consider themselves political activists, particularly women who might have been wary of a more militant approach. Ribbon board member Jean Cronin commented:

> What I recognized was that it allowed a great many people to take a stand, not feel threatened—I keep saying that over and over because I think it's important. It was nonthreatening because it was peaceful, nonviolent. It was standing up there displaying the things that were of greatest value to the participants.... Now when you tap that, you have, I think, tapped something. And we just simply asked people to put this down, to try and represent it in some way, and to do this in a totally nonviolent, nonaggressive way. This allowed people to do things that they would never, ever do in another situation. Like, they would probably never be able to walk a picket

line; they would probably never be able to go in a more politicized march of any kind.

Indeed, Mary Frances Jaster noted that on the day of the ceremony the singer Pete Seeger, one of the few "celebrities" who asked to participate in the project, declared it was the cleanest ("a group that picked up its own trash") and least disruptive protest he had ever witnessed.

On an individual level, those who came to The Ribbon with previous experience in needlework often learned their skills through generations of women who were "invisible" because they were not recognized as legitimate artists by others or by themselves. When Ribbon panels started arriving at the national office, Alice Coleman was amazed at the beauty and the quality of many of the panels: "I've always thought that artists were a small cluster of people. I found out that we've got thousands of artists in this country who are changing diapers and washing dishes, and they *are* artists!" Patricia Mainardi, an artist and art critic, notes that while needlework is one arena in which women have traditionally had control over the display and evaluation of their work, this autonomy may be due, in large part, to their invisibility in the eyes of the male-controlled art world: "Women quilt-makers enjoyed this freedom only because their work was not even considered art, and so they were exempt from the harassment experienced by most women artists" (1973:22).

In showing Ribbon panels to others, I have noticed that women, in particular, seem to be drawn to them as if they were decoding the panels on the basis of their own life experiences (cf. Radner, 1993; Radner and Lanser, 1987). Mainardi calls quilting, and I would extend this to needlework more generally, a "secret language of women" in which they are able to express their own convictions on a wide variety of subjects in a language that is, for the most part, comprehensible only to other women (1973:19). Moreover, sewing has long served as a medium for women's political discussion and statement. For example, Susan B. Anthony's first talk on equal rights for women occurred at a quilting bee in Cleveland (Mainardi, 1973:21), and earlier Sarah Grimké advised women to embroider antislavery slogans and images on domestic articles, urging, "May the point of our needles prick the slave-owner's conscience" (Hedges, 1980:17–18). More recent examples include midwestern quilters who expressed their support for the Populist crusade in a Women's Progressive Farm Association signature quilt of 1936–37 (Benson and Olsen, 1987:42), and there have been several peace quilts made in the last decade by the Boise Peace Quilt Project (Benson and Olsen, 1987:42, 53).[12] Some Ribbon panel makers similarly thought about their stitchery as encoded political statement, as was exemplified by one participant, who described

The Ribbon as "women using their traditional culture to challenge the Pentagon" (questionnaire response).[13]

And in another, more obvious way some of The Ribbon panels contain a "secret language." Through interviews with panel makers I discovered that many of them sewed into their work personal initials or symbolic images that only they can decipher—perhaps a way of leaving their mark on a historically invisible medium.[14] Mary Frances Jaster, for example, told me that a tiny sandcastle she embroidered on her panel was a symbol for her husband, one that developed during a religious retreat they shared together two years earlier. Similarly, Justine Merritt embroidered the name "Caspar" on one of her "name panels," a reference to Caspar Weinberger, the secretary of defense during the Reagan presidency. Lost in a sea of multicolored names, it is difficult to see. However, Merritt informed me with a chuckle that Weinberger's was the only name she outlined in red.

When other outlets seemed closed to them, needleworkers have sometimes used their sewing as a means of dealing with feelings of powerlessness, loss, or fear. In Chile women who made *arpilleras,* burlap-backed scenes depicting daily life under the Pinochet military regime, said that their needlework helped them in coping with and decrying their oppressive situation (Agosin, 1987). One *arpillerista* whose son was arrested by the military police and "disappeared" in 1974 commented: " 'I started to make *arpilleras* based on my grief and my anguish. It was a way we found of alleviating our pain because we could tell our story and at the same time denounce what happened to us' " (Agosin, 1987:15). The ability to work out anxiety onto cloth provided Ribbon participants a mechanism well suited to formulating a response to possible nuclear disaster. In her poem "Pieces to Peace" Merritt describes "the quilter's careful stitches holding her aching heart together after the evening's late news" (1985b:1). Mary Frances Jaster described the process of making her panel as a way of confronting her despair and reaffirming her ability to take action in what otherwise seemed a hopeless situation: "For me, it was mostly a sign of hope. I would see articles, or I would see movies about nuclear destruction or hear about more funding that's going into nuclear arms and feel somewhat discouraged and say: Is this ever going to end? Is there really going to be a nuclear war? And I think by sewing, actually making my Ribbon piece, and praying along with it, it continued to feed that hope that I have and the optimism that we can make a difference, that we can—that we can do something to prevent it."

Each of these aspects—the "gentle" staging of the Washington ceremony, women materializing beliefs, attitudes, and values in a medium few have considered "serious art," sewing their secret language, working through unvalidated hopes and fears with needle and thread—suggest that The

Ribbon is in part a work of invisible mending. But there is another, more crucial aspect of Marcus's metaphor that applies to The Ribbon. Her mother and aunt worked diligently not just to make their stitches invisible. They also were concerned with repair, salvaging the wholeness and integrity of the garment. Noting that in feminist scholarship "preserving the fabric of history is the same job as mending the family's jackets and sweaters" (1984:281), Marcus contends that as a feminist scholar she wants to "weave women's lives and works back into the fabric of culture, as if they had never been rent. It sometimes seems as if we are like Penelope, weaving by day and undoing our work by night, though it is others who seem bent on undoing what we weave. Penelope's shuttle, my mother's needle, and my pen are implements of order. They speak . . . not of destruction and war but of the preservation of culture" (1984:281). Preservation and restoration are also favorite metaphors for Merritt, who has described The Ribbon as "a lovely binding cloth to tie up a nation's wounds." And for other participants making a panel "meant a way of putting on fabric my feelings about preserving the earth and preventing nuclear destruction" (questionnaire response). For many panel makers a focus on protection and preservation, rather than destruction, attracted them to The Ribbon. One participant filled her panel with appliqués of large, open umbrellas, all sheltering the earth. Similarly, when asked why she became involved in the project, another panel maker responded: "I like The Ribbon emphasis on what we want to save" (questionnaire response).

Motifs expressing a concern for wholeness and relatedness are among the most plentiful in The Ribbon.[15] On a panel made in South Dakota are John Muir's words: "When we tug at a single thing in nature, we find it attached to the rest of the world." Ribbon panels depicting the interrelationship between nature and humanity, between peoples of different races and ethnicities, and between the personal and the political suggest that many participants were concerned with recovering that which they felt the dominant culture has wrongfully estranged. In writing about feminist perspectives on holism, theologian Penelope Washbourn suggests that "the feminist revolution is at its most fundamental a revolution that will involve the whole social fabric and our view of the human organism and its place within the fuller social order. . . . To be able to see the universe as a community of inter-related process is one of the most essential of modern tasks" (1981:102). Washbourn contends that particularly in patriarchal societies, women may be sensitive to the need for wholeness and integration, having been so largely alienated by androcentric modes of thought and order. Ribbon panels that focus on interrelationship suggest that it is the very notion of separation and individuation of oneself from the "other" that makes it possible to wage war, hence many panel makers accentuated the ways in which all things are connected.[16] With its interwoven threads, seams, and piecing, needlework lends itself to the expression of relationship. As one contemporary artist stated, "For women, the meaning of sewing and knotting is 'connecting'—connecting the parts of one's life, and connecting to other women—creating a sense of community and wholeness" (H. Hammond, 1977:67). The shared characteristics of peace-making and piecing were recognized by many participants, with variations of this wordplay appearing in countless slogans on Ribbon panels. In a poem that one participant wrote about the August 4, 1985, ceremony, women are characterized as both the "peacemakers" and the "piecemakers":

> The women
> Together
> Peacemakers
> Peacekeepers
>   Piecers of cloth
> Pieces one on the other
> Women together, who have picked up the pieces of a life
> At home
>   On the battlefield
>   Of a son, a husband, a father
> Piecing together lives without them
> Piecing together the words said so long ago
> Piecing them together so memories can remain.
>
> (Dougherty, n.d.)

Another way in which women panel makers attempted to materialize their concern for wholeness and relatedness is the use of a technique called "femmage," a term coined by the artist Miriam Schapiro, who has used needlework as a basis for her art (Meyer and Schapiro, 1978).[17] Contending that one important step in restoring recognition to women's art is the development of a terminology of its own, Meyer and Schapiro define femmage as various types of collage "practiced by women using traditional women's techniques to achieve their art—sewing, hooking, cutting, appliquéing, cooking and the like—activities also engaged in by men but assigned in history to women" (1978:67). They note that the creative work of women who have practiced femmage for centuries with fabric, needlework, paper, and, more recently, photographs was only recognized as art within the fine art world after male artists such as Picasso and Braque began using collage techniques in the early 1900s (1978:67). More than just randomly using readily available materials, femmage implies a sense of intentionality, the purposeful repositioning and recontextualizing of personal symbols in a manner that is particularly meaningful for the artist. Because it involves combining bits and pieces of materials that signify specific moments and relationships in the life of the creator, the practice of femmage is imbued with personal value and emotion.[18]

In Ribbon panels femmage manifests itself as a kind of collage that combines fabrics representative of bits and pieces of women's lives—such as lace from a wedding dress, yarn from a friend's favorite sweater, flannel from a baby's nightgown—allowing the artist to depict connections between life experiences in a graphic and tactile way.[19] For example, Ribbon participant Ariadne Wright's fond memories of her Polish stepmother, who died in 1980, prompted her to make a doll dressed in traditional Polish costume as the centerpiece of her panel (fig. 16.3). Her stepmother taught her to do needlework as a child, and after her death, Wright inherited her sewing basket and her collection of fabric. From these treasures, imbued with meaning, she crafted the elements of her Ribbon panel. The large crochet doily, which Wright made as a teenager when she lived with her stepmother in the Dominican Republic, reminds her of the happy times they spent together there. The smaller crochet doilies, sequins, yarn for the doll's hair, buttons for her eyes, ribbon, and bits of lace all came out of her stepmother's sewing basket. These are interspersed with scraps from the bridesmaids' dresses Wright made for her eldest daughter's wedding (the satin squares underneath the small snowflakes), green fabric she bought in Mexico sometime during the ten years she lived there (Christmas tree), and assorted materials from clothing she made in the past (doll's costume). Only the padding for the panel was newly purchased. In reflecting on her use of remnants, she noted: "Everything has a meaning from the past." Panel makers often used private symbols to convey a personal and more universal message simultaneously. Wright's Polish doll was one section of a triptych of panels created with two other Austin quilters, Mary K. Beard and Anne Long. Mary Beard made a Japanese doll and Anne Long designed an African doll so that the triptych would portray three different racial groups and geographic regions. On the backs of their panels they wrote: "The three dolls and their symbols represent the human race by three continents. We cannot bear to think of the extinction of one culture or continent, let alone the whole earth."

On a grand scale the entire Ribbon might be perceived as an exercise in femmage, a material tribute to the diversity and distinctive nature of women's values and aesthetics, particularly when juxtaposed with the Pentagon, a quintessentially male symbol of military might. One participant described The Ribbon as the delineation of "the incredible differ-

Figure 16.3. "Polish Doll," Ariadne Wright, Austin, Tex. (Photo by Linda Pershing)

ences between men's and women's worlds, thoughts and means of action" (questionnaire response).

Moving from Invisible Mending to Drawnwork: Accentuating Differences

Marcus's invisible mending metaphor is a useful interpretive device for understanding various aspects of The Ribbon. However, because the goal of invisible mending is to return the damaged garment to its original state, the metaphor is essentially restorative. It suggests a type of preservation that is self-effacing; invisible mending calls as little attention as possible to the stitches or to the women who skillfully executed them. Marcus notes that what is important is the repaired sweater, once again functional because the damage to the cloth—the holes and cigarette burns—cannot be detected. But, whereas both Marcus's invisible-mending metaphor and The Ribbon project emphasize restoration—restoring public acknowledgment of women's caretaking skills and contributions to society—the concept of The Ribbon differs from invisible mending in that it relies not only on invisible restoration but also on the disclosure of existing flaws, metaphorically accentuating what needs to be done to repair the damage. The technique of invisible mending repairs but does not significantly alter the garment, nor does it suggest ways in which the garment might be constructed differently. When this metaphor is applied to The Ribbon, it limits the project to an attempt to mend the social fabric—to consider alternatives to the nuclear arms race—without public criticism of the weaknesses and omissions of existing political and military policy.

But the organizers of The Ribbon had more in mind, although this was rarely an explicit part of the public presentation of the project. By encircling the Pentagon, an unmistakable symbol of national militarism, panel makers were commenting on the continuing escalation of nuclear weaponry that many feared would lead to the destruction of all they cherished. Despite the "nonconfrontational" way in which it was presented, social and political critique is implicit in The Ribbon in its encirclement of a primary masculinist military symbol. Lengths of splendidly decorated fabric upstaged the stone facade of the Pentagon, a flowing symbol of life and hope wrapped around what many consider a massive symbol of death and destruction. When examined in the context of a society that seldom values or encourages women's self-expression in the public arena, The Ribbon represents the voices of those who are often trivialized or ignored by legislators and policymakers. With their appliquéd diapers and embroidered flower gardens panel makers suggested that the details of their personal lives—details overlooked by "the powers that be"—were what led them to participate in a public demonstration and that these details were, in fact, the essence of their protest. Barbara Baer, a panel maker from California, commented:

> When I think of this Ribbon and the many more pieces that will be sewn to it, wrapped around the Pentagon, I think of all the details, the wonderful things people love—whether they put up their own food or make their own clothes or they walk somewhere or take their kids to play sports. And we hope that these people, mostly men, who work with such abstract weapons of destruction, will take a look at the particulars that we've chosen to paint and to sew onto these ribbons, just take a look. It's not canned. It's not laser-beamed. It's all done by hand, and I hope they take a look. (Hirschfield, 1985)

Given the element of heightened contrast so central to The Ribbon—lengths of flowing fabric encircling an immovable military complex—I suggest that another, more appropriate needlework metaphor can be found in a sewing technique called drawnwork, or *deshilado* (literally translated from Spanish as "dethreaded") as it is known in Mexican-American communities. Often using linen or high-quality cotton, the needleworker carefully counts and removes threads from a piece of cloth, creating a sort of negative space (Jasper, 1987). This hole is then transformed when new threads are inserted with a needle and the remaining threads are delicately bound or sewn together to make a new, often elaborate pattern. The aesthetic focus of the garment shifts to the way in which the fabric is fancifully rewoven (fig. 16.4). In her description of *deshilado*, folklorist Pat Jasper notes: "*Deshilado* is typically applied to the edges and trim of napkins, tablecloths, sheets, pillowcases, undergarments and other domestic linens, *thereby elevating the status of these everyday objects through the artful attention paid them*" (1987:3, emphasis mine). The mundane elements of women's experiences are accentuated. Extremely difficult work, drawnwork testifies to the unique skills and cultural competence of women who can do it. "The mathematical complexity of the 'count and draw' technique demands good memory, sharp eyesight, and exceptional dexterity" (Jasper, 1987:3). The maker of one piece echoed this by naming her design "Haz me sí puedes, y si no, déjame para las mujeres," or "Make me if you can, and if you can't, leave me for the women" (fig. 16.5).

In relation to The Ribbon, the drawnwork technique metaphorically emphasizes the critical aspects of reworking cloth that invisible mending neglects. Much like the practice of removal and innovative alteration that occurs in drawnwork, in The Ribbon women's fabric arts were used to critique existing U.S. military policies and to emphasize those values that participants believed had been slighted by governmental leaders. Damage and potential destruction—arms stockpiling and the threat of nuclear obliteration—were not simply accepted by participants as unavoidable. The strain on the social fabric that has been caused by the arms race, including the escalation of international tension during the Reagan years, spiraling military expenditures and budgetary deficits, and the fear of nuclear conflict and accidents, was not just "invisibly mended" by women's collusion. Rather, The Ribbon publicly accentuated the destructive potential of nuclear weaponry by weaving around the symbolic center of U.S. militarism with an abundance of personal imagery depicting those things that policymakers too often overlook in their military planning. Women's historical familiarity with needlework provided Ribbon participants an opportunity to express an alternative vision or a diversity of visions about the value and meaning of life. One panel maker noted: "The Ribbon makes a statement (especially a statement by women) that there are people who believe that war and armed conflict, as we have known it, are no longer feasible as a way to settle disputes between nations" (questionnaire response). Another participant described The Ribbon as "a symbolic way to let 'the powers-that-be' know that we want them to stop endangering our existence with their 'war-game' mentality. It especially appeals to women and lets them have their say in their own unique way" (questionnaire response). By wrapping the Pentagon with panels that portrayed such things as beloved pets, individual loved ones, musical notes, and favorite foods, panel makers sought to heighten the personal and the everyday and link it to the political. Using drawnwork rather than invisible mending,

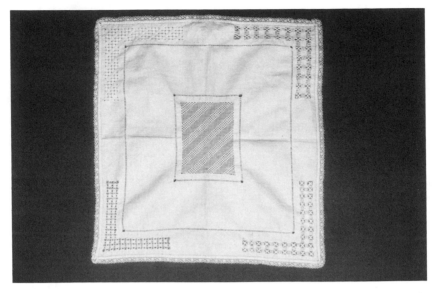

Figure 16.4. *Deshilado* sampler, Florentina Posada, San Juan, Tex., 1958. (Photo by Linda Pershing, courtesy of Texas Folklife Resources)

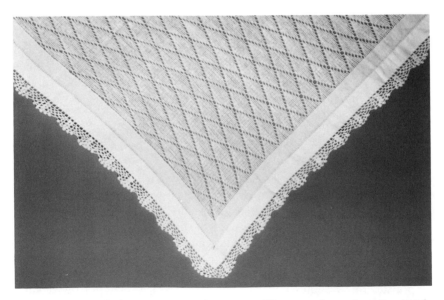

Figure 16.5. Detail of "Haz me sí puedes, y si no, déjame para las mujeres," or "Make me if you can, and if you can't, leave me for the women." Florentina Posada, San Juan, Tex., 1926. (Photo by Linda Pershing, courtesy of Texas Folklife Resources)

Ribbon participants responded to the torn social fabric as an opportunity to suggest the possibility of creative reconstruction.

Like *deshilado,* The Ribbon plays on symbolic inversions. In our everyday experience, ribbon commonly is used by women in service of something else, not as an end in itself. In unwrapping a gift, for example, we customarily toss it aside. Who would be more interested in the bow than what's inside the gift box? But in The Ribbon that which the dominant culture regards as unimportant—the way the damaged cloth is rewoven—is accentuated, and it is the stitching itself, the reconceptualization of society with women's expression about their everyday lives, that catches our attention. Here it is the creative manipulation of conventions and an intimate knowledge of fabrics—the result of years of careful attention to worn elbows and missing buttons—that ensures skillful mending. The vitality and uniqueness of the sewing is particularly striking when traditional forms of fabric art that are found abundantly in The Ribbon, such as quilting, appliqué, and embroidery, are transformed by new approaches, new messages, new media. The members of the Yellowstone Valley Quilters' Guild of Billings, Montana, for example, used the traditional pattern known as World without End to merge their message and their medium of expression (fig. 16.6).[20] This reworking and recontextualizing of women's traditional arts was a processual exercise. Ribbon participants indicated that it was the process of struggling with the terrifying prospects of nuclear annihilation by creating something beautiful in a medium familiar to them, the working out of tension onto fabric by individuals and collective groups of women, that they valued the most.[21]

Conclusion

Women's traditional needlework, weaving, and sewing recently have provided feminist authors a wealth of metaphorical imagery that they have used in their analyses of women's cultural practices. When feminist scholars use needlework metaphors, they often focus on the processes they represent, including the invisibility of women's culture, needlework as a secret language of women, needlework as a means of expressing emotion and overcoming feelings of powerlessness, and the way needlework lends itself to images of relationship, wholeness, and relatedness. These are all valuable metaphorical images frequently characteristic of women's experiences, and they are tools that can further our understanding of The Ribbon. In Marcus's invisible-mending metaphor, processual concerns are accentuated by paying attention to *how* the holes are mended, not just that they are. Similarly, in The Ribbon it is the *how*—the sewing, participation, awareness, personal growth, and opportunity for "safe"

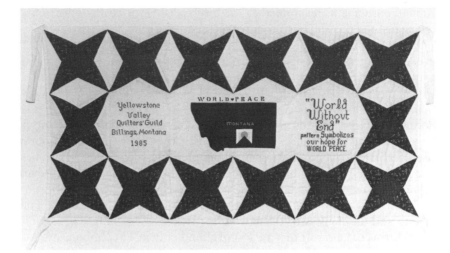

Figure 16.6. Detail of "World without End." The quilters' home state is depicted with pride in the center of the panel. (Photo by Linda Pershing)

social protest—that often was valued more than the potential results of the Washington, D.C., ceremony.

Most feminist needlework metaphors are based on quilting. However, there is a need to examine the whole variety of other needle art techniques as potential metaphors for women's experience, much as Marcus has done with invisible mending. These metaphors, arising directly from women's own artistic practices, can be useful in interpreting women's creative expressions such as The Ribbon. When viewed as a work of invisible mending, The Ribbon invokes the notions of salvaging, supplementing, and restoring that were important characteristics of the project. Other types of needlework, such as *deshilado,* better address the metaphorical *reworking* of existing structure. Drawnwork offers a metaphor suggesting women's evaluation, removal, or alteration of the status quo, and it implies that these processes and the possibilities they conjure for makers can be highly valued by women. Because of its potential for social critique, The Ribbon is much like drawnwork, calling attention to the flaws and accenting what is missing from the considerations of nuclear strategists and policymakers. It is a call for those in power to "cease to pose and bluff" and to "listen to women,"[22] for they may offer other voices and distinctive ways of redesigning the garment. Many panel makers used the particulars of their lives—specific loved ones, everyday events, artistic pleasures—to alert government officials to the reasons nuclear war must be avoided. "I dream of giving birth to a child who will ask, 'Mother, what was war?'" reads one panel made by women in Minnesota who envision a future in which parents do not have to wonder if there will be a next generation. Like drawnwork, in the process of making Ribbon panels women have metaphorically taken the damaged garment of U.S. nuclear arms policy and attempted to rework it, at times including the existing social fabric in their designs but also weaving other new and elaborate patterns not yet actualized.

Panel makers valued the "doing," the process of participation in The Ribbon and the opportunities for social commentary that participation provided for each individual. It wasn't just that the project worked, the Pentagon was encircled, or that the garment was repaired, with an emphasis solely on the results. What was important was *how* it was done, the careful reweaving of the damage, and the lives that were changed as a result. As an example, Justine Merritt likes to tell the story of how for Mary Anne DeVoe, a single parent whose mother had recently died, The Ribbon meant coming to terms with the past and regaining hope for the future. After her mother's death, Mary Anne discovered a picture of a farmhouse done in needlepoint by her mother. She also found, tucked away in her mother's belongings, a bright satin doily that her grandmother made years ago. Mary Anne stitched them both onto a piece of dark green fabric, the farmhouse at the bottom left corner, and the doily, fashioned into a sun, at the upper right. Between them she embroidered a representation of her own garden. Her sixteen-year-old daughter, named Strawberry, embroidered her namesake in the garden. Recalling the panel, Merritt commented: "And it is a work of heart.[23] Mary Anne has processed some of the grief of her mother's loss, some of her memory of her grandmother, some of her delight in her child, all on fabric 18 by 36 inches. And, as a result, she became a resource person for The Ribbon in her state. Lives have been changed."

Notes

My thanks to Ribbon panel makers and organizers Justine Merritt, Mary K. Beard, Alice Coleman, Jean Cronin, Ramona Elizalde, Marie Grosso, Pat Hutchinson, Mary Frances Jaster, Anne Long, Lucile Miller, Mary Jo Peterson, and Ariadne Wright. My friends and colleagues Kathy Wheeler Epstein, Elizabeth Warnock Fernea, Barbara Harlow, Gabriella Miller, Leslie Prosterman, Suzanne Seriff, Kay Turner, and M. Jane Young contributed greatly to the content and revision of this essay.

1. The project and the sum of all the individual panels were collectively called "The Ribbon" or "The Peace Ribbon." Individual segments or panels were, for the most part, 36 inches long by 18 inches high.

2. See Chicago (1977) and Chicago and Hill (1980) for a description of "The Dinner Party," a multimedia art exhibit created in the late 1970s. Chicago commented that it is "a work which uses women's traditional needle skills to record and celebrate women's lives and achievements" (Chicago and Hill, 1980:265).

3. Of the sixty state coordinators for The Ribbon (some states had teams of two), three were men (*Ribbon Tabloid,* 2–3). Concerned about including all who share her desire to work for peace, Merritt resisted the idea that The Ribbon was a women's project. She commented to the press, for example, "There are mostly women in this, but it's not a women's thing. We have two men on our board" (Kernan, 1984:B15). However, the medium suggested that participation would come predominately from women, as did an early flier from The Ribbon National Headquarters, which stated, "The Ribbon provides an opportunity for busy housewives, mothers, career women, and isolated farm and ranch people to be a part of the Peace Movement and share in the creation of The Ribbon" (undated flier).

4. Sociologists Gabriella Miller and Carol Cockrell at Texas Woman's University conducted two surveys of participants in 1985–86. Preliminary results are cited in Willcox (1985:18). Of the approximately 450 respondents to the first questionnaire, 98 percent were female. The majority were white, college educated, described themselves as more often "liberal" than "conservative," and ranged in age from fourteen to eighty-five.

5. Miller and Cockrell did not report on the economic status of questionnaire respondents. However, The Ribbon became largely the work of middle-class women. This occurred in part because of the way in which project information was passed on informally from friend to friend and through family networks, beginning with a small group consisting mostly of white, middle-class women. Failure to address the economic ramifications of the nuclear arms race during The Ribbon recruitment effort may also have limited the project's appeal to the lower-income population. Certainly there were exceptions, both on the individual and community levels. In Ignacio, Colorado, for example, an entire community of Native American and Hispanic women, many of whom were living below the poverty level, enthusiastically involved themselves in the project. Nonetheless, women of color, who may have perceived The Ribbon (and the entire anti-nuclear movement) as yet another social program controlled by white elites, and working-class or poor women, who lacked the time or financial resources to get involved and heard very little from Ribbon organizers about how funds diverted from the nuclear arms race could be better used in domestic social programs, did not comprise the bulk of Ribbon participants.

6. It should be noted that these reflections by participants were in hindsight, some months after the event. Of those I interviewed, Justine Merritt expressed the strongest feeling that The Ribbon might serve as a consciousness-raising device for legislators, but that this would take effect gradually through constituency pressure. During an April 24, 1986, presentation at the Ecumenical Center of St.

John's University in Collegeville, Minnesota, Merritt said of The Ribbon's impact, "I believe we have already changed history."

7. Mary Jo Peterson, a member of the board and the treasurer for The Ribbon beginning in October 1984, commented that "Reagan sort of blew off the whole thing. We could see him flying over us at the end of the day, when it was kind of disbanding. We later heard that he said that he didn't notice anything from the helicopter."

8. The Denver National Office for The Ribbon was closed by its founders, and the board was officially dissolved on October 24, 1986. Ribbon panels were dispersed to various museums and to state coordinators. Interestingly, however, The Ribbon continues to be used at exhibits and demonstrations, and collections of panels have appeared at numerous subsequent peace gatherings and other events. Merritt took panels with her to Geneva in October 1985 when representatives of Women for a Meaningful Summit attempted to meet with President Reagan and General Secretary Mikhail Gorbachev, and Ribbon panels were used in August 1986 at a peace vigil at the Nevada nuclear test site. Ribbon activities have taken place in various other countries, including Australia, Ireland, Japan, Kenya, the Netherlands, New Zealand, South Africa, Sweden, and the USSR.

9. See Limón and Young (1986:451) and Bronner (1982) for a more accurate account of the history of material culture studies.

10. To date there has been little investigation of the ways in which quilting can allow women to express contestation of social roles or to define themselves over and against the dominant culture. See Pershing (1993) for discussion of a quilting project in which women used their needlework to express critical commentary about pervasive social norms.

11. There have been some studies of various fabric arts, aside from quilting, both in the United States and abroad, but given the pervasive role of textiles in a wide variety of cultures around the world, much work remains to be done. See, for example, Sherzer and Sherzer (1976) and Salvador (1978) for analyses of Kuna needlework; Dewhurst, MacDowell, and MacDowell (1979) and Ferrero, Hedges, and Silber (1987) for the historical development of women's needle arts in the United States; Johnson (1985) for rag rug weaving; McDonald (1990) for the use of funeral ribbons by African American women in North Carolina; Yocom (1993) for knitting and doll clothes created by women in Maine; Hammond (1986) for piecework and appliqué textiles of Polynesia; Dewhurst (1988) for pleiku jackets from the Vietnam War; Agosin (1977) and Brett (1986) for Chilean *arpilleras;* Peterson (1988) for Hmong story cloth; and Weiner and Schneider (1989) for cross-cultural analysis of the role of fabric and the fabric arts in a number of widely differing societies.

12. The National Peace Quilt was the ninth made by the Boise Peace Project and their first overt attempt to influence policymakers. Benson and Olsen describe it as follows: "Fifty squares, each designed by children from one of the fifty states, surround a central panel which reads: 'REST beneath the warmth and weight of our hopes for a future for our children/ DREAM a vision of the world at peace/ ACT to give the vision life." The words on the panel are directed to the one

hundred United States senators who each were asked to spend one night sleeping beneath the quilt. The names of those who did so were embroidered below the blocks from their home states; the senators also were invited to record the dreams and thoughts stirred by contact with the quilt (1987:53).

13. This and all subsequent statements cited as "questionnaire response" are written responses to survey questions that are a part of research conducted by Gabriella Miller and Carol Cockrell (see note 5).

14. It is worth noting that women are not the only artists who sometimes secretly leave their mark on their expressive forms. See, for example, Hunt (1985:139) for mention of a male stone carver doing likewise at the Washington Cathedral. In this instance, the stone carver's encoded message might also be interpreted as an expression of resistance to contemporary social norms or events.

15. Complete records were not kept on the more than twenty-five thousand Ribbon panels. I base this assertion on my own observations, having seen about two thousand of them.

16. Carol Gilligan's (1982) suggestion that for many women moral decision-making is articulated through a distinct ethics of care based on interrelationship, likened to the imagery of the web, is apropros here. For further discussion of the imagery of women and webs, weaving, and spinning, see Daly (1978), Daly and Caputi (1987), and Weigle (1982).

17. Folklorist Kay Turner (1983a and 1983b) describes femmage as "the process of collecting and creatively assembling old or seemingly disparate elements into a functional, integrated whole" (1983a:7) and discusses women's home altar making in terms of this aesthetic. José Limón (1983) extends the scope of the concept of femmage to the sphere of verbal lore with the example of a Mexican-American women's narrative, and Barbara Babcock applies the concept to styles of discourse (1987:393).

18. Claude Lévi-Strauss uses the concept of bricolage to describe the developmental processes of mythical thought and expression (1966:16–36). His notion of bricolage is a derivative of the French term *bricoleur*, which he describes as someone generally handy but somewhat less trustworthy or respected than a craftsman (1966:16–17). In contrast, Meyer and Schapiro trace the origins of their notion of femmage to the vocabulary of the French art world; it is a feminist adaptation of techniques that traditionally have been called collage, assemblage, découpage, or photomontage (1978:66). For Lévi-Strauss, bricolage involves creating something from "whatever is at hand," combining seemingly unrelated bits and pieces "of a heterogeneous repertoire, which, even if extensive, is nevertheless limited" (1966:17). While this and the notion of femmage share the sense of recombining already existing materials that have had other uses in the past, Lévi-Strauss's concept does not articulate the important way in which artists may attribute personal meaning and sentiment to their materials, attempting to incorporate symbolic representations and images of their own lives into their work—an element that is central to Meyer and Schapiro's description of femmage. He contends, for example, that the bricoleur's "set of tools and materials . . . is always finite and is also heterogeneous because what it contains bears no relation to the

current project, or indeed to any particular project" (1966:17), while Meyer and Schapiro emphasize that the elements of femmage are selected precisely because of their relational meaning in the mind of the artist. They note, for example, that "collected, saved and combined materials represented for . . . women acts of pride, desperation and necessity. Spiritual survival depended on the harboring of memories. Each cherished scrap of percale, muslin or chintz, each bead, each letter, each photograph, was a reminder of its place in a woman's life" (1978:68). For a rather random list of criteria that the authors suggest can be used to determine whether a work can be called femmage, see Meyer and Schapiro (1978:69).

19. Elaine Showalter cites a wonderful example of needlework femmage in "The Patchwork Quilt," an anonymous essay by a factory girl, printed in the *Lowell Offering* in 1845. Showalter reports: "To the 'uninterested observer,' the narrator declares, it looks like a 'miscellaneous collection of odd bits and ends,' but to me 'it is a precious reliquary of past treasure.' The quilt's pieces, taken from the writer's childhood calico gowns, her dancing school dress, her fashionable young ladies' gowns, her mother's mourning dress, her brother's vest, are an album of the female life cycle from birth to death" (1986:230).

20. Elaine Reynolds of Ithaca, New York, also used the World without End pattern on her panel for much the same reason, noting that it was a symbol that "expresses my hope."

21. In her research on the Kuna, Mari Lyn Salvador (1978) found a similar dynamic at work in the ways that the molas made by the women reflect a cultural struggle between traditional Kuna values and the integration of outside Euro-American influences.

22. I found these words on Ribbon panels signed by Darbi Shakira Freeman and "Mae" respectively. Both panels are now in The Ribbon Archives at the Blagg-Huey Library of Texas Woman's University, Denton.

23. "A work of heart" is a turn of phrase that Merritt loves to use to describe The Ribbon.

References Cited

Agosin, Marjorie. 1987. *Scraps of Life: Chilean Arpilleras*. Translated by Cola Franzen. Trenton, N.J.: Red Sea Press.

Babcock, Barbara A. 1987. "Taking Liberties, Writing from the Margins, and Doing It with a Difference." *Journal of American Folklore* 100 (398): 390–411.

Bauman, Richard. 1975. "Verbal Art as Performance." *American Anthropologist* 77:290–312.

———. 1986. *Story, Performance, and Event: Contextual Studies of Oral Narrative.* Cambridge: Cambridge University Press.

Benson, Jane, and Nancy Olsen. 1987. *The Power of Cloth: Political Quilts 1845–1986.* Catalogue produced in conjunction with an exhibit by the same name at the Euphrat Gallery, De Anza College, Cupertino, California, Mar. 3 to Apr. 19.

Bergen, Fanny D. 1892. "Quilt Patterns." *Journal of American Folklore* 5 (16): 69.

Brett, Guy. 1986. *Through Our Own Eyes: Popular Art and Modern History.* London: GMP Publishers.

Bronner, Simon J. 1982. "The Hidden Past of Material Culture Studies in American Folkloristics." *New York Folklore* 8:1–10.

———. 1983. " 'Visible Proofs': Material Culture Study in American Folkloristics." *American Quarterly* 35:316–38.

———. 1986. *Grasping Things: Folk Material Culture and Mass Society in America.* Lexington: University Press of Kentucky.

Chicago, Judy. 1977. *Through the Flower: My Struggle as a Woman Artist.* Garden City, N.Y.: Anchor Books.

Chicago, Judy, with Susan Hill. 1980. *Embroidering Our Heritage: The Dinner Party Needlework.* Garden City, N.Y.: Anchor Books.

Clarke, Mary Washington. 1976. *Kentucky Quilts and Their Makers.* Lexington: University of Kentucky Press.

Cooper, Patricia, and Norma Bradley Buferd. 1977. *The Quilters: Women and Domestic Art.* Garden City, N.Y.: Doubleday.

Daley, Chris. 1985. "Local Peace Panel to Perambulate Pentagon." *Mountain Democrat and Placerville Times,* Apr. 24, A–1, A–3.

Daly, Mary. 1978. *Gyn/Ecology: The Metaethics of Radical Feminism.* Boston: Beacon Press.

Daly, Mary, with Jane Caputi. 1987. *Websters' First New Intergalactic Wickedary of the English Language.* Boston: Beacon Press.

Dewhurst, C. Kurt. 1988. "Pleiku Jackets, Tour Jackets, and Working Jackets: 'The Letter Sweaters of War.' " *Journal of American Folklore* 101 (399): 48–52.

Dewhurst, C. Kurt, Betty MacDowell, and Marsha MacDowell. 1979. *Artists in Aprons: Folk Art by American Women.* New York: Dutton.

Dougherty, Elayne. n.d. "A Ribbon around the Still Breathing Earth—August 4, 1985." Unpublished poem in possession of Ribbon Archives, Blagg-Huey Library of Texas Woman's University, Denton, Texas.

Ferrero, Pat, Elaine Hedges, and Julie Silber. 1987. *Hearts and Hands: The Influence of Women and Quilts on American Society.* San Francisco: Quilt Digest Press.

Gayton, A. H. 1945. "Unusual Patchwork Quilt Illustrated." *Journal of American Folklore* 58 (227): 52.

Gilligan, Carol. 1982. *In a Different Voice: Psychological Theory and Women's Development.* Cambridge: Harvard University Press.

Hammond, Harmony. 1977. "Feminist Abstract Art—A Political Viewpoint." *Heresies* 1 (1): 66.

Hammond, Joyce D. 1986. "Polynesian Women and *Tifaifai:* Fabrications of Identity." *Journal of American Folklore* 99 (393): 259–79.

Hedges, Elaine. 1980. "Quilts and Women's Culture." In *In Her Own Image: Women Working in the Arts,* ed. Elaine Hedges and Ingrid Wendt, 13–19. Old Westbury, N.Y.: Feminist Press.

Hirschfield, Barbara. 1985. *The Ribbon.* Videotape. Sonoma County Women's Action for Nuclear Disarmament.

Hunt, Marjorie. 1985. " 'Born into the Stone': Carvers at the Washington Cathedral." *Folklife Annual,* no. 1:120–41.

Ice, Joyce Ann. 1984. "Quilting and the Pattern of Relationships in Community Life." Ph.D. diss., University of Texas at Austin.

Ice, Joyce, and Judith Shulimson. 1979. "Beyond the Domestic: Women's Traditional Arts and the Creation of Community." *Southwest Folklore* 3:37–44.

Jasper, Pat. 1987. "Elpidia de la Cruz." In *Popular Arts/Artes Populares II.* Catalogue produced in conjunction with an exhibit by the same name at the Guadalupe Theatre Gallery, San Antonio, Tex., Nov. 13 to Dec. 23.

Johnson, Geraldine Niva. 1985. *Weaving Rag Rugs: A Women's Craft in Western Maryland.* Knoxville: University of Tennessee Press.

Jones, Michael Owen. 1980. "L.A. Add-ons and Re-dos: Renovation in Folk Art and Architectural Design." In *Perspectives on American Folk Art,* ed. Ian M. G. Quimby and Scott T. Swank, 325–63. New York: W. W. Norton.

Jordan, Rosan A., and F. A. de Caro. 1986. "Women and the Study of Folklore: Review Essay." *Signs* 11 (3): 500–518.

Kernan, Michael. "Ribbon around the Pentagon." *Washington Post,* Sept. 12, B–15.

Lark Books Staff and Marianne Philbin. 1985. *The Ribbon: A Celebration of Life.* Asheville, N.C.: Lark Books.

Lévi-Strauss, Claude. 1966. *The Savage Mind.* London: Weidenfeld and Nicolson.

Limón, José E. 1983. "Legendry, Metafolklore, and Performance: A Mexican-American Example." *Western Folklore* 42:191–208.

Limón, José E., and M. Jane Young. 1986. "Frontiers, Settlements, and Development in Folklore Studies, 1972–1985." *Annual Review of Anthropology* 15:437–60.

Lippard, Lucy. 1983. "Up, Down, and Across: A New Frame for New Quilts." In *The Artist and the Quilt,* ed. Charlotte Robinson, 32–43. New York: Knopf.

McDonald, Mary Anne. 1990. "Symbols from Ribbons: Afro-American Funeral-Ribbon Quilts in Chatham County, North Carolina." In *Arts in Earnest: North Carolina Folklife,* ed. Daniel Patterson and Charles Zug III, 164–78. Durham: Duke University Press.

Mainardi, Patricia. 1973. "Quilts: The Great American Art." *Feminist Art Journal* 2 (1): 18–23.

Marcus, Jane. 1984. "Invisible Mending." In *Between Women,* ed. Carol Ascher, Louise DeSalvo, and Sara Ruddick, 380–95. Boston: Beacon Press.

Merritt, Justine. 1985a. "Introduction." In *The Ribbon: A Celebration of Life,* ed. Lark Books Staff and Marianne Philbin, 11–13. Asheville, N.C.: Lark Books.

———. 1985b. "Pieces to Peace." *Ribbon Tabloid,* Aug. 4, 1.

Meyer, Melissa, and Miriam Schapiro. 1978. "Waste Not Want Not: An Inquiry into What Women Saved and Assembled." *Heresies* 4 (Winter): 66–69.

Morgan, Robin. 1982. "Piecing." In *Depth Perception: New Poems and a Masque.* Garden City, N.Y.: Anchor Press.

Paredes, Américo, and Richard Bauman, eds. 1972. *Toward New Perspectives in Folklore.* Austin: University of Texas Press.

Parker, Rozsika. [1984] 1986. *The Subversive Stitch: Embroidery and the Making of the Feminine.* London: Women's Press.

Parsons, Elsie Clews. 1919. "Folk-Lore of the Cherokee of Robeson County, North Carolina." *Journal of American Folklore* 32 (125): 384–93.

Pershing, Linda. 1990. "The Ribbon around the Pentagon: Women's Traditional Fabric Arts as a Vehicle for Social Critique." Ph.D. diss., University of Texas at Austin.

———. 1993. " 'She Really Wanted to Be Her Own Woman': Scandalous Sunbonnet Sue." In *Feminist Messages: Coding in Women's Folk Culture,* ed. Joan Newlon Radner, 98–125. Urbana: University of Illinois Press.

Peterson, Sally. 1988. "Translating Experience and the Reading of a Story Cloth." *Journal of American Folklore* 101 (399): 6–22.

Piercy, Marge. 1980. "Looking at Quilts." In *In Her Own Image: Women Working in the Arts,* ed. Elaine Hedges and Ingrid Wendt, 35–36. Old Westbury, N.Y.: Feminist Press.

Radner, Joan Newlon, ed. 1993. *Feminist Messages: Coding in Women's Folk Culture.* Urbana: University of Illinois Press.

Radner, Joan N., and Susan S. Lanser. 1987. "The Feminist Voice: Strategies of Coding in Folklore and Literature." *Journal of American Folklore* 100 (398): 412–25.

The Ribbon Tabloid. 1985. Newsletter passed out to participants of The Ribbon Washington, D.C., event.

Roach, Susan. 1985. "The Kinship Quilt: An Ethnographic Semiotic Analysis of a Quilting Bee." In *Women's Folklore, Women's Culture,* ed. Rosan A. Jordan and Susan J. Kalčik, 54–64. Philadelphia: University of Pennsylvania Press.

———. 1986. "The Traditional Quiltmaking of North Louisiana Women: Form, Function, and Meaning." Ph.D. diss., University of Texas at Austin.

Salvador, Mari Lyn. 1978. *Yer Dailege!: Kuna Women's Art.* Albuquerque: Maxwell Museum of Anthropology, University of New Mexico.

Sherzer, Dina, and Joel Sherzer. 1976. "*Mormaknamaloe:* The Cuna Mola." In *Ritual and Symbol in Native Central America,* ed. Philip Young and James Howe, 23–42. University of Oregon Anthropological Papers, no. 9. Portland: University of Oregon.

Showalter, Elaine. 1986. "Piecing and Writing." In *The Poetics of Gender,* ed. Nancy K. Miller, 222–45. New York: Columbia University Press.

Turner, Kay F. 1983a. "Mexican-American Women's Home Altars." *Lady-Unique-Inclination-of-the-Night* 6:71–82.

———. 1983b. "Why We Are So Inclined." *Lady-Unique-Inclination-of-the-Night* 6:4–18.

Turner, Victor W. 1974. *Dramas, Fields, and Metaphors.* Ithaca: Cornell University Press.

Vlach, John Michael. 1978. *The Afro-American Tradition in Decorative Arts.* Cleveland, Ohio: Cleveland Museum of Art.

Walker, Alice. 1973. "Everyday Use." In *Love and Trouble,* ed. Alice Walker, 47–59. New York: Harcourt, Brace, Jovanovich.

Washbourn, Penelope. 1981. "The Dynamics of Female Experience: Process Models and Human Values." In *Feminism and Process Thought: The Harvard Divinity School/Claremont Center for Process Studies Symposium Papers,* ed. Sheila Greeve Davaney, 83–105. Edwin Mellen Press Symposium Series, vol. 6. New York: E. Mellen Press.

Weidlich, Lorre Marie. 1986. "Quilting Transformed: An Anthropological Approach to the Quilt Revival." Ph.D. diss., University of Texas at Austin.

Weigle, Marta. 1982. *Spiders and Spinsters: Women and Mythology.* Albuquerque: University of New Mexico Press.

Weiner, Annette B., and Jane Schneider, eds. 1989. *Cloth and Human Experience.* Washington, D.C.: Smithsonian Institution Press.

Willcox, Don. 1985. "The People." In *The Ribbon: A Celebration of Life,* ed. Lark Books Staff and Marianne Philbin, 17–26. Asheville, N.C.: Lark Books.

Yocom, Margaret R. 1993. " 'Awful Real': Dolls and Development in Rangeley, Maine." In *Feminist Messages: Coding in Women's Folk Culture,* ed. Joan Newlon Radner, 126–54. Urbana: University of Illinois Press.

Politics and Gender: Geraldine Ferraro in the Editorial Cartoons

As the Democratic convention was gearing up in July 1984, there was talk of a female vice-presidential candidate on the ticket. (The Miss America Pageant was also on, but that is another story. Or is it?) On July 11 Geraldine Ferraro was named, and the joke cycle started. Two days later, in his *San Francisco Chronicle* column, Herb Caen noted that the "one-liners so far have been unprintable" (1984). Here's a selection of them:

—The Democrats picked a woman VP candidate because they've never had a woman in the White House.
—Who says they haven't? John Kennedy had hundreds.
—What do Reagan and Mondale have in common? They're both running with a bush.
—No matter how the election turns out, one thing's for sure. There will be a bush in the White House.
—If Mondale gets elected, it'll be Wally and the Beaver in the White House.
—Elect Mondale. Put three boobs in the White House.
—Did you hear Mondale was arrested over the weekend? He was doing 69 in his Ferraro.
—Did you hear Ferraro had to cancel a speaking engagement? Her tongue was on the fritz.

Or to sum it up,

Tits and Fritz.

But remember the Miss America Pageant (and the unfolding of the *Penthouse* photos drama):[1]

—Did you hear Mondale is going to ask Vanessa Williams to be his running mate? She's proved she can lick bush.

If the selection of a vice-presidential candidate is not ordinarily the subject of intense scrutiny, it *was* going to be during this campaign. The idea—and the subsequent reality—of a woman on the ticket offered an apparently irresistible array of possibilities for commentary. Rich lodes of gender lore were there for the taking. And they were strip-mined with gusto.

One source of sustained commentary within the mass media was the editorial cartoons. Since they rely heavily on images with which readers are already familiar, both visual and verbal, editorial cartoons offer up an inventory of the symbolism that is part of our social landscape. This study takes a look at the contents of that inventory for the 1984 vice-presidential campaign of Geraldine Ferraro.

Since editorial cartoons would, by traditional standards, be considered a popular culture form, it is perhaps in order to address the appropriateness of this topic for inclusion in a volume on folklore. The boundaries of these two areas, as treated in academic inquiry in recent years, seem to have become more permeable. Alan Dundes's and Carl Pagter's *Urban Folklore from the Paperwork Empire* (1975), and their follow-up *When You're up to Your Ass in Alligators . . . More Urban Folklore from the Paperwork Empire* (1987) are examples of a more inclusive approach. A number of scholars have addressed this theoretical issue in terms ranging from pointing out the ways in which folklore and popular culture are interdependent to regarding them as points along a continuum to questioning whether allowing the distinction to continue to shape our inquiry is more restricting than useful.

The publisher of *Media Sense: The Folklore–Popular Culture Continuum* asserts that the collection of essays in the volume make it evident that "folklore and popular culture are not *oppositional* cultural modes so much as *interdependent* categories of cultural activity in modern society- . . . [and that] making sense of the codes, messages and mechanisms of the folklore–popular culture continuum provides us with great insight into the nature of everyday life—our manner of interpreting and evaluating our experience, the development of our attitudes and beliefs, and the bases of our aesthetic actions" (Narváez and Laba, 1986:jacket copy). The editors offer the perspective that "artistic communication within small groups (folklore) and mass societies (popular culture) may be understood as polar types spanned by a complex continuum of different sized groups in which communications are transmitted via various configurations of sensory and technological media" (1986:1).

Michael Owen Jones, writing within the context of the study of "folk art," takes a different approach on this issue. Rather than recognizing folklore and popular culture as discrete entities but pointing out their interdependence, or reducing the degree of discreteness by locating them along a continuum, Jones reframes the issue by focusing on the objectives of the folklorist's inquiry, rather than on correct labels for categories of data bases. Asserting that "the potential contribution of folklorists . . . lies not in their ability to record and preserve seemingly old-fashioned ways of allegedly inarticulate people but in their capacity to solve some of the enigmas of human behavior" (1980:326), he recommends that we investigate the "hows" and "whys" of behavior rather than "origins of objects or texts." Noting that there has not been consensus on the meaning of such terms as *folk* and *tradition* (among others), nor consistent application of them on the part of scholars in their research and fieldwork, he argues that folklorists need to be open to considering new methods and new conceptual alternatives to inform their work: "Finally, *human behavior,* not folk or art or group or culture, should be the principal construct in the field of study called folkloristics. If 'behavior' is elevated to the status of a centrally informing concept in folkloristics, the kinds of problems encountered in using the word 'folk' or 'folklore' no longer plague research" (1980:355).

These theoretical perspectives can be applied to editorial cartoons in several ways. Editorial cartoons, in their use of metaphor, frequently draw on the material of folklore, thus illustrating the interdependence noted by Narváez and Laba. Examples (to identify just three) are Paul Conrad's Walter Mondale gazing into a mirror and asking who would be the best vice-president of all; Jack Higgins's Walter Mondale trying the slipper on the feet of potential vice-presidential candidates; and Tom Meyer's Geraldine Ferraro kissing Fritz as frog. Editorial cartoonists count on the reading public's ready recognition of such themes for the metaphor to work as persuasive argument. The work of editorial cartoonists can easily be seen as located along the continuum of artistic communication in societies that Narváez and Laba consider a rich vein to mine for greater understanding of how we interpret and evaluate everyday experience. Since the cartoonists rely on the reading public's familiarity with the themes and images that they use (the resonance of the metaphors), issues such as the nature of those themes and images, the ways in which they are used, and the frequency of their use (including the noticing of absence) are worth exploring for insights into the symbolic representation of common cultural assumptions. That femaleness is emphasized with such frequency in the editorial cartoons as a primary identifying feature of Geraldine Ferraro—and also the images that are used to accomplish that—are examples of phenomena worth exploring for insights into the symbolic portrayal of gender issues. (For other examples of research on images of women in cartoons, see Kramarae, 1974a, 1974b; and Meyer, et al., 1980.) This kind of inquiry seems consistent with the objective that Michael Owen Jones refers to as solving "some of the enigmas of human behavior." And finally, it is worth noting the perspective offered by Barbara Babcock in her examination of the use of the images of the Statue of Liberty. Asserting that "one of the problems in talking about folklore and feminist theory is defining not only feminist theories but folklore itself," Babcock remarks on the need for "cultural analysis from a feminist point of view and folklore analysis of woman as sign" (1987:380).[2]

This study is based on 155 cartoons gathered primarily from the July through November 1984 issues of eight U.S. newspapers.[3] There is, throughout this material, a striking recurrence of a specific group of themes—ones that are grounded in popular notions about gender. Of the 155 (133 researched systematically), the majority fall into at least one of these categories. During the period of selection of a vice-presidential candidate there is an interchangeability of "special interest groups," of minorities, and of women: they are categories rather than individuals. And they are pushy and demanding. A David Broder column entitled "Mondale the Hounded" refers to the "unceasing and increasing clamor from the constituencies of the Left in the Democratic party" (Broder, 1984); and the syndicated columnist Nick Thimmesch, in "The Crabby Women of NOW," reports that "citizens viewing their TV sets last weekend were treated to an unending sequence of close-up shots of *unattractive, belligerent* women demanding that a woman be installed on the Democratic ticket, NOW!" (Thimmesch, 1984, emphasis mine). After the naming of Geraldine Ferraro, the theme of interchangeability manifests itself again (as one, but not the only, example) in an association of Ferraro with Vanessa Williams (then deposed from her position as Miss America). In terms of Ferraro's relationship with Mondale, we see role reversal and domestic, romanticized, and sexualized contexts. The columnist Russell Baker uses the metaphor of courtship and marriage proposal as he writes of the vice-presidential selection process: "The Vice President Woos and Wins His Woman" (1984). The feminist columnist Ellen Goodman calls attention to the inappropriateness of such metaphors: "They Are a Team, Not a Couple" (1984b).

It is important to acknowledge at the outset that attention to female identity in popular treatment of this subject is to be expected. A woman vice-presidential candidate on a major party ticket is unique in this country's recent experience. (Patricia Schroeder was reported to have said, with respect to her decision to abandon a bid for the 1988 Democratic nomination, that she was treated more like a "woman running for the office" than a "candidate . . . who happen[ed] to be a woman" ["Schroeder Raps," 1987].) But if the attention is not surprising, nevertheless, what *is* worth examining is the repertoire of images that are drawn on in the process, whether in the joke cycle (freer for its anonymity)[4] or the editorial cartoons (necessarily more constrained in their references).

What follows is, first, an overview of the recurring themes in the cartoons and then an analysis that draws on four theoretical perspectives: the politics of humor, selected cartoonists' own philosophies of cartooning, the concept of metaphor as argument, and the concept of "symbolic annihilation."

The general themes are the following:

1. There are "special interest" groups trying to get into the action or even take over (fig. 17.1). Walter Mondale is repeatedly depicted as either a beleaguered and somewhat weary man trying to deal with this phenomenon (figs. 17.2–3) or as a cynical opportunist trying to capitalize on it in a blatantly perfunctory fashion (fig. 17.4). Mondale's staff is also frustrated by this pressure (fig. 17.5).

2. Women, constituting one of these "special interest" groups, are especially pushy or even threatening (fig. 17.6). They have placed Mondale in a no-win situation (fig. 17.7). They are domineering females who reduce Mondale to helpless submission (fig. 17.8), angry jilted lovers (fig. 17.9), or brides who wield their own shotgun (fig. 17.10). If not dangerous, they are, at least, annoying (fig. 17.11). Mondale would like to rid himself of the problem (fig. 17.12), but so great is the manipulative, coercive power of these women that Mondale's interaction with them has painted him into a corner on the issue (fig. 17.13).

3. As a group, women are interchangeable (figs. 17.14–15).[5] And interchangeability blends with romanticized context as Mondale tries the slipper on the feet of potential candidates (fig. 17.16) and with domesticity (albeit marital discord) as it is recast in the terms of the clichéd domestic metaphor of angry wife with rolling pin (fig. 17.17).

4. Gender roles and power are reversed (fig. 17.18). Ferraro upstages Mondale (fig. 17.19); she carries him as baggage (fig. 17.20); and, with a metaphor that blends role reversal and sexualized context, she carries him "to the threshold" (fig. 17.21). But can her strength prevail (fig. 17.22)? The role-reversal theme extends to other characters in the drama as well, as men are dressed up as women: this happens to Gary Hart (fig. 17.23) and George Bush (figs. 17.24–25), for hoped-for political advantage (which seems also to suggest unfair competition), and to John Zaccaro (fig. 17.26) for the apparent purpose of ridicule.

5. Ferraro appears in domestic or explicitly sexual contexts (figs.

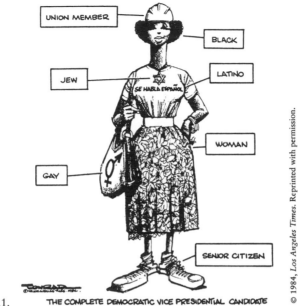

Fig. 17.1. THE COMPLETE DEMOCRATIC VICE PRESIDENTIAL CANDIDATE

"V for Vice Presidents... V for Vice Presidents..."

Fig. 17.2.

Fig. 17.3.

Fig. 17.4.

'Hey, No Kidding — I Found A Group That's Not Gonna
Fig. 17.5.　　　Force Fritz To Take One Of 'Em As Vice President'

Fig. 17.6.

Fig. 17.7.

Fig. 17.8.

Fig. 17.9.

Mike Keefe, the *Denver Post*.

Fig. 17.10.

Reprinted with the permission of Tom Meyer.

Fig. 17.11.

Fig. 17.12.

Fig. 17.13.

Fig. 17.14.

Fig. 17.15.

Fig. 17.16.

I SUPPOSE YOU'RE GOING TO TELL ME YOU WERE OUT OFFERING SOME WOMAN THE VICE PRESIDENCY...

Fig. 17.17.

Fig. 17.18.

Fig. 17.19.

© 1984, Newsday, Inc.

Fig. 17.20.

Fig. 17.21.

Fig. 17.22.

The dream ticket

Fig. 17.23.

'HOW SIMPLY DIVINE! THE FERRARO LOOK WAS JUST MADE FOR MR. BUSH.'

Fig. 17.24.

Fig. 17.25.

Fig. 17.26. 'I'M HOME, JOHN. ARE THOSE TAX FORMS READY?'

Fig. 17.27.

Fig. 17.28.

Fig. 17.29.

Fig. 17.30.

Fig. 17.31.

Fig. 17.32.

Fig. 17.33.

Fig. 17.34.

Fig. 17.35.

Fig. 17.36.

Fig. 17.37.

Fig. 17.38.   ONE GIANT STEP FOR WOMANKIND

Fig. 17.39.

Fig. 17.40.

Fig. 17.41.

Signe Wilkinson, *San Jose Mercury News.*

Fig. 17.42.

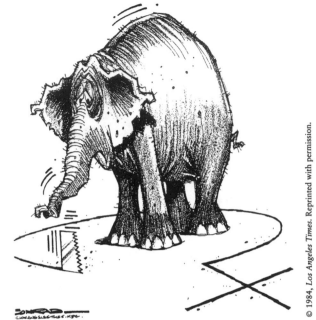

Fig. 17.43.

Fig. 17.44.

17.27–28). Her primary identity is that of housewife (fig. 17.29), and she and Mondale go over Democrats (lovers') Leap (fig. 17.30). She is a hula-skirted lure (fig. 17.31), a vehicle for "picking up chicks" (fig. 17.32) or one to be ridden herself (fig. 17.33), and, finally, an item of phone-booth graffiti (fig. 17.34).

6. The selection of a female vice-presidential candidate is linked to the selection of Miss America (fig. 17.35). Ronald Reagan dreams of Gerry Ferraro posing nude for *Penthouse* (fig. 17.36); and Republican campaign staffers, wishing to match the impact of Ferraro, get the bright idea of replacing George Bush with Vanessa Williams (fig. 17.37).

To return to the four theoretical perspectives for this discussion, let's look first at the cartoonists themselves and how the demographics of editorial cartooning illustrate what might be a "politics of humor." Editorial cartoonists are, with few exceptions, white men. (Only about 2 percent of editorial cartoonists in the United States are women,[6] and the number of minority men is equally low.) Why are there so few women? In an essay entitled "Why Women Cartoonists Are Rare, and Why That's Important," Betty Swords, whose cartoons appeared in the *Saturday Evening Post, Look,* and *Redbook,* among other publications, describes how her experiences in the world of commercial cartooning led her to conclude that "women don't make the jokes because they are the joke" (Swords, n.d.:8). This is a conclusion offered, in a variety of contexts, by a number of other analysts.[7]

Much has been written on the political and power dimensions of humor—for example, that in organizational settings, it frequently functions in a "downward fashion" to maintain the status quo, and those who are in power are empowered to make the jokes.[8] Jean Baker Miller, a psychoanalyst, in her discussion of traditional Freudian notions about women's "weaker egos," suggests that those theories "may well reflect the fact that women have no ego or superego at all as these terms are used now," since women have traditionally been denied one of the prime requisites for ego development—"the right or the requirement to be full-fledged representatives of the culture" (1986:73). Departing from this idea, it seems possible that one reason why female editorial cartoonists are so rare is that women do not enjoy socially sanctioned rights to joke about the social and/or political arrangements of the world (the essence of the editorial cartoonist's work) because it is not their world to joke about. Betty Swords suggests that "it had to be a woman who saw that the emperor wore no clothes" (Swords, n.d.:12). But as we know, that is not "the way the story goes." And so an important dimension of any analysis of editorial cartooning is to note the relative absence of women's voices and to consider whether there might be important consequences that flow from that absence.

A second theoretical perspective is the editorial cartoonists' own statements about cartooning:

Paul Conrad (*Los Angeles Times*): "A negative attitude is the nature of the art" (Adler, et al., 1980). "Cartoons are ridicule and satire by definition. I'm not sure that positive editorial cartoons say one damn thing" (Grecny, 1983).

Mike Peters (*Dayton Daily News*): "We all picture ourselves as the little kid looking at the naked emperor. That's our greatest gift to society" (Adler, et al., 1980).

Don Wright (*Palm Beach Post*): "The one element that everyone would have to have in order to understand [a] cartoon is to compare it with something they already know or something that is visible in the cartoon that they can compare the situation with" (Banks, 1980).

Jeff MacNelly (*Chicago Tribune*): "You can't really do two or three things at the same time [in a cartoon]" (Banks, 1980).

M. G. Lord (*Newsday*): "Cartoons both mirror and shape the public's perception of a candidate" (Lord, 1984).

The statements by Conrad and Peters, that cartoons are satirical by nature and that they thrive on calling attention to foibles, are both commonly understood ideas. The newspaper-reading public is accustomed to receiving and processing them in this way. And M. G. Lord asserts that they are both reflective and reinforcing of societal views and values. These comments suggest interesting questions with regard to some of the portrayals of the candidacy of Geraldine Ferraro.

Take the example of Conrad's editorial cartoon two days after Ferraro's nomination (fig. 17.38). I wrote to Conrad to ask for his thoughts on his previous questioning of whether "positive editorial cartoons say one damn thing." The reply from his office was that the intent of the cartoon was definitely positive, and editorial cartoons can be positive, "though perhaps more often they're not" (Janet Nippell to author, personal communication, June 12, 1986). (The issue of whether editorial cartoons are, of necessity, negative raises interesting theoretical questions about the essence of cartooning. Some *Newsweek* writers report that a few cartoonists, reflecting on the possibility of a favorable cartoon about Jimmy Carter, "reluctantly admit that it could be done," but only, they add, "by drawing him in opposition to something even worse—say Congress" [Adler, et al., 1980].) But accepting that Conrad's cartoon is meant to be positive, there are still some interesting questions to ask about the image used to communicate the message—the imprint of a woman's shoe. Let's integrate two additional perspectives: MacNelly's observation that a cartoon can really do only one thing at a time and the third theoretical perspective—the use of metaphor as argument in cartoons.[9]

Linking MacNelly's assertion that an editorial cartoon can't do two or three things at a time to Wright's observations that editorial cartoons rely on metaphors that must not contradict what is already known, we can take the analysis of Conrad's cartoon one step further. Even as the cartoonist means to be positive, can the image chosen convey a favorable impression—one that is unencumbered by negative connotations? Can that particular shoe imprint—pointed toe and tiny heel, separated one from the other—communicate strength and power, or is it too burdened with associations of weakness and vulnerability? Does the image's evocation of Cinderella (a la Disney), which is certainly what the reading public, at some level, "knows" about this metaphor, load it with ambivalence?

If the question related only to this one cartoon, it might be regarded as a happenstance instance of a problematic metaphor. But I think the question applies broadly and serves to highlight an intriguing issue: the repertoire of images available to us for positive statements about women. Note, for example, three other illustrations: figs. 17.18, in which gender roles are reversed; 17.27, in which a play on words has a Southern man relegating Ferraro to a domestic identity; and 17.34, in which two sailors spot a Ferraro message among phone-booth graffiti. Conrad and MacNelly had stated at the time, in general terms, that their cartooning about Ferraro was meant to be supportive, so let us assume, for example, that Ferraro is strong and competent (fig. 17.18), in fact so much so that she is the most, if not only, interesting personality in the Democratic cast of characters in recent years (fig. 17.34), and that if there is a problem it is not her gender, but rather some Southern male's neanderthal views (fig. 17.27). But if the cartoon cannot effectively attempt more than one primary message, and the metaphor employed must not be at odds with what is already known, is there a problem?

How are we to react to this image of a woman who "wears the pants," whose strength—metaphorically depicted as male—serves to highlight the man's weakness—depicted as female? If the intent is to say that she is a stronger person or candidate than Mondale, does the imagery nevertheless tap into latent sentiment that strength is incompatible with femininity or that a strong woman reflects negatively on the masculinity of the man beside her? And what about a woman who is the subject of phone-booth graffiti? Do the negative connotations of these images overwhelm and ultimately negate the positive intent?

Similarly, in the case of the iron as an image of domesticity (the source of the play on words), does the image more readily resonate with popular attitudes (one could argue that they are vast and deep) about the "proper place of women" than with a negative critique of Southern male gender politics? The *Newsday* cartoonist M. G. Lord, writing on the subject of cartoonists' treatment of Ferraro and critiquing specific cartoons (Wright's and MacNelly's among them), remarks that "some cartoons from the current campaign reveal more about the cartoonists' attitudes toward women than about their perspectives on the election," and she concludes that "rather than express ideas, [many of the cartoons] simply exploit the notion of a woman in a role normally filled by men" (1984). A final observation on this issue is that the above-mentioned cartoons are not isolated examples but are rather illustrations of themes that run throughout the cartoons that were produced about Ferraro and her candidacy.

The fourth theoretical perspective that I will bring to this discussion is the idea of "symbolic annihilation," a concept developed by George Gerbner (1972) and extended upon by Gaye Tuchman as it applies to the presentation of women by the mass media (1979). As pointed out by Gerbner, nonrepresentation or absence is one form of symbolic annihilation, but other more subtle as well as insidious forms may be "underrepresentation," "trivialization," or "condemnation." From this perspective, the relentless portrayal of Ferraro in domestic or sexualized contexts or through metaphors rooted in those allusions functions in an interesting way. By foregrounding her sexual identity, the imagery diverts our attention and obscures her role as a candidate for national public office.

A particularly dramatic example of this type of portrayal is the linkage of the candidacy of Ferraro to the Miss America Pageant, and, more specifically, to the issue of Vanessa Williams's having posed nude for photographs that were later sold to *Penthouse* (figs. 17.35–37). Barbara Ehrenreich and Jane O'Reilly, commenting on the concurrent events of the Democratic Convention and the unfolding of the Miss America troubles, observe that "in the hazy news overlap . . . , many viewers began to wonder, dimly, whether Geraldine Ferraro had any funny pictures in her past and whether Suzette Charles, the new Miss America, knew anything about foreign policy" (1984:11). The authors develop a wonderfully incisive satiric commentary on the whole issue, exposing the duplicity and hypocrisy of the protestations from pageant officials and miscellaneous others. They assert, in conclusion, that "the only real connection between the two events of July—the nomination of Ms. Ferraro in San Francisco and the impeachment of Miss America in New York—lies in the sleazy subconscious of American manhood" and that "for now, it appears that whether a woman wears a one-piece swimsuit and sash or a skirted suit and pearls, the boys see only tits and ass" (12). Her nomination, they remind us, was only "minutes" old when the "Tits and Fritz" buttons went on sale, people began joking about "bushes" in the White House, and Reagan campaign manager Edward Rollins told the press (acknowledging the double entendre but calling it a "Freudian slip") that Geraldine Ferraro would be "the biggest bust politically in recent history" ("Reagan Campaigner's," 1984).

It might well be asked, then, if it is possible to do a positive portrayal. I think it is. (It's broad appeal is another question.) Two pairs of cartoons, treating two different incidents during the campaign, can be used to illustrate the possibilities. The first is the subject of Ferraro's difficulties with the IRS as treated by Conrad (fig. 17.39) and by Signe Wilkinson of the *San Jose Mercury News* (fig. 17.40). Both are sympathetic to Ferraro's plight as well as cognizant of John Zaccaro's contributions to the problem. Conrad's Joan of Arc image is visually neat and aesthetically accomplished. The metaphor, however, is one of sacrifice and defeat—we know how that story ended. In contrast, Wilkinson's marathon runner offers a different kind of metaphor. Ferraro acts rather than being acted upon: she acknowledges what is going on, identifies the obstacles, and states her intention to continue. The first cartoon acknowledges victimization (accurate enough, but not enough); the second rejects it. As a story, the first is closed; the second is yet to be written.[10]

Another pair of cartoons treats an exchange between Ferraro and Mississippi agriculture commissioner Jim Buck Ross during Ferraro's first public campaign appearance in the South. Ross asked Ferraro if she could bake a blueberry muffin, to which Ferraro responded yes and asked if he could do the same. Ross then countered, "Down here in Mississippi, men don't cook" and went on to inform Ferraro that Mississippi had produced three Miss Americas ("Ferraro Quizzed," 1984). The media picked up immediately on the "newsworthiness" of these comments, and so, of course, did the cartoonists. Don Wright's treatment (fig. 17.27) and the problematic metaphor he uses leaves open the object of the put down: is it Ferraro or is it the Southern male chauvinist or is it both? Signe Wilkinson, once again, offers a contrasting perspective—one that frames the issue in such a way as to make it clear that it is the question (or questioner) that is flawed, not Ferraro (fig. 17.41).

There is one particular cartoon that could serve as a "centerpiece" cartoon for this whole discussion. Dan Wasserman's (fig. 17.42) captures a basic notion from which much of what was said and written on the subject of the selection of a vice-presidential candidate in 1984 flowed: the notion of the "otherness" of particular categories of people—most dramatically (although not exclusively, since there were class as well as race and sex issues), those who are not white males. This notion underlies the concept of "special interest group." Wasserman pinpoints the political nature of that concept, and he effectively reframes the issue by questioning the cultural exemption from it that is accorded to white males.

In the summer of 1984, just prior to the nomination of Ferraro, James Kilpatrick remarked in his column, in his customary style, "Now that [Mondale] is waffling on the matter of naming a woman to go on the ticket with him, voices are getting shrill. 'Heaven has no rage like love to hatred turned, nor hell a fury like a woman scorned.' . . . If this year's Democratic ticket does not include a woman, it seems a certain bet that in 1988 a woman will be up there" (1984). Well, the first came true, and the second seemed in the offing anyway (the first notwithstanding). But this is where we started: Pat Schroeder's experience was that things hadn't changed much in the media's handling of female personalities.

So what can we conclude about Geraldine Ferraro in the editorial cartoons? Obviously, there was a mix of cartoons that were meant to be supportive of her candidacy and those that were not. That much is to be expected. But we should examine closely the kinds of images that are called upon, regardless of whether the intent is supportive or critical, and how those images function. We've seen the themes around which the images clustered and the ways in which they are problematic. But perhaps more serious is the evidence that even statements intended as positive may be sabotaged by images that simply, and basically, are incompatible with that intent. If this analysis has some truth to it, it may well constitute a sobering insight into the issue of the images available to us for the positive portrayal of women and of female experience.

For many people the possibility of a woman on the ticket was an exciting one. Ellen Goodman wrote of the "goose bump" factor (1984a). That's one way to describe it. For many others it was a "specter"— unsettling, in part (to mix metaphors) because it threw people off balance, like a wild card in the equation, and threatened to "pull the rug out from under," turning familiar ground rules into thin ice, as captured by Conrad's elephant (fig. 17.43). It made the old rules insufficient and the new ones unclear, prompting a spate of columns on protocol—"ladies first" or presidents first? A "first gentleman"? (Beck, 1984; Buchwald, 1984; Dowd, 1984; Green, 1984; Randolph, 1984; Thompson, 1984; "The Two-Inch Gender Gap," 1984) But these questions, for now, are on hold.

In 1988 newspapers reported that "Americans expect to have a black president some day."[11] I read this news and, reflecting on language and gender assumptions, wondered if the "black president" in the minds of the poll respondents could possibly have been a woman.[12]

What will it take, really, to change the face of Mt. Rushmore (fig. 17.44)?

Notes

I want to express a special note of appreciation to my friend and colleague Beth Vanfossen, who has been both model and inspiration to me in my work in women's studies and for this project in particular. I began the research for this project in July 1984 as a participant in a National Endowment for the Humanities Seminar on Humor in Cross-cultural Perspective at the University of California at Berkeley. The seminar was directed by Professor Stanley Brandes of the Department of Anthropology.

1. Vanessa Williams was crowned Miss America on September 17, 1983, the first black woman to hold that title. She reigned for ten months. After the September 1984 issue of *Penthouse* published photographs of her (taken prior to her being named Miss America) in sexual poses with another woman, the pageant committee asked for her resignation. See the *San Francisco Chronicle,* Sept. 21, 1984, 3.

2. For additional discussion of the folklore/popular culture issue, see also Arpad (1975), Bird (1976), Burns (1969), and Denby (1971).

3. Cartoon material was researched from the following newspapers during the dates indicated: the *Atlanta Constitution,* the *Boston Globe,* the *San Francisco Chronicle,* and the *San Jose Mercury News* (July 1-Aug. 15, 1984); the *Chicago Tribune* and the *Seattle Post-Intelligencer* (July 1-Aug. 31, 1984); the *Washington Post* (July 1-Oct. 31, 1984); and the *Los Angeles Times* (July 1-Nov. 30, 1984). The above issues contained 133 different cartoons on the subject of either the selection of a vice-presidential candidate or the specific candidacy of Geraldine Ferraro. Syndicated cartoons that appeared in a number of papers were counted only once. In addition, I have included 22 cartoons from twelve other U.S. newspapers (July-Sept. 1984) that came to my attention in random fashion.

4. For recent folklore scholarship on the joke-cycle genre, see Kürti (1988), Oring (1987), and Simons (1986). Simons and Oring discuss the explosion of the space shuttle Challenger on January 28, 1986. Simons's work is of special interest here for its observations on the singling out of Christa McAullife; Kürti writes on popular response to the nuclear disaster at Chernobyl on April 26, 1986, and his comments that "one of the most popular forms of political expression is joking about...rulers" and "in the Chernobyl jokes...the populace articulated its deepest fears and anxieties" are of interest for their potential relevance to the Ferraro joke cycle.

5. See, for an unsupportive commentary, Geyer (1984).

6. Ed Stein, president of the Association of American Editorial Cartoonists, confirms that there are only a handful of editorial cartoonists on the staffs of U.S. daily newspapers who are not white males. Based on his past experience in working with college students studying to be cartoonists, Stein notes that the women tended to abandon plans for that career much more often than did the men, and he attributes that in part to what he perceived as the women's greater sensitivity to the attacks that go with the profession. He goes on to say that the women typically received much more "vehement reactions and criticisms" (of

their work) than did the men (from a telephone conversation, Mar. 29, 1988). Stein's accounting of his students' experiences suggests that there is less public receptivity to the idea of women cartoonists and seems to lend credence to the theory that women are not perceived as legitimate critics of societal arrangements—in short, that it is "not their world to joke about."

7. See, for example, Kramarae (1974a, 1974b).

8. See, for example, Coser (1959).

9. See Banks (1980) for an excellent and very thorough development of the subject as it relates to editorial cartoons.

10. For several examples of feminist writing that deal with the analysis of women's roles in humor (for example, as agents of change versus as victims) and the functions of feminist humor, see Clinton (1982), Kaufman (1977), and Weisstein (1973).

11. According to the report 62 percent of blacks and 56 percent of whites "believe the United States is likely to elect a black president within the next two decades" ("Americans Expect," 1988).

12. For a black feminist statement on the obscuring of black women's identity, note the title of the work *All the Women Are White, All the Blacks Are Men, but Some of Us Are Brave* (Hull, Scott, and Smith, 1982). The Affirmative Action expression *women and minorities,* for example, is an interesting one, in that it splits the identity of female members of minority groups. One could argue that a more logical Affirmative Action term would be *women and minority men* or *white women and minorities.* But perhaps the logic of the existing term derives from the fact that it reflects a conceptualization whose primary reference is the dominant group (white men); that is to say, the term doesn't so much identify who particular groups of people are as it calls attention to what they are not: not male (women) and not white (minorities). The conceptual ambiguity of the currently accepted usage is reflected in the following anecdote from Herb Caen's column (1984): "U.S. Atty. Joe Russoniello told Bill Cooney he was delighted that Mondale had picked—an Italian. 'Yeah, but what about the Italian being a woman?' asked Bill. Joe: 'Oh, that too.' " And Ellen Goodman makes specific note of the ambiguity when she observes that Jesse Jackson's comment that "the women got Ferraro; the South got Lance; what have the blacks got?" seems to obscure the fact that some of the blacks are women (Goodman, 1984c). But the usage is common: the *New York Times* reported that the National Press Club in Washington, D.C., "originally a white male bastion, . . . opened its doors to black people in 1955 and to women in 1971" (Gamarekian, 1988). A final comment on the political dimensions of this language issue is that perhaps the joining of the forces against racism and sexism is too threatening to be allowed to be identified accurately—it is a "coalition that has scared white men," Gloria Steinem observes (quoted in Mills, 1984). But its power can be diminished by the manipulation of language, which splits its component parts, permitting them to be seen as a collection of minorities rather than the majority that, together, they are.

References Cited

Adler, Jerry, Jane Whitmore, Phyllis Malamud, William D. Marbach, and Nancy Stadtman. 1980. "The Finer Art of Politics." *Newsweek,* Oct. 13, 74ff.

"Americans Expect to Have a Black President Some Day." 1988. *Rochester Democrat and Chronicle,* Feb. 28, 1A.

Arpad, Joseph J. 1975. "Between Folklore and Literature: Popular Culture as Anomaly." *Journal of Popular Culture* 9:403–22.

Babcock, Barbara. 1987. "Taking Liberties, Writing from the Margins, and Doing It with a Difference." *Journal of American Folklore* 100 (398): 390–411.

Baker, Russell. 1984. "The Vice President Woos and Wins His Woman." *Seattle Post Intelligencer,* July 5.

Banks, Barbara. 1980. "Metaphor as Argument in Editorial Cartoons." Ph.D. diss., Ohio State University.

Beck, Joan. 1984. "Ms-givings about Ms. Ferraro." *Chicago Tribune,* Aug. 8.

Bird, Donald Allport. 1976. "A Theory of Folklore in Mass Media: Traditional Patterns in the Mass Media." *Southern Folklore Quarterly* 40:285–305.

Broder, David. 1984. "Mondale the Hounded." *Boston Globe,* July 5.

Buchwald, Art. 1984. "Handshakes, but No Kisses." *Boston Globe,* July 24.

Burns, Tom. 1969. "Folklore in the Mass Media: Television." *Folklore Forum* 2:90–106.

Caen, Herb. 1984. *San Francisco Chronicle,* 13 July.

Clinton, Kate. 1982. "Making Light: Another Dimension. Some Notes on Feminist Humor." *Trivia* 1 (Fall): 37–42.

Coser, Rose. 1959. "Some Social Functions of Laughter." *Human Relations* 12:171–82.

Denby, Priscilla. 1971. "Folklore in the Mass Media." *Folklore Forum* 4:113–21.

Dowd, Maureen. 1984. "Goodbye Male Ticket, Hello Etiquette Gap." *New York Times,* July 18, part 1, p. 14.

Dundes, Alan. 1987. *Cracking Jokes: Studies of Sick Humor Cycles and Stereotypes.* Berkeley: Ten Speed Press.

Dundes, Alan, and Carl R. Pagter. 1975. *Urban Folklore from the Paperwork Empire.* American Folklore Society Memoirs, vol. 62. Austin: University of Texas Press.

———. 1987. *When You're up to Your Ass in Alligators . . . More Urban Folklore from the Paperwork Empire.* Detroit: Wayne State University Press.

Ehrenreich, Barbara, and Jane O'Reilly. 1984. "Sexual Foreboding: From 'Penthouse' to the White House." *The New Republic,* Aug. 27, 10–12.

"Ferraro Quizzed on Southern Issues—Catfish and Muffins." 1984. *Los Angeles Times,* Aug. 2, 6.

Gamarekian, Barbara. 1988. "Club's Rowdy, Irreverent Days Give Way to Age of the Yuppie." *New York Times,* Mar. 24, A32.

Gerbner, George. 1972. "Violence in Television Drama: Trends and Symbolic Functions." In *Media Content and Control: Television and Social Behavior,* ed. George C. Comstock and Eli A. Rubinstein, 28–127. Washington, D.C.: GPO.

Geyer, Georgie Anne. 1984. "The 'Any Woman Will Do' Circus." *Denver Post,* July 5.

Goodman, Ellen. 1984a. "Goose Bump Factor Enters the Election." *Boston Globe,* July 13.

———. 1984b. "They Are a Team, Not a Couple." *Los Angeles Times,* July 19.

———. 1984c. "Ties That Bind." *Boston Globe,* July 20.

Grecny, Jeff. 1983. "If It Stinks, Stir It: An Interview with Paul Conrad." *University Magazine* (Fall): 20–26, 59–60.

Green, Blake. 1984. "Should Fritz Kiss Gerry in Public?" *San Francisco Chronicle,* July 19, 28.

Hill, C. William. 1987. "Ferraro in Cartoon." *Target* 5 (22): 14–20.

Hull, Gloria, Patricia Bell Scott, and Barbara Smith, eds. 1982. *All the Women Are White, All the Blacks Are Men, But Some of Us Are Brave.* Old Westbury, N.Y.: Feminist Press.

Jones, Michael Owen. 1980. "L.A. Add-ons and Re-dos: Renovation in Folk Art and Architectural Design." In *Perspectives on American Folk Art,* ed. Ian M. G. Quimby and Scott T. Swank, 325–63. New York: W. W. Norton.

Kaufman, Gloria. 1977. "Feminist Humor." *Women* 5:42–43.

Kilpatrick, James J. 1984. "A Fair Chance for the Fair Sex." *San Jose Mercury News,* July 9.

Kramarae, Cheris. 1974a. "Folk Linguistics: Wishy-Washy Mommy Talk: Study of Sex Language Differences through Analysis of New Yorker Cartoons." *Psychology Today,* June, 82–85.

———. 1974b. "Stereotypes of Women's Speech: the Word from Cartoons." *Journal of Popular Culture* 8:624–30.

Kürti, László. 1988. "The Politics of Joking: Popular Response to Chernobyl." *Journal of American Folklore* 101 (401): 324–34.

Laba, Martin. 1986. "Popular Culture and Folklore: The Social Dimension." In *Media Sense: The Folklore-Popular Culture Continuum,* ed. Peter Narváez and Margin Laba, 9–18. Bowling Green, Ohio: Bowling Green State University Popular Press.

Lord, M. G. 1984. "Cartoonists' Art of Insinuation." *San Jose Mercury News,* Sept. 30.

Meyer, Katherine, John Seidler, Timothy Curry, and Adrian Aveni. 1980. "Women in July Fourth Cartoons: A One-Hundred-Year Look." *Journal of Communication* 30 (Winter): 21–30.

Miller, Jean Baker. 1986. *Toward a New Psychology of Women.* 2d ed. Boston: Beacon Press.

Mills, Kay. 1984. "Black Women Find Slights by Feminists, Others Galling." *Los Angeles Times,* July 20.

Narváez, Peter, and Margin Laba, eds. 1986. *Media Sense: The Folklore-Popular Culture Continuum.* Bowling Green, Ohio: Bowling Green State University Popular Press.

Oring, Elliott. 1987. "Jokes and the Discourse on Disaster." *Journal of American Folklore* 100 (398): 276–86.

Randolph, Eleanor. 1984. "Women Take to the Ferraro Trail." *Washington Post,* July 30, A4.

"Reagan Campaigner's Slipup on Ferraro." 1984. *San Francisco Chronicle,* July 25.

"Schroeder Raps Media's Questions." 1987. *Rochester Times-Union,* Nov. 23, 9A.

Simons, Elizabeth Radin. 1986. "The NASA Joke Cycle: The Astronauts and the Teacher." *Western Folklore* 45:261–77.

Swords, Betty. n.d. "Why Women Cartoonists Are Rare." Ms. Published in 1992 as "Why Women Cartoonists Are Rare, and Why That's Important." In *New Perspectives on Women and Comedy,* ed. Regina Barreca, 65–84. Studies in Gender and Culture, vol. 5. Philadelphia: Gordon and Breach.

Thimmesch, Nick. 1984. "The Crabby Women of NOW." *Boston Globe,* July 9.

Thompson, Robert. 1984. "Ferraro Should Be Treated as a Lady." *Seattle Post Intelligencer,* Aug. 6.

Tuchman, Gaye. 1979. "Women's Depiction by the Mass Media." *Signs* 4:528–42.

"The Two-Inch Gender Gap." 1984. *San Francisco Examiner,* July 23, B10.

Weisstein, Naomi. 1973. "Why We Aren't Laughing Any More." *Ms. Magazine,* Nov., 49–51, 88–90.

Straight Talk from "Crooked" Women

In connection with a study on the experience of disability in American culture, I documented personal experience narratives from nineteen women with physical disabilities (Phillips, 1984b). In this essay I will analyze the narratives that illustrate these women's perceptions of folk and popular images of their nonnormative (disabled) bodies. Stahl notes that personal experience narratives may function to affirm or deny a folk notion, to test the content of an otherwise idiosyncratic experience against the collective knowledge, and to acknowledge the narrator's affiliation to a set of experiences common to the population or community (Stahl, 1977a, 1977b). The women I interviewed not only provided biographical data and interpretive statements about themselves and their social circumstances but also recounted their life experiences in structured "self-oriented" stories that often focused on their bodies as texts (Stahl, 1983:270). Although I was a stranger to all of these women prior to entering the field, as a disabled woman I shared with them the vulnerability of being an outsider in the culture, having the same social minority status (Gliedman and Roth, 1980). These women were very forthcoming, not surprising considering the relative ease with which insiders may establish rapport (Phillips, 1983). In telling me their most intimate stories they "authored" themselves, their narratives richly illustrating how their "deleted" and "crooked" bodies function as cultural metaphors (Myerhoff, 1978; Rich, 1982; Frank, 1988). They shared with me their own body images and their perceptions of how their forms function symbolically in society.

These women's narratives do not suggest that the disabled body acts as symbol and memory of the "deep fears of childhood": disembodiment and castration anxieties (Bettelheim, 1977; Fiedler, 1978). Nor is the disabled body equated with the anomalous forms associated with magical rites—potent sources of good and evil. Rather, an analysis of these women's texts affirms that the disabled body, like the female body, is a socially constructed symbol of powerlessness and deviation, created by social organizations and imbued with meaning by cultural ideologies (Bogdan, 1988). By documenting disabled women's stories, folklorists not only are providing new texts but also are broadening the feminist canon to include the experiences of all females.

A Description of Those Interviewed

The majority of those interviewed resided in a small midwestern university town where I lived for an eighteen-month fieldwork project. These women ranged in age from early twenties to midfifties. All except two were Caucasian, these two being racially mixed but reared in predominately Caucasian environments. Fifteen had been disabled since childhood, and eleven had some or all of their early education in segregated settings (Phillips, 1985a). All had finished high school. Ten held undergraduate degrees; four had master's degrees; and three were ABD. Of those continuing their education, five were enrolled in undergraduate programs and five in graduate programs. Regarding their employment status, six were on Social Security Disability Insurance (SSDI) benefits, one employed part-time, and two employed full-time. Three had children, and of the four who had been married, three were divorced. These women were well above average in their educational achievement, not unusual for a population traditionally encouraged to emphasize education in light of limited employment prospects (Fine and Asch, 1981). Many were involved in mainstream disability activism, ranging from association with disabled students' organizations to involvement with centers for independent living. Some were friends, especially those who were students at the university. Others had casual acquaintanceship with one another through the local disability networks. Collectively, they had no single affiliation in common. Individually, they had unique and diverse personal interests. Often, they held differing disability ideologies, including various preferences for self-referential language (Phillips, 1986).[1] The interviews I conducted with these women were private and confidential. To preserve their privacy, those cited here are referred to by pseudonyms.

Theoretical Frameworks: The Study of the Body in Culture

That the body acts as a cultural metaphor or as a sign for social interaction is not a new notion.[2] Historically, the concept derives from the late nineteenth-, early twentieth-century controversy between scholars who believed that bodily expression is genetically determined and therefore universal cross-culturally and those who believed that bodily expression is environmentally determined and therefore culturally relative. It was Darwin who argued that bodily expression is a cross-cultural genetically determined universal, innate or inherited, "not [having] been learnt by the individual" (1965:23). Those following the Durkheimian L'Annee Sociologique tradition, among them Robert Hertz and Marcel Mauss, postulated that although bodily expression is predicated on physiology, in addition there are social origins of certain physiological behaviors (Hertz, 1960; Mauss, 1935). Mauss argued for the total influence of culture on the "education" of the body, insisting that there were no universals, including knowing and learning the conditions of body behavior.

The branch of research that followed the Maussian program of cultural relativism serves as a dominant framework for my analysis and is consistent with more contemporary symbolic and semiotic interpretations of the body. These theories may identify the body as a text for metaphoric interpretation (Sontag, 1978). Or, they may interpret the body as a code for deciphering social interaction, as in the branch of kinesics research that studies the body as a communicative system (Birdwhistell, 1971). Certainly Mary Douglas affirms the physical body to be the symbolic medium through which we express social relations that enable us to know our own society (1973), and Brenda Beck acknowledges that "symbolic and social structures must be recognized as inextricably connected to cultural meanings about the body" (1975:486). Ironically, however, some who study the body in culture limit their focus only to "somatic states and capabilities that normal organisms can share" (Blacking, 1977:12). It would seem evident that it is the nonnormative body that should be central to any investigation of the symbolic meaning of physiology in culture. As Barbara Babcock has observed, what a group shares in common cannot be understood without recognizing that which is *not* shared by "significant others" (1972).

If scholars study nonnormative bodies at all, they tend to study them as anomalies, the unordered physiologies of marginal persons who are simultaneously dangerous and awesome (Douglas, 1966; Fiedler, 1978). Perhaps we should investigate why nonnormative persons occupy actual and symbolic realms that are inversions of the conceptual frameworks for cultural appropriateness (Jackson, 1972). Why certain physiologies are considered nonnormative may provide the key to understanding the dimensions of "normality" in various cultures.

Two questions are central to an investigation of the meaning of the nonnormative (or disabled) body in culture: How does the culture shape (as Durkheim and especially Mauss would argue) not only the "normal" body but also the disabled body? And how does the disabled body shape culture, specifically social perceptions and social interactions? How culture shapes the disabled body is pertinent to those pinnacles of a "healthist culture," medicine and rehabilitation, both of which professions quite literally seek to re-form the nonnormative body (Zola, 1982). Several of the women I interviewed who are amputees discussed their difficulty in achieving closure in their rehabilitation, noting how prostheses for females are perceived by the medical profession to function primarily as cosmetic appliances that reshape the female form. Jane Geyer, born without fore-arms and without one leg, recalled the pressure placed on her to wear cosmetic hands:

> When I was in tenth and eleventh grades, I wore my arms, and when I was in the twelfth grade, I decided not to anymore. Well, I always kept one on, but they aren't very efficient because you [can't] hold a pencil and write very well. Better for opening doors. Plus, there was a glove that gets dirty really quick. And you can't clean it, and it costs a lot, and you have to send away [for new ones]. So, on special occasions I'd wear both [cosmetic] hands. I never wore them after school. I only wore them to school, because, you see, [rehabilitation counselors] used to ask me if I was wearing my arms, and they would scare the hell out of me, and I'd say yeah. Of course, what they meant was *after* school. And I never did. And I used to, oh my God, I used to lie! But as soon as I got home I used to take them off. I just knew how well I could operate without them.

In this chapter, I emphasize the second question: How does the disabled body shape culture, particularly social perceptions and social interactions? In other words, how do members of a society decipher the culturally coded disabled body and what meaning do they derive from these physiological texts (Scholes, 1982)? Primarily, I base my analysis on the texts of those women I interviewed. In addition, I utilize popular media images and references to further illustrate how disabled female bodies function as cultural metaphors and signs for social interaction (Zola, 1985). In the disabled women's narratives I collected there are three major themes related to body image: the concealment of the body, the mechanization of the body, and the body as metaphor for "the cripple."

The Concealment of the Body

In studies on the cultural history of women's fashion, concealment is discussed both as re-shaping and as hiding the female form (Hess and Nochlin, 1972). Chinese foot-binding is an example of reshaping the female physiology to meet male criteria for beauty and eroticism in prerevolutionary China. Howard Levy suggests a relationship between the symbolic binding of women to their social roles, as women were "inaccessible to view [and] concealed within the women's apartments," and the quite literal repression through binding and reshaping women's feet in order to "achieve[e] the criterion of beauty" established in that culture (n.d.:23). Concealment is also the hiding of natural forms to create an illusion of physiological acquiescence to culturally prescribed norms for eroticism, a phenomenon common cross-culturally. David Kunzle describes corseting as "instruction" of the female body; for example, in eighteenth-century French society, the stay maker was "required to 'educate' the body of the young into the newly fashionable slenderness [with the goal of] inflam[ing] the desires" of men (1972:95).

The narratives of women with disabilities illustrate the kinds of culturally imposed concealment intended to hide their crooked forms. Yet women with disabilities have two struggles: to assert their femaleness without submitting to the trappings of femininity and to reject cultural criteria for normalization without yielding to the cripple role.

The "Sunk and Shrunken" Eyes of Kelly Holt

Kelly Holt has rejected a specific requisite for normalization—that the "bad" parts be covered up. Totally blind since age eleven, Kelly had cataract surgery on her left eye at age twelve. She did not regain sight and the procedure caused her left eye to appear "sunk and shrunken":

> My family and the people around me taught me to be ashamed of the way I looked and to hide. I was really encouraged to wear dark glasses, and I was taught to think of myself as being ugly, and to hide behind the glasses. I think [those images] still haunt me. I don't think I'm going to fully recover from some of them—being unfeminine, being ugly. The rest of my body is supposed to make up for my blindness, and, in that sense, I'm connecting what my mother always said about my being ugly and unfeminine, with the fact that I'm blind, so that the rest of me has to be feminine enough, attractive enough to cover up! [This guy's] planning to invite me to this party. Here he is, he's not going to show up just with a woman—they're going to look me over anyway. But he's showing up with a *blind* woman! Which in their eyes, I don't know, may not be a woman at all. And I have this uncomfortable feeling. I don't want to be on display, and yet I know that in very subtle ways, I'm always on display. But in this situation, I feel nervous. You know how guys rate the other man's woman. And in some ways, if we don't go, I think I'll be glad.

When she went away to college, geographically and emotionally a thousand miles from home, Kelly became involved with student disability activist groups. Eventually, she discarded her glasses: "I rather hate them, 'cause they're symbolic now." Yet, for others, her uncovered eyes continued to symbolize weakness and unattractiveness: "Sometimes, when people are having some kind of conflict with me, they're drawn to the left side of me, because they see that as being weak, as opposed to the right side of my face. And I see my face, almost cut in two, like the right side of my face is normal and healthy and pretty, and the left side projects someone who is ill or vulnerable."

Certainly revolutions of the spirit are not unlike political revolutions: we carry with us the baggage of old worldviews throughout the process of self- and social redefinitions. In uncovering her inappropriate shape, Kelly liberated herself both from the traditional feminine role and from the stereotypical cripple role. One consequence, not regretted, was that changing her self-image further shamed her family. She remains ambivalent, however, about the extent to which her "sunk and shrunken" eyes are perceived to be signs of weakness, passivity, illness, and vulnerability. The next challenge, to effect a change in her social image, that is, to redefine social images of disability, is not Kelly's alone. Among those whose consciousness must be raised are the very feminists who have most vehemently argued that the objectification of the female form is demeaning to all women (Phillips, 1984a).

In a popular article on women's bodies, Gloria Steinem urges women to rid themselves of the "commercial, idealized image that diverse female bodies rarely fit" (1982:29). She praises obese and slender women, small and tall women, women who look like pear-shaped Buddhas, and women with stretch marks and appendectomy scars. Yet among ninety diverse bodies she praises, there is not one missing a limb or two, none withered on one side or the other, none dancing spasmodically with palsy, and none with "sunk and shrunken" eyes like Kelly's. As if an afterthought, Steinem concedes that "even mastectomies and other realities [now] seem less terrifying" (32). Her euphemism "other realities" is quite telling: implicit in this otherwise liberated view of the diversity of women's bodies there remains a dread and repulsion of crooked forms.

The Mechanization of the Body

The narratives of these women affirm the degree to which disabled persons are persistent consumers in rehabilitation and medical spheres. It is notable that the disabled men I interviewed during the eighteen-month project generally spoke of rehabilitation in the past tense, their narratives set in almost mythical time during which they optimized, or perceived that they optimized, their physiological functions but not their forms.

Whether the men accepted or categorically rejected mechanical mobility aids, for them mechanization was less mortifying. Mechanization could even be intriguing, and sometimes they "souped up" wheelchairs to their own specifications. In contrast, the disabled women spoke of rehabilitation in the present and future tenses. Sometimes they were engaged in an ongoing and seemingly endless process of physiological restoration, primarily of form, not function. They tended to express greater ambivalence about mechanizing their bodies than did their male counterparts (Phillips, 1985b). In addition, a distinction between the men and the women is that those women most active in the disability rights movement were more conscious of the external origins of their body images and far more assertive than men in expressing symbolic and real liberation from socially imposed criteria for normality. The women's narratives were filled with accounts of social reactions to their mechanized bodies and more clearly illustrated the symbolic relevance of such mechanical aids. That is, orthopedic braces, wheelchairs, and prostheses may serve to aid mobility, but they also function to reshape physiologies for appropriate social interaction. Jane Geyer notes how often people like "Shriners come up [on the street] and say, 'You know, we can provide money.' and I say, 'No, those [cosmetic hands] don't work very well.' I mean, they are really inefficient." The crooked form is straightened. The deleted form is supplemented. In effect, the mechanized and re-formed body shapes self-perception and predicts social interaction (Goffman, 1967).

Have You Met Iron Hook Yet?

Jaclyn Stuart was cognizant of the dehumanizing appearance of her hook prosthesis: "I've gotten too many shudders, too many people who draw back from me. When you have mechanical parts, you know, it's Captain Hook!" It is significant that Jaclyn refers to herself as having mechanical parts when she wears her hook prosthesis. Implicit in this metaphoric association is the transformational character of such mechanical devices, particularly on a disabled woman's body image. Jaclyn notes the importance of gender as a critical factor in the social image of her mechanized and deleted forms: "There's this guy in town who has a hook, but people don't react to him like they react to me. I guess it's appropriate for him, more macho."

Jaclyn, born without a left forearm, explains that she has evolved through three body images: from the natural look without a prosthesis to the normalized look of the artificial (cosmetic) hand to the utilitarian look of the hook prosthesis. She is most comfortable au naturel, a self she reveals only to close friends and family (Goffman, 1959). The cosmetic hand, uncomfortable and hot and totally useless, serves as costume when she enters the other world:

> The changes that hand made in the way that people perceive me really freaks me out. I expected to appear clumsier, because I was clumsier with that hand. But all of a sudden, when I had that damn, heavy, horrible, but *real-looking* artificial hand—well, I wear it when I go dancing because otherwise [if I wear my hook] the whole dance floor goes crazy! Just having that thing on. I couldn't really do anything with it. I couldn't really hold anything, but people treated me like a *real* person. Imagine, after twenty-six years, a real person. They didn't stare at me, they started to treat me like I was really attractive, and all of a sudden my social life went up 3,000 percent! And so I fell into wearing it for about a year, and I wore that goddamned thing no matter how hot it was.

On the surface, there is a rather obvious interpretation of the meaning of mechanization to Jaclyn, a kind of Lévi-Straussian binary opposition: mechanization is hard and male, whereas the female form is expected to be soft, pliable, and, yes, feminine. Yet, Jaclyn does not totally reject the hook prosthesis. Although she admits that when she first obtained the cosmetic hand her primary motivation for using it was social acceptance, increasingly she has settled for her hook prosthesis, the mechanical device that permits her functional independence. Jaclyn is keenly aware of the management of her public presentation of self, and therefore she chooses which image to "wear" depending on the nature and purpose of the social interaction. She is amused when she recalls her reactions to seeing her reflection in store windows:

> Yeah, I look all the time. I never failed to get a reaction from people, so I always looked too. What the hell are they looking at? [So] I looked and I saw a woman with a *surprisingly* short arm! But when I got the [cosmetic] hand, I looked and I thought, oh my God, that's what I would have looked like! And I saw this person that I would have been. But maybe I would have been an asshole just like all the rest of them. That's not fair, but that *is* what came to mind. And when I see the hook [now], I say, boy what a *bad* broad. And that's the [image] I like the best.

Jaclyn developed survival skills in an upper middle-class "regular" public school, where she was called "the one-arm bandit" by the "snots" whose social hierarchy was predicated solely on appearance: "All the fat girls, all the ugly girls, and me hung around in the same group. We, the fat girls and the ugly girls and the cripple, got so angry at these snots. Taught me a very good lesson: make them afraid of you. That's your only choice." It is notable that not only adolescent "snots" but also adult

co-workers are apt to make snide remarks about her deleted and mechanized body: "I was in one of the bathroom stalls when these two women
came in. Click, click, click—heels. And I heard them talking. And I knew
one of them, who it was. And I was going to come out and say something
to them, because you're supposed to be real friendly there. All of a
sudden, the first one—do you know what she said? 'Have you met Iron
Hook yet?' And so I flushed the toilet, and then I heard, click, click, click.
Click, click, click. Out. I was so mad and afraid of blowing my cool. I
hope to God I didn't."

A fear of being labeled paranoid often silences persons with disabilities.
Although Jaclyn refuses to be silent, she is also concerned that if she is the
least bit vocal, the least bit temperamental, people will say: "Well, she's
got a hook instead of a hand, and she can't handle it." Active in the
disability rights movement, Jaclyn confided how this ideology has affected
her redefinition of self. Although for Jaclyn mechanization is unfeminine,
increasingly she has become less interested in presenting herself as feminine than in managing her own body in social interactions: "Believe me,
they will [make snide remarks]! I cannot be assertive, strong, and myself
without being called a bitch. But I'd rather be a bitch than poor Jaclyn. I'd
rather be Iron Hook."

The Body as Metaphor for the Cripple

The third theme in these narratives concerns the metaphoric traits of "the
cripple" associated with disabled women's bodies. Feminists have long
decried the negative signing of the female physiology. Objecting to the metaphoric association of the female-body-as-sex-object, they have also rejected
the companion notion that the female body is a sign for passivity, weakness,
frailty, and dependency. The physiologies of disabled persons, and especially of disabled women, are also metaphorically signed—perceived to be
passive, weak, frail, and dependent. Thus, the disabled body, like the
female body, is culturally imbued with what Sontag has called "punitive
or sentimental fantasies" of metaphoric thinking (1978). Both notions—the
feminine and the cripple—may arise from the oppressive realities we all
construct (Berger and Luckman, 1967).

Demetaphorizing the Cripple from Her Body

Jessica Howard, thirty-three, graduated from college with a degree in
cultural geography. A sixties political activist, she has continued to be
involved in collective politics. Married for seven years, she was divorced
nearly one year before the onset and diagnosis of multiple sclerosis in
1977. The progression of MS has been rapid: "I walked for eight months

with one cane and then eight months with two canes and then the wheelchair." Once a year Jessica spends ten days in the hospital for intravenous steroid treatments that help her speech and swallowing. Although Jessica attends MS Society self-help meetings, she finds that her presence makes others anxious: "They see the disease could get worse for them, 'cause everyone is walking still. [They] don't like to have me there. It reminds them. But that just makes me be more positive. [My MS is] very manageable, although it is getting worse."

At the onset of MS in 1977, Jessica had been a manager of a bookstore. After her diagnosis, she transferred to a clerking position for about a year. Once she began using a wheelchair, she worked in the office as an assistant to the bookkeeper. She had to quit that job after her physician limited her work week to twenty hours. For nine months she was a receptionist. Then, for fifteen months, she was employed by a telephone answering service, work she did from her apartment. Increasing fatigue required that she stop working altogether. She now receives SSDI benefits. Once a week she volunteers as a counselor at a local outreach center. She enjoys crisis counseling, most done on the phone, but some with walk-ins. A few of her clients themselves have disabilities: "I'm really good at working with people with disabilities, but I haven't had a lot of that yet. Like, for instance, there's one man. He's epileptic and mentally retarded. And, I've opened myself up to him, saying, "Call me." And so, he calls a lot. And nobody [else] knows what to say to him, and I'm much better able *not* to feel sorry for him, and go ahead and like him!"

Jessica believes she is responsible for her own destiny. She has also learned, in part as a result of her disablement, to redefine what it means to be a successful human being and to change her idea of what independence means: "Health is not all there is to being alive. I guess I think there's other things that make me a valuable person besides my body."

For Jessica, a major turning point occurred after a particularly severe exacerbation left her quadriplegic. She spent one month in the rehabilitation unit at the hospital, where she was told that she could no longer live independently:

> They said, "Well, you can't transfer yourself to and from the wheelchair. Therefore, you can't live alone. You can live with your family or in the nursing home." And I chose the nursing home over my family, and since then I've discovered that there are other choices that they didn't suggest. [But] I lived in a nursing home for two months. And [there] they assumed that your body was all there is, and I just couldn't stand it. All there was was watching TV and making my body work better, and if it couldn't, *I* was a failure! And so eventually I left, realizing I don't have to be here. This was my choice. And I chose to leave. There was this feeling [there] that if you

have progressive disease, your life is hopeless. And I feel that *can't* be true, that it's not possible! I don't believe in giving up on anyone's life. There must be a way to live a fine life, no matter what.

Observing the interaction between the staff and the residents, Jessica concluded that "the people there gave up real easy." Since they were "treated like they couldn't be responsible for themselves," they began to believe that they were incapable of controlling their own lives. They became passive, weak, frail, and dependent. In effect, the two months of institutionalization had even severely depressed Jessica. After leaving the nursing home, she spent nine months reasserting control over her life. At first, she moved into a house owned by a woman who immediately took control over Jessica's life. Faced again with the prospects of emotional dependency, Jessica found a roommate to *share* an apartment with her. In exchange for room and board and a small salary, the roommate assisted with some of Jessica's physical needs. (Jessica also received daily assistance from state-provided attendant services.) Finally, Jessica felt "completely in charge" of her life as she began the process of demetaphorizing the cripple from her body.

Conflicts or Connections?

The three themes of concealment, mechanization, and metaphoric coding of "the cripple" are prevalent in the narratives of many of the disabled women I have interviewed. Certainly, such narratives reveal disabled women's conflicts between liberating their bodies from negative metaphoric associations while asserting and manifesting their femaleness. Whatever the impetus for their redefinitions of self, their liberation experiences are similar to what the women's movement calls consciousness-raising. Indeed, it is plausible to think of both kinds of emancipations as being empowered by a demetaphorizing process.

Certainly there are parallels between the processes of demetaphorizing the feminine and demetaphorizing the cripple. First, many disabled and nondisabled women share a resistance to the medical or male draping of their shapes. Second, many disabled and nondisabled women share an ambivalence toward mechanization and re-forming of their physiologies. And, third, many disabled and nondisabled women share a desire to liberate their bodies from the culturally imposed metaphoric traits of passivity, weakness, frailty, and dependency (Fine and Asch, 1981). Yet, some nondisabled feminists remain alienated from those disabled women whose withered and deleted bodies they associate with cripple/feminine traits. On the one hand, disabled women are characterized as traditional women—passive, weak, frail, and dependent. On the other hand, disabled women often are denied access to traditional sexual and gender roles (Rousso, 1988; Harris and Wideman, 1988). Such rolelessness results in their being "a kind of social nomad" (Blackwell-Stratton et al., 1988:307).

Why are disabled women, virtually invisible within the society and absent from both traditional and nontraditional roles for women, equally invisible within the women's movement? Because there, too, they are perceived to be asexual. It is paradoxical that *not* sharing the culturally imposed metaphor of woman-as-sex-object may be central to this alienation. Nondisabled women in the process of demetaphorizing the feminine-from-female should feel camaraderie, if not sisterhood, with disabled women who are in the process of demetaphorizing the cripple-from-disability. However, many disabled women report experiences of exclusion from the feminist dialogue, and even Fine and Asch conclude that the women's movement has had "an exploitative and embarrassing history vis à vis the politics of disability" (n.d.:1). Ironically, the feminist ritual of the *de*-object-ification of the female body may be a rite of passage denied women whose bodies are *not* perceived to be sexual objects. What feminist folklorists can offer the women's movement, literally and figuratively, is a new text. By documenting disabled women's stories, folklorists not only are providing new texts but also are broadening the feminist canon to include the experiences of females in all their diverse forms—be they straight or be they crooked.

Notes

Aspects of this essay were included in presentations at the following meetings: the 1982 meeting of the Michigan Women's Studies Association, the 1982 meeting of the American Folklore Society, the 1984 Symposium on Issues of Women and Disability at Barnard College, and the 1986 meeting of the National Women's Studies Association.

1. There continues to be controversy within the disability movement, particularly in the United States, on politically correct referential language. In this essay I alternately use the two terms (*disabled women* and *women with disabilities*) most widely accepted in the rights movement. Some individuals would argue that we are people first and therefore should be referred to as "persons with disabilities." Others argue that we are disabled more by our environment than by our physiologies and therefore should refer to ourselves as "disabled persons." The term *the disabled,* considered to be caustic and demeaning, is avoided, although it does have impact when purposely used to focus on the social minority status of an

otherwise heterogeneous population. Referential terminology most disparaged include the euphemistic terms *physically inconvenienced* and *physically challenged.* In an attempt to create a unifying terminology, some activists in Michigan lobbied the state legislature to legitimize the term *handicapper* (as in, "I am a handicapper"). Outside of Michigan, *handicapper* is perceived to be a personality cult term and usually dismissed as such. Inside Michigan, however, its usage has caused divisiveness and sometimes bitterness among different disability populations. The term *differently abled* may have had its genesis in feminist music festivals and is attributed to Holly Near. Although a small number of disabled feminists use this term, it is usually attributed to AB's (able-bodied), and is generally disparaged in the disabled activist community. I agree with Rae that "apart from its superficiality, it also feeds the myth that we are somehow compensated by Nature with extraordinary cheerfulness, courage, an extra 'sense'" (1989:3). Increasingly, the otherwise denigrating term *cripple* is used in radical contexts yet is still essentially an in-group term—never to be spoken in polite conversation with outsiders. Given the "burden of historical connotations" associated with most terminology in use, some have suggested coining completely new terms (Acton, 1989:3). Such a luxury, unfortunately, may not be available to a population that continues to face serious social and economic discrimination and multiple barriers to full participation in society.

2. The inclusion of four panels on bodylore in the 1989 American Folklore Society meetings in Philadelphia suggests a serious scholarly interest among folklorists in the emerging field of the folklore of the body.

References Cited

Acton, Norman. 1989. "Impairments, Disabilities, and Handicaps or Krezdorgs, Stanyrgys and Dommapsas?" *International Rehabilitation Review* 40 (June): 3.

Babcock, Barbara A. 1972. "Introduction." In *The Reversible World: Symbolic Inversion in Art and Society,* ed. Barbara A. Babcock, 1–12. Ithaca: Cornell University Press.

Beck, Brenda. 1975. "The Anthropology of the Body." *Current Anthropology* 16:486.

Berger, Peter, and Thomas Luckman. 1967. *The Social Construction of Reality: A Treatise in the Sociology of Knowledge.* Garden City, N.Y.: Doubleday.

Bettelheim, Bruno. 1977. *The Uses of Enchantment: The Meaning and Importance of Fairy Tales.* Alfred A. Knopf: New York.

Birdwhistell, Ray. 1971. *Kinesics and Context: Essays on Body-Motion Communication.* Philadelphia: University of Pennsylvania Press.

Blacking, John. 1977. "Towards an Anthropology of the Body." In *The Anthropology of the Body,* ed. John Blacking, 1–28. New York: Academic Press.

Blackwell-Stratton, Marian, Mary Lou Breslin, Arlene Byrnne Mayerson, and Susan Bailey. 1988. "Smashing Icons: Disabled Women and the Disability and Women's Movements." In *Women with Disabilities: Essays in Psychology, Culture, and Politics,* ed. Michelle Fine and Adrienne Asch, 306–32. Philadelphia: Temple University Press.

Bogdan, Robert. 1988. *Freak Show: Presenting Human Oddities for Amusement and Profit.* Chicago: University of Chicago Press.

Darwin, Charles. [1872] 1965. *The Expressions of the Emotions in Man and Animal.* Edited by Francis Darwin. Chicago: University of Chicago Press.

Douglas, Mary. 1966. *Purity and Danger: An Analysis of the Concepts of Pollution and Taboo.* London: Routledge and Kegan Paul.

———. 1973. "The Two Bodies." In *Natural Symbols.* New York: Vintage Books.

Fiedler, Leslie. 1978. *Freaks: Myths and Images of the Secret Self.* New York: Simon and Schuster.

Fine, Michelle, and Adrienne Asch. 1981. "Disabled Women: Sexism without the Pedestal." *Journal of Sociology and Social Welfare* 8:233–48.

———. n.d. "Dialectics of Disability and Reproductive Rights for Women." Ms.

Frank, Gelya. 1988. "On Embodiment." In *Women with Disabilities: Essays in Psychology, Culture, and Politics,* ed. Michelle Fine and Adrienne Asch, 41–71. Philadelphia: Temple University Press.

Gliedman, John, and William Roth. 1980. *The Unexpected Minority.* New York: Harcourt Brace Jovanovich.

Goffman, Erving. 1959. *The Presentation of Self in Everyday Life.* Garden City, N.Y.: Doubleday.

———. 1967. *Interaction Ritual.* Garden City, N.Y.: Doubleday.

Harris, Adrienne, and Dana Wideman. 1988. "The Construction of Gender and Disability in Early Attachment." In *Women with Disabilities: Essays in Psychology, Culture, and Politics,* ed. Michelle Fine and Adrienne Asch, 115–38. Philadelphia: Temple University Press.

Hertz, Robert. [1909] 1960. "The Pre-eminence of the Right Hand: A Study in Religious Polarity." In *Death and the Right Hand,* ed. R. Needham and C. Needham, 91–113. New York: Cohen and West.

Hess, Thomas, and Linda Nochlin, eds. 1972. *Woman as Sex Object: Studies in Erotic Art, 1730–1970.* New York: Newsweek Books.

Jackson, Bruce. 1972. "Deviance as Success: The Double Inversion of Stigmatized Roles." In *The Reversible World,* ed. Barbara A. Babcock, 258–75. Ithaca: Cornell University Press.

Kunzle, David. 1972. "The Corset as Erotic Alchemy: From Rococo Galanterie to Montaut's Physiologies." In *Women as Sex Object: Studies in Erotic Art, 1730–1970,* ed. Thomas B. Hess and Linda Nochlin, 90–165. New York: Newsweek Books.

Levy, Howard S. n.d. *Chinese Footbinding: The History of a Curious Erotic Custom.* New York: Bell.

Mauss, Marcel. 1935. "Techniques of the Body." *Economy and Society* 2:70–88.

Myerhoff, Barbara. 1978. *Number Our Days.* New York: E. P. Dutton.

Phillips, Marilynn J. 1983. "The Fieldworker as Insider/Outsider." Paper presented at the annual meeting of the American Folklore Society, Nashville, Tenn.

———. 1984a. "Disabled Women and Feminism: Ambivalence in the Struggle for Inclusion." Paper presented at the annual meeting of the Mid-Atlantic Women's Studies Association, Philadelphia, Pa.

———. 1984b. "Oral Narratives of the Experience of Disability in American Culture." Ph.D. diss., University of Pennsylvania.

———. 1985a. "Not So Special Education: Oral Narratives of the Experiences of Childhood Disability and Special Education." Paper presented at the annual University of Pennsylvania Ethnography of Education Research Forum, Philadelphia.

———. 1985b. "Try Harder: The Experience of Disability and the Dilemma of Normalization." *Social Science Journal* 22:45–57.

———. 1986. "What We Call Ourselves: Self-Referential Naming among the Disabled." Paper presented at the annual University of Pennsylvania Ethnography in Education Research Forum, Philadelphia.

Rae, Anne. "What's in a Name?" *International Rehabilitation Review* 40 (June): 3.

Rich, Adrienne. 1982. "A Woman Dead in Her Forties." In *Ordinary Lives: Voices of Disability and Disease,* ed. Irving Kenneth Zola, 217. Cambridge, Mass.: Apple-wood Books.

Rousso, Harilyn. 1988. "Daughters with Disabilities: Defective Women or Minority Women?" In *Women with Disabilities: Essays in Psychology, Culture, and Politics,* ed. Michelle Fine and Adrienne Asch, 139–71. Philadelphia: Temple University Press.

Scholes, Robert. 1982. "Un-coding Mama: The Female Body as Text." In *Semiotics and Interpretation,* 127–41. New Haven: Yale University Press.

Sontag, Susan. 1978. *Illness as Metaphor.* New York: Vintage Books.

Stahl, Sandra. 1977a. "The Oral Personal Narrative in Its Generic Context." *Fabula* 18:18–39.

———. 1977b. "The Personal Narrative as Folklore." *Journal of the Folklore Institute* 14:9–30.

———. 1983. "Personal Experience Stories." In *Handbook of American Folklore,* ed. Richard M. Dorson, 268–76. Bloomington: Indiana University Press.

Steinem, Gloria. 1982. "Feminist Notes: In Praise of Women's Bodies." *Ms,* Apr., 28ff.

Zola, Irving Kenneth. 1982. *Missing Pieces: A Chronicle of Living with a Disability.* Philadelphia: Temple University Press.

———. 1985. "Depictions of Disability—Metaphor, Message, and Medium in the Media: A Research and Political Agenda." *Social Science Journal* 22:5–17.

Contributors

ROBBIE E. DAVIS–FLOYD is the author of numerous articles on the cultural treatment of reproduction in the United States and *Birth as an American Rite of Passage*. She is currently working on a study comparing the self- and body images of pregnant professionals and home birthers and teaches at the University of Texas at Austin.

JENNIFER FOX is a doctoral candidate in anthropology at the University of Texas at Austin, currently researching poetic inspiration in the *cantoria* tradition of northeastern Brazil. She is a research associate with the Pauline Oliveros Foundation.

MARJORIE HARNESS GOODWIN is a professor of anthropology at the University of South Carolina and the author of *He-Said-She-Said: Talk as Social Organization among Black Children*. Currently she is investigating interaction within multiactivity work settings.

RAYNA GREEN is currently director of the American Indian Program at the National Museum of American History, Smithsonian Institution. She has published *That's What She Said: Contemporary Fiction and Poetry By Native American Women*, *Native American Women: A Contextual Bibliography*, and *Women in American Indian Society*.

SUSAN TOWER HOLLIS, author of *The Ancient Egyptian Tale of Two Brothers: The Oldest Fairy Tale in the World*, is currently working on a book on the major ancient Egyptian goddesses of the third millennium BCE. She is a professor in the College of Undergraduate Studies at the Union Institute.

LINDA A. HUGHES is an assistant professor in the College of Education at Millersville University. She received a Ph.D. in human development from the University of Pennsylvania in 1983. Her primary interests are in the culture of children's peer groups and in play and gender.

JOYCE ICE, who earned her Ph.D. in anthropology and folklore at the University of Texas, is the assistant director of the Museum of International Folk Art in Santa Fe, New Mexico. She has served as staff folklorist for the Delaware County Historical Association in upstate New York and as a teacher of folklore and English at Northern Arizona University.

DEBORA KODISH is the author of *Good Friends and Bad Enemies: Robert Winslow Gordon and the Study of American Folklore* and is at work with Roger Abrahams on a book on Almeda Riddle, a traditional singer. She is the director of the Philadelphia Folklore Project, an independent not-for-profit folk arts organization.

ELAINE J. LAWLESS is professor of English, folklore, and women's studies at the University of Missouri–Columbia. She is the author of *God's Peculiar People: Women's Voices and Folk Tradition in a Pentecostal Church, Handmaidens of the Lord: Pentecostal Women Preachers and Traditional Religion,* and *Holy Women/Wholly Women: Sharing Ministries through Life Stories and Reciprocal Ethnography.* She is currently researching female homiletics and sermon style.

JUDITH LEVIN is a Ph.D. candidate at the University of Pennsylvania. She is writing her dissertation on folklore and housework while editing children's books in New York City.

VERA MARK is an assistant professor in the Department of French at Penn State University. She has published articles on Gascon ethnic jokes, folk poetry, and the intellectual discourses of southern French regionalism. She is currently finishing a book on the representations of self of Pierre Sentat, an unpublished twentieth-century cobbler poet and folk artist.

ELAINE K. MILLER is an associate professor of Spanish and women's studies at the State University of New York at Brockport. She is the author of *Mexican Folk Narrative from the Los Angeles Area* and has produced a videotape on the vice-presidential candidacy of Geraldine Ferraro entitled "Running Mate: Gender and Politics in the Editorial Cartoons."

CAROL MITCHELL is an associate professor at Colorado State University and previously chaired the women's studies program. Her publications have focused on jokes and joke-telling.

LINDA PERSHING is an assistant professor in the Department of Women's Studies at the State University of New York at Albany. Her principal areas of interest are feminist folklore theory, peace studies, and the intersection of gender, race, class, and sexual identity as they are expressed through folklore performance and folk art.

MARILYNN J. PHILLIPS is an associate professor of English and Language Arts at Morgan State University. She is currently writing a book on the significance of poster child campaigns in framing cultural attitudes toward disability.

RACHELLE H. SALTZMAN is staff folklorist at the Delaware County Historical Association in Delhi, New York. Previously, she was employed as a visiting assistant professor of English and folklore at the University of Delaware and before that as folklife programs administrator at the Bureau of Florida Folklife Programs. She is currently working on a manuscript entitled "A Lark for the Sake of Their Country: Upper-Class British Play Genres and the Maintenance of Social Class."

PATRICIA E. SAWIN does research on personal narrative, the politics of cultural representation, and the use of performance to negotiate gendered identity. She is a past editor of *Folklore Women's Communication*.

SUZANNE SERIFF holds a Ph.D. in folklore from the University of Texas at Austin. She is the author of the forthcoming book *Snakes, Sirens, Virgins, and Devils: The Politics of Representation of a Mexican American Folk Artist*. She is currently working as consultant and co-curator of two museum projects on ephemeral and recycled folk arts and toys.

AMY SHUMAN is an associate professor in the English Department at Ohio State University. She is the author of *Storytelling Rights: The Uses of Literacy by Urban Adolescents* and articles on conversational narrative. She is completing a manuscript entitled "Authentic Copies," a study of artisan technology and culture in an Italian community of stone carvers.

KAY TURNER holds a Ph.D. in folklore from the University of Texas at Austin. She has published widely in the area of folklore and women's studies and is currently working as a free-lance folklorist and lead singer in the all-woman band Girls in the Nose.

MARGARET R. YOCOM's fieldwork has taken her home to her Pennsylvania German family, away to the Inuit of northwestern Alaska, and then on to New England. Her articles on feminist and family folklore have appeared in several books of essays. She is the assistant editor of *Ugiuvangmiut Quiliapyuit,* a collection of King Island Inuit folktales, and is currently writing *Generations in Wood,* a book about the folk art of the Richard family of Rangeley, Maine. An associate professor of English at George Mason University, she teaches folklore and United States studies.

M. JANE YOUNG is an associate professor in the American Studies Department at the University of New Mexico. She has conducted extensive fieldwork at the Pueblo of Zuni in New Mexico, where she produced a traveling exhibit of rock art of the Zuni-Cibola region in conjunction with the tribal museum committee. She has written *Signs from the Ancestors: Zuni Cultural Symbolism and Perceptions of Rock Art*.